A
PORTRAIT
OF
WAR
1939-1943

A
PORTRAIT
OF
WAR
1939-1943

Richard S. Malone

COLLINS
Toronto

First published 1983
by Collins Publishers
100 Lesmill Road, Don Mills, Ontario

Canadian Cataloguing in Publication Data

Malone, Richard.
    A Portrait of war, 1939-1943

ISBN 0-00-217105-8

1. World War, 1939-1945 — Canada. 2. World War,
1939-1945 — Great Britain. 3. Malone, Richard.
4. Canada. Armed Forces — Biography. 5. World War,
1939-1945 — Personal narratives, Canadian. I. Title.

D768.15.M34   940.54'0971   C83-098316-3

Printed and bound in Canada
by John Deyell Company

CONTENTS

A
PORTRAIT
OF
WAR
1939-1943

Introduction

There are many advantages, but also some disadvantages, in attempting to record wartime recollections some 40 years after the event. With the passing of time, there is always some risk of an inadvertent slip of memory. But also, over the years, additional facts come to light, and it is possible to be more objective.

Being directly involved in the great drama of World War II, I was not always able to see the entire picture. While a person might accurately interpret and record decisions and consequences at one level of command, he might not fully appreciate at the time, the factors involved at higher military or political levels, or the agonizing decisions which led to various courses of action.

Official war histories provide us with fairly precise records of battle dates, casualty statistics and map locations. But such official accounts, perforce, pretty well present the picture as the authorities would have us believe. Most of the human aspects — the humorous incidents, the blunders, the personality clashes and the backroom dramas, all essential to the real story — have to be omitted. Similarly, little is recorded about the personal struggles and sacrifices of the principals involved, or about the political pressures at play as the nation mobilized for war.

It must be realized that politicians and commanders on the spot, despite the fog and confusion of battle, were frequently obliged to make major decisions, sometimes in minutes, based on the information available to them at that time. Some of that information was to prove false, but the decisions were made in the sincere belief that the actions taken would best defeat the enemy. Certainly, mistakes were made because of personal pride, ambition, anger and bullheadedness. Hindsight, in consequence, can often be very deceptive; at times, it can distort the actual scene.

Inevitably in the years following a major war, a great body of myth builds up and, for a period, becomes gospel. Similarly, official records at times simply suggest the merest whiff of some unpleasant or embarrassing truth, or ignore it entirely, as it might put some official in a bad light.

Fortunately, as more time passes, additional information and important facts come to light. Confidential reports are made public, enemy intelligence digests are discovered and private diaries and letters turn up to help fill the gaps in the picture. Even today, fresh details are being discovered about such battles as Waterloo and Balaklava.

There still remains much to be told about World War II — not only the political rows happening behind the scenes, but also the many personal trials, tragedies and triumphs which led to victory.

A Portrait of War is not intended as a history or a complete account of World War II but simply an attempt to fill a few of the gaps in the Canadian record, to capture some of the colour of that exciting period and to describe the roles played by many of the leading actors.

By good fortune, I had an unequalled opportunity of participating in many of the major events of the war and seeing at close range most of our senior commanders and wartime political leaders.

Before the war, as much as a crowded newspaper life permitted, I served with various militia units such as the Queen's Own Rifles in Toronto and the 12th Machinegun Battalion in Regina and completed a number of militia courses in different parts of the country.

During the Depression years in Saskatchewan and while associated with the Regina *Leader-Post*, by chance I joined in with a number of Permanent Force army officers, stationed at the local Military District HQ, to occupy a very comfortable "bach" house. It was operated by a former World War I nursing sister, Miss Davies, together with her very able Chinese staff, Hom Dow and Hom Dot.

It was a very lively and sociable household, run rather on the lines of an officers' mess, and had an ever-changing list of occupants. Parties were frequent, and a poker game ran almost non-stop in the little card room. There was always a waiting list for any vacant room.

Other lodgers at that time included such personalities as Captain Guy Simonds, later to become a Lieutenant General and Commander of the Canadian Army, and Sammy Sansom, subsequently to command 2nd Canadian Corps. Additionally there were Brigadier Howard Penhale, wartime commander of 3rd Infantry Brigade, Brigadier Pat Kelly, director of army pay services (a good man to know and an expert poker player), Captain Chris Vokes, later to command the 2nd Brigade in Sicily and the 1st Canadian Division in Italy, Sparky Sparling who achieved the rank of Major General in the war years, and a score or more of other PF officers, including Colonel Frank Ovens, de Loeb Panet and the colourful "Baron" Van Den Berg. The friendships formed at that time were to prove of value when the dark years of war arrived.

Early in the war I was seconded from my regiment, the PPCLI (Princess Patricia's Canadian Light Infantry) to serve as Staff Secretary to Canada's Minister of National Defence, Colonel J. L. Ralston. I accompanied the minister, together with Canada's Chief of General Staff, General H.D.G. Crerar, on a mission to England for meetings with Winston Churchill and other members of the British government to co-ordinate mobilization plans.

Later on, after completing the War Staff College course, I was posted overseas again and served with both 1st and 3rd Canadian Infantry Divisions, as well as the 5th Armoured Division.

As brigade major of the 2nd Infantry Brigade, I participated in the planning and D-Day landings in Sicily, and was then appointed personal liaison officer to General Montgomery and participated in the D-Day landing in Italy.

Returning to England in time for the D-Day landings in Normandy, I had charge of all Canadian press and psychological warfare activities on the Canadian front: censorship, war correspondents, transmission, broadcasting, film and photo units, enemy propaganda, and the establishment of the Canadian Army newspaper, the *Maple Leaf*.

Throughout the campaign in north-west Europe, I maintained my close association with Field Marshal Montgomery. Although holding staff appointments at both SHAEF (Eisenhower's HQ) and 21st Army Group (Monty's HQ), I participated in all major operations of the Canadian Army and was fortunate in being among the first Allied troops to enter Paris and Brussels, and, later, Tokyo.

After the Rhine crossing, on instructions from Ottawa, I headed a

10

mission to General MacArthur's HQ in the Pacific, and visited the HQ of U.S. Admiral Nimitz in Guam. I had the honour of representing Canada in the Philippines when the Japanese emissaries arrived to negotiate terms of surrender. In the airborne landings in Japan, I was able to participate with the U.S. assault troops from the island of Okinawa.

On V-J Day I was aboard the USS *Missouri* for the formal Japanese surrender ceremonies. Following this I had the responsibility of liberating the Canadian prisoners of war captured at Hong Kong, and establishing first Canadian Army contact with the Nationalist Chinese Army.

Soon afterward I returned to Canada and Civvy Street and had an opportunity to visit the United States. I was shocked at what appeared to be a deliberate campaign to belittle, if not destroy, the reputations of both Colonel Ralston and Field Marshal Montgomery. Although pitched into the midst of a prolonged newspaper strike, almost as soon as I returned, I quickly wrote the book *Missing from the Record* in an effort to halt the vicious propaganda. Chapters dealing with Montgomery appeared in the *Saturday Evening Post* under the heading, "You Yanks Never Gave Monty His Due." Other chapters appeared in England in one of the larger Sunday newspapers, while the chapters on Ralston were serialized in *Maclean's* magazine.

Although the events I recorded at that time were entirely accurate, I did not use all the documentation available to me nor did I expand the report beyond the essentials, to avoid needlessly offending those involved.

As nearly 40 years have now elapsed since the publication of *Missing from the Record*, I have attempted in this book to present a more detailed picture, based not only on first-hand knowledge but on letters and diaries written by some of the principal figures and wartime cabinet ministers, which have not yet been made public.

In the years after the war, I also had the opportunity to recheck many of the facts in long talks with Sir Winston Churchill, Field Marshals Alanbrooke and Montgomery, Lord Beaverbrook, General Price Montague, General Simonds and such members of the wartime cabinet as Howe, Macdonald, Crerar and Ralston. In the course of this book I shall include further details, based on personal recollections, of many wartime events that were purposely withheld from the earlier book.

In the prospect that the author would some day find the opportunity to record something of his wartime experiences and some of the behind-the-scenes aspects of Canada's war effort, a number of Canada's wartime leaders were kind enough to leave in my custody their own hitherto unpublished memoranda and personal accounts of important events. Where relevant, these first-hand recollections have been incorporated into or quoted in this book. Some personal and incidental anecdotes have also been included, to give a sense of immediacy and human emotion to the story.

It may be clever, in retrospect, to pontificate as to what might have happened if this or that course of action had been taken, or to compare the abilities of various generals. This is a rather futile exercise, however, and certainly not the author's purpose in these memoirs.

As the great historian Macaulay wrote, "No history can present us with the whole truth; but those are the best pictures and the best histories which exhibit such parts of the truth as most nearly produce the effect of the whole."

Touching on the matter of memory, Sir Winston Churchill once advanced an intriguing theory on this subject. It was the summer just before the great statesman's death, while we were both visiting Lord Beaverbrook in the south of France. Sitting in the sun, overlooking the Mediterranean, we spent the afternoon reminiscing about World War II and such subsequent developments as Suez and the Common Market. At his advanced age, Churchill paused frequently, trying to recall a forgotten name or date.

Then Beaverbrook switched the conversation back to events in World War I, covering the period when he and Churchill had served together in Whitehall; Churchill in the Admiralty and Beaverbrook in Wartime Information. I was astounded at the clarity and the precise detail of their recollections. Beaverbrook laughingly recalled how, after Churchill had been forced out of office at the Admiralty and was leaving for France to serve in the trenches, he had gone to Churchill's London home, to wish him farewell. Churchill's tin army boxes were all neatly packed and piled in the hallway, together with his sword and several boxes of champagne and luxury canned food.

It was a Saturday morning, according to Beaverbrook, who was able to recall his rude remarks at the time about Churchill's boxes of goodies and the futility of taking a sword for fighting in the trenches. Churchill added some additional details to top the Beaver's story.

I commented on how good their memories were for detail.

"The memory of youth," Churchill replied.

He then went on to expound the theory that when a person is young, the brain is soft and pliable. Events are easily implanted and leave their imprints. As one gets older, however, the brain gets tough and leathery like an old liver, and very few events leave any permanent trace or indent.

"Now I often can't remember where I was yesterday," he commented sadly.

It is the author's sincere hope that the "memory of youth" has not betrayed him, and that the following recollections will serve in some measure to round out the picture by relating something of the individual endeavours and human dramas which punctuated those tragic years of challenge, during which Canada played a courageous, unselfish and creditable part.

For readers of the current generation, a proper appreciation of Canada's role in World War II is hardly possible without some understanding of the Canadian scene and the mood of her people just prior to the outbreak of war.

Canada has never been a military-minded country, and her armed forces in peacetime have traditionally been starved and forgotten. Regular and reserve forces have been kept to a minimum. Between wars, government practice has been to appoint to the defence portfolio only ministers who would not cause trouble — keeping things quiet, cutting costs, shielding the department from public controversy.

Consequently, in times of national emergency and during both world wars, Canada has had to rely primarily on her militia; that is, her volunteer reserve army, navy and air forces.

Surprisingly, however, in 1914 and again in 1939, when war was declared Canada's response was immediate and her military contribution was of the highest order. The Canadian Corps of World War I established a high reputation for both efficiency and gallantry in action. In the devastating battles of Flanders, they were repeatedly employed in the role of shock troops.

In the new arena of air combat, Canadian flyers such as Bishop, Barker, Collishaw and dozens of others, were recognized among the top Allied aces.

Similarly, in World War II, Canada's contribution in the air, at sea, and with her land forces, was outstanding. The first Allied divisions to reach Britain's shores, to help resist the Nazi aggressors, came from Canada.

Back in the days of the Napoleonic wars, Britain's celebrated commander, the Duke of Wellington, who had never visited the colony, made some penetrating observations about Canada's defences. It had been feared that while Britain was fighting for her existence against Napoleon's victorious armies, the United States would seize the opportunity to invade Canada. Wellington had been asked to come to Canada to organize Canada's defences and bring with him trained British regiments. Deeply committed in the Peninsula campaign, Wellington could not be spared; but working from maps of Canada, he did draft out an appreciation and offered some comments. As he had repeatedly done in England, he urged the authorities, "Never, never forget your militia." It was not possible, he reasoned, for Canada to support a large standing or professional army to guard her vast borders. He could send out a few veteran brigades of British infantry, but they would only serve as a small mobile nucleus. For the most part, Canada must rely on her local militia units and independent Rifle companies. "Treat your farmers well," Wellington cautioned. "In times of peril, they will fight for their homes."

Following World War I, Canada faced many difficulties. Some 60,000 of her young men had paid the price of war with their lives, and many of those who returned could not find employment. A general strike in Winnipeg had to be brought under control by military force. Before there was any real economic recovery from the weary years of war, the great Depression struck. The Conservative government, under R. B. Bennett in Ottawa, vainly employed trade tariffs in an attempt to "blast our way" into world markets. Meanwhile, camps for single unemployed men had to be established, under army supervision, to provide food and shelter for thousands of hungry and disillusioned. Years of drought, great dust storms, and repeated grasshopper plagues destroyed successive prairie grain crops.

Absorbed by her own trials, Canada had little interest in world affairs — such as the League of Nations, or the growing dictatorships of Hitler and Mussolini. The Canadian mood was isolationist. Her people wanted no further involvements in Europe or adventures in far-off Asia. Everyone longed for peace. There could be no more Great Wars.

Prime Minister Mackenzie King, on forming his government in 1935, obliged Canada's representative at the League of Nations to reverse our country's endorsement of sanctions against Mussolini for his brutal bombing of Ethiopia. Following a friendly visit to Germany to meet the new Nazi dictator, King saw no real danger ahead. Talking to Bruce Hutchison on his return to Canada, King described Hitler as "a simple peasant." In a private memo to the Governor General, King recorded that he was "perfectly certain that the Germans are not contemplating war."

When Hitler attacked Czechoslovakia and Chamberlain flew to Munich with an appeasement package for "peace in our time," King congratulated the British Prime Minister in a cabled message, "Canada rejoices at the success of your efforts . . . "

As for weapons and munitions, Canada was totally unprepared for war. None of the militia regiments had any vehicles. There was no armoured corps, and there were only two demonstration tanks in all of Canada. Our artillery consisted of some obsolete guns, left over from World War I. Our supply of rifles and machine guns, also of World War I vintage, was so limited that, when war broke out, only a 90-day training period could be adopted under our national service program. Even our supply of Ross rifles, condemned early in World War I, had to be sent to Britain to equip the Home Guard.

As the war clouds gathered, bringing back memories of 1914-18, advocates of neutrality and isolation spoke out in Ottawa. Any attempts to increase Canada's limited defence budgets, prior to the outbreak of war in 1939, were strongly opposed in Parliament.

Yet when Hitler invaded Poland and Britain declared war, Canada's response to the challenge was immediate. Britain declared war on September 3, and that same day Mackenzie King, the most improbable of war leaders, issued a statement clearly committing Canada as well. There followed the formality of parliamentary approval and a formal declaration on September 7. When the vote was taken in the House of Commons, only one member, J. S. Woodsworth, the C.C.F. leader, voted against war.

Even the Quebec Members of the House, led by Justice Minister Lapointe, Public Works Minister Cardin, and Chubby Power, later to become Minister for Air, supported the declaration, though wholeheartedly registering their opposition to any form of conscription.

Canada's total population at the time was just over 11 million, yet within the next few years Canada had more than 740,000 fully equipped men under arms. Starting from scratch, RCAF squadrons were operating in all European fronts, and through the great Empire Air Training Scheme, Canada had undertaken the training of thousands of pilots and air crew for other nations of the Commonwealth. At sea, her destroyers, corvettes and frigates were patrolling the sea lanes of the Atlantic and guarding convoys to the Middle East and northern Russian ports.

Canadian factories were supplying vehicles, guns, ammunition and war supplies of all sorts to equip not only Canadian forces, but also to help our British, Polish, French and Russian allies. Canadian farms and mines established production records to back the war effort. Prices and wages on the home front were frozen. Financially, every effort was made to support a pay-as-you-go policy. After the first three years of war, Canada's national debt was only five billion dollars — truly a staggering performance. The scale of this achievement will be difficult for present-generation Canadians to appreciate. Today, after some 40 years of peace, incredibly Canada's national debt has soared to greater than $160 billion, and Ottawa, year after year, is unable to bring in a balanced budget, control inflation or create jobs for our young people. These debts will never be repaid except by devaluation, inflation or repudiation.

But Canada's great war effort was not without its heartbreaks, pettiness and personal tragedies. As the truth emerges with the passing years

14

and more becomes known of the personal sacrifices and individual achievements, it is perhaps sad to realize that praise may come too late to serve many who are gone. Some whose names commanded newspaper headlines 40 years ago are hardly recognized by many Canadians today.

To assist younger readers, a capsule biography of a few of the leading actors in the great drama of World War II is given at the back of this book.

Doubtless some historians will disagree with my views or find some error to harpoon. They may well be right, but what follows is the picture as it appeared to the writer from a ringside seat. If any errors have been made as to exact dates and places, they are quite unintentional and certainly regretted.

ONE

Mission To Britain
November, 1940

WORLD SCENE

*Following the collapse of France and the British
evacuation at Dunkirk, Canada is urged to expand and
speed up mobilization of army, navy and air forces for
defence of Britain. Canadian industry is asked for
all-out production of war supplies. Canadian mission
visits England to co-ordinate plans with British cabinet
and defence chiefs.*

The army staff car swung into Downing Street and eased to a dignified
halt before Number 10. Immediately ahead of us was a military van
painted drab camouflage colours. In accordance with my careful staff
work, the moment our car came to a halt the back doors of the van were
thrown open by our army driver. A wheelchair was quickly off-loaded
and wheeled to where Colonel Ralston, Canada's Minister of National
Defence, and I were to have our first visit with Britain's Prime Minister,
Winston Churchill.

It was November 1940. The tragic but miraculous evacuation of Dunkirk had been carried out. Belgium and Holland had fallen, France had
collapsed. The first of Churchill's great wartime speeches — "if necessary alone" — which were to rally the Commonwealth and inspire the
Western world, had been delivered in the House of Commons. Except for
two Canadian infantry divisions, which were now equipped and concentrated in south-east England, together with what had been salvaged from
France, Britain stood almost disarmed. The bulk of the British Army
field equipment had been left on the beaches of Dunkirk. Only 25 tanks
had been brought home from France. Units evacuated from France needed
time to refit, reorganize and fill up the ranks. The Battle of Britain had
been raging in the skies since July. RAF fighter squadrons were still
fighting back the massive Luftwaffe attacks. On 82 of 85 consecutive
nights, hundreds of German bombers rained explosives on London.

The name of Churchill was everywhere. In the public mind he stood
forth like Gibraltar, the champion of the Western world. It was during
these weeks of high drama that I had my first contact with the great man
of history, Winston Churchill.

The moment of truth had come to England. The appeasers and
defeatists had vanished. The Piccadilly soldiers disappeared and in their
place were seen men in battle dress, regulars and territorials, carrying gas
masks and pistols. During lunch breaks, older men from offices, wearing
Home Guard uniforms, carried out platoon tactics in the parks or dug slit
trenches. Young women in ATS, WRENS and MTC* uniforms were seen

*British women's services: Auxiliary Territorial Service (ATS), Women's Royal Naval Service
(WRENS), Motor Transport Corps (MTC).

driving lorries and staff cars, manning AA guns or down on their knees scrubbing out barracks and mess halls. Everyone suddenly had a purpose. Nowhere was there panic or despair; simply, a national determination to win a seemingly impossible war.

Today when thousands of people drift neurotically, trying to find some reason for life, some challenge, some belief or national purpose, it is strange to look back and recall that great transformation in England. Young mothers with children to look after, on short rations, no cars, their husbands away in the Services, not only did volunteer work during the day but then spent long nights huddled in air-raid shelters, or took turns as roof watchers to put out incendiary bombs, or, in country points, acted as air-raid spotters for fighter command. Above all, they were cheery and pleasant with one another.

While the war was being taken seriously in Canada, it was still a great contrast, in those early days, to arrive in London and grope your way along the streets in the blackout, in the midst of an air raid, watching searchlights and tracer shells decorate the sky while bits of shrapnel hit the pavement.

I was accompanying Canada's Minister of Defence, Colonel J. L. Ralston, in the capacity of staff secretary. Considerable importance was attached to Ralston's visit, both in England and in Canada. As a senior member of Canada's wartime cabinet, Ralston, in his rushed visit, was to negotiate and draw up a program with the British government for the full-scale development of Canada's military and industrial potential to help win the war.

Ralston's trip started disastrously. I had arrived in England by ship a week earlier, to set up all our meetings, but Ralston had flown to England in an unheated bomber. He suffered a severe chill which affected the sciatic nerve and muscles of his lower back, with the result that he was badly crippled for nearly two weeks. So painful was his condition on arrival that he could only walk with crutches or be moved in a wheelchair. He was taken directly to the Dorchester Hotel, where despite his protests, he was ordered to bed by an army doctor.

Furious and impatient with his unexpected infirmity, Ralston was still in bed raging and protesting when Captain Anthony Eden, Britain's Secretary of State for War, arrived to extend an official welcome on behalf of the British government. Complaining bitterly at his ill fortune, Ralston assured Eden that he would be up and well by the next day. Regardless of his condition, he insisted, none of his heavy schedule of meetings should be cancelled. He was determined to get on with his conferences, including his meetings with Churchill.

The only solution was the use of a wheelchair. I took Ralston secretly in the wheelchair down the freight elevator at the Dorchester to the service entrance, where I had a limousine waiting. A truck was to go ahead and have the wheelchair ready outside Number 10 by the time we arrived. The secrecy of the operation was imposed by Ralston's order, as he was determined to avoid any photographers and any chance of a picture with him riding in a "baby carriage," as he called it, appearing in any of the papers in England or Canada.

From Fort Osborne Barracks To Whitehall And Downing Street

I had known Ralston very slightly back in 1934-35, when I had been a very young member of the Parliamentary press gallery in Ottawa. On the outbreak of war, I was in Winnipeg with the *Winnipeg Free Press* and at once volunteered for overseas service. After waiting for several weeks, I was called up for duty with the Princess Patricia's, one of Canada's elite Permanent Force infantry regiments. On mobilization, the Patricias found themselves in the position of having several of their regular officers "boarded out" on medical grounds. By chance, I had the necessary qualifications for company commander and was available to fill one of the gaps. Newspaper work was a trade rather looked down upon by regular army officers in those days, but I was accepted with only slight disdain.

When Ralston took over as Minister of Defence, early in the war, he had me posted to NDHQ (National Defence HQ) for a week to help sort out press problems and to assist with plans to promote recruiting and the war effort generally.

As each day passed, however, and a new crisis arose, he kept employing me on short notice rather as a trouble shooter or jack of all trades. One day I might be sent flying off to Halifax to see about coast defence guns, another day writing a speech for Ralston or preparing a report for Parliament. Other days I might have to accompany him on an inspection or attend a conference. Sometimes I had to sit in for him at committee meetings when he was unavoidably delayed.

Ralston worked nearly 18 hours a day and I was happy to help wherever I could. There was always action, and I found it an exciting change from the rather formal and ordered regimental life. Seemingly he found me useful, as I was given an office adjoining his own in the Woods Building and told I would be on special duty with him until further notice.

Working so closely with him, privy to all the great secrets, was a rare privilege for a junior officer and ex-journalist. It was even more flattering and challenging to be selected to accompany the minister as staff secretary on this historic and crucial mission to London. Needless to say, this same delight was hardly shared by many of the more senior, regular army officers at NDHQ, over whom I had been chosen.

Accompanying Ralston to London, besides myself, were Major-General Harry Crerar, Canada's Chief of General Staff, and Alan Magee, a corporation lawyer from Montreal who had seen overseas service in World War I and was presently serving as an executive assistant to his long-time friend, Colonel Ralston.

Magee, besides being a very clear-headed and competent lawyer, was blessed with a very relaxed manner and a quick sense of humour. There was a generation difference in our ages but we got along famously together. Crerar, on the other hand, treated me very coldly and maintained the traditional frozen-faced front of the regular soldier.

Despite my regimental posting, I was still a militia man, a civilian Tuesday night soldier, and worst of all a newspaper man, as far as Crerar was concerned. He continued to look down his nose at me until one day, several years later in Italy, when very humbly he was obliged to seek my private advice to extricate himself from a humiliating run-in with his superior, General Montgomery.

At that time I knew little about higher military echelons and the maze of headquarters operations. Possibly my chief asset to the minister during that early mobilization period was that I simply didn't understand regular channels, established authorities, precedents and regulations. Used to cutting every possible corner and bypassing obstacles in my civilian newspaper work, to get a story and meet deadlines, I assumed that this was also the practice to follow in the army when a war was on. Having the authority of the minister behind me, I fear many senior toes got trod on, and I made more than a few enemies among the regular and qualified staff officers at National Defence Headquarters when I went around them or over their heads to meet Ralston's orders to get something done quickly.

It is now safe to relate that while carrying out missions for Ralston, I always carried with me a good supply of the crimson-embossed official stationery, "From the Office of the Minister of National Defence." In any real emergency, to carry out the minister's orders quickly and cut through the red tape, I did not hesitate to issue for myself authorizations "to whom it may concern," and then sign "J. L. Ralston," without a qualm. The war had to be won — the war on red tape.

While I never specifically informed Ralston of my unorthodox methods, and he certainly never gave formal approval, he was quite aware of my many indiscretions. Indeed on one occasion when I had resorted to a Minister's Order to obtain a plane reservation back from Halifax, Colonel Ralston pulled my leg gently on the subject. After I had reported my urgent mission accomplished, Ralston thanked me for the speed of execution but added, "I have just received a complaint from a very important man that he was bumped off a flight from Halifax on the personal orders of the Minister of Defence, to make room for an officer on top priority — I don't recall ever signing such an order." "I don't know how that could happen Sir," I replied. "Well, don't cut your own throat. Thanks for your good work but be careful," he said and smiled.

I have seldom enjoyed a relationship of such trust and confidence as I was able to establish with Ralston during that period. It was to serve us both well, and also the war effort, in the war years ahead, in many curious ways at critical periods.

Very early I realized, as all others did who worked closely with Ralston, that he was a man of absolute integrity and conscience. While he had great difficulty in ridding himself of detail, his capacity for work and sense of duty were unlimited. Later I shall trace the political manoeuvres of Prime Minister Mackenzie King which forced Ralston's ultimate resignation from the cabinet. Suffice for the moment to say that despite all the in-fighting and heavy political, public and general staff pressures, I never once saw Ralston make a dishonourable decision or take the easy way out to save his own reputation.

London Meetings

When we arrived in Downing Street, neither Ralston nor I had ever before met Churchill. Why I had been selected to accompany Ralston on this first visit with the British Prime Minister, instead of Alan Magee or General Crerar, I don't know. Possibly I was better at handling the wheelchair or had a better working knowledge of Ralston's files. Crerar and Magee were certainly more knowledgeable than myself on many army matters. But in planning the trip, it had been my job to draw up our agenda and prepare the supporting documents; I could also help now in preparing official statements or press releases.

Highly polished riding boots and proper "brass hats" were still in evidence in Whitehall, and I must confess that my first encounter with the British general staff and the War Office had been a bit awe-inspiring.

Arriving at 10 Downing Street, I was properly turned out and very alert to avoid any slip in protocol which might disgrace the senior Dominion. According to standing orders, I carried a service revolver on my belt, and over my shoulder was an issue gas respirator and "tin hat." On our arrival in England, General Crerar had painfully pointed out to me that in London, as staff secretary to the minister, I should be wearing the scarlet and black brassard with the Royal Cypher on my arm to signify General Staff. I had immediately purchased this essential item of dress, but inadvertently mounted it on the wrong sleeve of my jacket. It was somewhat humiliating to have this pointed out by a junior at Canadian Military HQ, London.

With the help of the army driver at 10 Downing Street, I was able to transfer safely my sadly crippled chief from the car to the wheelchair, and we proceeded toward the entrance of the Prime Minister's official residence. The bobbie on duty asked our business, and I carefully explained that my passenger was the Canadian Defence Minister with an appointment to see Mr. Churchill. We were waved forward. Next came a Scotland Yard man and we went through the same procedure. Then after wrestling the wheelchair up a few steps into the vestibule, the explanations were repeated to an inside doorman in a dark suit.

A few steps further and a tall figure in a black jacket and striped trousers approached us — undoubtedly the butler. Again I went through my words of explanation. "Yes, I know," answered the man. "I am Mr. Churchill. I have been expecting you." I had seen dozens of pictures of the great British war leader, but I had always gained the impression of a short, stocky, bulldog figure chewing a cigar — and was completely put off the track by his height and the decided touch of red in his hair. Ralston had also failed to recognize our host, but Churchill put us immediately at our ease and was very solicitous about Ralston's state of health. Ralston brushed aside his temporary infirmity.

We then proceeded to an office or, more properly, a small sitting-room, to get on with our business.

Churchill's first words were, "So you have come over to find out how the hell we're going to win this war." In this he was mischievously repeating Ralston's own words and obviously had been talking to Anthony Eden. When we had first arrived at the Dorchester Hotel, Anthony Eden was most distressed to observe the extent to which Ralston had been crippled by the Atlantic flight and the degree of pain he was suffering. He had urged Ralston to delay all his meetings for a few days to get some rest and medical treatment.

Furious with himself and his physical incapacity, Ralston had roughly dismissed any suggestion of postponing our meetings. There was too much to be done. Matters were too important, the meetings must go on as scheduled. Many decisions regarding Canada's military participation all had to be completed in the next few weeks before Ralston's colleague, C. D. Howe, Canada's Minister of Munitions and Supply, arrived with a mission to work out all the equipment schedules to implement our own military commitments as well as help in re-equipping British formations.

In a burst of irritation with himself, Ralston had rather exploded to Eden with the statement, "We've come over to find out how the hell we're going to win this war. It won't wait."

At that moment, with London under bombardment, British Home Forces desperately weak, lacking equipment and devoid of European allies, it was hard to see what possible hope Britain had of defeating Nazi Germany.

Ralston's blunt remark had been passed on by Eden to Churchill earlier in the morning and Churchill very accurately recognized that this was indeed the primary purpose of Ralston's visit. It was at once evident that little time would be wasted in pleasantries and preliminaries between these two. They both understood the need for plain talking and action.

It is not possible now to recall or to summarize all the details and technicalities of the ensuing discussion with Churchill, which ranged over the whole spectrum of current military requirements and planning. The minutes can all likely be found in official records in Ottawa, as well as in the Ralston diaries, which were missing for some years after the war but are now safely lodged in the Public Archives in Ottawa as a result of my own strenuous efforts after Ralston's death.

About one o'clock we adjourned and went down in a small elevator at the rear of the residence to an underground dining room which had just been constructed to protect Churchill from German bombing raids.

Churchill was rather contemptuous and apologetic of this underground apartment. He explained that his colleagues had insisted upon it although it struck him as a rather cowardly practice when other Londoners had to take their chances eating above ground.

As I was able to observe several times at future meetings with Churchill, his habit was to change the conversation away from business during meal times. He talked of his family, his country projects, the hardships of the working people, horses, the theatre and news items in the London press.

Following a pleasant lunch, members of Churchill's war cabinet started to assemble in the small council room on the main floor. As I was quite properly not to attend this formal meeting of a cabinet within a cabinet, Churchill indicated I would find a sitting room upstairs where I could make myself comfortable with some cigarettes and magazines, and could ring for a drink if I wished.

Sitting in this historic home of such great leaders as Gladstone, Disraeli, Wellington and Lloyd George, while Hitler's battle for Britain was at its height, rather sparked the imagination. Given by George II as the official residence to Prime Minister Sir Robert Walpole in 1725, it had witnessed the great cabinet consultations which decided the course of Empire since before the American Revolution. Here control of the Suez Canal was worked out, and here the German Kaiser's ultimatum was debated in 1914. Here, too, Prince Lichnowsky, the German ambassador, broke in on Prime Minister Asquith's breakfast and then broke into tears at his failure to prevent an earlier war between England and Germany.

Now in the small council room downstairs another war cabinet was meeting to develop mobilization plans for the Commonwealth and the exiled governments of her allies. Canada was well represented by the determined minister, a veteran of the previous world war, who sat in the wheelchair. Ralston was a modest, quiet man, but there was no questioning his character, courage or mental capacity.

I had been sitting, smoking and reading in the upstairs room for 20 minutes or so, when the door to the room opened and a woman in a rather plain housedress entered. My back was somewhat to the door and the woman was careful not to disturb me, so I gave her only a casual glance as she quietly proceeded to tidy up the room, shaking up the cushions and putting books away. I assumed she was the housekeeper, so continued with my reading. I looked again. Yes, it was Mrs. Churchill, the wife of the Prime Minister, and there I sat like an oaf reading the *Tatler* and puffing a cigarette. What would she think of Canadians? I leapt to my feet with apologies. She was very gracious about my unintentional rudeness and waved it aside. She then begged me to be seated and sat talking easily with me for the next half hour. While I only had the good fortune to meet Lady Churchill on one other occasion, I could accept entirely all the great tributes paid to her by her husband both publicly and in several private conversations, during and after the war.

Prior to our arrival, Ralston had instructed me to take careful notes of the points discussed with Churchill. This was rather a new role for me, but I did my best at the job. Later, back at our hotel, Ralston, who had a highly trained legal mind, complained to me that I had done it very badly. He was quite correct. With my newspaper training and complete fascination with Churchill as an individual, my notes looked like a news report; I had concentrated on the highlights in terms of their news value.

"And look, you've got down nearly everything that Churchill said and not a word of mine," he protested. I was quick to assure him it would not happen again, though I had no idea how this was to be accomplished. I had not studied shorthand, nor had my previous military or newspaper training provided me with any secretarial skills. I still had much to learn as a military staff secretary.

Ordered To Hospital

After the first week in London it became apparent that Colonel Ralston would have to get some rest and treatment for the pain in his back. Propped up in bed, he would work on his files and memoranda until two or three in the morning. Then after only a few hours of sleep, off we went with his wheelchair to the endless meetings and conferences. He finally agreed to go to hospital for a few days, and I arranged to have him admitted to the Royal Masonic Hospital in London. He insisted that I keep his hospitalization entirely secret; nothing was to be reported to the press or back to Canada.

The Royal Masonic was an ancient hospital, and the travelling carriage that Florence Nightingale used at the Crimea was enshrined in the lobby. The nurses all wore enormous starched caps and costumes of an earlier century. All in all, rather an intimidating institution, although I did discover that one of the cute little nurses, peering out of a great bonnet, came from Maple Creek, Saskatchewan. The trip to the Royal Masonic, however, proved a wasted effort. The doctor prescribed deep-heat treatments, but the apparatus required could not be operated in the London area, as it interfered with some electronic air defence device for spotting enemy planes. Following a fast negotiation the next day with Dr. Stan Conn at CMHQ, I arranged to have the colonel transferred out of London to a Canadian Army hospital established at Taplow on the Cliveden estate of Lord Astor, where the formidable Nancy Astor dominated both the estate and the hospital. The much publicized Cliveden set, with its tolerant views of Hitler in the prewar Chamberlain period, was now in considerable disarray, though Lady Astor still attracted many interesting house guests for the weekends.

Two events remain in my memory about the stay at the Taplow hospital. The colonel had insisted on bringing a carload of files to the hospital, and no sooner did the medics have him stretched out on the narrow hospital bed than he started to work again on the everlasting reports and minutes. Despite his great pain, he got propped up with a support for his back, set his pince-nez in place and off he started.

It was at this point we became acquainted with the powerful personality of nursing sister Marnie Hearn. Marnie had served overseas as an army nurse in World War I, and in her long army career had the experience of dealing with some thousands of male patients. There was little she did not know about army customs or how to handle the youngest subaltern, the old sweat or the crusty general.

As Colonel Ralston worked away in the little hospital room, a young orderly opened the door to wheel in the large deep-heat apparatus. Without looking up from his papers, Ralston gruffly demanded what he wanted. When the orderly explained his mission, the colonel brushed aside the interruption — "Come back later; I'll tell you when I'm ready for my treatment." The hapless orderly, on receiving this command from "God" — the Minister of Defence himself — quickly backed out into the hall, where he ran into Marnie, who was in charge of that wing. On hearing the orderly's explanation, Marnie, at her majestic best, sailed straight into the room. "Son," she said to Ralston, "around here I give the orders." Then before Ralston realized what was happening, she stripped back the blankets, rolled the minister over on his tummy and gave him a sharp slap on his bare behind. This was the only occasion on which I saw the colonel forced to capitulate. As Marnie then issued her orders that treatments would be carried out according to schedule, the colonel spoke not a word of protest — nor did he attempt to disobey her orders in future.

In passing, it could be added that while Marnie was something of a tyrant and an established character at Taplow, some hundreds of badly wounded Canadian soldiers in two world wars remembered her with affection.

Dramatic Meeting With McNaughton

One critical event, which happened while we were at the hospital, was the first official or business meeting between Colonel Ralston and General McNaughton, who was then Canada's senior field commander in England.

General McNaughton, an artillery staff officer of some distinction in World War I, had been appointed to command Canada's 1st Division early in World War II and proceeded overseas with this formation. In time, this force would be augmented by an additional two infantry divisions, two armoured divisions, two army tank brigades and various ancillary army troop formations of artillery, engineers and so forth. McNaughton was widely recognized at the start of the war as Canada's senior professional soldier. He also enjoyed a high reputation in the scientific aspects of war. He had a commanding presence and made an imposing figure with his iron grey hair, piercing eyes and bushy eyebrows. Despite his subsequently proven inability to command large formations in the field, he unquestionably was a man of marked ability, determination and great self-confidence. It is fair to say that in matters of character, his only serious fault sprang from vanity when he refused to recognize his own limitations. When, ultimately, he was obliged to resign his command later in the war, pride led him into serious errors of judgment and vindictiveness against those, including Ralston, whom he wrongly blamed for his removal, on what he imagined were entirely political grounds.

In some measure, McNaughton was the innocent victim of an excessive publicity build-up early in the war, which served to distort his personal vanity. This publicity build-up was due to the fact that for mobilization purposes, Canada desperately needed the image of a strong war leader, a Kitchener, a Churchill, a Smuts or a de Gaulle, around which the nation could mobilize. Canada had found a purpose but desperately needed a national hero. Mackenzie King, our Prime Minister, although a shrewd political leader, was hopeless as a hero-image, with his short stature, bald head, glasses, rotund little figure and pedantic oratory. As a result, it was McNaughton's picture that appeared on the front pages, on the posters, the newsreels and magazine covers. He was, for a time, tipped as the probable commander of all Allied forces for the Second Front.

All of this had been pretty heady stuff. Soaring on the wave of public acclaim, McNaughton on arrival in England had assumed great authority, made great decisions and commitments for Canada without any approval from the government in Ottawa. Overseas he became rather a law unto himself, brooking no interference.

Colonel Ralston, a prominent corporation lawyer in Montreal, had been brought back hastily into the government and subsequently appointed senior Defence Minister on the tragic death of Norman Rogers in a plane crash. Along with Ralston, Mackenzie King had commandeered for his wartime cabinet such other forceful personalities as Angus Macdonald, C. D. Howe and J. L. Ilsley, who together with Chubby Power as Air Minister, T. A. Crerar and James Gardiner, formed what was undoubtedly the strongest cabinet in Canada's history.

While all these ministers accorded the fullest measure of loyalty to Mackenzie King, it was to Ralston they looked as the strong man to prosecute the war effort. Ralston was one of Canada's foremost corporation lawyers and had served in the trenches during World War I as Colonel of the Nova Scotia Highlanders. He was a man of integrity, with an immense capacity for work, a penetrating mind and a toughness which was accentuated by a strong protruding jaw. He came from dour Scottish-Maritime stock and in the prewar years had served in earlier cabinets. During the R. B. Bennett government, he had been the chief financial critic in the Liberal opposition. Twice previously he had retired from public office.

The day of the first overseas meeting between the minister and McNaughton saw considerable excitement at Taplow Army Hospital. I had set up in one of the large sunrooms a long board table and easels. Then a convoy of staff cars arrived with pennants flying and a motorcycle escort from the Army Provosts' Corps. McNaughton, attended by a large retinue of senior staff officers, complete with polished riding boots, Sam Browne belts and red tabs, stamped importantly along the hospital corridors.

I pushed Ralston in his wheelchair into the conference room. Still hunched over from the pain in his back and wearing a faded blue hospital-issue dressing gown, he sat in marked contrast to the smartly uniformed officers about the table.

With only a passing deference to the minister, McNaughton proceeded for the next hour to deliver a rather condescending report on our overseas forces and, as an afterthought, outlined the various new agreements he had entered into with the British over the use of reinforcements, the reorganization of units and the creation of new ad hoc units — none of which had been approved by or even communicated to the government in Ottawa.

Ralston listened carefully throughout, then spoke very slowly and precisely. "Those decisions which you have just reported, General, are all matters which will be properly decided by the Canadian government, not independently by yourself."

There was a complete and icy silence in the room for the next few minutes. McNaughton stared into Ralston's steady gaze and then slowly sat down. There was no doubt left in anyone's mind as to where authority rested or who would exercise it.

Some Amusement At Cliveden

To divert briefly, it is perhaps of interest to recall in passing my introduction to the "Cliveden Set" while I was filling in time at Taplow Hospital. Lady (Nancy) Astor, the "American Cyclone," as she was called by the army doctors, invited me to one of her famous intellectual weekend gatherings at Cliveden, her nearby estate. She was certainly a woman of strong opinions and rather an aggressive manner, but she could also be extremely kind and entertaining. It was a large house party of colourful people, mostly civilians, whom I knew only by reputation. During that era Nancy Astor was acknowledged to be England's most brilliant hostess.

The light chit-chat before dinner was on a rather ethereal plane and rather escaped me. Being a bit lost the first night at the pre-dinner gathering, I wandered about loosely from group to group, seeing where a colonial officer might unobtrusively fit in. Finally I spotted a fellow journalist and former Canadian, Beverly Baxter, who had become a British MP and whom I had known slightly in Canada. He was holding court with great words of learning to a small admiring audience, so I gathered in to absorb his wisdom.

All was going well till he made the rather fatuous statement that this war would not be won by tanks and guns, but by imponderables. In my more limited grasp of affairs, it rather came to me that if imponderables were the big thing, obviously all the efforts of Churchill, Ralston and others to produce tanks and guns were being wasted, so I innocently asked what were these "imponderables" and where could we get some. Baxter turned slowly and gave me a fishy stare. He had not recognized me in uniform at first, but then came to realization.

"You are from the *Winnipeg Free Press*, aren't you?," he demanded. With that, he gave me his back and walked off.

As a great Tory, Baxter had nursed a deep loathing for the Liberal *Free Press* and, in particular, for one of our chief editors at that time, George Ferguson. George had always delighted in pulling Baxter's leg each time one of his under-the-table columns appeared in *Maclean's* magazine.

It is a peculiar English custom in some circles that nobody bothers to introduce people to one another. It is considered that everyone of importance either knows the others, or should not show their ignorance. This is not really a matter of rudeness, but simply "form." The correct and accepted response is a very superior stance and the "back-of-the-hand-to-you" approach. People then wonder just who you are . . . maybe they should know. As one of my experienced social friends in England once explained, "If you act like a nobody, they treat you like a nobody."

However, I next managed to strike up some light conversation with a bright, older man, who allowed that he was half Canadian. His father or mother had once owned some coal mines in Nova Scotia. He was highly informed about the Middle East, had been a close friend of Lord Allenby and the legendary Lawrence of Arabia. His name was Sir Ronald Storrs and he had been the first governor of Jerusalem, after the liberation of the Holy City back in 1918. His book on the subject, which he subsequently sent to me, is still must reading for students of the Arab-Israeli conflict.

Very strict rationing of electricity had just been imposed in England. You could only have so many light bulbs burning at any one time, in strict ratio to the number of permanent residents. This was periodically checked by the local bobby. With true patriotism, the rule was strictly enforced by Nancy Astor, regardless of the number of her guests or the countless rooms in Cliveden. As a result, when our party moved into the dining hall, the rest of the mansion had to be plunged into utter darkness so the many lights in that large room could be turned on. The description of utter darkness is no exaggeration; every window and door chink had to be completely blacked-out with air-raid curtains or black paint.

Seated beside Storrs, I found him an excellent and witty storyteller. The long dinner went well enough, except that I developed a strong urge to find a men's room as time passed. Excusing myself quietly, I slipped out of the great dining room and went groping along endless dark hallways, with only the aid of an austerity cigarette lighter. It was a hopeless exploration and I was lucky even to find my way back to the dinner table. In some desperation, I then asked Storrs, as one Canadian to another, "where in hell do they hide the loo?"

A second safari saw me resort to a rather difficult manoeuvre, which I have had to employ on a few similar occasions when I groped about some strange darkened room. I was able to find a window where the slats on the shutters could be opened a few inches.

On returning to the table, I found the elderly Sir Ronald chatting-up and enthralled by a gorgeous young lady of about 19, seated across the table. It seemed they shared a deep love of music. The young lady played piano and Sir Ronald was rather an authority on the subject of Bach, Beethoven and Chopin. Acceding to Sir Ronald's urgent request, the young lady agreed to play for him in the music room after dinner.

Though Lady Astor had been seated some distance down the table from us, none of the table chat escaped her sharp ear. As we paraded out of the dining room to a great hall where fireplaces blazed, Sir Ronald, very pleased with himself, led his trusting young partner off into the pitch dark music room. At this precise moment I felt the strong fingers of Nancy Astor seize my left ear, as she marched me rapidly toward the music room with the words, "I wouldn't trust Sir Ronald alone in there with a young girl for two minutes. You are to stay in there until they leave." It seemed an odd mission for the secretary to the Minister of

Defence having to play "gooseberry" for a former governor of Jerusalem, but I carried out my orders.

It should be recalled that even after Munich, the intellectuals of the Cliveden Set still hailed Hitler as the saviour of Europe and assailed Churchill as being a warmonger.

TWO

Back To Whitehall

WORLD SCENE

*1940 draws to a close — a grim year. Alone in Europe
and threatened by invasion, Britain turns to Canada
for immediate help. Hectic meetings in Whitehall to
speed the supply of Canadian forces, munitions and
supplies across the Atlantic. Empire Air Training
Scheme and destroyer construction in Canada to
be expanded. London's worst air blitz. Canadian
Corps created.*

The few days' rest at Taplow gave Ralston considerable relief, so back we
raced to London. My notebook for the following week records meetings
with Britain's First Sea Lord, A. V. Alexander; Sir Archibald Sinclair,
Secretary of State for Air; Sir Charles Portal, Chief of Air Staff; C-in-C
Home Forces, Sir Alan Brooke; Minister of Munitions, Sir Andrew
Duncan — and dozens of others. Preparing minutes of all these meetings
and then gathering papers for meetings the following day kept me
working till nearly dawn each night. Sleep was pretty well out of the
question anyway till dawn, as the air-raids were continuous every night
and the anti-aircraft guns in Hyde Park blasted periodically.

Mike Pearson, at that time Secretary at Canada House, was of tremendous help to us. It was Mike at his best. He knew the form in all official
circles and had personal contacts everywhere. There was seldom a day
when he did not turn up at the Dorchester to give us a hand.

I won't attempt to record all the endless meetings. Much of this record
can be found in the daily notes for Ralston's diaries, and in his formal
reports to the government made after we returned to Ottawa. But a few
of the meetings and the circumstances surrounding them are worth
special mention.

Among the matters considered top secret at that time were tentative
plans to move the Royal Family to Canada in the event Hitler's forces
were able to invade England. Similar consideration was also given to
having the British navy based in Canada, to continue the war if Britain
was overrun by the Nazis.

There was one situation which caused a little embarrassment during all
the London meetings I attended and was pictured at, arising from my
modest rank of captain. Anthony Eden, Britain's Secretary for War, who
also attended many of the meetings, was referred to as Captain Eden at
that time, and his successor was also addressed as Captain Margesson.

By accident, several times my name appeared in the British press as
Captain Eden Malone. I corrected this error each time, but it didn't sit
too well with Vincent Massey, Canada's High Commissioner in London,
or with Harry Crerar.

Massey was rather sensitive on matters of protocol and a bit jealous of
his official position as Canada's senior representative in England. Under-

29

standably, he was disturbed when, due to the urgency of war, commitments were made in England by Ralston, Howe, McNaughton, myself and others, direct with members of the British war cabinet or chiefs of staff committee, to avoid the delay and red tape of going through Canada House, and for reasons of security.

Similarly, Massey's nose was out of joint sometimes at official functions, when either McNaughton or Price Montague, in general's uniform and red tabs, got the spotlight in the British press as representing Canada.

It was amazing to see how, under the pressure of war, the business of government could be accelerated. Prolonged negotiations, studies and the protocol of polite exchanges were all swept aside by the driving energies of Ralston and Howe. Almost instant commitments were given to expand the Empire Air Training Scheme, build destroyers and tanks in Canada, supply cars and trucks to the British army, send hard rock miners to Gibraltar, a forestry corps to Scotland, more armoured and infantry divisions to England, and establish Polish training centres in Canada. It was a staggering program, bearing in mind that Canada had started almost from scratch in many cases.

As an instance of Ralston's consideration and generosity of spirit, I should mention that he paid a great tribute to me when reporting later to Parliament. He touched on his own illness and periods of incapacity in England, and stated that without the hard work of Malone in assisting him, his mission and program could not have been accomplished. This was high praise indeed for a rather junior militia officer, but it didn't help my military career much with the Permanent Force brass in Ottawa.

The night of the famous fire bombing of London, Ralston and I went up together to the roof of the Dorchester Hotel, where we were staying, to witness the awe-inspiring spectacle. The Luftwaffe on this particular night had launched its entire bomber strength in an effort to destroy London. The crash of heavy anti-aircraft batteries, a few hundred yards away in Hyde Park, added to the din of ambulance sirens and the wails of air-raid warnings. Beams from huge searchlights raked the skies and the entire city was lit up from the hundreds of separate fires caused by incendiaries. It was past midnight, but we could clearly see the dome of St. Paul's Cathedral far away down in the City, and off to the right the great cranes in the dock area, the House of Parliament and Westminster, all seemingly floating in a sea of flames.

Each night after dinner in the hotel, the elderly dowagers could be seen gathering in the rotunda, ready to retire to the shelters for the night when the blitz started up. Many of these older women would have their mink coats on over their night attire, and in their hands would be clutched their jewel cases and frequently a bottle of whisky or brandy.

Ralston insisted on touring the east end and the poorer sections of the city, where entire blocks of flats and other dwellings had been smashed to rubble, and the air-raid wardens helped the homeless hundreds in trying to salvage a few pitiful remains or recover the bodies of their loved ones.

Unquestionably, scenes like this gave him an even greater determination that Canada's war effort must be pressed to the limit. And it was little wonder that he found the restraint in Canada, of only voluntary enlistment for overseas service, almost unbearable during the next two years.

Despite our heavy schedule, there were also a few lighter moments. Not that they were important in themselves, but they will perhaps recapture a bit of the colour, emotions and atmosphere of those days, when Britain was preparing for a German invasion.

As mentioned, Ralston's question on his arrival in London — "how in hell are we going to win this war?" — had gained some circulation among cabinet circles in London. One evening after dinner, Mr. Churchill, fortified with several drinks, got up from the table and proceeded to answer Ralston's question in very vigorous, free-swinging language as he marched around the table. At one point, he seized an orange from a plate on the table to illustrate his point.

"We'll Namsos* these bastards yet," he growled. "We must fight to regain our mobility at sea. Britain has never been a great land power. We must always preserve our freedom of movement around Europe with our navy and air force . . . then choose the time and place of our attack." Here, he jabbed his finger into various sides of the orange. "The rotten spots will show up; then we will know where to attack."

The first essential, he argued, was to clear the Mediterranean. He expected Gibraltar to fall to Hitler and Mussolini, but we must keep the sea lanes open. We must clear the enemy out of North Africa. He forecast the date when this would be accomplished.

In actuality, he was wrong in his judgment that Gibraltar would be captured and he was about six months premature in his date for the clearing of North Africa. In general terms, however, his assessment and forecast even at that early period proved substantially correct.

His words were to come back to me repeatedly as the war developed. Alanbrooke, Montgomery, Wavell and Admiral Cunningham, as well as Churchill, all understood the use of naval power, the importance of keeping the sea lanes open and the Mediterranean free in any European war. It was an historic strategy** fully appreciated by Nelson more than a century before, when Britain alone had faced the great land armies of a Europe dominated by another tyrant. By keeping her own supply lines open, the enemy ports blockaded, and with the mobility to concentrate and quickly move her small army to threaten every coast, Britain had triumphed.

Tragically, it was a factor that the United States in World War II failed to grasp.

Despite all Churchill's powers of persuasion, President Roosevelt, backed by his Generals Marshall and Eisenhower, together with Admiral King, insisted on the one great assault across the Channel. They refused to co-operate in any drive across the Adriatic into the Balkans to block the Soviet armies from seizing Vienna, Prague and Berlin. They could not appreciate that by threatening the underbelly of Europe in this way, a great number of Hitler's divisions would have to be withdrawn from France. To them it appeared as simply a useless adventure. They did not understand the politics of Europe or the ultimate Soviet threat. Albania, Yugoslavia, Hungary, Austria and Romania were far-off lands of little interest to Washington then.

Similarly they did not appreciate that Hitler's failure to reach Moscow in 1941, before the onset of winter, was largely due to the delays caused by the Nazi divisions having to intervene in Greece and Yugoslavia.

*Namsos: Small Norwegian port, target of a British diversionary attack in 1940.

**This strategy (brilliantly outlined by the historian, Sir Arthur Bryant, in his book *Years of Endurance*) was something never fully understood by the continental powers, or by either Napoleon or Hitler until it was too late.

As became known after the war, General Von Branchitsch, Hitler's Chief of Land Forces, fully understood the critical importance of securing the Mediterranean, through the seizure of Gibraltar, Malta and Egypt, before tackling Russia. His efforts to convince Hitler of this fact only produced one of Hitler's most furious outbursts and a tirade of abuse.

Back at the Dorchester Hotel the day following our meeting with Churchill, Ralston and I tried to put together the essentials of Churchill's after-dinner lecture in the form of a written memo or minute. As Ralston observed, "It is terribly important for us to know exactly what this man is thinking, so I can report to the cabinet in Canada, despite his many drinks and the fact it was a private dinner."

As I drafted the memo, I tried as far as possible to record Churchill's actual words and such phrases as "We'll Namsos these bastards yet."

Several days later, we reached a point of some serious dispute with the British. I was not particularly experienced in the practice and protocol required of a staff secretary operating at such dizzy international heights. Each night at the Dorchester, a special uniformed messenger from Downing Street or Whitehall would arrive and deliver to my custody a beautiful red-leather despatch box containing page after page of minutes of our various meetings, held three or four days previously, all finely typed on onion skin paper. On top would be a brief note on crested stationery, addressed to myself. "My dear Malone," or "Dear private secretary" — would you kindly have your chief initial the dozen or more minutes of our meetings at the Ministry of Supply last Thursday, etc.

These daily despatch boxes were a source of great irritation to Ralston, and he would fume and sulk every time the great masses of onion skin paper arrived. He would stuff them back into my hands at first and tell me to check them over. A few minutes later, he would either send for me or burst into my room at the hotel to recover them and then sit down to work them over. His years of training as a lawyer would not allow him to pass all this fine print in any casual manner. Out would come his pen, and correction after correction would be scribbled across each page. "We didn't agree to that," he would shout. "They have changed it all. We didn't agree to supply that and we won't pay for this." And so it went.

Finally, one day he lost his temper over this situation and he challenged Churchill directly on this manner of doing business with the British government. I was much impressed with the vigour and directness of Ralston's complaint to Churchill. If there were any doubts whatever as to exactly what was agreed to, a stenographer should be called in at the time and the minute dictated and signed immediately by all present, he contended. We can't go on this way, trying to approve minutes of meetings held several days before, when we were now working on entirely different subjects. I can't keep going back over the old files days later, he protested. Churchill listened thoughtfully and then quietly agreed.

Then, rather to relieve the tension but also to relieve his own conscience a little, Ralston jokingly informed Churchill that he had taken the liberty of having me record, in memo form, Churchill's own freewheeling remarks at the dinner party.

The Prime Minister was immediately alert. Turning to me he said, "Well, send those minutes over for my signature if you please." Recalling the easy manner in which these minutes were drawn with the use of the odd profanity and description, I tried to avoid his requirement, protesting that they were simply some rough notes I had written. Nevertheless, Churchill demanded to see them. In due course, they were returned to me with all Churchill's own corrections marked by himself in green ink, deleting the profanities and correcting my grammar.

As this memo was obviously of some historic interest — it recorded Churchill's personal views at the time — I asked Ralston to let me keep the original. Quite properly, he refused, saying it must go with his diary notes back for cabinet information. He assured me, however, that he would let me have a copy of his diary covering those weeks together, along with the Churchill memo, when the war was over.

Some 36 years after this event, I was intrigued to read a passage in the book, *A Man Called Intrepid*, about an old wartime friend, Sir William Stephenson, the famous Chief of Intelligence and Espionage. It told how he had used an orange to explain Britain's continental strategy, in almost identical terms, to President Roosevelt at the White House in 1942. Out of curiosity, I wrote to Sir William in Bermuda, asking about this odd coincidence. It was no coincidence, he replied. Sir William had seen my secret, free-swinging memo of the Churchill talk and, two years later, used the same orange idea to illustrate Britain's thinking to the American President.

As an indication of Mr. Churchill's thinking at that period, the following is a more formal memo covering an earlier meeting that Colonel Ralston and I had with him on December 17, 1940.

Notes on Mr. Churchill's Conversation
of Tuesday 17th December 1940
(as corrected by Mr. Churchill)

Mr. Churchill said the first consideration was, of course, survival. We are building a fine army. Men from the new battalions are manning the beaches, giving the older troops a chance to train.

Within six months Italy may be eliminated from N.E. Africa. We shall go as far as possible in the present operations in Libya. We shall certainly send more troops there.

The revolt in Abyssinia is going well. We may put in additional troops there and we have to consider troops as well as equipment to help the Greeks. We may want to use troops in North West Africa to overshadow the West Coast. We may want to help Spain.

I [Ralston] mentioned that in Canada already there had been newspaper reports already, intimating that it was proposed to send Canadians to the Middle East. I had advised the Government that such a proposal had never even been put forward and I intimated that we would assume that employment of our troops, outside of the United Kingdom, be left for our suggestion. His reply was, "of course."

He said that one is always trying to appraise what the enemy is up to and out of the several possibilities some move in Spain seemed the more probable. He spoke of invasion as always being a very real threat and here the Canadian forces in air and the navy had most important roles.

On the point of building up air superiority, he believes that we may do it in less than six months, counting what we can get from the United States and bearing in mind the German air preoccupations on other fronts.

Regarding aggressive operations we have two or three plans for activity where we can muster superior forces on account of Hitler's distractions elsewhere. He has taught us a great deal with "wise recklessness."

He didn't discuss any measures to meet the increased U-boat menace, except the need for more destroyers.

Regarding gas warfare, we shall not initiate it; but we have considerable counter measures prepared.

Speaking of production, he said it was not seriously menaced as yet, by air raids. He was confident that notwithstanding an apparently great military superiority he is quite sure we can survive and eventually defeat him. Victory might, however, take years.

I suggested that the practical possibilities of ultimate victory seemed to lie along the line of disintegration on the continent, with which he agreed.

Sikorski — A Gallant Patriot

Among the many world figures we met at that period was the colourful General Sikorski, President of Poland, then leading his exiled government and military headquarters in London. (Many years after his tragic death during the war, an irresponsible and libellous story was circulated that his death was plotted by Churchill to get him out of the way.) Canada had undertaken to handle recruiting of Polish nationals in Canada for the Polish Army, as well as Polish-American citizens who came up to Canada from the United States. For this purpose, we were establishing, at Canadian expense, a Polish Army training centre. Because of this, General Sikorski, as well as the British military chiefs, were anxious to arrange a meeting on the subject while Ralston was in London.

While it was a matter of considerable import to the Poles, the meeting had to take a lower priority with Ralston and Ottawa. We were sadly pressed just then with dozens of problems, of greater urgency, in our own mobilization.

An appointment was made to meet with General Sikorski, despite Ralston's impatience to get on with other, more pressing items. As Ralston still had difficulty in getting around, the meeting was to be held in his suite at the Dorchester, a few days later. On the day of the meeting, Leopold Amery, Britain's Secretary of State for India, suddenly arrived unannounced at our Dorchester suite, just a few minutes before Sikorski, and demanded to see Ralston.

In passing, two famous utterances by Mr. Amery in the British House, spoken just before the fall of the Chamberlain government, may be recalled. When Hitler marched into Poland, Chamberlain had risen in the House the next day to make a temporizing statement, which was ill received by Parliament. Arthur Greenwood next rose to speak. It was then that Amery had shouted from the opposition the historic phrase: "Speak for England." Then later, on May 7, 1940, when Chamberlain attempted to explain Britain's lack of early action and the failure in Norway, Amery was cheered from all sides when he quoted to him Cromwell's famous words: "You have sat too long here for any good you have been doing. Depart, I say, and let us have done with you . . . in the name of God go." Considered to be the most romantic Tory of that era, Amery was a former schoolmate of Winston Churchill.

Later, I came to know Mr. Amery well, and on one of his visits to Winnipeg I was interested to learn that he had once worked on a ranch near Calgary and was also noted as a cross-country runner. To train for some race back in England one time, he told me he had run behind a buckboard all the way from Calgary to Edmonton. Mount Amery in the Canadian Rockies, he said, was named for him to recognize his interest in mountain climbing.

At the time of his visit to the Dorchester, however, I did not know him very well but I did point out that the President of Poland was due and Ralston could only spare a few minutes before this formal appointment. With this caution, I showed Amery in to Ralston's sitting room.

Promptly at four o'clock General Sikorski — in full service uniform, complete with riding boots and spurs — and three members of his staff, stamped into our ante room.

Through Sikorski's interpreter, I explained that Mr. Amery would just be a few minutes; Ralston was expecting them, and they should be seated.

They took their seats rigidly and made no further comment. Some 10 minutes elapsed and no sign of Amery's departure, so I broke in on his visit and announced that the President was waiting. Amery was holding forth at great length about India, which was not a pressing subject with Ralston. Ralston replied in pointed fashion that Mr. Amery was just leaving, and would I explain and apologize to Sikorski. Outside again, I asked the interpreter to explain the short delay to the Polish President. Another 10 minutes elapsed; more embarrassment. Sikorski got up and started to pace the room. Again I broke in on Amery's visit to report Sikorski was getting impatient. And so, obviously, was Ralston, but Amery refused to take any hint.

When I returned to the ante room, it was already too late; Sikorski was leaving with Imperial decision. As his staff members followed in dignified exit, I did my best to offer apologies and explanation. The entire business put Ralston out of humour and we tried to forget the unfortunate incident in the days following.

Then came an urgent plea from the Foreign Office. Sikorski, as Head of State, considered himself to have been deliberately affronted. Ralston was entreated to see Sikorski to try to patch up matters before we returned to Canada. By this time, our program was entirely booked up. In desperation and irritation, Ralston directed that I should go and make an official call on the President, extend his formal apology and discover what exactly was troubling Sikorski. Alan Magee would accompany me on the visit.

Two days later, with my buttons polished, red brassard, swagger stick, pistol and all, I paid a visit to the Polish headquarters. Some 16 senior Polish ministers and military officers were seated around a council table with General Sikorski at the head. After a very formal round of introductions, Alan Magee and I took the two vacant seats at the near end of the table. Black cigarettes were then offered all round, and a spokesman rose on Sikorski's left and demanded, did we speak Polish. Magee and I expressed our regrets. General Sikorski would speak in French then, as he could not use English. I explained that my limited

French was not equal to the occasion; the exchange must therefore be through a Polish interpreter. And so the lengthy negotiations began, but they were entirely one-sided. As each of the Polish officials spoke, another one of his colleagues would violently inject himself into the oratory before the poor interpreter had a chance to translate the previous speaker to us. This bewildering performance continued for more than an hour, while Magee and I listened bug-eyed.

Finally, from a few garbled words the interpreter was able to interpret, I came to the appalling realization that the Polish staff had concluded that Magee and I had agreed to all their requests. Canada would pay to clothe, feed, equip and transport overseas all the Canadian- and American-Polish recruits. Obviously, my first diplomatic mission had run completely out of control.

In something of a panic, I conveyed this horrible suspicion quietly to Magee. His apprehensions were similar to my own, and he whispered hoarsely "What do we do now?" In desperation a flash of inspiration came to me. Raising my voice above the torrent of Polish, I impressed on the interpreter that "of course all the verbal discussions could only form the basis of an *aide memoire*, which we would be glad to submit to our government for consideration." The day was saved and Magee and I quickly made a formal departure.

I had only heard of this handy little instrument, an *aide memoire*, a few days before. In diplomatic parlance it is a "memorandum sent by one government through its ambassador to the Foreign Minister of another government, summarizing points made by word of mouth."

In the event, while Canada did not in the months ahead extend all the support General Sikorski demanded, we did assist the Polish Army very substantially by establishing a Polish Army training centre near Owen Sound, Ontario, and we processed and equipped many reinforcements for the Polish units in England.

Throughout the war I held a particular sympathy for the exiled Polish forces, who had been driven from their homeland but had been rallied by Sikorski to continue to fight with great effect in the air, at sea and in infantry and armoured divisions in Italy and north-west Europe. Several years later, when serving on General Montgomery's 8th Army staff in Italy and with 21st Army Group in France, I was able to assist the Poles on many occasions — fighting to get them more vehicles, intervening on their behalf for Polish war correspondents, their own censors in the Polish language and a share of transmission facilities, and so forth. Later I came to know both generals, Anders and Matcheck, and was with their units in action at times.

Immediately after the war, I was also able to assist in plans for resettling in various parts of Canada some thousands of Polish war veterans, who were stranded in Scotland. They were a courageous and cheery lot, but we failed them in the end. It has always distressed me that these wartime comrades, after fighting as our allies, were never able to see their homes again. I think perhaps my affection for the Poles stemmed from those first meetings with Sikorski and his defence staff.

Although considered a bit mad at times, with their reckless courage in action, the Polish units were well respected by the Allied forces. Their divisions frequently trained and served alongside the Canadians, sometimes as part of the Canadian Army. Many Canadians were transported across the oceans in such Polish ships as the *Batory* or flew in formations with Polish air squadrons. The early Polish-Canadian co-operation, negotiated with President Sikorski, proved of substantial value and did much at that time to preserve the identity of a tragic country, which through betrayals and brutal deceits had been torn asunder between Germany and Russia. Remembering the Polish corps in World War II, it is hard to believe that the trumpet of freedom will not some day be blown again in Warsaw.

Endless Round Of Meetings

Each week in London brought a fresh round of meetings as other British officials sought out Ralston to arrange further assistance from Canada. One day it would be Lord Hankey and Clement Attlee. The next day, Lord Cranbourne. And so it went, keeping me swamped with memos and minutes till the early hours each morning.

There was a dinner one evening of only a dozen or so officials from the supply services, where matters of timber, coal, wheat and machinery were to be discussed. In attendance was a rugged British cabinet minister, who got very tipsy and sorrowful to the point of tears as the dinner progressed.

He had come up the hard way, from a childhood spent as a pitboy in a Welsh coal mine. Because of his knowledge, capability and the respect in which he was held by the unions, he had been appointed by Churchill to the cabinet, to help encourage the miners in longer work hours and maximum production.

After many drinks, the minister, to our astonishment, suddenly rose to his feet and made a very passionate and unscheduled speech. Tipsy though he was, our Canadian group was profoundly moved at his words. With tears in his eyes he told how, at the age of eight, he had been harnessed to pull coal carts through a Welch mine, along tunnels that were too low to permit the use of a donkey.

Throughout his life as a miner he had struggled to reach the top of his union, with the sole purpose of improving conditions in the mines. Now he had achieved a position of cabinet authority and should be able to do things. But the war had defeated his purpose. Many of the younger miners had been enlisted in the army and, instead of improving conditions, he was obliged to drive the older men and youngsters harder than ever. With their food reduced by rationing and their towns hit by Nazi bombs, all he could do was repeat the critical call for more coal to win the war. Having reached the top, there was now nothing he could do to achieve his dream.

This great burst of unexpected oratory rather concluded the party, but it certainly brought home to us the demands and sacrifices Britain was facing on all fronts.

Another meeting which remains in my mind was one Ralston had secretly at the Dorchester with Pierre Dupuy. Dupuy at that time was in charge of the Canadian legation in German-occupied Paris, where he maintained constant contact with the Vichy government. Very few people in Canada or in any of our Allied countries realized then, or even realize now, that Canada did not sever diplomatic relations with Vichy, France during the war.

In Volume I of *The Mackenzie King Record* by Jack Pickersgill, there is a single paragraph reference to Mr. Dupuy, who before the war was a member of the Canadian legation in Paris. Pickersgill records simply that, "Mackenzie King read his [Pierre Dupuy's] confidential report and found it an exceedingly interesting and able document. Felt very proud that a Canadian could have played so immensely important a part . . . as Churchill himself cabled me, Dupuy was the one effective link the British government had."

Pickersgill makes no attempt to explain the nature of this report — how Dupuy got the report out of Vichy, France, or any details as to the nature of Dupuy's mission. It is likely that Mr. Dupuy will someday give a complete account of these events himself, but as I heard Dupuy's personal report at the time when he visited Ralston secretly at the Dorchester Hotel, I shall give a brief outline here.

There was some mystery and there were also some protests in the press and Parliament of Canada, after the fall of France, over why Canada did not sever diplomatic relations with France as England had done, and why the French minister was allowed to remain in Ottawa. Any time the question was raised in Parliament, it was quietly quashed, and the questioner was answered privately, outside the chamber. Some suggestion was made that this was because of the small French islands of St. Pierre and Miquelon, which were the cause of some squabbles with General de Gaulle. Another suggestion was that Mackenzie King did not wish to risk asking Quebec Members of Parliament to vote on any bill declaring war on France.

Undoubtedly, Mackenzie King was very conscious of this latter situation, but the real purpose of Dupuy remaining in Paris was for him to act as an invaluable go-between for the Vichy authorities and the British government.

When Dupuy came to see us privately at the Dorchester one night, he had just slipped out of Paris through Portugal, to bring a secret personal appeal direct from Marshal Petain to Churchill. Details of his trip, as well as his message, he confided to Ralston and myself.

After the fall of France and his return to Paris, Dupuy had experienced considerable difficulty at first in establishing trustworthy contacts either with Vichy authorities or members of the resistance movement. Vichy officials were very gun-shy of him, as Dupuy was kept under careful watch by the Nazi Gestapo. For some time he was unable to have any reliable talks with Vichy officials, and there was no opportunity for any completely private conversation with Petain. As Dupuy related, however, at the instigation of Petain himself, he was approached by a Vichy agent and a most secret rendezvous with Petain was effected. Petain wished to get a personal message to Churchill in London.

He appealed to Churchill in the strongest possible terms, begging him not to attack the French naval units in the Mediterranean. He pointed out that possession of the French fleet was vital to France. It was the last bargaining card he had with Hitler to preserve any measure of French control in France. Petain gave Churchill his solemn and unqualified pledge that the French fleet would never be allowed to fall into German hands or be used against the Allies. They would scuttle it if necessary.

In getting this message back to England, Dupuy had motored out of Paris and reached the border before the Gestapo could catch up to him. He had used an old Buick, which had formerly belonged to the embassy in Paris and was much faster than the Volkswagen of his pursuers; Dupuy was not certain whether the Germans would ignore his diplomatic status and risk arresting him, once they saw him headed for the border. He had stopped for lunch at a small town, feeling he had given the Germans the slip, but just as he finished his meal, he saw the Gestapo men driving furiously up in their smaller car. At this point Dupuy repaired hastily to the gentlemen's room, tore up the pages of his notebook and hastily flushed them down the toilet. These exciting accounts and details of his discussions with Vichy and resistance leaders in France were reported back to Mackenzie King. They formed the basis of the Dupuy report mentioned in Pickersgill's book.*

Another Canadian to visit us at the Dorchester then was a young naval lieutenant. I don't recall his name but he was on naval intelligence work and told us some surprising details of his work. He had been in the shipping or marine insurance business before the war and he was experienced in assessing hulls, capacities and cargoes of merchant ships. Seemingly, he was able to slip over to the continent as a civilian whenever he liked through Sweden or Norway, and then he would wander about the major ports in Europe as a broker or something, sizing up all the enemy merchant shipping, departures and cargoes. He would then report his observations to London through Lloyd's Insurance. It was a dangerous assignment but he seemed quite unconcerned with the risks. Lloyd's Insurance, I might add, secretly operated all through the war as the centre of shipping intelligence for the Admiralty. I was taken into the heavily guarded ops-room one day to see how the set-up functioned. Apparently Lloyd's Insurance brokers at European ports were still able to record, in London, details of all the sailings of merchant ships, their cargoes and destinations. Large maps on the walls gave the picture in daily detail, showing the positions of various ships. Needless to say, such information was of tremendous value, not only to the Admiralty but also to Bomber Command.

London, at that time, presented an exciting picture. Everywhere there were uniforms of all varieties. Besides the British services, there were the Free French, Polish, Canadian, Home Guard and Air Raid uniforms. The fronts of larger stores, banks and official buildings were sandbagged to door-top levels. Each night the air-raid sirens wailed in the dark; soon the bombs would start to fall, and people trooped to nearby air-raid shelters. But many of the restaurants, theatres and hotels, bottle clubs and night clubs, provided attractions for the troops on leave. The Berkley, Buttery, Savoy, Bagatelle, Le Suivi, Ciro's, The 400, Claridges, Kempinsky's

*In his memoirs, Churchill records that following receipt of Petain's appeal through Dupuy, he was forced to make a decision that he considered "the most unnatural and painful with which I have ever been concerned." The risk of the French fleet falling under German control was too great, and the British Navy was ordered to attack at both Oran and Dakar.

Oddly enough, this incident was related by a French lawyer many years later and after the death of Marshal Petain, in an appeal to reconsider the Marshal's conviction of collaborating with the Germans and to restore his honour.

The lawyer produced a report dated December 19, 1940, by Lord Halifax, recording the meeting between Petain and his second-in-command, Admiral d'Arlan, and Dupuy. Dupuy had been assured that "there was no question of letting the Germans seize the French fleet or use French bases in Africa." The ships would either sail to Allied ports or be scuttled. D'Arlan also assured Dupuy that he would delay and resist German pressures to attack French African colonies which had joined General de Gaulle. This was advanced as evidence that Petain wanted Britain to win.

and the Haywire Club were favourite Canadian gathering places, as were such bottle clubs as the Mayfair and Liaison Club after midnight.

The Beaver

It was during this visit to England that I formed a lasting friendship with the colourful, unpredictable and much criticized Lord Beaverbrook — whose explosive career, both in journalism and politics, is too well known to require any review here. I had met the great Press Lord briefly before the war, at a newspaper gathering. As in World War I, he was now a minister in the British government, to which he had been called by his friend, Sir Winston Churchill.

Beaverbrook had many enemies who deeply resented his overbearing manner and his bullying autocratic actions. There were many, including Lady Churchill, who could not understand or appreciate the great loyalty and affection which Churchill accorded this ruthless and difficult Canadian newspaper baron. With Churchill's backing, Beaverbrook tramped roughshod over everyone in his responsibilities as Minister of Aircraft Production.

During World War I, Beaverbrook had also been a focus of conflict and controversy. Indeed, as I was to discover in subsequent years, one of his greatest delights was to stir up a first-class row on every possible occasion.

From childhood I had heard of Beaverbrook's controversial conduct. My father, who commanded a Canadian regiment during the first war, became so enraged with him that he once sued him in the courts and secured damages against him. This was a subject that was always tactfully forgotten during my many visits with The Lord, as he was called by his household staff.

Ralston and Beaverbrook were both Maritimers and they had known each other for many years. Neither Ralston nor myself, however, were quite prepared for the dramatic reception which was shown us when we paid our first visit to Beaverbrook's office at the Ministry. Everything was done with a tremendous rush and efficiency. We were first shown into a general waiting room which was decorated with broken airplane propellors and sections of shot-down Nazi planes. Clerks and officials scurried in and out of doors as we watched in amazement. But we were not kept waiting. As soon as we got the general effect, another door was swung open for us and we were shown into a second, private waiting room. Then, with crisp efficiency, we were ushered into the great presence. At the end of the large private office behind an enormous desk sat the terrible little man with his sharp eyes, beneath untidy eyebrows, peering out from a wrinkled face. He looked like one of the wicked leprechauns or imps from an ancient book of Irish fairy tales, magically transformed into twentieth century England. The top of his desk was covered with a disarray of open newspapers, and on one side was a whole battery of coloured telephones. The red one was a direct line to the War Office; the blue one to the Admiralty, the green one to Downing Street, and so forth.

His lordship peered up from his work, then bounced to his feet. "How are you, Layton?" he roared at Ralston. And with a great fling of his arm, he swept all the newspapers off onto the floor. "Glad to see you. Have a chair."

Next came a demanding ring from the red telephone. Beaverbrook seized it forcefully, barked a few comments — a growl or two, several profanities — and bang went the receiver. Then back for a few more words with Ralston and myself when the green telephone rang. He had just dealt with this urgent priority when a male secretary bustled in from a side door, bearing an enormous leather blotter on which lay several crested letters requiring immediate signature. Without even a glance at them, Beaverbrook dashed off his signature with a side flourish while continuing his machine-gun conversation with us. And so it went for nearly an hour, when Ralston and I staggered out into the relative calm of the Strand.

We were to visit Beaverbrook for the weekend at his country place, Cherkley Court, near Leatherhead. It promised to be interesting. Some 20 or more high officials were also to join us for dinner there on the Saturday evening. The first showing of some movie in his private theatre was also promised.

The following Friday we paid our weekend visit to Cherkley. On the way I was first to have a meeting with General Guy Simonds, an old roommate from my days with the *Leader-Post* newspaper in Regina. At that time Guy had been a young artillery captain on the district staff. It had been several years since I had seen him. I knew he had moved ahead very rapidly in the army and I was to discuss with him some details for setting up a Canadian staff course in England. I was not, however, prepared for the reception I received. Far from any friendly or relaxed greeting from an old friend of our rowdy bachelor days, I was accorded the strictly formal, frozen Permanent-Force treatment with the clipped sentences and raised eyebrow. Thank heaven I remembered to salute him, as I was, still, only a mere captain then.

I was to see much of Guy in the years ahead but his manner was always unpredictable: at one minute the formal general, and on our next meeting the old friend of prewar days. He was to prove, by long odds, the most capable battle commander produced by Canada during the war years.

Following this rather sobering encounter, I set off with the staff car, two briefcases of papers and a batman-driver, to meet Ralston at Beaverbrook's country estate. I approached the imposing entrance, I thought, in some style. My personal luggage consisted of a single haversack, with a change of socks, shorts and shirts, pyjamas and a shaving kit.

Nockels, Lord Beaverbrook's valet, welcomed me with great condescension. "The Lord was not expected until five o'clock," he informed me, but he would show me to my suite.

"Had I brought a man with me, or would he unpack me?"

I explained that my batman-driver could take care of unpacking my haversack, but Nockels would have none of it.

Off the driver was dismissed with the car to the servants' quarters in the rear, and Nockels marched me solemnly up the stairs. I had some work to do on the files before dinner, so got busy at the desk, telling Nockels not to bother about the haversack. But Nockels was not to be diverted from his responsibilities. I watched as he rather disdainfully laid out a clean khaki shirt and placed my colonial brands of toothpaste, shaving soap, comb and razor all in line on the dresser top.

Then came the very formal demand, would he draw my bath for me? I waved him grandly off, saying not to bother, I had some work to do first, then I could "draw" my own bath. This, however, would not do for Nockels, and a sort of thing developed between us, simply because he was determined to run the bath. I was to pull the bell when I *was* ready, and he would come to manage the tub. Rather than prolong the minuet any longer, I capitulated and told him he could fill the bath now.

Then came Nockels' coup-de-grace: "What temperature would you like?" he asked with great deference. The bastard had me. I had no idea what temperature you have in a bath. Looking Nockels dead in the eye for a moment, I said, "Make it damn good and hot." He did, as I discovered a few minutes later when I had shut the bathroom door behind me. Then I was able to use an ingenious implement I had not seen before, to check the tub before I jumped in. It was like a small canoe paddle, with a thermometer recessed in the blade, which one used to stir the tub. Quite clearly, Canada still had a few things to learn.

In fairness I must add that in future visits over the years, while Nockels retained a great formality, we got along very well together, indeed were subsequently allied in several difficult situations stirred up by the Beaver.

There was always a colourful and controversial crowd at these weekend visits with Beaverbrook, either house guests or people who came in on Saturday evenings for the dinner party and movie in his private theatre.

Brendan Bracken and Lord Castlerose were pretty regular guests, together with an assortment of service chiefs, cabinet ministers and at times Winston Churchill, any visiting Canadians such as Bickell, Howe and Taylor, and Beaverbrook's current lady friend, who lived nearby. There was no shortage of drinks and there were never any lulls in the conversation, which became very forceful and abusive at times. Beaverbrook always delighted in getting an argument started. Indeed, he frequently plotted and deliberately provoked many first-class rows to make things lively.

It was during this first visit to Cherkley Court that I got a pathetic telephone call from Lord Bennett of Mickleham, Canada's former Conservative Prime Minister, asking me to intercede with Ralston on his behalf. On assuming his British title, R.B. had gone to live in England and had a country home near Leatherhead, across the valley from Beaverbrook. Though a powerful figure in Canadian politics, he had sunk into oblivion in England. Now that Canada, his homeland, was at war, he was desperately anxious to make some contribution, to take on some war work or responsibilities for Canada even in a minor role, perhaps as Canadian Red Cross representative in England or anything else where his considerable abilities could be employed once more.

I had been in the parliamentary press gallery in Ottawa when R.B. was Prime Minister. I had repeatedly attacked him in my articles to our western Liberal newspapers, and he had been very angry with me at times. On one occasion he had threatened to have me called before the Bar of the House and expelled. But he had also, on more than one occasion, shown a kindness to me as a young journalist, despite his high office.

In his present obscurity I felt genuinely sorry for him and approached Ralston privately to see if something could not be found for our former Prime Minister. In opposition when Bennett was in power, Ralston had no particular love for R.B., but he gave the request a sympathetic hearing. After considering it for a couple of days, he felt obliged to reject the proposal. Knowing R.B.'s forceful nature, Ralston feared that he would simply stir up further problems to embarrass or discredit the Mackenzie King government. "We just can't risk having to fight R.B. again and a war at the same time," Ralston told me. It was my unpleasant job to relay this answer diplomatically to R.B.

Bennett had achieved all his ambitions, high office, wealth, and nobility, but now he was merely a tragic figure when Canada faced a national crisis. Perhaps there is truth in the old saying, "There is nothing so dead as a dead politician." The public's memory is very short.

Lord Haw Haw

Back again in London on Monday morning we continued our endless meetings. Nazi air raids hammered London both day and night. Every evening, as the sirens wailed their warnings, people would file down into dark air-raid shelters, the underground railway stations, and basements of buildings, with blankets and their valuables, to spend the entire night. They would hear the BBC news broadcast, with its familiar identification call of "V" for Victory sounded in a musical bar — dot dot dot dash, from Beethoven's *Fifth Symphony* — and then off to the catacombs.

At that same period Lord Haw Haw,* the British traitor, was also broadcasting regularly to Britain over Nazi radio stations. His information was surprisingly accurate at times, as when he correctly noted that Big Ben, the great clock at Westminster, was two minutes slow one evening. The members of our Canadian mission were also surprised to hear Lord Haw Haw broadcasting from Germany the night after our arrival, that "senior Canadian officials had just checked into the Dorchester Hotel." Obviously Hitler's spies in England were well informed, and I quickly made a point of seeing that an armed sergeant was always on duty and slept in the room which we used as an office at the Dorchester, for each day top secret memos and minutes of meetings were delivered to us from the War Office and other ministries.

Another of Lord Haw Haw's broadcasts touched a raw spot on the Canadians in England. Lord Haw Haw offered the witty observation that if the Canadians were left in Sussex long enough they would never see any fighting, as they would all either kill themselves on motorcycles or run off with the English blondes. In point of fact the Canadian regiments stationed in Sussex were experiencing some girl trouble. But more damaging were the endless motorcycle accidents caused by the winding English roads, long night convoys in the blackout, and driving on the left with no lights showing. While motorcycles had their uses and were essential in many circumstances, they were often a menace. After passing my own motorcycle tests I never rode one again in the U.K., and later, in action, I always insisted that liaison officers on important jobs should travel by jeep instead of risking their lives on a "stink-wheeler."

Ralston's mission to London had been programmed on the basis that his group would first negotiate and co-ordinate with the British the whole range and composition of Canada's further overseas war contribution in army, navy and air force units, together with such back-up establishments as shipbuilding, the Empire Air Training Scheme, convoy work and munitions programs.

*Lord Haw Haw was in real life William Joyce, an American citizen who, having lived in England for some years, passed himself off as an Englishman. Captured after the war by the British, he was tried and hanged for treason. Although the U.S. was not at war when his crimes were committed, it was held by the British that, as a non-national, he had enjoyed England's hospitality and protection.

When these broad areas had been defined, C. D. Howe, Canada's dynamic Minister of Munitions and Supply, was to arrive with a group consisting of Eddie Taylor, Billy Woodward and Gordon Scott, to determine how the production and supply aspects were to be developed and the munitions allocated.

Howe and his mission were to come by sea, sailing on the *Western Prince*. A few days after they sailed from Canada, we were shocked to receive a signal from the Admiralty that the ship had been torpedoed and sunk in the North Atlantic, with no word of any survivors.

THREE
C. D. Howe's Ship Torpedoed

WORLD SCENE

*Nightly blitz of London continues. Over 23,000 to date
killed in Britain by German air raids. Australian and
British capture Bardia and Tobruk in Libya from
Italians. German troops sent to Africa to bolster
Italians. Canada extends compulsory military training.
Canadians of Japanese origin ordered to register.*

As the members of C. D. Howe's mission were all close personal friends of our own group, we were stunned at the report that their ship had been sunk. Apart from personal feelings, we also realized that Howe, and the information he was bringing in respect to Canada's industrial capacity and resources, were essential to the second phase of our negotiations with the war cabinet in England.

I believe it was two days later that we received a second report from the Admiralty. A signal had been picked up from a small ship sailing out of convoy, which simply read "have picked up some survivors of *Western Prince*." There was no indication of how many had been saved, and further communication with the rescue ship was impossible due to the imposition of rigid wireless silence. The single message received had been transmitted visually by Aldis lamp.

The only additional information we could obtain was from Shipping Control HQ. From their calculations, the rescuing ship, which had a slow rate of speed, would likely dock at either Greenock or Gourock in Scotland, in two or three days' time. Following a flurry of calls and consultations with the Prime Minister in Canada and with Canada House, it was determined that in view of Ralston's condition, I should pick up Howe's young son who was attending a naval college in England, break the grim news to him and then take him with me to Greenock to await the arrival of the rescuing ship in the hope that C.D. would be among those who had been saved.

Naval Cadet Bill Howe accepted the disturbing news calmly, and we caught the night train to Glasgow where I arranged for an army car to drive us to Greenock. Here we booked into a small and ancient seafront hotel. I had often experienced -40° temperatures in western Canada, but I can truthfully say I never felt so cold as in this grim little stone hostel. It was impossible to keep warm either in bed or at the bar. We huddled there for two days, wearing all the clothing we had with us, trying to eat our porridge without milk or sugar and then shivering in the bar when it opened, sipping whisky most of the day to keep warm.

Finally the ship arrived. Howe was safe, as was Eddie Taylor, Billy Woodward and also a very old friend of mine, Jim Bone, the much loved London editor of the Manchester *Guardian*. I had last seen Jim in Ottawa several months earlier when Victor Sifton had given a rowdy dinner party for him at the Chateau Laurier. Howe, Chubby Power, Tom Crerar and several other cabinet ministers had attended, as well as Grant Dexter and myself. I use the term rowdy, as Grattan O'Leary, editor of the Ottawa *Journal*, turned up very late, fresh from some great financial victories at the race track which he had been celebrating in good Irish whiskey. Rather than eat his dinner, Grattan took over the party with an impromptu speech, employing his wild Irish oratory to the full. Jim Bone, our guest of honour, a little man aged about 70 then and full of Scottish wit, was delighted with this development in an otherwise formal dinner. He proceeded to heckle Grattan all during the speech.

Finally, Jim's sallies proved too much for Grattan and in frustration he turned on the little Scotsman. "What the hell are you talking about?" Grattan exploded. "The damned Scotch stopped fighting 300 years ago — but the Irish are still fighting the bloody British." With that, Grattan subsided into his chair with a glass of Scotch, which he substituted on occasion.

Following this party Jim had undertaken a tour of the United States, visiting top American editors. After the tour, he underwent a serious operation in New York. Determined to get back to England without further delay, Jim had insisted on sailing on the *Western Prince*, and was taken on board in a wheelchair, direct from the hospital.

The survivors of the *Western Prince* had spent many hours in an open lifeboat in the North Atlantic in midwinter, and I was amazed that old Jim had survived the ordeal. One of the Canadian party, Gordon Scott, had tragically been crushed between the side of the sinking liner and the lifeboat he was trying to board as the waves bounced about. He had dropped beneath the waves before anyone could reach him.

I had the party taken at once to Glasgow, where I had booked them into the Central Hotel. They were all suffering from the ordeal and, after a good meal, took to their beds. An hour or so later, after I had got messages away to the families and the government, I made the rounds of their rooms to see if all was well. Looking in on Jim Bone, I asked if there was anything more he needed. "Yes," said Jim. "Get me a typewriter and a bottle of whisky." The barman was able to supply the bottle and the hotel office lent me a typewriter. To my amazement, Jim banged out a news story about the sinking of the ship, which I filed to the *Guardian* for him, knocked off most of the bottle and then caught the night train to London that same evening. As I was to discover repeatedly in the years ahead, the Bones were indeed a hardy family of little Scotsmen.

Within a few days Howe's party joined us at the Dorchester Hotel, and our heavy work schedule redoubled. Besides the loss of time and the rescheduling of many meetings, we faced a serious handicap, in that all the files and important data accompanying Howe's party now lay at the bottom of the Atlantic. In some cases duplicates were ordered from Canada, but in most instances Ralston and Howe, with their tremendous energy, worked long into the night, recreating from their own knowledge the necessary documents for the next day's meetings. This, in turn, placed an enormous workload on our small clerical staff, particularly as Ralston with his legal background made endless revisions in all our briefs and draft agreements.

In reconstructing the lost files, largely from memory, Ralston's capacity for detail far outshown that of his more impetuous colleague, Howe. It was during this trying period that I began to appreciate the iron determination, dedication and utterly selfless contribution of these two ministers at a time of national crisis, all without the slightest regard to their own health or energy.

I can recall Eddie Taylor's first night at the Dorchester. He was still a bit shaken after his shipwreck and had never experienced an air raid before. We had been invited out to a dinner party, and agreed to meet together first in the Dorchester bar, from where I undertook to find our way through the blackout to the home of our hostess. Just as Eddie joined me in the bar, the first air raid of the night began. The sirens wailed — then the drone of enemy bombers, the heavy crash of bombs which shook the hotel; next, the beep of police and wardens' cars, followed by the shattering crash of heavy AA guns firing only a few hundred yards away in Hyde Park. As the massive symphony continued, Eddie looked far from happy and suggested we have another drink before heading out into pitch black streets. Having experienced several weeks of this nightly nocturne, I had become rather acclimatized and fatalistic. However, I fully sympathized with Eddie's further suggestion of let's have another — and wait till it clears. As I recall, I don't think we ever did get to that dinner party.

A week or so after Howe's party arrived, C.D. and Taylor had a meeting at the Beaver's office. Later, Eddie related their experience to me. In every detail, it was an exact rerun of the earlier performance for Ralston and myself: first the red telephone, then the blue, next the secretary. And, of course, the newspapers on the floor. The script had been identical. Do you suppose, I asked Eddie, that as each delegation leaves, the old man pushes the button and the props are set for the next performance? Just the same, and despite all his stunts, Beaverbrook made a vital contribution to the Allied war effort at that time.

Sir Frederick Banting's Request

A rather sad recollection of that period concerns a job we had been asked to do in London by the world-famous doctor, Sir Frederick Banting, the co-discoverer of insulin. It concerned a brilliant young doctor from Canada, who was doing research in England.

Just before Ralston and I had left Ottawa for England, I was surprised one day to notice a very untidy major in a World War I style uniform, sitting with a row of other people in Ralston's ante room, waiting his turn to see the minister. Because of the rumpled old uniform, I took another look at the officer and recognized my old Toronto friend of many years before, the Nobel Prize winner, Sir Frederick Banting. He told me it was most important that he see Ralston without delay — before we left for England. I got him in to see the minister forthwith. He told us a surprising story and made two urgent requests.

He explained that in some aspects of chemical warfare, Canadian scientists were far ahead of such research in England, but the British simply couldn't believe this. German bombers were trying to destroy London, and Banting was fearful that in desperation, Hitler might be tempted to bomb English cities with germs or poison gas, provided the RAF were not able to retaliate with equal or greater effect. It all concerned vaporization and density of the gas with regard to humidity, altitude, temperature and so forth. It was most urgent, said Banting.

A young doctor was employed in England on research for a substitute for quinine; apparently, the enemy could cut off our supplies of quinine, badly needed to fight malaria for our troops in the Middle East and Asia. The doctor, however, was also a leading expert on vaporization, and Banting begged Ralston, on his visit to England, to convince Churchill to have the doctor released to work on chemical warfare in Canada. Banting felt this was far more important for Britain's safety. Banting's other request was for a large area of several thousand acres in Canada, where tests of chemical warfare could be carried out before Germany got the jump on us. The area required was to be uninhabited, but with roads and, as far as possible, the same atmospheric conditions as Western Europe.

To meet this second request, we called in experts from the land departments of both the Canadian Pacific and the Canadian National Railways, with the result that the necessary area was located for Banting in Alberta.

Insofar as getting the young doctor returned to Canada, we failed in our mission. The British obviously did not accept Banting's claim that Canadian research in chemical warfare was ahead of theirs. They insisted that the doctor's work in England had far greater priority. After our return to Canada, I reported our failure to Banting and he was greatly disappointed.

Some weeks later, walking along Sparks Street in Ottawa about midnight on my way back to the Chateau Laurier, I ran into Banting again. He told me he was leaving early the next morning to fly over to England. As room service at the Chateau Laurier was then closed, we walked along the street till we found a Honey Dew shop, and we had a cup of coffee together.

Sir Frederick told me that he was taking some of his research data over to England and, amongst many other things, still hoped to convince the British on the extent of Canadian discoveries and get the young doctor back.

The next day at my office, I was shocked to learn that Banting's plane had crashed in Newfoundland and he had been killed. Although the plane had been checked out before the flight, both engines had mysteriously failed after a refuelling stop at Harbour Grace, and the plane had crashed on the east coast. Banting lived for a few hours after the crash. The U.S. pilot survived, though injured. The other two crew members were killed instantly. It was reported that when the pilot regained consciousness after the crash, he found that his injuries had been bandaged by Banting. Then, before dying, Banting had tried to dictate some information to the pilot. As I recall, the notes made by the pilot, when studied, did not make sense. It was officially reported that Banting was studying such things as pilot stress and the physical problems of airmen.

After the war it was discovered that the German Army had stockpiled several tons of nerve gas, as well as other deadly chemicals, which they could have employed during many critical periods, with devastating effect. There was one key deterrent, however; they were aware that the Western allies, thanks to Sir Frederick Banting and other scientists, were in a position to retaliate on a much greater scale.

Besides taking the results of his chemical warfare tests with him to England on his fatal trip, Banting also took details of the world's first anti-gravity or "G" suit, which he had invented, working with his Toronto research associate, Dr. W. R. Franks. This Canadian invention was the forerunner of today's space suit.

For some curious reason, the cause of the crash was never investigated by the Canadian government. Seemingly, the matter of ferrying aircraft to England came under Lord Beaverbrook in the U.K., and the investigation was made by Britain and the Newfoundland government. Subsequently, Canadian Air Minister Powers stated that he had no knowledge of what was contained in the report of the crash.

Two weeks later the New York *Herald Tribune* carried a report credited to "reliable informants and authentic" that the bomber had been sabotaged and that sand and grass had been placed in the oil supply system.*

Authorities in Ottawa were sceptical of this story. Then the Newfoundland government announced that it had received a report from the Court of Inquiry, but it would not be made public. Publication of the report, it said, "would not be in the public interest." And that was the end of the matter.

An Historic Speech

One day I got a call for help from Jim Bone, who was now back at his *Guardian* office on Fleet Street. Hamish McGeachy, a former newspaper colleague from the *Winnipeg Free Press*, was in deep trouble in Dublin . . . bottle trouble. Hamish was a colourful and widely known newspaper character. He had a lively wit, a touch of brilliance, a great circle of friends — but an unending battle with the bottle.

Jim claimed to be Hamish's godfather. (He may have been, at that, though Jim was godfather to nearly all stray journalists as I remember.) Seemingly, Hamish was right on his uppers this trip. Could I help in a rescue operation, get him on his feet and use my influence to get him a job, perhaps in the British Ministry of Information or the BBC. There was no questioning Hamish's ability if he could be kept sober, so I did my best. The trick was to convince people that he had something special to offer. We finally sold the idea that he would be ideal to produce a broadcast series on the BBC called *Empire Talks*. The first distinguished guest on his program was to be Ralston, the Canadian Minister of Defence . . . visiting the heart of the Empire . . . pledging Canada's support. I never told Ralston that I had any hand in the affair, as he was very much against it. Finally, when I undertook to write the speech for him and told him the British felt it was most important for Empire morale, he reluctantly agreed.

I put my heart into the text, with all the heroics and dramatic touches I could muster. I had Ralston announce the formation in England once more of the Canadian Corps, which had been famous as shock-troops in the battles of World War I. (We had just about enough participants for a corps in England by now.)

Ralston read my emotional script and was seized with the drama of such a timely announcement, so much so that he said he couldn't make such an important statement. He wouldn't steal Mackenzie King's thunder. The Prime Minister himself should make the statement from Ottawa. Ralston would cable the text to King at once. In short, I had overdone it and struck out. Prime Minister King on Christmas Day announced there was to be a Canadian Corps again, "marking an epoch"

---

*A subsequent rumour had it that the sabotage agents had been captured and executed. This was immediately ridiculed in Ottawa. What the real facts were I still don't know, and I'm surprised that no additional information has come to light since the war.

in Canada's war effort. According to the official history, "it evoked proud memories of 1914-18 . . . the triumphs and sacrifices on hard-fought battlefields." Poor Hamish. And I had promised to deliver on this one.

I tried hard to get Ralston to tackle another broadcast for Hamish a little later, but he refused absolutely. Badgered by Hamish, I resorted to subterfuge. Ralston was going down to the Aldershot area a few days later to speak informally to some troops in our 1st Division. In speaking to troops, Ralston was excellent. He spoke forcefully in a language the men understood. As an old combat soldier himself, he pulled no punches.

We had arranged for loudspeakers and microphones. Unknown to Ralston, one of the microphones was for Hamish's radio broadcast, *Empire Talks*, which we duly put on the air without the minister's knowledge. Ralston was at his best, with a great fighting speech telling the men exactly why Canada was in the war and what their job was.

It was back in London that night before Ralston learned that he had been on the air, and he was really furious with me. He couldn't remember what he had said in his impromptu remarks, and he was very concerned. After giving me a rocket, he retired to his room in deep dudgeon.

By next morning, however, I was saved. Congratulations for his splendid talk started to flow in to Ralston by cable from Canada and South Africa, from Churchill and Eden; also, quotes in the morning papers. A triumph.

After breakfast, Ralston came into my room a bit shamefaced, rather apologized for his reprimand the night before, then added, "But don't you ever do that to me again."

Hamish was now safely on the rails, but in passing I might record that he had a narrow escape a few nights later during an air raid. The central section of the Ministry of Information building was supposed to be bomb resistant in some degree, and when the alarm was given from the roof watchers, staff members were to rush from their offices into this structure.

An enormous land mine was spotted floating down on two parachutes, heading directly for the building. When the warning sounded, Hamish dashed for cover. Then suddenly remembering the brand new typewriter we had bought him, virtually his only possession and source of livelihood, he dashed back and gathered it into his arms — just in time to be thrown forward flat on his face from the blast . . . the new typewriter all smashed to hell. Following the war years Hamish returned to Canada and, after a rather hilarious and noteworthy stint at the *Winnipeg Free Press* with his old cronies George Ferguson and Archie Dale, left to join *The Globe and Mail* and later the *Financial Post* in Toronto for several years before he died, a much beloved and legendary figure in newspaper circles.

Mike Pearson — The Diplomat

It was while arranging all our detailed agendas and meetings that I first observed the great efficiency and diplomatic skill of Mike Pearson. Despite the long hours of work, the nightly blitz and pressures of the negotiations, Mike was always able to come up with a laugh and a smile. Among many amusing incidents was one involving an early morning arrival by Mike at the Dorchester Hotel, where our mission was staying. I was shaving when Mike burst into my room and demanded to know which was Crerar's room. An urgent coded signal had arrived for the general, and Mike had brought it personally to the Dorchester.

I told Mike that Crerar's room was the third room around the corner of the corridor, and Mike dashed off. Seconds later he returned, visibly shaken. "Good God, why didn't you tell me Crerar was keeping a woman in there with him," he blurted out.

Apparently, the door had not been locked, so Mike had simply knocked and walked in — and was shocked to see a very attractive young lady in the nude. As a comparatively junior officer at the time, and still regarding generals with some awe, I was likewise startled by Mike's revelation. What to do? If Mike went back or telephoned the other room, it could be embarrassing for all parties concerned. Ever the diplomat, Mike decided to pretend the awkward intrusion had simply not happened. He would go down to breakfast with me, and then when Crerar joined us, there need be no mention of his earlier approach.

During breakfast we both regarded the CGS in a somewhat different light, despite his usual stuffy and very military manner. It was not until two days later that Mike and I discovered that in our minds we had unfairly underrated or overrated the capacities of our general. Mike had opened the third door on the right; Crerar's room was the third on the left. A few days later we spotted "Crerar's girl" in the dining room, and fully clothed she was still a knock-out.

All during our stay at the Dorchester, various gifts of liquor would arrive as a form of hospitality from well-wishers, a bottle of good brandy or port, a dozen bottles of claret or a case or two of champagne, apart from the odd bottles of whisky and gin.

The irony of this hospitality was that Ralston was a staunch Baptist and strict teetotaller. "Good heavens," he would mutter when the porter's desk sent up some more bottles. "We'll put it in the closet," he would say, and then promptly forget all about the substantial cellar which was accumulating. With the existing premium on and rationing of good liquor, Alan Magee and myself were hopeful that Ralston might think of sharing the booty, but no luck; it never even crossed his mind.

Finally in mid-January we were ready for our return to Canada. We were to slip quietly out of the Dorchester after dark, for security reasons, then catch the ghost train for Glasgow, from where we were to be taken out in a lighter to the old battleship HMS *Ramillies*, which was being refuelled at sea for the run to Halifax.

We were packing up in the morning when Ralston suddenly recalled the closet full of booze. Unable to think of any other solution, he simply told me to "get rid of it."

What to do in the few remaining hours? Each of us packed a bottle of the excellent brandy in our luggage in case of shipwreck, but then we were stumped. Well, what about an instant cocktail party this afternoon, I suggested. The situation was desperate; we couldn't just leave it all there. We immediately started telephoning any friends within quick reach as well as any pals at CMHQ such as Pat Kelly, Howard Penhale, Stan Conn and Alan Embury, together with Mike Pearson and others from Canada House.

When our cocktail party assembled we did not have a single female; it was entirely stag, a poor show indeed. At this point I suddenly thought of our neighbour at the Dorchester, "Crerar's girl." I scribbled a quick invitation for her to join us and rang for the floor waiter to deliver our note.

The waiter hesitated and coughed a few times when I gave the instructions, and then deferentially submitted that "perhaps the captain might not like it." "What captain?" I demanded. We were then discreetly informed of the fact that had entirely escaped our notice. "Crerar's girl" was in fact a prominent London model who was sleeping with a young Guard's officer at the hotel. Such are the hazards of war.

In the event, we did our best to dispose of the surplus supplies till the porter came to take down our bags. As I walked through the rotunda of the hotel and passed the main dining room, I paused to take a look at the festive scene. Every table was occupied with officers in various uniforms, and many of the girls with them were also in uniform. At one table I spotted four or five young Canadian officers, with their girl friends, on a 48-hour leave. The inspiration was instantaneous. I signalled the head porter, gave 10 shillings and told him to go up to our suite and bring down the case of champagne together with the other assorted bottles, then take it to the Canadians' table, case and all, and simply say, "Compliments of the Minister of National Defence." I was not able to watch the presentation, nor did I ever learn the identity of the officers. Fortunately, they did not have a chance to thank Ralston for his unknown generosity.

The original plan had been that I would disguise myself as a civilian and fly back to Canada via Portugal to get our war plans back to Ottawa as fast as possible. The plans were all packed in a leather box with a great slab of lead at the bottom, with holes in it. If my plane was shot down or crashed, I was to hurl all our plans into the ocean to sink to the bottom. The box was to be chained to my wrist at all times, except at the airport in Portugal, where someone from the embassy would hold it with immunity as a diplomatic pouch.

This seemed all rather exciting secret agent stuff, but I did wonder how I was to get my best uniform back to Canada if I posed as a civilian — and also, what happened if I forgot to unchain myself when I hurled the secret plans into the ocean? The intelligence people at the War Office rushed me to a studio where I changed coats with the photographer and had a photo taken. An hour later I was supplied with a faked Canadian passport, complete with the Canadian Secretary of State's signature and Canadian coat of arms.

Then the adventure was called off. I was to take the plans back on His Majesty's battleship *Ramillies*. The reason given was that German planes were also using the neutral Lisbon airport, and spies were lurking about there. I had always wanted to be a smooth, secret agent-type, and this seemed rather a reflection on my capacity in undercover work.

Making up for my disappointment, however, I noted that on board the *Ramillies* all the naval types gave me a promotion in rank and addressed me as major. Either they didn't know the insignia of army ranks or, who knows, maybe at long last I had been promoted from captain. After a bit in the ward room, I finally asked when I had been promoted. "A mere courtesy old boy," was the answer. "You see, on a ship we have only one captain."

Given the admiral's quarters on the ship, complete with separate sitting room, dining room and galley, we considered ourselves well provided for, until we hit some heavy winter storms the first day out. It became at once apparent that situated right in the stern, over the screws, the admiral had the worst space in the ship. Trying to shave each morning in time with the slow heave and shudder, I could look through the weathered oak lattice flooring in the washroom and see pools of rusty water, which had sweated down the steel plating, all swishing about. Ralston stuck it out without being seasick, but Harry Crerar left the table every so often on short notice. For my part, each morning I would make a zigzag course through the alternately sealed bulkhead and passageways, through the great ship, till I found the officers' ward room. Here I discovered that if you sipped small glasses of brandy frappé during the day, it sort of pulled you together.

Working my way along a narrow corridor one day and dodging hammocks, I found my passage blocked by a small gathering standing about a lectern. A naval commander was conducting what in the army would be called "orders." A prisoner between two guards was being tried, so I stood back to watch the naval version of Orderly Room, a procedure I had conducted many times in the army. The charge was striking a petty officer, and from the evidence it was quickly established that able seaman McSnook had indeed bashed the PO.

Seemingly, the ship's crew had not had any shore leave for some months, as Britain's convoy system was being taxed to the limit with Allied shipping being sunk each day by torpedoes. Returning from a long stint in the "Med," the ship's crew had all expected leave when they reached Scotland. But shore leave was cancelled; the *Ramillies* was oiled and provisioned at sea for a fast turn around and then ordered to take up patrol duties in the Atlantic.

In consequence, McSnook was a bit bloody-minded when the PO had given him the sharp edge of his tongue one morning. And in the mood of the moment, he had slugged the PO without delay.

The procedure of the trial was very similar to army custom, except that I was shocked to hear the man awarded the lash. In the army this would likely have netted about 30 days of hard labour. I thought the lash had gone out in Nelson's day.

Later, up in the ward room, I discussed the severity of the sentence with the ship's MO, who had to attend the carrying out of the sentence. The MO assured me that the lash was the only realistic way to meet the situation when at sea on duty. Even the culprits would prefer to get it over with rather than be held in irons or in the brig below decks should the ship suddenly have to go into action.

For the first day or so, Ralston, Crerar, Magee and I were able to busy ourselves tidying up the mass of files and notes we were taking back to Canada, but then, cooped up below decks, we found the time dragged slowly. In a heavy sea the *Ramillies* tended to go through the enormous 30-foot waves rather than ride them, with the result that the maindeck and most of the 10-inch gun deck were under great mountains of green water much of the time, and we could not get out on deck.

To pass the time, Ralston taught me a card game popular in the Maritimes. "Forty-fives," I think he called it, and he enjoyed it immensely, slapping his knee when he won. He also told me endless funny stories about his early days on court circuit in the Maritimes, and talked about the ramifications of early party politics in the Maritimes. Crerar kept himself aloof from these mundane amusements and sat in a corner by himself reading military appreciations.

One day in the midst of a card game Ralston demanded, "What day is it?" When I informed him it was Sunday he banged down his cards and got up from the table — furious with himself for having played cards on the Sabbath, against all his Baptist principles.

He was fond of reading detective stories, so he rustled through his bags to find a paperback he hadn't read. Before sailing he had asked Mike Pearson to pick him up a couple for the voyage. I don't know whether Mike was up on his detective stories, but among the titles he had given Ralston was a paperback, *The Cautious Amorist*.

I observed Ralston quietly as he launched into the purple pages in the belief it was a mystery story. As I watched his frown develop and his eyes start to pop a bit, I asked innocently, "Sir, do you think reading is better than cards on Sunday?" That was the end of *The Cautious Amorist*. I never even got to read it myself, as it went overboard.

As Ralston and the others retired to their cabins early each night, I frequently made my way forward to the ward room where a game called "liar dice" (or "beat that, you bugger") was played for drinks, to pass the time. During the day I would spend some time having one of the RN types take me around the ship and explain its workings. A few weeks earlier, the *Ramillies* had participated in what was known as the Italian Boat Race, in the Med. Repeatedly, the British Navy had attempted, without success, to intercept lighter and faster units of the Italian navy as they ran convoys of supplies over to their own and German forces in North Africa. One morning the dawn broke in the British favour. The Italian battleships were spotted at first light, and it was estimated that the *Ramillies* with its slow speed but enormous guns might get within shelling range, if they were not spotted by the Italians for another hour. It was all-speed ahead, but no luck. When they needed only another 20 minutes' sailing they were spotted, and the Italians took off — being no match for the heavy British guns. The race continued for some time, with all guns of the *Ramillies* firing at extreme range in the forlorn hope of a lucky hit.

As a result of this last chase, the liners on the big guns of the *Ramillies* had to be replaced. With this job now completed, a practice firing of the guns was to be carried out in the next day or two. I had been ragging the redheaded gunnery officer a bit with the theory that if they fired all four turrets of their big guns, all at the same time and all over the same side, it would turn their old tub upside down. He was very hot in rejecting this view . . . said his father had written the book on naval gunnery.

To back up my claim, I accepted a few bets on the matter from everyone in the ward room crap game. After various consultations the next day and a posting of the stakes, it was announced that, as the guns did have to fire a practice round, the captain had agreed they should all be fired simultaneously over the same side.

This was a new bit of excitement for me, and when the practice time arrived, I asked just where I should stand to observe this great performance. Also, I wished to see the shells actually roar through the air, which the RN officers claimed was possible.

I was directed to stand on the 10-inch gun deck just above the great turrets of 16-inch guns. And there I stood as the salvo was fired . . . but what effect it had on the ship itself, I never discovered. I simply recall a blinding flash of red flame and billows of smoke, as I was hurled flat on the deck from the blast. Apparently, everyone on the ship, except myself, knew that an exposed position on the 10-inch gun deck makes the worst possible grandstand for a firing practice. When I was able to gather my wits again, I managed to stagger back to the ward room — quite happy to pay off my debts, and drinks all around.

The navy, I might record, paid about sixpence per drink at that time. Later in the war, when I was stationed briefly at RCAF fighter stations, I discovered that pilots got fed with beefsteaks — and both services slept in beds at night. In the poor bloody infantry some months later, sleeping on the ground in the wintertime with our NAAFI* whisky ration of half a bottle a month and living on tinned Spam and M&V (meat and veg.), I figured this seemed rather unequal.

After about five days on the *Ramillies*, I felt we should be reaching Canada very shortly. I enquired casually about when we would arrive. Just as casually, one of the ship's officers asked in reply, "just where were you going?" This seemed a bit of nonsense, as he would at least know where we were headed. When I finally explained we were going to Halifax, my reply caused quite a bit of amusement.

They were all in on the little game. The fact was that the previous day or so, wireless orders had diverted the *Ramillies* from her course and we were now somewhere south of the Azores. There were reports that a German raider or pocket battleship was charging about somewhere, and the only ship in the vicinity with heavy enough guns to sink it was the *Ramillies*. I never heard all the details, but we never caught up with any enemy. For another few days, however, there was just nothing the Canadians could do about the situation. We couldn't signal Ottawa, so with all our great war secrets we continued to sail around the Atlantic looking for Germans.

When we finally reached Halifax, Ottawa was notified of our arrival. It was arranged that a small plane on skis would be waiting at an airfield opposite the harbour, to rush me — together with the files — through to Ottawa as fast as possible. I have never been mad keen about flying, and I doubt that the war would have come to an end if I had just taken a comfortable compartment on the train to Ottawa.

The plane was a little two-seater job, and once I climbed aboard, the pilot revved the motor, the whole crate started to shake — but nothing happened. The pilot roared the engine repeatedly, but there we stayed. The wretched skis were frozen on the ice. After getting chopped free, we at last took off; then, in a couple of hours, we were lost in a dense fog. Then followed several more hours of utter madness trying to find an air strip that was open, so we could set down again. At last we made it to Moncton, where conditions cleared for a moment. I sent a signal to Ottawa that I would try to come on by train.

Gambling that the *Maritime Limited* from Halifax to Montreal would be running late, I grabbed a taxi and raced for the railway station. By great luck not only was the train late, but hitched to it was one of the government's private cars — running empty, except for its porter who was well known to me. After some debate, the conductor reluctantly allowed me to take over the private car, where the great plans would be safe.

*NAAFI: Navy, Army and Air Force Institutes.

55

Further along the line some hours later, the conductor came back to see me. All was well. He had wired ahead about my privacy, and Ottawa, no doubt relieved to know what had happened to me, had wired back instructions; when the train reached Montreal, my car, with the precious plans, was to be hitched to an engine and run through to the capital that night. It was the only time I have been able to arrive home in such style.

FOUR

Ottawa Moves Into High Gear

WORLD SCENE
Canadian industry and Canada's defence chiefs,
Ralston, Howe, Power and Macdonald, cut red tape to
speed Canada's war effort. U.S. Congress, despite
neutrality, approves Lend-Lease Bill to aid Britain.
British navy sinks 11 enemy ships off Norway. Rommel
launches offensive in North Africa. British navy sinks
five Italian warships off Cape Matapan.

On our return to Ottawa, the first few days were completely taken up with Ralston's report to the Prime Minister and the cabinet, then to the House of Commons, and finally to the nation by radio, announcing all our new wartime commitments to the Allied cause.

The details of all the many official meetings and agreements worked out in England by Ralston and Howe were of staggering proportions, but they make dull reading now; I shall not attempt to cover them in these rambling reminiscences. They are all fully recorded in the official files or the pages of Hansard.

Ralston made one omission from his report to Ottawa, which embarrassed me then and has rather haunted me since, as it was formally (and accurately) recorded that I knew nothing about women.

In the early months of the war and prior to our departure for England, the women of Canada had been raising hell about forming women's corps — such as ATS, WRENS, WAAFS and God knows what — just as they had in England. They demanded to know why the government didn't move on this. They wanted action. The truth of the matter was that we really didn't know then how England employed ATS and WRENS. We didn't have jobs for them, nor did we have any female uniforms or barracks.

We couldn't even produce enough trousers and great coats for the thousands of men being mobilized, let alone find any skirts. But the women were becoming militant. Demands were being made in Parliament, and in some instances, women were organizing themselves into unofficial volunteer corps. Others were wangling their own way overseas to join up in various limey corps.

I recall landing with Ralston at an airfield, either at Sudbury or North Bay, when we were surprised to see a complete honour guard of females drawn up in review order waiting to be inspected. It had no official status; they were insurgents or guerrillas, Ralston muttered. Having no more understanding of women than I possessed, Ralston simply chickened out. I was in uniform, so I was ordered to inspect them. I started off in the approved manner, looking the women up and down from head to toe; but after a few cold stares, and a few quite improper winks, I turned my eyes away and marched straight ahead, praying that the pictures being taken would never be seen by my fellow officers in the Princess Patricias.

As soon as Ralston finished reporting to Parliament, a female Member immediately demanded, "And what about women's corps?" Ralston rather paled at this, as we still had no plans for the women or a clue about how to employ them just then. Rising bravely to the attack, Ralston gave some tortured explanation . . . that the government was indeed aware of the value of women's corps. We were right on top of the game, and in England his staff secretary (myself) had carried out long negotiations on the matter with the British. Canada's plans for women were well in hand following Malone's studies. This was the closest I ever heard Ralston come to an outright fib. The Member of Parliament's subsequent retort was to the effect that it was, "quite obvious that Captain Malone knows absolutely nothing about women."

There had been a slender thread of truth in Ralston's remarks, however, which can now be related. In London, Ralston had sent me over to talk to Lady Reading and other leaders of the various women's corps at the War Office, to discover what they did with all these thousands of women. In point of fact the record was very impressive. Women were not only handling anti-aircraft units and ops-rooms at fighter commands, they were also running lighthouses off the coast of Scotland, and driving lorries and almost everything else you could name. The War Office supplied me with scores of pamphlets setting forth the war establishments of all the various women's units. Among the many pamphlets was one showing the organization of a nursing unit for expectant mothers. Seemingly, with thousands of women in the services such establishments had been found necessary.

Reporting back to Ralston at the Dorchester after these investigations, I placed the "expectant mother" pamphlet on top of the pile. That rather did it as far as Ralston was concerned. "Good heavens," he exclaimed. "We can't get into all that." How could the government answer in the House as to how they allowed the girls to get pregnant? That had closed the file for the moment.

Greater Effort Needed

After we had seen England's fight for national survival, Canada's leisurely approach to war was painfully apparent as soon as we returned to Ottawa. Although in time Canada was able to mobilize a tremendous effort and contribution to the Allied cause, both in men and arms, our preparations at that period were moving slowly. Canadians had not grasped either the magnitude or the urgency of our commitment. The war still seemed remote for most people. It was not that the country did not back the war effort in spirit; quite the reverse. More volunteers had come forward than we could possibly equip, train or accommodate. Our problem lay in moving into high gear on organization, in finding an effective administration to direct the war machine.

Many of the senior officers in the various services responsible for war mobilization had, through the simple circumstance of peacetime seniority, been promoted to jobs of top responsibility miles beyond their abilities. In some cases they were too old for the challenge and too rigid and limited in their views. A complete revolution was required in the Ordnance Branch to cope with a modern army on wheels, with thousands of vehicles and tanks, new armoured units, new style battle dress, mechanized artillery — and tens of thousands of portable wireless kits and walkie-talkies to replace such things as field telephones, signal flags and heliographs.

At the start of the war, we were still using some horse-drawn limbers, and we still had mounted cavalry and horse artillery. Officers were taking annual equitation courses. Enough saddlery was held in depots to equip two entire cavalry brigades.

Since World War I there had been no proper designing of or provision for modern equipment, and our handful of ordnance officers were employed largely to operate stores, depots and the warehousing of obsolete equipment.

It has been traditional in Canada that, between wars, neither the public nor the politicians gave a damn about the militia.

A picture of Canada's armed forces just prior to the outbreak of war is perhaps best given in the following extracts from a letter by a senior Regular Force officer who held an appointment, about that period, at NDHQ.

In the inter-war period pacifism ruled. There was a long succession of weak ministers. It [Defence] was not an important portfolio.

Mr. X was minister when I joined the General Staff and it may interest you to hear that he did not conduct one solitary meeting of the Defence Council during the next four years. He never even entered his office in the Woods building, except to greet the staff at Christmas.

The Department was run by the deputy minister. He used it entirely for patronage purposes and a long line of patronage seekers waited daily at his door. He treated the military members with contempt and did all the hiring and firing from patronage lists. The Department was notorious.

In those inter-war years the Permanent Force could only turn out one, two or three candidates yearly for the Staff Colleges. In 1939, there were about 30 graduates, and almost every one of them had been assigned to the General Staff either in Ottawa or in the Districts.

The other staff branches got only second stringers, and by 1939 the AG branch was quite moribund, and incapable of handling a war.

The Navy was formed in 1910 in a separate Dept., under its own Act. It remained that way until the Department of National Defence was formed in 1922. It took its orders straight from the [British] Admiralty right into the Second War. The Chief of Naval Staff consulted the Admiralty on everything. It was an entirely colonial arrangement. So much so that we in the Army were astounded that the government tolerated it.

The Air Force dated from 1924 and the Army was mainly responsible for its administration right into the war. There was nothing like an "Air Council" until Chubby Power created it.

About the same time as I had been seconded from the PPCLI to join the Minister's Office in Ottawa, Victor Sifton, my colleague and chief from the *Winnipeg Free Press*, had also been invited to Ottawa, for a conference on how to promote our mobilization plans and rouse the needed press and public support to back Canada's war effort in all areas: manpower, production of munitions and financing. Recognizing Victor's great ability and courage in slicing through red tape, Ralston insisted that Victor stay on in Ottawa as an executive assistant.

There was an unfortunate aspect of Canada's military structure which had prevailed, in rather bitter form, from the very earliest days right up till Canadian militia regiments saw action in World War II. Between wars, Canada has never maintained a large permanent force. For the most part our Permanent Force officers, or regulars, were graduates of various British courses and staff colleges. They had been trained in the style of British regulars, and they spoke with the peculiar clipped jargon and accent of their English brothers at Whitehall, Sandhurst, Camberley, Woolwich and Quetta, miles removed from the Canadian civilians they would command in wartime.

In times of national emergency, however, Canada has always had to call on her militia, the amateurs or Thursday night soldiers. Local militia units had very little training, but with their business experience, when called to active service these men quickly established themselves as practical and competent soldiers. All too often militia men held PF officers and NCOs with contempt, regarding them as arrogant, impractical and useless producers of red tape.*

These feelings were so strong in some districts that some militia regiments would pool their annual pay so that they could hire their own drill sergeants rather than have "any PF bastards mucking about their armouries." Similarly, on courses and at camps, militia officers at times would establish their own messes rather than drink with their PF brothers who, in turn, looked down on the civilian tyros. These attitudes, hiding just below the surface when war was declared, proved very difficult to overcome. From the standpoint of scale alone, the Permanent Force could not possibly cope with full-scale mobilization; yet for the first year or so of the war they jealously guarded what they imagined to be their sole preserve and tried to resist the inevitable civilian deluge.

This intolerance and resistance to change, backed by a very powerful old boy PF network, had completely defeated several of Canada's former defence ministers and also proved a major frustration for Ralston in his efforts to produce our overseas army. As indicated in many of his private letters, memos and conversations, he complained with justification of the obstructions he faced on all sides by the PF establishment, led primarily by Crerar, the Chief of General Staff himself. As a tough corporation lawyer and practical politician, Ralston found it a heavy cross to bear.

It was not a new situation for Ralston, however. In World War I, as a commander of a militia regiment, serving in the front line trenches, he had experienced the red tape of Argyle House.

He had been seriously wounded, won the DSO and bar for gallantry, and was twice mentioned in despatches. Twice Ralston had given up his law practice to serve his country as a cabinet minister at the request of Mackenzie King.

Having some knowledge of the prewar army situation at Defence Headquarters, with its old boy PF network, Ralston quickly brought in from Civy Street such businessmen as Alan Magee, George Currie, Sandy Dyde, Jimmy Delalan, Victor Sifton and many others.

It was not that the PF people were bad or lazy. It was simply that after 20 years of barracks life, on a reduced establishment, isolated from civilian

---

*Happily, this animosity practically vanished on active service, once Militia and Permanent Force units operated together in the field and shared common dangers. To a considerable degree, a much better relationship continued after World War II.

life and the modern world of business and manufacturing, they were just not equipped for large-scale mobilization and mechanization. When money was suddenly poured at them, they didn't know how to make use of it or free themselves from peacetime procedures. Following regular channels, it required two to three days, for example, to get a travel warrant from the Movement Control Office for an officer to proceed from Ottawa to Halifax, even though he was on an urgent mission.

The PF, with their military knowledge, were invaluable in getting the war machine started and establishing training camps. In many cases, however, they were soon thrust aside by the complexities of the problems. Although I had many friends among the Permanent Force, I must confess to a certain bias. Observing the inner conflicts, dramas and obstructions, my sympathies were certainly with Ralston in his battle with the Permanent Force and red tape.

Victor Sifton

Problems, particularly in the Ordnance Branch, had soon reached crisis proportions. Thousands of men were joining up, but the masses of clothing and weapons to equip them were, in many instances, not even on order. In desperation, in July 1940, Ralston fired the Master General of Ordnance and asked Victor to take over as MGO and a member of the Army Council.

Although Victor had served as a battalion commander in the trenches in World War I and was anxious to contribute his full energies to the war effort, he had no real qualifications for this job of equipping the army . . . other than his ability to rip through red tape. He telephoned and invited me to drive down with him for a weekend at Assiniboine Lodge, his summer house in Brockville. He wanted to talk over and consider Ralston's proposition with me, counting on my knowledge of the workings of the Minister's Office and Army Council policies. I urged him strongly to accept the responsibility as I was aware of the need for a vigorous hand and action in Ordnance affairs. In this post and as a member of the Army Council, Victor would have to sign up for the duration and put on a uniform again, with the rank of Major General. He was uncertain about exactly what he could achieve in these duties, which were foreign to him, but reluctantly agreed he could not refuse Ralston. He went up to the third floor of the ancient lodge and dug out his old World War I uniforms, to see if they still fitted.

But suddenly a hard look came into his eyes. "To heck with it," he exclaimed. "I'm not going to place myself into a position where I have to obey Harry Crerar or be crowded by the PF because I'm in uniform and a serving officer. The only out would be court martial or to be relieved of command. I'll either serve as a civilian or not at all. Then I can speak my mind and resign if they don't like it, or they can fire me without any fuss. I won't be on any payroll." This was a pretty independent position to take, and I doubted he could make it stick at NDHQ. There had never before been a civilian MGO on the Army Council.

But I was wrong. Victor did make it stick. He had originally urged that they get Phillip Chester, operating head of the Hudson's Bay department stores, for the job, Chester being experienced in matters of supply and purchasing. Ralston wouldn't accept this, but agreed to bring him in as

61

joint MGO with Victor. Then if it worked out, Victor in time could step out. However, Ralston held Victor responsible for this odd arrangement, as equipment matters were now critical. Despite many resentments in Ordnance circles at this appointment of civilian outsiders, Victor quickly established his authority and the impact on the branch was immediate.

One of his early steps was to fire a full colonel in the regular Ordnance Corps whom he had previously warned about drinking. In front of other members of the staff, Victor simply told him he was fired and to get out then and there.

The shock waves of this direct action by Victor registered instantly in all departments of Defence Headquarters. An immediate roar came from the Adjutant General's Branch. Victor, told that he had no authority to fire an officer, was summoned to a hastily convened meeting of the Army Council to account for his actions. It was an historic meeting. Victor listened in silence while his sins were related. Then in ice cold terms, Victor replied that the officer in question had been properly warned about his drinking, and as far as he, Victor Sifton, was concerned, either the colonel remained fired or they could find a new MGO. There were a few blustering noises, but no one was ready to tackle Victor or challenge his decision.

There were times when the force of Victor's personality and his choice of words explained matters very clearly. The colonel remained fired from the army, though the old boy network did wangle a new appointment for him a few weeks later in the RCAF, unbeknown to Air Minister Chubby Power.

A few days after Victor took over the office of MGO, his staff secretary placed on his desk an enormous report with sections for every division of the Ordnance Branch — technical stores, clothing, vehicles, barrack stores, explosives, and so forth — which Victor was to sign. It was the weekly report for the Prime Minister's Office. After the MGO's signature was in place, the papers would go forward to the Chief of General Staff for collating with similar reports from the A&Q, the Adjutant General and the G Branches.

This great mass of paper would then be added to similar collections from the navy, the air force and the War Supply Ministry each Thursday, so it could all be placed on the Prime Minister's desk each Friday morning.

After surveying the mountain of paper placed before him, Victor ordered the elderly captain to take it away. He had no intention of signing it. He wasn't going to sign something he hadn't read, and he had no intention of reading "all that bumf" — even if he had the time. The secretary was flabbergasted. "But, Sir, it's for the Prime Minister. It has to be in every Thursday; it is laid down in orders by the CGS himself."

Victor remained quite unmoved. Everyone was aghast. The unspeakable happened — the orders of the CGS were ignored. The great report went forward to the Prime Minister minus any section from the Ordnance Branch. As this great weekly pile of paper was never read anyway by the Prime Minister, he did not notice the deletion. The G Branch, however, was furious. But for many weeks to come there was no weekly pile of paper from Ordnance.

One of the many great problems facing the Ordnance Branch at that time was the problem of suddenly producing uniforms and boots fast enough to equip all the tens of thousands of men being recruited by units all across the country. As winter was approaching, the most urgent need was for great coats. But the battle with paper and red tape was being lost. Indeed, due to government regulations and rules about procedures, tendering, registration of patterns, restricted lists of approved suppliers, and so forth, the orders hadn't even been placed or the manufacturers selected.

The degree of Victor's frustration reached the boiling point. He summoned his staff secretary and announced there would be a report from the MGO this week for the Prime Minister. The little man was delighted. Light, sanity and proper procedures were to prevail once more. "I will notify all the sections immediately, Sir, so they can get the typing in hand."

"No," said Victor. "Get me a piece of paper and a red pencil. I will write it myself — it won't be typed."

Then as the secretary looked on in shocked disbelief, Victor wrote in bold letters across the single piece of paper:

"Mr. Prime Minister. Unless someone has the authority to break all the rules around here and quickly, the Canadian Army is going to damn well freeze this winter."

"There," said Victor. "Send that over to the PM and just as it is written." Needless to say, this was the only part of the report the Prime Minister did see, and it produced action. Victor was given immediate and full authority to produce great coats by whatever means were necessary. He at once picked up the telephone and called Eaton's, Simpson's and the Bay to locate the most experienced buyer of men's clothing in the trade, one who knew all the clothing factories and their production capacities. They came up with a fine, tough old boy named Switzer, whom Victor immediately put in uniform with the rank of full colonel and complete authority as a director to produce the coats and ignore the red tape. The plan worked.

Switzer didn't know anything about regular channels and didn't wait to find out before telling the factories to get busy, even though it might be months before the paper work caught up. But then as expected, came the PF counterattack from the AG Branch. Victor had no authority to give Switzer an officer's commission or promote him to colonel. Why, Switzer had not had any basic infantry training, not even attended a summer militia camp. Switzer would at least have to attend the Junior Officer's Training School at Brockville for three months before he was commissioned, to do his drill, route marches, range tests and so forth.

Victor was quite unperturbed and simply advised the AG that Colonel Switzer had already taken up his duties as an officer and could not be spared for three months of training. Victor had no intention of sending him to Brockville, as Switzer's duties did not require him to fire guns, fight with a bayonet or do ceremonial drills. Indeed, as he was 60 years of age, a route march would likely kill him. He had been enlisted as the best qualified clothing man in Canada. Again, Victor's decision stuck, but there was much muttering, sulking and wringing of hands in PF circles at this further outrageous action by a civilian.

It is difficult now to describe all the confusion and complexities of suddenly mobilizing a nation for war.

The problems of gearing up to wartime needs were, of course, not confined to the Ordnance Branch. The battle against red tape, apathy, entrenched peacetime procedures and the normal morbid pace of Ottawa was being waged on all fronts. In the RCAF, Chubby Power, with a host of vigorous imports from private industry, was fighting to create a totally new service as well as the vast Empire Air Training Scheme, without the benefit of sufficient training planes or instructors.

At Camp Borden, Worthington was trying to create an armoured corps out of cavalry regiments — and without the benefit of tanks. Toward this end, he gathered about him a collection of pirates and rascals who never bothered to read the military manuals.

One subject dealt with extensively in England during our negotiations with the War Office had been the matter of tanks and armoured formations. The blitzkrieg's tactics of Germany's armoured columns racing through Holland and Belgium, had introduced a different concept of battle. The great emphasis now was toward tanks and mechanized infantry.

General McNaughton made brave statements about the total mechanization of the Canadian Army, and Worthington was rushed to Camp Borden to start a tank training school and begin to organize an Army Tank Brigade. There was one small problem for Worthy — we didn't have a single modern tank. There were three or four World War I style tanks and a couple of French armoured cars somewhere, and he put some canvas frames around old Model T Fords to make them look like tanks, but that was it. Perhaps we could borrow some secretly from the U.S., and Ralston would see what the British could do to help when we got to England. We didn't have any blueprints or plans for building them in Canada.

During our conferences in England, I noticed that Churchill kept talking about Canada supplying "armoured divisions." We told the British that, back in Camp Borden, Worthy was busy setting up an Army Tank Brigade. In my ignorance at that time, I assumed this was part of an armoured division. As I listened to Churchill, however, a certain doubt entered my mind, so I passed a note along the table to Ralston, asking, "Is there any difference between an Army Tank Brigade and brigades in armoured divisions?" Ralston accordingly raised this naive question, and we were astonished when the British generals gently explained that these were two quite different animals. Ralston was nonplussed. "Well, just which is it you want?" he demanded, "Army tanks or armoured divisions?" The answer was that both were needed and as fast as possible. I would like to have seen Worthy's face when our urgent signal arrived from England to produce both formations — without any modern tanks. It was also amusing when we returned to Canada to hear Ralston explaining in Parliament that army tank brigades and armoured brigades were "vastly different" — as if we had known all along.

In the possibility that Britain might be overrun by the Nazis or her tank factories destroyed by the air raids, it was decided that complete plans for building tanks in Canada should be sent across the Atlantic without delay. Steps were also taken to start developing a Canadian designed tank to be called a RAM I.

There was great hilarity in Ottawa around NDHQ when a senior supply officer rushed to Halifax once word was received that the secret plans for the latest British tank had arrived by ship. He took with him a briefcase to carry the plans back to Ottawa, but was staggered to see enormous crates of blueprints being off-loaded, which would require several lorries to transport.

About this time, General McNaughton made the announcement in England that the Canadian Army was to be a mechanized army, complete with armoured divisions and mechanized artillery and infantry — everything on wheels.

To the dismay of Ralston, who was trying to sell the idea and need for costly mechanized divisions to the cabinet and the country, the Quarter Master General in a rousing public speech made the fatuous statement that the war would be won not with fancy new machines but, as always, by a man with his feet in the mud and a bayonet in his hand. This illuminated revelation, which so clearly exposed the Stone Age thinking of some of our PF generals, was seized on with delight by the press all across the country. At the time we were trying to build confidence in Canada's war effort; encourage recruiting for a modern army able to cope with the Nazi armoured columns and blitzkrieg tactics. For public relations reasons alone, the poor general was quietly replaced.

As Victor Sifton studied the needs of a mechanized army in the way of trucks, transporters, tanks, and vehicles of all sorts, he began to worry about the problems of mechanical maintenance. No one at Defence Headquarters had apparently considered just how many mechanics might be needed to keep all these thousands of engines running or wheels and springs replaced . . . or where all the mechanics were to come from.

General McNaughton, in England at the time of his announcement of Canadian policy, had not seriously applied his imaginative mind to this practical and all-important consideration.

Before McNaughton went soaring too far off into a fantasy world, Victor insisted he be told that unless thousands of mechanics could be conjured up by some miracle, Canada's mechanized army could well grind to a dead halt after one week of operations.

Turning again to Civy Street, Victor then started to phone about to find some expert on trucking and motor transport. He was told that the biggest fleet operator of trucks was a man named Francis Farwell in Hamilton. Victor called him to Ottawa at once to work out with him such matters as how many mechanic hours were required to keep a thousand vehicles on the road per month, and how long did it take to train a mechanic. The results of these simple calculations applied to the number of vehicles called for in our army plans completely staggered Victor. He called for an immediate meeting of the Army Council. All training came under General Crerar's G Branch, which had to confess there were no plans whatever to train mechanics on this massive scale.

"Well, what's the sense of my producing thousands of vehicles if they are all going to be bogged down through lack of maintenance in a few weeks' time?" Victor demanded, and the fight began again.

Ralston was shocked at this lack of foresight, indeed negligence, on the part of G Branch — going gaily along with McNaughton's dreams, with no serious concern about the training of motor mechanics. In consequence, the responsibility for recruiting and training thousands of mechanics was taken from G Branch and placed under Victor's control. He moved at once by press ganging Francis Farwell into the army and ordering him to take over some signals barracks near Kingston to start up a large mechanical training centre — by whatever means necessary and with whatever equipment was available, anywhere.

Truck Production

In the matter of trucks — or lorries, as they were called in the army — the situation was much the same. Plans for the mass production of military type trucks, on the scale needed, simply did not exist. Meetings were held with representatives of C.D. Howe's Department of Supply, and officials from General Motors, Ford, Chrysler and Willys car companies. The G Branch produced the army-approved plans and specifications of the trucks required, and the motor company officials were asked to see how they could pool their resources toward joint production.

The motor officials, taking one look at the obsolete plans and specifications, recoiled in horror and disbelief. The army vehicle designs, inherited from World War I models with a few improvisations by some PF officer in peacetime, were hopelessly out of date and totally removed from modern manufacturing processes. The motor companies, with the full backing of both Victor and Howe, put their own design people to work at once, to come up with some standard vehicles which all the companies could produce quickly and in quantity.

In fairness to the army, as far as the trucks were concerned it should be recalled that at the outset of the war, Britain had urged Canada not to waste time in manufacturing army trucks in Canada. With ships so badly needed for food, lumber, minerals and troops, sending trucks to Europe would use up valuable space. British motor factories, Britain said, could produce all the vehicles necessary, not only for British forces but also for Canadian formations as they arrived overseas. Besides, Britain badly needed the foreign exchange from vehicle production.

After Dunkirk, however, when the British Expeditionary Force had to abandon their vehicles on the beaches and the Nazi bombers started to destroy British factories, the picture altered very suddenly. Not only could Britain not supply any vehicles for the Canadian Army, but she needed all the vehicles Canada could produce to help re-equip her own armies.

The manner in which Canadian factories met this challenge was a tremendous tribute to the entire motor industry in Canada. Their combined production in the next few years exceeded all early forecasts. Canadian trucks and other vehicles supplied not only our own forces, but also British troops in England and North Africa; some vehicles even went to Russia.

It was the same with signals and wireless equipment. The new-style army called for tens of thousands of wireless sets of all descriptions. Every infantry platoon, every tank and scout car, every headquarters — all required modern receivers, portable sets and walkie talkies. Long-range transmitters were needed for headquarters and for army-air communications and assault landing operations. Up until the start of the war, our army was still thinking largely in terms of signal flags, Morse keys and field telephone lines of World War I vintage.

When Canadian electrical companies such as RCA, Westinghouse, General Electric and Marconi were called together, to plan for co-ordinated mass production, their representatives gazed in disbelief at the outdated prototypes and specifications demanded by the army, which still called for bakelite panels and other such obsolete parts — about one step removed from the crystal set era.

Similarly, the Canadian electrical industry, starting from scratch, astonished everyone in the next few months by their combined capacity to design and mass produce thousands of modern wireless sets for different requirements, not only for our own army but for many Allied forces as well. Some of the designs, such as the Maple Leaf C-33 set, were to prove outstanding in field operations in all theatres.

These were only a few of the enormous problems which had to be met by Victor and his new team in Ordnance, working with C. D. Howe's department.

As Victor had done, C.D. simply commandeered the services of top civilians across Canada, wherever they were needed. Without exception these executives, when called upon, responded at once. Released by their companies, most served without pay, becoming known as the "dollar-a-year men." They numbered in the hundreds and included such well-known figures as Al Williamson, Eddie Taylor, Smoot Mavor, H. R. MacMillan, Edgar Burton, Tommy Davis, Billy Woodward and Ed Bickell. All of them were business managers or professionals, used to direct action and knowing little about the niceties of civil service procedures. Their great value lay in the fact that they spoke out courageously and acted vigorously according to their conscience, free from political considerations and not fearful of civil service seniority, their job security or personal finances. Regrettably, very little has been written about their enormous contribution to our war effort during that hectic period.

Like Victor and myself, many of these executives lived at their own expense at the Chateau Laurier. Each evening, a group would gather together for dinner at the Chateau before returning to their government offices again in the evening, often working till the early hours of the morning in their efforts to drive Canada's mobilization into high gear. It was an exciting but exhausting period, with endless frustrations. Entrenched civil servants and Regular Force officers were fighting a rearguard battle according to the book — a book which none of the amateurs understood, or had ever read.

At dinner each night at the Chateau, stories would be exchanged about the tangles of red tape and massive brick walls being encountered. The situations every day were quite hilarious, almost slapstick comedy at times.

One day, to his utter amazement, Victor learned about the enormous depot, somewhere near Montreal, for the storage and maintenance of sufficient saddlery and harnesses to equip an entire cavalry division. This wasn't simply dead storage; a staff was maintained to keep the harnesses greased and the saddles properly polished — and there wasn't a single mounted unit left in the entire Canadian Army. For fear of ridicule we kept this one rather hidden till we were able to sell the harnesses off at bargain prices to some Latin American government.

Forestry Corps Embarks

Another event which comes to mind was a chance encounter I had one evening at Standish Hall in Hull, Quebec, where I had repaired for a beer after working till a late hour with Ralston. At the bar was a colonel of the Canadian Forestry Corps, rather drunk and pouring out his woes and frustrations, damning in a loud voice all higher authority and stupidity. He fastened on to me and I listened sympathetically as he seemed to have a point.

In answer to an urgent call for lumber in Britain, Canada on short notice had undertaken to mobilize quickly lumberjacks and bushworkers from all across the country. They were to be formed into units, supplied with equipment and then rushed over to cut down the forests in Scotland. This improvisation was due to shortage of shipping space for Canadian lumber as a result of U-boat warfare and the need for food in England.

It seemed that my new friend, the drunken colonel, was a top forestry manager with very little knowledge of the army or military procedures. He had managed by a gigantic effort to get his lumber camp boys into uniform and concentrated in Halifax. They were due to embark in two days' time.

It was then discovered that not a single piece of the promised portable saw mill equipment had reached Halifax, and his entire corps would arrive in Scotland quite useless and unable to function. No one knew where the equipment was — or whether it was even on its way to Halifax.

In great heat and desperation, the colonel had flown to Ottawa, where he had been calling hopelessly at government offices all day. "No one knew and no one cared where all the bloody equipment was . . . all was lost . . . there was nothing left to do but get drunk." Drunk as he was, his answers to my questions seemed valid enough so I told him I would take him to a man who would look after everything. Although it was two in the morning, I bundled him into a taxi and took him to Defence Headquarters, where I knew Ralston would still be working. Without explaining where we were, I got him seated in the minister's ante room while I barged in to see Ralston.

I explained to Ralston that I had a drunken colonel in tow, but wanted him to overlook his condition as I thought he had something to say which Ralston should hear. Tomorrow would be too late.

Despite Ralston's fishy look, I marched the Colonel into the ministerial office and told him to tell his story. Ralston listened with a grim expression, then reached for a telephone. He got Howe out of bed, then the president of the CNR, then Movement Control in Halifax. The lost equipment and machinery were located, the right of way cleared to Halifax, and all was saved.

By the time this was completed an hour or two later, the Forestry colonel was rather shaken and nearly sober. As we left Ralston's office, the minister called to me, "Don't let anyone see him going out of my office in that condition at this hour of the morning."

About this period, the U.S. Army sent us up a new experimental army vehicle they called a "jeep." As the American people were not at war, the army wanted us to try out the vehicle and give our opinion. We gave it every test we could think of, under every possible condition. Victor sent it to Camp Borden and to Petawawa, where they bashed it over rocks, through water, sand, mud and snow. It was tried hauling guns and bouncing off trees, and it gave an amazing performance. Victor and I were quite ecstatic after driving all about Ottawa one day, so he sent it over to G Branch, which had to approve any new equipment.

Unbelievably, the CGS, Harry Crerar, sent it back to us a few days later saying that G Branch had tried it and, while it was an interesting novelty, determined that it would have "no practical value in modern warfare." For anyone who saw active service in any theatre during World War II, comment is unnecessary.

At that time a series of embarrassing articles appeared in the Toronto *Telegram* under the by-line of Judith Robinson. We had to admit the articles were entirely accurate and we were amazed at all the technical detail covered. But after a couple of weeks of the writer's screaming attack for greater priority on tank production, I started to smell a rat. I phoned Camp Borden and got General Worthington on the line.

"Those articles of yours in the Tely are pretty close to the bone, Worthy," I said. I knew Worthy of old. He had been told to produce a tank brigade fast and that he was proceeding to do, regardless of methods to be employed. He had been quietly supplying ammunition to Judith for her columns, to get faster action from Howe's Department of Supply.

Ottawa Livens Up

With all the strangers pouring into Ottawa at that time, the city suddenly took on an entirely new look. A new zest and vitality was apparent. Uniforms were everywhere, not only our own service uniforms but also those of missions from the British, French, Polish, Dutch and Belgian armies. Hotel accommodation was at a premium. Men's canteens and officers' clubs sprang to life under the auspices of women volunteers. The Badminton Club became a quick lunchroom, and the Chateau Grill was jammed every night with young officers dancing to Len Hopkins' band. To help my friend Carol Gibbons and his band at the Savoy in London, I several times arranged for Len to send over the latest orchestrations through the co-operation of some RAF pilot ferrying bombers to London.

There was one dashing and well-heeled young liaison officer of the French Army, cutting a big swath with girls in Ottawa at that time with his champagne lunches. I was later to see this same young officer at a bar in Paris when the city was liberated, again surrounded by girls and champagne, though then he was disguised as a commando.

Some amusement was caused when a well-known young Ottawa girl and her RAF fiancé were married in bed. The young flyer had been able to arrange for only a 48-hour leave to get married. He had roared into Ottawa to discover that his bride-to-be had developed measles. Before the day was out he had also broken out in a rash of measles and had to go to bed. He didn't know when he might be granted another leave, so it was decided to go ahead with the wedding, with both principals in bed together and with all their friends invited.

There was a big formal dance one evening at the Royal Ottawa Golf Club. While I was dancing, a little wisp of a girl I knew grabbed my arm and demanded that I get her over to England by hook or by crook. She was convinced that in my position as Staff Secretary to the Minister, I could wangle a job of some kind for her in London. As I tried to convince her it was impossible, Mike Pearson danced by. He was also back on a short trip to Ottawa. Seeking an escape, I directed the young lady to Mike. "Get after him," I said. "He is the only man I know who can fix it for you or give you a job."

Some months later in England, when I was on the staff of the 5th Armoured Division at Hindhead, I received a wedding invitation — for the marriage of Hope Gilmour of Ottawa to Allistair Buchan (son of former Governor-General Lord Tweedsmuir). Scribbled across the invitation was a notation to me from Hope, "I made it."

Staff Duties

Of note at that period was the arrival back from the U.K. of Colonel Tommy (later Lieutenant-General) E. L. M. Burns and my old friend Brigadier Penhale of Regina days in the thirties. They were both PF officers with World War I experience. Burns had been Chief of Staff to McNaughton in England and Pen had been at CMHQ in London. Burns was to become V/CGS in Ottawa and, with Pen, was to start up a new section in the G Branch called Staff Duties Directorate — largely because the War Office had one in England.

In my view, it was a completely useless appendage, simply Empire building, as the directorate duplicated work already being done. By superimposing another level of control, however, it gave more power to the CGS, Harry Crerar, on the theory that everything should be co-ordinated for the CGS as though he were a commander-in-chief.

In my innocence, and at Pen's request, I agreed to become, temporarily, SD-4, whatever that meant, to help him get things started, though Ralston still insisted I also be available to him for special assignments from the Minister's Office, on short notice.

Besides Penhale, the Director of Staff Duties, there was also to be two assistant directors and then subdivisions SD 1, 2, 3, 4, etc. We were to see all the files that went whirling about between the G Branch, the AG Branch, QMG, MGO, etc., and the various technical directorates such as National Research. All of which we were supposed to co-ordinate in some curious manner by attaching snotty little notes in crisp military style such as: "to review and report," "for information only," "for action forthwith," "your opinion please." Then you would stick on a red tag meaning urgent, another meaning secret — or perhaps top secret, "for Directors' eyes only" — and so forth. You next made notes and wrote dates on the cover of the file ... recorded the number of the file in a diary (so anyone could tell where any of 10,000 files currently in the stream had gone, and you could blame someone else).

It was all quite marvellous. You sent files up or down, or if your desk got stacked up too badly at the end of the day you simply "minuted" some over to a pal in another department and called an orderly to clear your basket. The files would go back to the Central Registry — apparently a great sinkhole somewhere down in the catacombs of the Woods Building. Here, an ancient cave dweller would stir them up every few days or so and shoot them off to someone else. If there was anything of real urgency, you simply picked up the phone or dropped down the hall to chat with the other man. Still, the file system had to be observed as it was laid down in Standing Orders — or some other orders, someplace. No one really understood, but it was a jolly paper war if you wished to play it. I found it all quite hopeless and must now confess I merely went through the motions.

I kept my eyes open for anything urgent or serious and conducted any real business first hand, which of course often landed me in trouble. From my daily contact with the Minister's Office, I frequently knew that decisions were already taken on matters still being shuttled back and forth in files between Central Registry and some directorate.

In no time, of course, our new SD directorate had to be subdivided again — with more lieutenant colonels to head up each split; and they each needed additional captains as assistants, and this called for more staff clerks, which warranted more orderlies on the establishment ... and so forth.

They never threw files away in Central Registry. I believe there were files still active then covering the Boer War. One day the branch responsible for the Veterans' Guard enquired about the use of shotguns for prisoner-of-war camps, then being established in Canada. I accordingly requisitioned from Central Registry the "shotgun file." Sure enough, up it came with the last entry, a memo, dated in 1916. That memo was from the trenches in France, signed by an officer in the 48th Highlanders, obviously with a sense of humour. His note had gone to Brigade, Division, Corps, and so forth, then to Argyle House in London, then finally back to Central Registry in Ottawa.

In correct military, third-person jargon, it recorded that thought had been given to the practical value of 12-gauge pump guns in clearing German trenches on night raids. It then related that two subalterns had been detailed to visit a well-known gunsmith in London on their next leave to obtain said weapons for the use of ... Following several paragraphs of officialese, the officer concluded that after the pump guns had been tried out an unfortunate incident took place: "the red band on a staff officer's cap had been mistaken for a rising pheasant, at which time the weapons had been withdrawn from service."

One of the deathly and serious secrets at that time was the disturbing fact that the defences of Halifax, our all-important port for convoys, did not include any long-range guns capable of shooting a German battleship, should it choose to raid the docks or steam right into Halifax Basin — where a hundred or more ships might be at anchor. Guns had been ordered from England, the shells from some place in Canada and electrical plotting gear from the United States. Concrete emplacements were still being constructed. This embarrassing oversight in our defences was kept very secret while we waited impatiently for the guns to arrive.

One morning the long-awaited signal came in code. The guns were arriving that week; everyone was to be alerted so the installation could proceed at once. This indeed called for instant action — no sense waiting to draw files from Central Registry and all that nonsense. I took the decoded text, pinned a small scribble to it: "CGS, AG, MGO and QMG. For your information and immediate action." I signed my name to the chit — which I did not bother waiting to have typed — put a red tag on it and had an orderly circulate it to the offices of the respective chiefs direct, all within a matter of minutes. What a sad mistake.

Four days later my poor little chit arrived back on my desk. Now attached to it were five long official letters (or rockets) from on high, castigating me in the most icy terms.

It started off with a long typed observation on the letterhead of the CGS, addressed to the Vice CGS, and ran: "I do not approve of this informal manner of addressing the senior members of the army staff. Please have this matter dealt with so it does not happen again and report ... " And so it went down the line, each sub-chief adding his own reprimand. The last letter was from the Director of Staff Duties, "to note please the critical observation ... Please refer to standing orders No. XXX and refer to manual of ... In future kindly ... "

My chit had made the rounds in record time and had been properly noted, but obviously I could never really adjust to life at NDHQ. I should try once more, I decided, to get back to my regiment overseas, a matter of debate between Ralston and myself.

During this period in Ottawa, I was fortunate in having a very able ally in the person of Miss Olive Waters, Ralston's private secretary and one of the most able women I have ever known. She knew all the ropes in Ottawa, how the civil service worked and how to expedite everything. She was on my side from the beginning and knew how to handle ministers, deputies and PF generals. She was accorded the unofficial title of General Waters by her many admirers among the civilian imports.

There was considerable surprise and many questions raised when General Burns had suddenly returned to Ottawa from overseas, where he held the appointment of senior staff officer to General McNaughton. Burns had graduated from Camberley with high acclaim, and was recognized as a brilliant staff officer. The fact of the matter was that General Burns, in a private letter to a friend in Canada, had indiscreetly criticized his chief, Andy McNaughton, in very frank language. By some prescience it was his opinion that McNaughton was not competent as a field commander.

This damaging letter was intercepted by the postal censors and directed to the minister's attention. Here was a dilemma for Ralston. What to do? It couldn't exactly be considered a security matter, he reasoned. After pondering the problem for a day, he simply sent the letter overseas to McNaughton, with the comment, "for your information and such action considered necessary." As Ralston explained, it might not be a security matter, but at that important level, if the letter truly represented the views of McNaughton's chief staff officer, it would be both wrong and unfair to leave Burns in that sensitive position without McNaughton's knowledge. This was the overriding consideration with Ralston at the time. Though this was perhaps the first intimation that McNaughton was not the man to command the army in action, this consideration was barely noticed. Tragically, in a year or so, Burns's assessment would prove to have been correct.

Ever since the start of the war, the government had seemed cursed with bad public relations and press relations, subjects of which the armed forces of the time seemed to have very little understanding. For a year or more there was complete chaos. Generals repeatedly put their foot in it, making speeches and discussing government policy. The admirals, on the other hand, stolidly maintained the traditions of "the silent service" and refused to give the press even legitimate news about the navy. Then, when mistakes were made in the forces, futile whitewash jobs were attempted, which always backfired. It ran all the way from false press releases to attempts at censorship, restricting areas to the press, and feuding endlessly with editors. Reporters were regarded as traitors who, in the national interest, should be shot for obstructing the war efforts.

It was all quite hopeless. There was a single junior officer, Captain Tommy Wayling, a former member of the Parliamentary press gallery, who was put in uniform with the title Chief Press Liaison Officer (CPLO). He had no direct access to the minister, but he alone was supposed to handle all press matters for the entire army from coast to coast. Every general who gave a silly statement to the press, or gave his opinion on how to win the war, later claimed he was misquoted by the press.

It was always Wayling's fault; he should have controlled the press. Staff officers and deputies from every branch of the service gave Wayling contradictory orders. Regularly, once or twice a week, Wayling was fired.

Unbelievably, the Chief of the Naval Staff one day went so far as to issue a directive that newspapers in Canada should cease to publish daily weather reports, on the grounds that it might tip-off the enemy about convoy sailings. He couldn't grasp that U.S. radio stations broadcast weather bulletins every hour and that the German Navy knew as much about the weather on the Atlantic coast as we did. This endless nonsense resulted in an angry press and a furious opposition in the House.

A Job To Be Avoided

Repeatedly, Ralston asked me to take on the army press job, but knowing it was a hopeless proposition I steadfastly refused. From the Chief of Staff down through all the Permanent Force, there was not the slightest understanding of either the need or functions of a free press in peacetime, let alone in war. Granted the press did at times shoot from the hip without all the facts, but the fault lay largely with the army high command who tried to keep everything secret and hidden from the press, instead of properly briefing the reporters and broadcasters who were as anxious as the generals to win the war. The press felt victory could only be achieved if weaknesses and inefficiency in our mobilization program were exposed and the nation fully informed of problems and needs. There was no chance that any militia officer could have the generals accept this.

I discussed the situation with Victor Sifton several times, and he entirely backed my decision to keep out of the mess. As I believe William Pitt once said, it was obvious that "the fruit was not yet ripe." The post could only be a graveyard till the army was prepared to listen to advice and give a press director some proper authority, as well as keeping him totally in the picture at the very top level. The role and support of the press in wartime mobilization are of vital importance, not only in matters of public trust, understanding and national morale but also, as I was to discover later, in the matter of information to our own troops and information and misinformation to the enemy in the area of psychological warfare.

Much as I wished to help Ralston in this difficult situation, I knew it would be a death sentence at that time for anyone to attempt organizing an army press section. I could not, however, refuse to carry out some special projects requested by Ralston in the area of public information, concurrently with my duties as his staff secretary and my work in the new Directorate of Staff Duties.

Frequently, I became involved in the frustrating and tiresome job of drafting some of the many speeches the minister was obliged to make. I say tiresome, as Ralston, with his legal training, could not resist endlessly editing every paragraph, removing all the punch lines, till the piece emerged more like a legal brief than a ringing call to arms in the Churchill fashion. He would revise every speech a dozen times or more, driving myself and others who helped, including Miss Waters, nearly insane. Several times I jumped the gun on him, releasing to newspapers and wire services the early drafts of the speeches, and just ignoring his subsequent drafts.

73

One speech, which he was to make in the United States — the first speech by a Canadian cabinet minister in that country since the outbreak of the war — was considered of great importance and sensitivity. Ralston kept us until three o'clock in the morning, rewriting it time after time. Finally we convinced him to wind things up so he could go home, have a few hours of sleep and a shave before taking his early plane to the States. I stayed on another hour or so to get copies printed and distributed in advance to U.S. and Canadian wire services, then staggered off to bed. To my horror, when I returned to Defence HQ about 9 a.m., I learned that aboard the plane Ralston had been at it again, having signalled back about 50 more corrections to be made before the speech was released. It was quite hopeless. Canadian-American relations might be in jeopardy, but I simply pretended that the corrections hadn't reached me through signal services. As in the past, Ralston forgave my dereliction. He understood his own weakness in this regard.

Similarly, I was at times conscripted to help draft an important and supposedly rousing warlike speech for the Prime Minister. Trying to make King sound warlike and heroic was an exercise in futility. His appearance, delivery and public image were all against it. The army held him rather in contempt, and the fact that he had remained in the United States during World War I was not forgotten by the public.

In one instance, when King was to speak in Parliament on the war effort, Hutchison, Dexter and I worked for hours polishing some historic and rousing phrases for his speech, marking the particular words to be emphasized for the headlines. But it was all in vain; he blew it completely when he stood up to speak. With his tubby little figure, his bald head covered by a few wisps of hair, and his precise formality, he was the furthest thing imaginable from a national wartime leader.

In flat tones he plodded through the script with no sign of any emotion. Then when he reached the key sentences he halted entirely for a minute or two while he located his pince-nez, which hung round his neck on a black ribbon. Then carefully adjusting them on his nose, he peered at his notes while he blandly read off our purple passages. Watching him from the gallery, we realized it was a lost cause.

Leonard Brockington, QC, at that time hailed by both the public and himself as Canada's leading orator, was then secretly brought into the act for the next speech, in the hope that he could "raise the heather." His experience, however, was exactly the same. Listening to King massacre his speech in the House was too much for Brock, and he retired to the Rideau Club to drown his grief in Scotch. Close to tears, he very foolishly complained loudly to everyone within hearing range about how King had ruined his speech and destroyed his reputation. As was usually the case, King heard about Brock's indiscretion in a matter of hours. Brock was not asked to write any more speeches for the Prime Minister.

As further revelations about Mr. King come to light from his diaries and from private sources, the question grows as to how King was able to direct Canada effectively all through the war years and control what was possibly the most powerful cabinet in our history, composed of such forceful and independent characters as Howe, Ralston, Macdonald, Ilsley, Lapointe, Gardiner, Power and Crerar. Here was a pedantic politician, distrusted by much of the country as a trickster, despised by most of the army, regarded as a bit potty on social welfare and human relations issues.

Unquestionably, King's greatest accomplishment lay in his understanding of the need, with the country at war, to surround himself with strong colleagues, men of action whom the country could trust and respect, to cover his own deficiencies. Equally important was his ability to harness and firmly control this powerful team, by clever manipulation and playing one against the other.

Mrs. Angus Macdonald later told me that when her husband was urged to join the federal cabinet, she tried to dissuade him from this step. At a meeting of Ralston and Ilsley with the former Premier of Nova Scotia, Mrs. Macdonald warned them all not to trust Mackenzie King. "He will use you all and when he is finished with you he will hurl you from the battlements." In this, her warning proved entirely accurate. King made use of their abilities and public respect, but in the end he betrayed them and discarded them ruthlessly. At the time of Ralston's death shortly after the war, King attended the funeral for appearance's sake, but Mrs. Ralston refused to meet him.

As Bruce Hutchison relates, King never forgave Ralston. Apparently, King destroyed Ralston because the PM knew that Ralston was the one man who, in fact, had defeated him.*

By some magic King was able to hold his team together till the conscription issue of 1944. The report that in his desk King held undated letters of resignation from several of these ministers, is quite correct.

I was privileged in counting many members of King's war cabinet as my friends, and I had many talks with them both during and after the war on the subject of their relations with King. One of my oldest friends, T. A. Crerar, was King's only contemporary in the cabinet after Lapointe's death, and was King's seatmate in the House for many years. In the election of 1921 it was Crerar, then leader of the Progressive party, which had captured 65 seats, who made it possible for King to form his first government. In my many talks with T.A. in later years, when he retired to the Senate, he explained one facet of King's curious and complex make-up which I think is vital in understanding some of King's actions and beliefs.

According to Crerar, King was at times capable of great self deception. As political situations developed he would, over a period of weeks, gradually convince himself that what he wanted to believe was true — in complete disregard of the facts. He would then, with great skill, set about convincing his colleagues and also the nation.

*As for the others, Hutchison, in his book *The Incredible Canadian*, about MacKenzie King, has accurately written: "Crerar, Ilsley and Angus Macdonald he could barely tolerate as the war progressed and they reciprocated his feelings." Gardiner he feared and regarded as eccentric and uncontrollable. Howe, as Jack Pickersgill relates, King did not understand at all. In Bruce Hutchison's words he regarded Howe as a political ignoramus.

FIVE
Press And Propaganda

WORLD SCENE

*A costly summer. Yugoslavia surrenders. Greece
surrenders and British withdraw. Rudolf Hess
parachutes into Scotland on private peace mission.
Six British ships sunk off Crete. Crete evacuated.
HMS* Hood *sunk by German battleship* Bismark.
*Germany turns on Russian ally. Japan moves into
Viet Nam with approval of Vichy, France. Germans
drive into Ukraine, encircle Leningrad.*

Quite early in the war a group of newspaper men and writers, including myself, were called to a meeting in Ottawa for the purpose of planning a build-up of public support for Canada's war effort in areas such as recruiting, financing, munitions and arms production, and general patriotism. This informal, temporary group was in fact the forerunner of Canada's Wartime Information Service and, later, the Press and Censorship sections connected with the three armed services and External Affairs.

While I can't recall all the names, the original group did include Grant Dexter, Bruce Hutchison, Charlie Vining, Joe Clark, Dave Rogers and, I believe, Wilf Eggleston.

Our big handicap was the impossibility of projecting an image of Willie King as a war leader to rally and inspire the nation. We did what we could, but all our efforts were a flop. Finally we decided that McNaughton, with his bushy eyebrows and penetrating eyes, was our best bet. Accordingly, we built him up to the heavens. We had his speeches quoted on every occasion and scores of photographs were distributed showing him in every sort of heroic and forceful pose. As well as a steady exposure in Canadian publications, a wide release of McNaughton pictures and statements was also made to British and American publications.

Propaganda In The U.S.

Another task undertaken quietly by several members of this group was the distribution of wartime information within the United States. The Roosevelt administration knew that sooner or later the United States would be caught up in the war with Hitler and likely with Japan as well. As Eleanor Roosevelt recorded in her diary, the President longed to strike. Isolationist feelings ran high, however. Politically, it was impossible for Roosevelt to move his country toward a war footing. Powerful blocks of voters kept up an anti-war campaign, and the cry was "no involvement in Europe."

Roosevelt was fully aware that in the Battle of Britain after Dunkirk, England was, in effect, America's first line of defence, and her struggle gained time for re-arming America. The visit by King George VI to Roosevelt in Washington, shortly before the outbreak of war, undoubted-

76

ly contributed greatly to Roosevelt's resolve to support Britain in the fight against the horrors of Hitler's Germany.

But it must be remembered that after 1920, the United States had virtually shut out the world. Having refused to join the League of Nations, the U.S. had retired in sullen self-righteousness. The American peace movement lobbied to outlaw war, little realizing the encouragement given to the aggressor nations. Roosevelt also faced the U.S. Neutrality Law, a strong German Bund organization, the complexities of party politics, and American intellectuals who remained totally blind to the moral question at issue in the war against Nazi Germany. There were restraints and limits to preparing the U.S. for war and to the degree to which Roosevelt could actively assist Canada and England, until the American public was prepared to back him.

Roosevelt was deeply concerned lest Britain attempt some propaganda to bring the U.S. into the war, as in World War I, which might backfire on his own efforts. It was therefore arranged with Churchill that no efforts at propaganda would be undertaken by the British.

This undertaking, however, did not embrace Canada. Proceeding carefully, with the blessing of England we began to send a flow of information to the United States from Ottawa, concerning Canada's mobilization and the operations of naval convoy work, the Empire Air Training Scheme, ship construction and so forth, in an effort to bring home to our neighbours that the war was not in some remote part of the world but right next door; their turn could be next. We stressed that if Britain were invaded, it was planned to continue the war from Canada. While much of the American press gave full support to the Allied cause, many newspapers still followed the isolationist line and some were openly anti-British.

The American armed forces realized they would soon be at war, but it was almost impossible to get any large war appropriations for new equipment through Congress. In Ottawa, we had a close liaison with the U.S. Department of War, and there was an easy flow of information between staffs. Many teams of U.S. officers in civy clothes visited Canada to exchange information and to share in tests and weapon design.

Quite unknown, however, even by many senior U.S. officers at that time, top level staff talks were also going on between the British and United States. As early as June 1941, this joint study initiated a highly secret strategic plan, code named Rainbow V, by which the war in Europe was to receive top priority when the U.S. entered the war. Operations in the Pacific were to be of a defensive or holding nature. The plan also envisaged the withdrawal of U.S. forces from the Philippines should these islands be attacked by Japanese forces.

Because of the strong isolationist forces in America, all this had to be kept under heavy wraps. One of the chief victims of this isolationist mood was General Douglas MacArthur, whose headquarters I would join in the years ahead.

As commander of the Philippine forces before the war, he called repeatedly on Washington for modern weapons, tanks, men and aircraft. But Congress would not pass the needed appropriations. His cries were ignored.

The U.S. War Department, however, did not object to our efforts to bring the realities of the war home to the American public. *Time* and *Life* magazines as well as *Collier's* and the *Saturday Evening Post* accepted our invitation to send some of their top feature writers up to Canada. In addition, we arranged to supply well-known American writers, connected to U.S. newspapers, with good copy to capture headlines in the U.S. press.

We also arranged for and briefed prominent Canadians visiting U.S. cities to speak at meetings of Rotary clubs, chambers of commerce, and so forth.

This was a sizeable project, and Bruce Hutchison* and others were kept busy turning out scores of speeches to be delivered all the way from Boston to San Francisco.

As Ottawa, perhaps with encouragement from London, was anxious to expand this activity, I hit on a plan which would reach all the major U.S. newspapers. My plan involved the use of the Canadian Press, Canada's national news service, as a cover. I arranged for the government to invite Canadian newspaper publishers and editors, as members of Canadian Press, to undertake a major tour of Canada's war effort, visiting important installations and training establishments of the army, navy and air force. They would travel by a special train and witness field exercises, artillery shoots, tank exercises, and so forth — and also be taken to sea on destroyers accompanying a North Atlantic convoy out of Halifax.

The Canadian Press members were invited to include on the tour some U.S. publishers and editors — quite incidentally of course — as their guests. Needless to say, we hand-picked all the most important publishers in the United States to be included on the invitation list. My old friend, the late Senator Rupert Davies, was at that time president of Canadian Press. At my request, he came down to Ottawa and, after consulting his board, agreed to co-operate in the national interest. The Canadian government, of course, would pick up the tab for this sizeable project, which required a tremendous amount of staff work. I had to work Rupert pretty hard signing scores of letters to U.S. editors and arranging to act as host for countless functions. At one point, when he had removed his jacket, then his vest, then loosened his tie and rolled up his shirt sleeves as he slugged away in my office, he finally ran his fingers through his hair and shouted, "Good God, you're going to give me a heart attack."

All the American papers accepted our invitation. Representatives included Hansen Baldwin, of the New York *Times*, considered the leading military writer in the United States. I don't recall all the other names, but also of importance were Ogden Reid of the *Herald Trib* and Hal O'Flaherty of the *Chicago Daily News*. O'Flaherty had been pursuing a very anti-British line on his editorial pages.

It might be argued that we were using the CP for propaganda purposes, but the government was simply extending complete facilities for publishers and editors to see our whole mobilization, have access to defence information, and then write or not as they saw fit. No false information or political angles were promoted. Senior officers and supply officials travelled on the train with the party and were available to supply facts and figures or give any briefings requested.

In getting approval for the operation, several members of the cabinet as well as some of the Defence chiefs were rather sceptical and critical of my idea.

*Earlier, under the guise of covering the U.S. election campaign, Bruce had been sent to join the press corps on Wendell Willkie's special train for the purpose of influencing public opinion. Travelling about the country for several weeks, he was able to talk privately with many prominent American politicians and political writers.

78

Results, however, far exceeded even my own estimates. Following the tour, I had a newspaper clipping service in New York monitor and clip all related stories appearing in American newspapers. From these hundreds of clippings, two enormous scrapbooks were compiled for the benefit of cabinet ministers. They were highly pleased with the results.

It will be recalled that the U.S. during this period did start to extend every assistance possible to Canada, allowed by the rules of neutrality. This assistance not only took the form of financial loans and purchasing credits arranged through Secretary of Treasury Henry Morgenthau, but also the supply and loan of U.S. aircraft and badly needed destroyers. American war planes were pushed close to the Canadian border; Canadians pulled them across the line, and the 50 over-aged destroyers, minus their guns, were turned over to the Allies at a very critical period in the battle of the Atlantic. There was, I should add, no great public outcry in the U.S. More than 600 Americans came to Canada to help as instructors in the RCAF for the Empire Air Training Scheme, and more than 10,000 Americans crossed the border to join the Canadian forces.

It was considered that the CP press tour had contributed greatly toward public acceptance in America of this important and neighbourly help. It was also possible for a meeting to be arranged between Roosevelt and Mackenzie King, at Ogdensburg, New York, when Roosevelt issued his historic statement on America's position on the defence of North America and the leasing of air bases for that purpose.

One incident on the press tour remains vividly in my mind. We were returning from Halifax where our American guests had been taken to sea on a destroyer. In the cold, grim freight sheds of Halifax harbour they had silently watched as long rows of Canadian soldiers in battle dress, helmets, respirators and full marching order filed up the gangways of the great troop ships, all painted in camouflage colours. Then on a destroyer in early dawn, they had sailed out past the anti-submarine booms and witnessed the great naval convoy form up with rows of battleships and escort vessels. It was a very sobering experience for the Americans, being tossed about on the waves of the North Atlantic.

On the train trip back to Montreal we had three hospitality cars attached, where drinks and refreshments were available. A number of the American writers sat up drinking with us till a late hour, debating the problems of war. They were under no illusions whatever as to the purpose of our tour, which they accepted without protest despite an ill-timed remark by Billy Woodward who, with several others, represented C. D. Howe. With one drink too many under his belt, Billy, in sweeping generosity, encouraged our guests in a loud voice to "drink up the liquor . . . the Canadian government's paying for it." Someone managed to get Billy off to bed, but the incident created the new nickname of "Billy Woodwind."

The Americans fully recognized the danger to the United States if Hitler invaded England and then proceeded to dominate the Atlantic and direct his attacks on Canada. They explained to us the great problem of reversing isolationist feelings in the United States, despite the great dangers which threatened. America, they felt, would never fight again. Their youth had gone soft, they argued. All the WPA projects during the thirties and Roosevelt's welfare programs had taken the fibre and initiative out of the country. They dismissed my views to the contrary, saying I just didn't know the U.S.A.

Having experienced the London air raids and witnessed the tremendous surge of purpose and discipline in England after Dunkirk, I assured them they were quite wrong. America's whole history was a record of fighting, adventure and violence as her people had fought their way across the continent. These fighting qualities were not suddenly bred out in a single generation. Indeed, I argued, it would only take a single Nazi Focke-Wulf bomber to fly over New York and drop one single bomb, and they would quickly discover whether their nation would fight or not. They dismissed this theory entirely. America had become indifferent and self-centred, they said.

A year or so later, the day of Japan's attack on Pearl Harbor, I happened to be in London on a short leave from my unit on the Sussex coast. I went at once to the British Ministry of Information, where I knew there were long-range radio receivers. We tuned in dozens of American radio stations to hear the news that evening. The American eagle was screaming all the way from Oregon to Maine. Recalling the press tour with the Americans in Canada, I could not refrain from sending a few cables. I forwarded messages to the five American friends who had debated with me on the train to Montreal. The message simply read: "So America won't fight."

Toronto Occupied

Another war promotion effort I undertook about that time, between my duties in the SD Branch and assignments in the Minister's Office, had to do with the capture and occupation of Toronto.

Ralston and others in the cabinet complained that the country still hadn't realized we were truly at war. In Toronto and our other larger cities, life seemed to go on much as usual once the early novelty of war had worn off. There was no great sense of urgency in industry or in public attitudes. Although British forces were being driven back in North Africa and an invasion of England still threatened, the Canadian Army was still not in action. Ottawa knew this was a lull before the storm, but there was still no great sense of urgency. Churchill once wrote in a purple passage that it was "a world of monstrous shadows moving in convulsive combinations through vistas of fathomless catastrophe." Couldn't we do something to shake up Toronto, Ralston asked.

By this time, Worthington, at Camp Borden just north of Toronto, had his armoured training centre pretty well organized, as well as elements of our 1st Army Tank Brigade. Alongside him, General Ernie Sansom was in the process of concentrating our 5th Armoured Division. The happy thought came to me that I might have these "brutal and licentious" armoured columns seize and occupy Toronto in a surprise attack, after the style of the Nazis' panzer blitzkriegs. This could show Canadians what enemy occupations in Europe were like — and stir things up.

Worthy and Sansom, both old friends, enthusiastically fell in with my plan, and Sansom set his staff to work out detailed operation orders for seizing radio stations and newspaper offices, occupying railway yards, placing guards on public buildings and bus depots, and demanding identification papers from Toronto civilians. We used the code name Shamblitz for the operation.

80

Under cover of darkness, armoured columns would move on Toronto, using three axes of advance. By daylight, everything would be accomplished and Toronto would awaken to see troops, in battle dress and with fixed bayonets, patrolling the streets and checking all civilian movements. A full regiment of field artillery would have their guns in place in Queen's Park, to dominate the Ontario Legislature. A corps headquarters, established in the rotunda of the Royal York Hotel, would be complete with wireless centre and security troops. General Sansom would go on the air with radio messages ordering the public to remain calm till we had rounded up all the subversives and collaborators.

The troops would camp in the open with suitable checkpoints and defences. Field kitchens and outdoor latrines would be operated in the downtown park areas. Apart from anything else, the event would give the troops a change of routine as well as being a good exercise for rapid movement and occupation, and we had great fun planning the lark.

Everything went swimmingly at first; the newspapers and radio stations played right along with the stunt. They had received no advance warning, as our security was excellent.

During the morning of occupation the publicity effect was marvellous. But a few sour notes started to creep in by mid-afternoon. Coming out of the *Star* building, a very crusty and difficult columnist of the Toronto *Star* was stopped at bayonet point by an enthusiastic young trooper who demanded an identification card. This the writer refused to produce, demanding to know when the hell was military law declared in Canada . . . what authority had the trooper to detain him and restrict his movements . . .

He had a good point, so the young trooper, uncertain, sent for his Sergeant who in turn sent for the troop commander. Their orders had not specified what action should be taken when a civilian refused to produce identification.

At this point the imp of all newspapermen, Greg Clark, happened along and joined the small crowd gathering now on King Street. "Arrest him at once," Greg urged, despite the fact that he could have readily identified and vouched for his newspaper colleague. After further urging from Greg, the columnist was taken into custody and marched off under escort to the nearby armouries.

In due course, a telephone call from Sansom's chief staff officer, Garry Lee, advised me about the prisoner and asked what should be done.

"Is he mad?" I asked. The staff officer left the phone to investigate, then came on again. Yes, the prisoner was indeed mad. He was marching up and down the room in which he was confined, breathing vengeance and blasphemies. "Get him a drink at once," I ordered. "I will be right over."

Before I could leave the hotel there was another telephone call, this time from the Vice-Chief of the General Staff in Ottawa, demanding to know just what in hell was going on. In my enthusiasm over the whole project I had omitted to tell the G Branch in Ottawa about the Toronto caper, and Worthington and Sansom, because of my association with the Minister's Office, assumed that NDHQ had been clued in and approved the exercise. It seemed that the Premier of Ontario was very annoyed to arrive at his office in Queen's Park to find himself surrounded by a regiment of artillery with all their guns pointing at his legislative buildings. Outraged, he got on direct to the Prime Minister's Office in Ottawa. The

Toronto city health department next got into the act about the outdoor latrines in the parks. Our finale wasn't as good as our first act.

After seeing the withdrawal of the occupation forces back to Camp Borden the next day, I returned to Ottawa to confess my sins and face the music. Meekly and apologetically I accepted a "royal rocket" from the office of the CGS, but Ralston's only comment was, "Well, you certainly woke Toronto up." Indeed, the exercise had served its purpose in publicity, and the people of Toronto had enjoyed the stunt, as well as an opportunity to see our new armoured division in battle order for the first time.

Although it was kept fairly quiet, there was at this time a developing liaison between the defence staffs in Ottawa and Washington. Groups of American officers in civies frequently visited Canadian defence establishments. In several minor ways, I was able to co-operate with these U.S. officials, particularly in respect to the problems and delays in putting larger defence appropriations through Congress.

The American National Guard units held a large summer camp that year just across the border at Ogdensburg. Through friends at *Look* magazine and other publications, it was arranged to secure photographs of these reserve units' training exercises with their mock-up or improvised training aids. Pieces of ordinary stove pipe, for example, were used to simulate non-existent three-inch mortars, and old Ford cars were built up with painted canvas frames to give the silhouette of a tank for firing practice. Photos of these make-shift stage props appeared in U.S. picture magazines with such captions as, "This is what defends American democracy." As soon as they appeared, a loud yell of protest and anger came from Washington. I was held partly responsible. Instead of helping, I had simply brought the United States Army into ridicule and made it a laughing stock, they said.

A few weeks later, when arms appropriations started to get fast approval through Congress, I had many words of thanks from my American friends. It was simply the age-old story in publicity: to get public support and understanding, tell the truth and beat the critics to the punch.

A quiet haven for Canadians visiting New York on wartime missions at that period was the Chatham Hotel. It was there that I first met Sir William Stephenson — the "Man Called Intrepid" — the legendary Canadian millionaire who headed up one of the great Allied spy rings, operating out of New York and other centres. While I got to know much of Sir William's work during the war, I never asked too many questions as to his sources of information. I knew quite a few odd things were afoot, but I cannot claim to have had any direct knowledge of "enigma" or "purple" — though I was unknowingly using "purple" facilities later on in the Pacific. When Stevenson's biography was written after the war, one reviewer in England quite properly commented that "he deserved a better biographer."

At the Chatham one might run across someone from Howe's Supply Department, or Air Marshal Billy Bishop, Joe Clark, Canadian treasury officials or goodness knows who — all working on some aspect of Canadian-American defence co-operation. A permanent apartment was maintained in the Chatham by Harry Sedgwick, and a spare bed was always available there on short notice if you couldn't get a room in one of the crowded New York hotels. Cecily Vaison, Harry's secretary, was an expert in handling any emergency for Canadians short of money, air reservations, a change of clothes, theatre tickets or a bottle of V.O.

A Naval Mission

Shortly after Angus L. Macdonald, the Premier of Nova Scotia, had been appointed Minister of Naval Affairs and gone to Ottawa, I was returning to Ottawa by plane from Halifax, after completing some job for Ralston. Because of fog my plane was forced to land at Moncton, where Macdonald was also grounded on a flight to the Atlantic ports, where he would be reviewing some of his naval units for the first time. He was a little apprehensive about the drill and parade formalities connected with his inspection and insisted I turn about and go back with him to Halifax, as a sort of ADC. I had arranged all that type of thing dozens of times for Ralston's visits with army units and besides, I could help him with the press and security aspects, he reasoned.

Knowing little if anything about naval protocol and drills, I tried my best to beg off, despite my high regard for and friendship with Angus. To settle the question, Angus telephoned Ralston in Ottawa and I was ordered to turn about and go with Angus. It was a nerve-racking experience. We made many mistakes. I knew enough to salute the quarter-deck, but that was about all. I did not realize that when the official party was invited below to the captain's quarters, the captain is the last one to leave the deck but the first to come up from below. Our errors were duly noted by many of my friends from civilian life, now wearing sailor suits at various RCN depots and in ships' companies. As they stood at attention, a look of horror crossed their faces as they saw me — in army uniform — appear with their minister.

Angus was a great loyalist and student of Scottish history. His loyalty, however, went back to the Stuart kings. Whenever a toast to the King was drunk, I noted that Angus always passed his drink over a tumbler of water. It was the ancient and silent toast of the Scots to the exiled "King over the waters."

On a subsequent trip with Angus to Halifax basin, I became good friends with a naval Commander, Johnny Farrow, who was married to the movie star Maureen O'Sullivan and was later the father of Mia Farrow.

John, who had a very engaging personality, had been a film director in Hollywood at the outbreak of war. He was also a commander in the reserve of the RN, so he came to Canada when the war started, to offer his services. Needless to say, his gorgeous wife caused quite a stir when she arrived in Ottawa. In fact, on public appearances the naval brass took a back seat when she was on deck. This never went down too well with the admirals.

Partly at my suggestion, Angus Macdonald had Farrow appointed Director of Naval Information. This annoyed Farrow intensely as it meant desk work in Ottawa; he was determined to go to sea.

I reasoned that Farrow, who was an excellent writer, would together with his wife have a high public profile, as well as some understanding of press matters and publicity. In addition, there would be some propaganda value in the United States, where he was well known, in his support of our war against Hitler and the Nazis.

83

Shortly after his appointment, two matters of concern arose regarding press releases and wartime security. One was the difficulty of announcing the sinking of the Canadian ship HMCS *Margaree* with a heavy loss of life, and the other concerned a vital press blackout on news that 50 over-aged U.S. destroyers had been quietly assembled in Halifax basin prior to making the dangerous run across the Atlantic. The danger was that the destroyers would have to travel at reduced speed, due to limited fuel capacities; also, as required by the rules of neutrality, they had been turned over minus their guns. In short, they would be sitting ducks if the Germans learned of their sailing dates and course. Apart from the value of the destroyers in guarding Britain's convoys, their safe arrival in Britain would have a tremendous propaganda value, clearly indicating American aid and support for the Allied cause at a critical period. They would not only encourage England in her desperate struggle, but the message would also be clearly heard in Moscow, Berlin and Vichy, France. In return for the destroyers, the United States was to obtain leases on naval bases in Newfoundland, Bermuda and the West Indies. It would be seen that Roosevelt's pledge at Charlottesville, Virginia, of aid to Britain, was not an idle threat. It would demonstrate his intention to act with executive authority alone, despite a hesitant Congress.

Fifty strange destroyers in Halifax, of course, could not be hidden from view. But if the details could be kept out of the press until the destroyers reached England, the risk would be reduced.

Regarding the sinking of the *Margaree*, there was a humanitarian, as well as a security, aspect involved. A delay of a few days in the announcement would allow time for next of kin to be notified and spared the shock of reading it first in the newspapers.

In these circumstances, I advised Macdonald to call a press conference behind closed doors, take the press into confidence, brief them fully on both events and ask for their co-operation. I assured him, if given the full facts, the reporters could be trusted.

In the case of the destroyers it was clearly a matter of operational security. The story could be censored in Canada, but we had no control over stories filed to newspapers or radio stations in the United States or other neutral countries.

Angus called the press conference and followed my advice. With only one exception, the correspondents recognized the vital need for security respecting the destroyers and did not break the news blackout till the destroyers were safely across the Atlantic. The single exception was the British United Press.

Suspecting that there would be an announcement regarding the destroyers and an embargo placed on the story, Bob Keyserlingk, head of BUP in Canada, under some arrangement with his reporter, released a speculative story the moment the conference was over — to get a beat on the other news services. When it was realized that Bob came from one of the Baltic states in central Europe — and was Count Von Keyserlingk, with family roots in Prussia and Russia — he immediately came under suspicion of being an enemy agent. He was investigated by the RCMP, and the military authorities urged that he be arrested. His explanation — blaming the slip up on a misunderstanding by his junior reporter — was not entirely satisfactory. Steps were taken at once to restrict the BUP story as far as possible and, luckily, no harm was done. Needless to say,

Angus became rather sceptical in the future of my assurance that the press could be trusted where operational security was involved.

What the full facts were I never discovered, but it was the only time in my considerable experience with press matters during the war, that a correspondent jumped the gun on a secret briefing. Keyserlingk and his reporter were given the benefit of the doubt and were not arrested, though they were kept on the suspect list for some time.

Just at the end of Macdonald's press conference, when a few questions were directed at the minister, one reporter stood up and said, "I understand your Director of Naval Information [Johnny Farrow] does not like desk work and wishes to go to sea . . . Can you confirm this?"

Angus was caught off guard, as the question was completely out of context and had no relation to his announcement of the *Margaree* casualties or U.S. destroyers. Angus brushed the question aside saying simply that he was not aware of the matter.

The moment the conference closed, poor Johnny was paraded before the Chief of Naval Staff for a fearful tongue lashing.

Who the hell did he think he was . . . who gave two goddams if he went to sea or rotted in Ottawa. Didn't he know that men's lives were lost, and here he was trying to gain some benefit from the tragedy with some of his cheap Hollywood publicity. He would get to sea when they were bloody well ready to send him and not before. Meanwhile, he could forget his movie stuff.

It was all very unfair. Farrow had not raised the subject, though some weeks before he had certainly expressed his desire to get into action and away from Ottawa, where it was impossible for his actress wife and himself to have any privacy.

Farrow was in a blind rage after this rocket, and came up to my room at the Chateau for a drink while he cooled down. We both had the same problem in trying to get posted back overseas.

To add to Farrow's problems was a question raised in the House of Commons by one of the Members who demanded to know by what right a member of Canada's armed forces was wearing an "Axis decoration" on his uniform.

Some years prior to the war, Commander Farrow had been awarded a special papal decoration by the Pope. Quite properly he wore the ribbon on the right side of his jacket. This incident had also been reported in the press, to Johnny's further embarrassment.

I listened sympathetically to John's lamentations. His tribulations were simply due to being a Hollywood celebrity, although David Niven, Clark Gable, Douglas Fairbanks, Jr., and other film personalities did manage to switch over to military service without too many problems. At Farrow's request, I did intercede for him later with Angus Macdonald to obtain an overseas posting.

Press Relations

In some respects I was in the same boat as Farrow. Every time I raised the issue of getting back overseas to a field formation, Ralston immediately came up with a dozen reasons why I should remain a bit longer in Ottawa. With the mobilization machinery for both men and equipment in Canada now moving into high gear and our overseas army starting to take shape, it was quite clear to me that the centre of action would soon be with the field formations.

In the matter of press relations, one great obsession still persisted in higher staff levels in Ottawa: that any information about the armed services which was embarrassing, put some general or politician in a bad light or exposed some inefficiency, should at once be censored as a security matter. After all, we were at war. The army could not grasp that the public had a right to know what went on — and that the sooner some stupidity was exposed the sooner it would be corrected. They could not accept that the only information which should be censored, was "information which would help the enemy win the war."

Invariably, senior officers would try to cover up mistakes, classify information as "top-secret" and refuse to answer legitimate questions from the press. Things always leaked out, of course, and boomeranged, causing far greater harm than if the truth had been announced at once. There would be furious rows at times when the press got hold of so-called secret reports. The newspapers would be denounced as irresponsible — threatening national security — acting for the enemy, in fact. And the poor CPLO would be hauled up on the mat for not controlling the press.

A classic illustration of the boomerang from a cover-up had to do with German prisoners of war held in Canadian internment camps.

Several hundreds of prisoners in the early stages of the war had been sent to Canada for internment, to ease the problem of trying to guard and feed them in England, where rations were short and invasion threatened.

Called upon, on short notice, to establish these camps and provide guards, Canada did what she could. Huts and wire enclosures were erected in remote northern bush areas such as Kapuskasing, Ontario. Members of the Veterans' Guard, though they had no previous training as prison guards, were mobilized to operate the camps.

In consequence, a number of the prisoners — whose duty it was to escape — did just that for the first few weeks, till the camps were properly organized.

This was a matter of great embarrassment, not only to the Defence Department but also to the government, when every few days there would be reports in the press of new escapes. More questions would be asked in the House as to why our army could not keep a few unarmed Germans behind barbed wire.

After each escape, frantic efforts would be made to hide it from the newspapers. I did not gain any popularity by laughing at all the futile efforts of the generals to cover up the facts, and I was considered quite crazy when I advised telling the truth, asking for public support to catch the fugitives and flying up some reporters to see the conditions of our camps.

I was in bed one night at the Chateau when the telephone rang about three in the morning. It was the Director of Canadian Internment Operations calling about a great emergency. Five more prisoners had escaped. I must use the authority of the Minister's Office to keep the news from the press.

When I told the Colonel that I could do no such thing, he nearly exploded with anger. It was an order, he said . . . the news had to be censored. I asked how it could possibly help the enemy win the war, knowing that a few prisoners were running loose in Canada. He simply wouldn't listen to my arguments, and when I had to refuse his demands he banged the phone down saying he would take other steps.

Half an hour later, the Colonel was on the phone again to report smugly that he did not need my assistance. He had arranged for complete censorship by going through the Department of External Affairs. In checking his manual, he had discovered that prisoners of war were covered by the Geneva Regulations, which in Canada came under External Affairs, not Defence. He did not need my help.

"Well bully for External Affairs," I answered. "It's a mistake and you will live to regret it." With that I rolled back into bed to get some sleep.

My forecast came true faster than I thought. Retribution took less than 12 hours. Two of the escaped prisoners managed to hitch-hike across the American border, where they turned themselves over to the authorities and then gave interviews to the American radio stations.

When Canadians from coast to coast turned on their radio stations for the morning news, they had all the details first hand. What happened next was quite hilarious. By the time I got down to the Woods Building, alibis and explanations were flying. Everyone was trying to cover his backside, including External Affairs. And, of course, it was all the fault of Tommy Wayling, our single Chief Press Liaison Officer. He didn't handle it properly. He should have controlled the radio stations this time. Then at 3 p.m., when the House of Commons met, the first question on the order paper was, "Why do Canadians have to listen to American radio stations to learn what is going on in their own country?" The government simply had no defence and, in great confusion, announced that the Director of Internment Operations was fired. Incidents like this gradually made the Defence Department realize a different approach was needed on press matters.

At the start of the war, press censorship and censorship regulations constituted a complete mare's nest. Not that the newspapers and reporters weren't ready and willing to co-operate; simply, no one, either press or armed services, knew where real authority lay or what constituted a war secret. Every general and admiral, of course, together with every deputy and directorate, wished to censor anything that reflected adversely on his department. All the fat-headed blunders must be covered up, and reporters who tried to expose stupidity and waste were obviously traitors.

The key to the problem was simple. People were concerned about the war and wanted to know what was going on. They did not wish to be lectured or misled with evasions by pompous and tight-lipped civil servants and senior officers.

Finally, by 1941, the situation started to take shape. Walter Thomson, PR director of the CNR and well respected by the press, was appointed Director of Public Information in the Department of War Services. He issued guidances and directives to the press, and regional censorship offices were established. Fortunately, experienced newsmen were appointed to these offices, rather than armed forces personnel. Although Colonel O. M. Biggar took over the job as National Director after Walter Thomson, Wilf Eggleston, a former colleague in the press gallery, was placed in charge of English-language censorship — and brought some sanity to the operations. Except for the communist Toronto *Clarion*, no daily Canadian newspaper was suspended or closed during the war on grounds of security, and only a few token fines were levied covering accidental breaches.

Until the U.S. entered the war, however, Canada could not be entirely insulated from Axis information agencies and enemy propaganda via U.S. radio stations and magazines. For example, when a writer in *Life* magazine commented that the government in Ottawa was being "blackmailed by the crudely pro-Axis French-Canadian minority (an ideal Nazi fifth column)," the magazine could have been banned in Canada. Fortunately, the Canadian censors refrained from acting on the grounds that such action would be counter-productive and only draw greater notice to the paragraph in the American press. In point of fact, *Life* and *Time* magazines, on balance, were very helpful to the Allied cause by awakening the American public to the dangers and horrors of Hitler's war.

In England, Churchill fully grasped the dangers of German propaganda and also the importance of public and press relations in supporting mobilization and the government's war effort. He also understood the tactics of releasing news quickly, particularly bad news, before it leaked out, was magnified by gossip or exaggeration and brought charges of cover-up. Ottawa still had much to learn.

The escaping prisoner episode was only one illustration of hundreds of similar instances at that period — and there were several sequels to the prisoner saga. While I was travelling with Ralston to Halifax a few days later in one of the private government railway carriages, a telegraph message was delivered from Ottawa.

More bloody prisoners had escaped. This time a dozen or more in a single breakout. Ralston was beside himself, as he envisioned all the newspaper headlines and editorials about army inefficiency and more questions in the House of Commons.

"Send a signal to the Chief of the General Staff," he said. "Have him order an immediate Court of Inquiry, with a board of five senior officers. We must impress the public that we will get to the bottom of this once and for all. Have him appoint the Adjutant General himself as president of the board, and name the Vice Chief of Staff and other senior officers to act with him."

I drafted out the signal, but then turned to Ralston. "Do you really want me to send this?" I asked.

"At once, and write a press release saying we are taking instant action on the matter."

"You know what the press reaction will be?" I questioned. "All the members you are appointing to the board are senior Permanent Force officers. The press will at once claim that the stage is being set for another major snow job. Regardless of what your board finds, they will be suspected of protecting their pals."

Ralston seemed dumbfounded. "Well, what do we do?"

"Get some prominent board members from outside the army staff, men whom the public knows and trusts. Find some prominent Tory, a militia officer, some member of the bar, someone who hates the Liberals and couldn't possibly be accused of being soft or partisan. Then let the chips fall properly where they may. Tell the public about the problems of creating instant internment camps. That's the only way you can get the press and public on-side and create trust in the department. What about getting old Judge Embury from Saskatchewan to preside? He was a tough militia general in the last war and is miles removed from the Ottawa scene. He is known far and wide as a deep-dyed Tory, but he will be fair. More importantly, he will be trusted by the public."

Ralston was inclined to question my reasoning at first, but on thinking it over, said, "Go ahead. See if General Embury will act."

Embury did agree to act and did a thorough job of it. His findings and recommendations were accepted without question by the press.

Despite my efforts to keep clear of these rather hopeless and unhappy squabbles, I found myself being dragged into one press crisis after another — by Ralston, as well as by many of my former newspaper colleagues when they were in trouble.

Quebec Problems

At the time the Mobilization Bill, calling for national registration, was passed in the House, a tense situation developed in respect to Quebec. Although registration was supported by such Quebec Members as Lapointe, Cardin and Power and had the solid endorsement of the provincial Liberal party, resistance was voiced in some areas of the province.

Camillien Houde, Mayor of Montreal, openly defied the legislation and urged French Canadians to ignore it, although he had been advised in advance that he would be liable to arrest for such actions. At once Ottawa became haunted with the spectre of the conscription fights in Quebec in World War I.

A night sitting of cabinet was called in the East Block to which Walter Thompson and I were summoned. Walter was a legendary figure, widely respected by the press in Canada, England and the United States. He was wise and experienced from many years of handling critical situations with great diplomacy and advising on such matters as royal tours and rail strikes.

Mackenzie King was obsessed with fears of riots, demonstrations and violence in Quebec. At the same time he could not afford politically to ignore such an open challenge to the authority of Parliament in wartime.

The special cabinet meeting continued to a late hour under great strain, particularly for such ministers as Power and Lapointe. Thompson and I were asked for our views and advice in respect to probable press reaction if Houde were arrested, either by the federal or provincial authorities; he might be charged in court or simply interned by the military authorities, where there would be less chance of courtroom dramas and emotional statements.

Thompson and I were in complete agreement on the advice we offered, but we did not seem able to get our points across. Finally we left and walked together down the dark little path from Parliament Hill which runs along the bank of the Rideau Canal. I was angry that the cabinet seemingly would not accept our advice, and as we walked in the moonlight I raged at the stupidity and indecision of all politicians. My friend Walter, a much older man, had long accustomed himself to the realities of politics. "Cool down," he said, "you were asked for your opinion. You gave it honestly and they gave you a proper hearing. That's all you can do. You don't have to make the decision or carry the responsibility — so what are you angry about?"

In the event, Houde was arrested and interned over the weekend and many of our suggestions regarding press releases, briefings and advance tip-offs were adopted. The arrest was a 48-hour wonder and passed off with no immediate political threat to the government. As it transpired, King was needlessly alarmed over the possible reaction in Quebec to the National Mobilization or registration program. A motion in the Quebec Assembly, condemning the bill, was soundly defeated by a vote of 56 to 13.

Due to my close association and easy access then to Ralston, I came under some pressures in those days from my old regimental associations. The "black network" of the Queen's Own Rifles wished to have a complete rifle brigade formed with their own unit, the Royal Winnipeg Rifles and the Regina Rifles. Similarly, the Highlanders wanted a Highland Brigade of the 48th, The Black Watch of Montreal and the Seaforths of Vancouver. It seemed a dandy idea to me — being myself a member of the black network — so at a convenient moment I put the proposal before Ralston.

He listened quietly but completely rejected the idea. "And then we would have French-Canadian Brigades — and create divisions and differences. The Canadian Army overseas must be simply Canadians integrated, regardless of province."

As I was to observe over the next few years, Ralston's judgment in this was quite correct. Overseas soldiers, regardless of language or ethnic origin, shared a common pride in their brigade, their division and the Canada shoulder title on their uniforms. The old prejudices faded quickly when the soldiers faced action together overseas in composite brigades.

By the spring of 1941 Canada's defence programs were all moving into high gear. The 1st and 2nd Divisions, as well as Worthington's Army Tank Brigade, were now concentrated overseas in the south of England, together with a great complement of Corps Troops and such auxiliary units as extra anti-aircraft regiments, field hospitals, special engineer units and the Forestry Corps. The 3rd Division was moving overseas. The 5th Armoured Division would join them before the summer was out. The Empire Air Training Scheme was now going all out, and the Canadian Navy had been able to take over a wide area of convoy responsibility in the North Atlantic.

Tens of thousands of military vehicles and other war equipment were pouring from the assembly lines of our factories for both Canada and her allies. But much of the fun and early mobilization excitement was going out of Ottawa by then. The relentless fog of civil service procedures and endless red tape were descending once more, now that the invasion of mad civilians had started to spend its force. No longer could you get away with hair raising projects on the plea of ignorance as to how the system worked.

Clearly it was time to get back overseas if I wished to get in on the action, so I raised the matter once more with Ralston. He agreed to consider my wishes, but later on. There was another job I had to tackle first. It had been decided that maybe I had been right in some of my views on press relations, and I would be given the green light to set up a complete public relations and press service for the Defence Department, along the lines I had advocated and following the policies and procedures considered essential. I was "hoist by my own petard."

All my recommendations were accepted; there would be a press officer with newspaper training in every military district. The senior PR officer in Ottawa would have direct access to the Minister's Office and not be subject to dozens of conflicting orders by his subordinates. He would sit in at meetings of the Army Council when policies were decided — not with a vote but simply to offer advice before decisions were finalized, so that serious mistakes would not be made in public relations matters. In short, instead of trying to cover up or pick up the pieces after the event, he could, perhaps, head off many unnecessary headaches before they happened.

Senior officers across Canada would work through their local press officer to avoid making some frightful gaff in a speech or public statement. They would also leave statements on policy matters to the Minister's Office or to deputies delegated by the minister. There would be no more holding back of news or any censorship to destroy public confidence, except for reasons of operational security. Censorship in the services would be determined only by the G Branch through the Director of Intelligence. Censorship guidance to newspapers and radio stations would be issued through an independent civilian board, to be headed by veteran journalist Wilf Eggleston. Except for strictly service matters, all other wartime information and publicity — for matters such as war savings drives, munitions production and rationing — would become the responsibility of a large wartime information bureau now developed under the new Department of War Services.

It was a difficult position for me. I was anxious to get back to a field unit, but how to duck out of the job they had tailored for me? Ralston had insisted that I should set up this new service, but he didn't say I had to continue operating it. After thinking it over for a few days, I told Ralston I would make a deal with him. I would go all out and set up the new service, which I was certain I could do in three months. Then, all the defence information services of the army, navy and air force should be brought under one director: Joe Clark, a veteran flyer from World War I and a well-known advertising agency man now working with Chubby Power on RCAF matters. John Farrow could build up the navy's public relations service.

If I took on the organizational work for three months, I asked Ralston, could I then have the first available vacancy to the Staff Course? By watching the Junior and Senior Selection Committees at work in Ottawa, as they made appointments to staff and command in our rapidly expanding army, I had discerned one essential requirement. Almost regardless of ability or experience, if an officer had either of the magic initials SC (Staff College) or RMC (Royal Military College) after his name — in that early period — his file was given precedence over other Canadians. It looked like a long war, and SC was certainly something I should have.

"So you're going to horse trade now over how you serve in the army?" Ralston demanded. He had every right to be angry, but I knew my man. He would have done exactly the same thing. I smiled as I made my case. I had forfeited my seniority as a company commander in the PPCLI to come down to help him out and work at a desk job. I had worked hard, and felt I had earned this consideration. Ralston knew I had not joined the army for a desk job in Ottawa, and he quietly agreed. I assured him I could get a complete press and PR service set up for the Defence Department, with qualified press officers in each district, within three months. I would then be free for the first Staff College course starting at that time.

91

Having the okay from the Minister and a completely free hand, I then raced about recruiting experienced newspapermen I knew across the country and set up a proper press headquarters in Ottawa, complete with sections for film and photo, broadcasting, press releases, promotion and recruiting, together with Liaison or Conducting Officers for magazines and visiting journalists. Contact with the press would now be through qualified press officers, rather than regular army types who, in most cases, considered reporters the scum of the earth. It would be an open door policy, with the local press invited to attend training areas and visit all defence establishments.

In short, the principles set forth very clearly in King's Regulations and Orders prior to the war, were to be re-established. Only the minister or his delegate had authority to speak for the department, or on government policy. All branches of the staff were told to keep hands off, except on normal matters of news — no comment on policy without the minister's approval or without clearance through the local PR officer, who had fast access to the Minister's Office. On matters of operational security, the authority was the Intelligence Branch, but they had no authority to impose any policy censorship. Under this new set-up, the endless controversies between Parliament and the press, over defence matters, soon started to subside.

Forty-eight hours before the starting date of the staff course at RMC, I reported my mission accomplished to Ralston.

Though I can't recall the details now, some new crisis had arisen in Ralston's office when I reported. Another brush fire to be put out and I was again elected, despite my protests.

As it was, I was only one day late arriving at Kingston, but even one day late makes for a bad start at any Army Staff College. A signal had gone to the college over the minister's signature, advising that I was delayed by important duties. Needless to say, this special treatment did not endear me particularly to the Directing Staff. In fact, it was nearly a kiss of death.

Staff College

Most of the senior instructors were regular officers, graduates of either Camberley in England or Quetta in India, and spoke in the affected PF jargon with clipped English accents. Fortunately, I did know a few of the instructors, such as Colonel Lister and Colonel Saunders, who were more typical Canadians.

During World War I, British staff officers had on one occasion been said to possess "bird brains and the manners of Potsdam." The higher-ups at this first staff college were not quite at that level, but there were a few similarities, which I shall touch on briefly. Britain had to supply many of the officers to staff the Canadian Corps HQ in World War I; this time, Canada was determined to fill all her own field staff appointments.

For the first couple of weeks, the officers clearly took a very poor view of me at the college, and it was quite obvious that I had been preceded by some lurid tales of my unorthodox activities while working for Ralston.

The subject of the first lecture I attended was, The Precise Use of Military English. First, we were handed some mimeographed sheets providing a glossary of military jargon and fashionable Staff College terms —

which illiterate officers from the militia and field regiments are not expected to know — that included "bumf, allez-allez, bicycle-up, laid-on, swan about, and the form." This was obviously to set staff officers apart and to ensure that they wouldn't be understood by the common herd.

Next, the colonel instructor very pompously explained that we "must remember that in military writing, we were staff officers and gentlemen and not a goddamned bunch of newspaper types." He then held up a copy of a sports page from the local newspaper and pointed to the heading, "Yanks Down Sox in Ninth."

"Now, gentlemen, I ask you, what does that drivel really mean?" he demanded. Everyone in the room knew damn well what it meant, but none of us lowly types opened his mouth for a minute. Then I suddenly started to get the message. I looked about and realized I was the only "goddamned" newspaper type in the room. This was obviously all for my special benefit. Rising from my seat, I politely stated that I took exception to the colonel's remarks. There was a frozen silence for a moment, and then my temperature started to rise. I explained that for the past few months I had been occupied in developing a press service, which would cost many thousands of taxpayers' dollars, simply to overcome the bad public image of our regular services — an image which had been created by the very attitude he had just displayed. By encouraging staff officers to adopt the same poor attitude toward the press, he would ensure that the money would be wasted and the army would continue to be looked upon as a bunch of bigoted blimps.

The colonel's eyes bulged from their sockets as he stared at me. "I don't understand a word you are saying, Malone." "That seems apparent, Sir," I replied, and sat down, boiling inside.

At the end of this lecture the Chief of the Directing Staff sent for me. "Malone, do you expect to pass this course?" he demanded. "That was my purpose in coming here, Sir," I replied rather meekly. "In that case, I should tread very gently." Then he confided, "There are some members of the staff here who would be very happy to see you fail. You have to play the game our way while you are here — do you understand?" He was quite right, of course, and his advice was good.

Next, to my amazement, came our first big field exercise, on a divisional level, complete with supporting engineers and artillery, conferences, umpires, appreciations, O Groups, operation orders down to battalion levels and so forth. It was a two-day exercise or TEWT (tactical exercise without troops) — a trench raid based on World War I experience. Having recently been briefed in England about mechanized warfare and the advent of armour and blitzkrieg tactics, I felt we might just as well have gone back to cavalry charges and siege warfare. However, the Directing Staff was mad keen on the project, so we all got lost in the dark out on Barriefield Common one night and learned how to clear enemy trenches.

The next highlight on the course was a syndicate production of a major thesis on the subject: Give Your Views on the Reorganization of the Canadian Army after the War. The topic seemed to me a bit premature, and the thought crossed my mind that the time might be better spent on the subject of organizing to win the war first. However, this was a subject that did stir my interest; having seen first hand some of the bonehead performances by our Permanent Forces when it came to mobilizing for war, I felt this was one subject I could deal with to perfection. The idea of four-man syndicates, to write these papers, was to develop staff co-ordination and the art of working as a team.

Our syndicate gathered for a night session to get the job in hand. Being able to operate a typewriter and with some newspaper facility on the writing side, I started to bang away non-stop. Indeed, I could hardly get at this chore fast enough. They had asked for it.

Gradually, as my team members read some of the purple prose issuing from my typewriter, I gathered they were not really with me. In fact, as I went on they were horrified to see the treason and revolutionary madness I had advocated. All flatly refused to put their names to the document. It would be committing suicide they said, thanks particularly to suggestions that our staff officers stop trying to "talk with phony English accents so as to be further removed than ever from the Canadian troops, which they would some day have to lead in action."

I had been in Ottawa when mobilization had been ordered, when the guts of the Canadian Army, after 20 years of peacetime neglect, had to be exposed. I could document my case. There were things that should be said. But my arguments with the other syndicate members were in vain. Having warmed up to the project by then and being in a rather bolshy mood at that period, I said I would write the entire treatise myself and just put my own name on it, which I did.

A week later candidates all got their marked papers back . . . all except myself. I let a day elapse and then gently enquired about my marks. Very curtly I was informed that due to the outrageous nature of my solo paper, it had been forwarded to the Director of Military Training in Ottawa, for his information and determination as to my continuing the course. In retrospect it was an act of insanity, but the luck of the Irish held. The paper was returned to me in due course and all across the folder cover was scribbled in heavy red crayon, "'O' . . . your remarks are considered most offensive."

Despite all these minor trials and trivialities of the service, they did let me pass the course in the end. Although the preceding comments are on the critical side, I must in fairness also record that we did receive some very valuable instruction at the college, particularly in matters of army organization and field administration, together with planning procedures and large-scale movement operations by road, rail and sea. For the first time, I had an appreciation of artillery and air support, which stood me in good stead in the next few years. Also, I made many great friendships. And almost without exception, graduates from that first Canadian Staff Course all gave good accounts of themselves in action.

At the end of the course, we were all given a few days' embarkation leave and then ordered back overseas on a convoy, leaving from Halifax just before Christmas day.

As I stood on the deck of the troopship SS *Batory* a few days later, watching the last detachments climb the loading ramps from the cold freight sheds in Halifax harbour, an announcement came over the ship's loudspeaker system; there was an urgent message waiting for me at the ship's wireless office. I opened the army signal from Defence HQ. It read, "Report back forthwith to Minister's Office Ottawa. Ralston."

"There will be no acknowledgment," I told the ship's operator. Half an hour later, when the *Batory* had cast off and was safely out in the channel, I slowly crumpled the message and smiled as I dropped it overboard. Much as I admired Ralston and wanted to help him, I knew he would understand.

With all mobilization plans now well in hand, it was quite apparent that Ottawa would shortly become simply an administrative centre for co-ordinating the supply of reinforcements and equipment for overseas formations. Activity in Ottawa at NDHQ would soon become "properly" organized and routine as the bureaucracy regularized procedures again. Certainly, it was no place for me now.

The real excitement would be overseas, when the Canadian Army got into action. A complete Canadian Army was now taking shape in England. The 3rd Division had joined the 1st and 2nd Divisions overseas together with the Army Tank Brigade. The 5th Armoured Division was on its way and the 4th Armoured was being concentrated in Canada for overseas service. Because of Britain's critical situation at that period, our Canadian divisions assumed an importance far beyond their actual number.

From 1940 to 1942, after Dunkirk and the Spitzbergen expeditions, the Canadian troops in England had been carrying out endless training and exercises, awaiting the expected German invasion. In the villages of south-east England they had worked with Britain's Home Guard units, mined beaches on the coast, constructed tank traps, road by-passes and emergency air fields.

In May 1941, there had been a suggestion of Canadian divisions going to Egypt to reinforce General Wavell's hard-pressed forces, but the defence of Britain was held to be of greater priority. The Canadian cabinet had no objection to the use of Canadian troops outside of Britain at that time, but Churchill's reaction was, "If you Canadians were to leave England, I could not sleep at night."

In Scotland, the Canadian Forestry Corps were now chopping down trees faster than the Scots had ever seen it done. Canadian lumbering techniques seemed like desecration in the Highlands, but the saving of shipping space across the Atlantic was vitally important.

Canadian hard-rock miners from northern Ontario and Quebec were now operating in Gibraltar, drilling great caverns and emplacements in the rock.

Hong Kong C Force

On short notice, Canada had also despatched a brigade of troops to Hong Kong at the urgent request of the British. Japan had not yet entered the war, and in the view of both London and Washington there were some signs that Japan was softening its attitude toward Britain and the United States. The United States had recently reinforced the Philippines, and Britain had strengthened Malaya. It was felt that even a modest reinforcement of Hong Kong, if it could be done quickly, might considerably influence Japanese decisions. In addition, it would reassure Chinese Generalissimo Chiang Kai-shek.

With British forces badly pressed and scattered throughout the world, and looking to Canada's particular interest in the North Pacific, Britain asked for Canadian assistance.

In these circumstances Canada, not wishing to disrupt the unit formations destined for Europe, secretly rushed to Hong Kong the Winnipeg Grenadiers and Royal Rifles of Canada. Their training was not complete, nor was it possible to have their full complement of vehicles and heavier weapons accompany them in the first ship convoy.

Canada's C Force arrived just three weeks before the outbreak of war and the attack on Pearl Harbor. The fall of Hong Kong was not long delayed. In the defence of Hong Kong, some 23 Canadian officers and 267 other ranks were killed, and the remainder of the force became prisoners of war. I had known the Winnipeg Grenadiers well at the start of the war, and it would be my job after the Japanese surrender, several years later, to release many of them from prison camps and return them to Canada.

As soon as the surrender of Hong Kong was announced, George Drew spearheaded a great political attack against the government in Ottawa, charging incompetence and mismanagement in despatching the force. A Royal Commission was appointed but proved little. Canada had taken a calculated gamble and lost. A few days had been gained. Japan, with General Tojo as Prime Minister, had not been deterred.

U.S. Wishes To Command Canadian Forces

Several months prior to Pearl Harbor and the American declaration of war, the U.S. section of the Canada-U.S. joint board on defence advised Ottawa that if the United States entered the war, that country wished to take over supreme command of the Canadian forces.

The Americans were prepared to allow Canada only tactical command of its own forces in a few places, such as the Gulf of St. Lawrence and the Bay of Fundy, and within 30 miles of defended ports, such as Halifax.

Needless to say, this proposal from a country still sitting on the sidelines was given a very caustic reception in Ottawa. Although I knew about it from Ralston, it was kept highly secret at the time and only became public in 1972. Understandably, the idea was vigorously rejected, both by the Canadian cabinet and the Defence Department. Washington was advised that only in the event that Britain had been knocked out of the war and the United States had declared war on Germany, would Canada consider an overall or supreme U.S. command.

SIX
Back To England

WORLD SCENE

Japan attacks Pearl Harbor — U.S. declares war —
Hong Kong and Singapore fall — Japanese invade
Philippines, Malaya and Burma — General MacArthur
reaches Australia. 5th Canadian Armoured Division
arrives in England — 1st Canadian Army formed in
England for anti-invasion role under General
McNaughton. National plebiscite gives Ottawa power
to impose overseas conscription — "if necessary."

Crossing the Atlantic that December gave me one of the roughest trips I can remember. The SS *Batory* had been designed as a cruise ship for southern climates. She had no stabilizers to check her roll in the huge Atlantic seas. And she was jammed to capacity with thousands of troops who took turns in the bunks and sleeping in the passageways. As the ship lurched about in the rollers, it was impossible to remain on deck for more than a few minutes. At one point, the great doors into the main dining salon came crashing down. The hot smells of the engines, packed humanity and men being seasick made life a bit trying, but the hardier souls managed to keep some poker and crap games going nonstop in all quarters of the ship.

For once I had absolutely no shipboard duties or responsibilities, and I had a sure cure for seasickness. Long ago I had discovered that if you quietly sipped brandy all day long, in the Cyprus manner, it settles the stomach and lifts you above the swings and lurches. The trick is to have the brandy on crushed ice, so you can't smell it. By the end of the day, you find yourself more than a trifle boiled . . . but still fighting.

There was no trouble finding friends aboard the *Batory*. From Regina days there were Emmet McCusker and Beatty Martin, both doctors in the Medical Corps, who knew how to enjoy life. From Winnipeg there were Art Snell, a former roommate and ex-badminton champion who had just qualified in the RCAF as a navigator, and Brigadier Spike Birmingham, Commander, Royal Engineers of 5th Division, ex-RMC and, in civilian life, a successful harbour construction engineer.

These, together with scores of other rowdy friends from all across Canada, made the trip almost enjoyable. Birmingham was a good two-fisted drinker and provided entertainment by pounding the piano and reciting "The Hermit of Shark Tooth Shoal." He had been working night and day for months, building airfields, and was determined to enjoy a blow-out before taking command of his divisional engineers at Aldershot. Art Snell teamed up with me to introduce high-low, a new game of poker that we had learned in western Canada, to our eastern shipmates. The introduction was most successful; between us, we pretty well cleaned up the ship.

In the bowels of the *Batory* was a pendulum which shows the degree of roll measured against the critical point at which a ship is supposed to tip over. The pendulum on the old *Batory* was swinging well into the red danger zone most of two days, but we finally docked safely at Liverpool, a port where I had landed once before in wartime, as a small boy. During World War I my mother had packed the family all off to England to be nearer my father, who was serving in France. This was not unusual in those days. We had sailed on the *Ausonia* and had stood by our lifeboats all one night when chased by a German U-boat. On both occasions, I was greeted at Liverpool with an air raid; a Zeppelin bombing in the first war, some Focke-Wulf in World War II.

Following our movement orders, Emmet McCusker, Beatty Martin and I found ourselves stuck in a dreary and very cold Nissen hut at a godforsaken holding unit, somewhere in Surrey, the day before Christmas. We each knew which unit we would be joining, but the system had to be followed — and so we would be processed through the transit holding unit. Our baggage had been lost and we only had with us the contents of our haversacks. We suggested to the officious young adjutant of the camp, that we be allowed to continue on to our designated units or go up to London for Christmas day and come back when he had all the paper sorted out.

The adjutant rejected these ideas at once, and furthermore, in accordance with his standing camp orders, we were to turn out for a six-mile march with all ranks the next morning, even though we only had our serge uniforms and dress shoes with us.

Emmet and Beatty were both old hands from World War I. Within the hour we had quietly packed our haversacks and caught the next train for London . . . to hell with that little bastard.

When we got our eyes open about noon on Christmas day at the Ritz Hotel, after a night on the town, I managed to locate and get a trunk call through to my regiment, The Queen's Own Rifles, which was then encamped at Pippingford Park, not far from East Grinstead. While I had joined up with the PPCLI in western Canada, my original unit was the QOR, in which I had enlisted in militia days in Toronto, swearing I was 18 years of age (and being sworn in by an uncle who knew my real age was 14). Three generations of my family had served in the QOR, and my brother was presently with the regiment.

Like most regiments, they had a saying, "Once in the QOR always in the QOR." Every unit or ship's company, of course, always promotes its own, and is rightly convinced that it is the best in the service. Many years after the war, when Paul Hellyer became Canada's Minister of Defence, I tried to explain something of this to him when, under his nightmare of unification, he decided to replace unit identifications with a weird green uniform for all three services. This long-recognized asset of regimental pride, however, was something Paul simply couldn't grasp at the time. (Several years afterward, when Paul tried unsuccessfully for the Tory leadership, he did confide to me that unification was the greatest mistake he had ever made.)

Another long-established army principle is that "The regiment always looks after its own." As soon as my call got through to the QOR, I was home in the family once more, though it had been many years since I had worn their black buttons.

Before the afternoon was out, a QOR lorry had picked up both myself and my lost baggage and I reached Pippingford Park in time to enjoy a

Christmas dinner with old friends, the Pangman and Dalton brothers, Jock Sprague, Dampier, Delamere, Lett, Downie, my brother and many others.

In the army, regimental life is by long odds the happiest form of military service. There are always one or two SOBs, of course, but in a regiment people become individual human beings again. Within platoons and companies, close comradeships form from sharing common dangers and hardships, as well as achievements and recognition. I knew that my period with the QOR again would be short, as I was slated for a staff appointment with the 1st Armoured Brigade as soon as the 5th Division was assembled in England. The QOR was commanded by Harry McKendrick at the time, who had been with the regiment back in 1924 when I had first enlisted. It was a happy and efficient militia outfit, and it was a great change for me to enjoy training with men again — giving grenade instruction, carrying out company exercises, having war games with the Home Guard in local villages on weekends and visiting nearby pubs.

As my brief tour with the QOR came to an end, I was approached by the unit padre, Captain Jack Clough, with a request. There was a very bright young rifleman in the unit, by the name of Cliff Manser. He could do everything from handle a Bren gun to drive carriers, organize the officers' mess or whatever else was required of him — except march. He simply didn't have marching feet. Each time the unit went on a long route march, Manser ended up back in the sick bay with badly swollen feet. He had tried everything, but the feet couldn't perform and he was scared of being sent back to Canada.

The padre rightly surmised that in an armoured division where I was going, there wouldn't be much marching and I would likely be able to take my own batman with me. What about it? It would break Manser's heart to be sent home before seeing any action. This seemed a reasonable proposition and Manser looked as good as his reputation, so I took him on. It was a happy decision. He showed tremendous loyalty in the next few years, as he stuck with me through various invasions in Sicily, Italy, Normandy and during my subsequent tour with Monty at 8th Army HQ. He saw all the action he wanted.

The 1st Armoured Brigade was quartered about the Hazelmere area in the south of England, when I joined them and was commanded by a very old friend, Brigadier Tommy Rutherford of Owen Sound. He was a militia officer and in World War I had served under Victor Sifton in the 4th CMRs. He had also been a friend of my father's, and I was delighted to be on his staff. He was a little out of date on modern tank warfare, but he knew men and how to organize his brigade. His dominating passion was to train everyone to kill Germans. He sat beside the gunner in nearly every tank on the firing range, always coaching him in getting the first shots off fast ahead of any enemy. Questions of supply, harbouring and movement control, he pretty well left to myself and other members of his staff. These were mere incidentals to him; the real job, as he saw it, was outshooting German tanks. There were four regiments in the brigade: the Strathcona Horse, the Fort Garry Horse (commanded by my cousin), the Hussars from London, Ontario, and a motorized infantry regiment, the Westminsters from British Columbia — all first-class units. It was an interesting period for me, learning about tank tactics and swanning about the countryside in ACVs, scout cars and the newly adopted Canadian-made tank called the RAM.

From time to time, we carried out sham battles with and against the newly formed Polish Armoured Division, who were a carefree crowd with all the dash of Cossacks and Polish cavalry despite their rather worn-out equipment at that time.

A number of my friends from the Staff College had also been posted to staff appointments in the 5th Armoured Division, including Bill Murphy and Jean Allard, and I knew many of the others, such as Chip Drury and Bob Moncel on division staff. Commanding the division was General Sammy Sansom, my associate in the Shamblitz raid on Toronto, which had gotten me into so much trouble. I also had some civilian friends in the neighbourhood, including Uncle Jim Bone, London editor of the Manchester *Guardian*, who had been on the ill-fated *Western Prince*. Jim lived in the little village of Abbots Holt, on the edge of Frenchman's Common. He was in residence each weekend, so I was able to have many pleasant weekends with him and also keep in touch a bit with the newspaper world. Jim was a great supporter of Canada and kept a friendly eye open for our interests on Fleet Street.

Every so often our division would be visited by the Army Commander, General Andrew McNaughton. When some of Andy's great inventions were to be tried out on us, he would often be accompanied by some high-ranking brass from the War Office. On one occasion, some hundreds of officers, both British and Canadian, were gathered to watch a mine-clearing experiment. A complete mine field had been laid across one of the nearby moors, or commons as they were called. The idea was that one of our tanks would push enormous lengths of eight-inch flexible pipe across the field of land mines. The pipe was packed solid with explosive. Then the boys in the tank would detonate it, which in turn would detonate all the mines in the vicinity.

It was a marvellous show. We had never seen such a bloody explosion before as the pipe, and scores of mines all went off together. The ground shook under us and all the windows in the hamlets for miles around were shattered.

On another occasion McNaughton conceived the idea of a tank being waterproofed, with the exhaust pipe turned up like a great mast, and waddling its way across a fair-sized river. The big audience watched with interest as one of our brand new RAM tanks started bravely out into the stream. About mid-current something seemed to go wrong. Before our eyes the tank simply started to disappear. It had hit quicksand. There was nothing that could be done. In some panic, the tank crew scrambled from the hatch and swam to shore while our tank slowly sank from sight forever, bringing the show to a rather sober finale.

General McNaughton had formerly been head of the National Research Council in Canada and was a highly qualified engineer. There is no doubt that some of his ideas did bear valuable fruit, but the War Office and his immediate superiors in SE Command rather wished he would spend more time directing and learning to handle his army in manoeuvres than experimenting with new gadgets.

Another frequent visitor to our division at that period was the noted British tank expert, General Martel, who was assigned to give us a hand in training our tank formations. He stayed at our mess several times and was most helpful in his advice.

Martel's first inspection of the 5th Division shortly after it arrived in the U.K. had not gone very well. Sammy had taken him over to the old

100

Wellington barracks at Aldershot, where the CRE, Brigadier Spike Birmingham, was to have all his engineer companies and field sections on parade, en masse, for the first time. Since the start of the war, Spike had been kept busy constructing airfields, and it is doubtful that he had been on a parade ground since he had left the Royal Military College as a cadet many years before.

The inspection was a shambles. Spike had forgotten the words of command. Everything got twisted backward. When the situation was all beyond recovery, Spike hopefully suggested that maybe Martel would be more interested in an inspection of the barracks. Martel dryly commented that anything might be an improvement, so the official party moved off to take a look at the ancient block of barrack building, which had remained unchanged since the Crimean War.

This was an even worse snafu. A filthy dirty sapper coated in coal dust happened to be cutting through one of the mess halls and panicked when he saw all the brass. In a desperate effort to appear occupied, he seized an armful of bread and marched smartly past them. His name was taken. In the next barrack block, the drains had burst and water was spurting through the ceiling. And so it went, Birmingham wildly ordering the adjutants and RSMs to place men on charge, till in final desperation he thought of his new mobile workshops. They were his own invention. Maybe they could save the day.

Would the general care to see these marvellous new Canadian developments, a complete tinsmith's shop on wheels, an electrical repair van and a collapsible portable plumbing works.

"Anything," said Martel, in a ghostly voice.

It was at the mobile tinsmithy that Spike reached his triumph. Noting that Martel was evincing some interest for the first time, Spike became enthusiastic and proceeded to demonstrate personally how all the gadgets worked. Then very cleverly in his excitement, he showed us how to chop off the end of his finger with a guillotine chopper, with blood everywhere.

There was no change of expression whatever in Martel's frozen features, as he suggested that perhaps they could now go someplace where he could have a drink. They repaired to Sammy's newly established General's "A" mess, where his newly appointed ADC, Arthur Reid, was quickly ordered to produce some drinks.

Arthur stuttered a bit and managed to draw his chief quietly to one side, where he conveyed the embarrassing information that they didn't have any booze in the mess yet. After an explosive blast, Reid was sternly informed that as ADC it was his duty to see that there was some booze available when the general invited a guest to his mess. Reid was to take some mess funds and a station wagon the next morning and visit the wine merchants in London, to see that this never happened again.

It must be explained that in civilian life, Arthur Reid wrote plays for the stage in London and New York, but with the call to arms he knew his country needed him, and by some miracle he became an officer. It had always been difficult to find a job for Arthur, as he approached life and spoke just like a character from one of his delightfully silly plays would — all wit and nonsense. His friends had rescued him just in time from General Guy Turner's staff, before he was boiled in oil. Then, with all his charm, worldly experience and many social graces, they felt the real job for Arthur was ADC to a general.

The next morning, Reid drove up to London in style, with a station wagon and driver, together with £86 of mess funds, to shop for liquor, which was not easy to come by. Toward noon, with his shopping completed, Arthur spotted a charming young lady he had known in his stage days and he properly invited her to lunch at the Ivy, a gathering spot for theatre folk. The driver was dismissed with a grand flourish. He was to get himself a sandwich and meet Arthur back at the Ivy at 3 p.m. That, of course, was the last that was seen of the driver, the station wagon and the load of booze.

Arthur took the train back to Aldershot. It was all very sad. Sammy, when he cooled off, ordered a Court of Inquiry . . . mess funds were involved. The driver, with a granddaddy of a hangover, was dredged up by the military police in due course, but the booze and station wagon never surfaced. At the hearing the driver, in righteous terms, allowed that, "It was all Captain Reid's fault. He gave me 10 bob and told me to get a beer someplace and I don't remember another thing."

Arthur, in his gentle way, never quite understood the army. Two years later, during the battles of Normandy, we were to meet again. At that time, Arthur was in the historical section — "hysterical section" as he used to call it — and attached to Army HQ. He was close to tears. He had written a beautiful official account of the day's fighting, he explained, but General Crerar had changed it all about and deleted some sections, as it put some of his pals "in a rather bad light." When the war ended, Arthur returned happily to the world of stage and film.

In passing, Spike Birmingham and his engineers, while they did not shine on the parade square, performed miracles later when blasting through the German concrete on the invasion beaches of Normandy and bulldozing roads through the rubble of Caen under heavy shelling and bombing.

After a dozen or so brigade exercises, roaring through the countryside of Surrey, I became absorbed with armoured tactics and often debated the fine points with General Martel over a friendly nightcap.

Our Canadian troops were all too friendly and trusting, Martel complained . . . no sense of security. "It would only take a couple of blondes to defeat the entire division," he maintained. To prove his point, one day he rounded up a couple of attractive tarts and had them take a stroll down a country road, past a large tank parking area, where two Canadian troopers with fixed bayonets guarded the entrance to the enclosure. Martel won his bet. In less than 10 minutes, the cheeky little dolls had our two brave troopers behind the hedges and rolling in the hay.

An historic problem in infantry-cum-tank attacks, Martel explained to me, was that tanks move across country at about 20 mph, while infantry can move at only 3 mph, and it is impossible to keep them together very long. If the tank waits for the infantry, it becomes a sitting duck for the enemy. Efforts made to marry-up the different elements on a second or third phase line are never too successful in the excitement of action.

This matter I applied my mind to for some days, till I arrived at a possible solution. On the following Saturday I was visiting Jim Bone in the nearby little village, and we sauntered down to the local pub for a beer. Here we were joined by one of Jim's old village cronies, who was wearing a worn tweed jacket and shapeless corduroy bags.

As we drank our beer, I expounded my great tank invention to the two of them.

What was needed was a quantity of Canadian-style toboggans, which could all be stacked in a single lorry. Then when the tanks were to operate with infantry, they would each drag a couple of toboggans behind. Each toboggan would carry five men, the leading man holding a three-inch mortar and smoke bombs. The infantry, instead of making a tiring tramp through the mire and meadows, would have a happy ride into action, crouching low on the toboggan. When the tank came under fire, the forward man would bang off his mortar; then, under the cover of smoke, the men would roll off and disperse in order to "winkle out" the enemy anti-tank guns. Meanwhile, the tank would have a temporary smoke screen while it got into a hull-down position. It was absolutely marvellous, as I described it.

Curiously, Jim's village drinking pal seemed very interested and asked many questions. Would I write a memo about it all and draw him some pictures. Jim had omitted to tell me till now that his rather shabby pal was a Sir James Grigg, then Britain's Secretary of State for War, later Lord Altringham. I stayed up all night writing the memo and making drawings in the form of a comic strip, to show my toboggans in action. As I despatched this brilliant concept off to Whitehall, I did not consider it necessary to tell Sammy that I was now dealing direct with the British cabinet on how to win the war. This was an error, a fault I never really got over during the war years.

In the weeks which followed, I was intrigued to read in the confidential army bulletins on equipment research that trials were being held with the newly developed tank toboggans. Whatever went wrong with the idea, I never heard. As the months went by there was no further mention of my brainchild. Later, I still thought they would have been dandy for sliding over the deserts of Africa.*

As our division became more proficient, orders were received that we were to move our entire brigade, including tanks, to Wales, to some tank firing ranges at Linney Head where we could race over hills and fire out to sea. The move was to be carried out secretly at night so the Germans would not know all our tanks had left the south-east coast. About a dozen trainloads were needed for the move; it would be a tricky business loading dozens of 40-ton tanks in the dark onto flat cars.

I was sent down to the Guards Armoured Division in advance to learn the technique. The tank driver can only see out a small aperture, and he has to steer his great machine up a narrow ramp, with no lights. His tank treads overhang the edges of the flat cars on both sides. The limey troopers did the job efficiently by having a man with a lighted cigarette butt in his hand walking ahead of the vehicle.

We had all the regiments practise this drill; then the big move was on. There was to be a junior officer in charge of each train. According to instructions, I lined up all these men and read them their orders from the manual. The regulations were most explicit. Each officer was charged with the responsibility of personally checking the great chain shackles which tied the tanks to the flat cars and held them in place when the train went around curves. Secondly, he was to ensure personally that the tank

*Many years after the war a report on the assault landing at Anzio in Italy recorded that infantry tank toboggans had been tried out in action without success.

103

turrets were securely locked so that the great cannons could not swing sideways en route.

Everyone understood his orders and everything was reported correct, so the trains started off from the marshalling area . . . one every 15 minutes.

All went well, so I went back to my office to clean up the paper work. About half an hour later the telephone rang. The worst had happened. One of the turrets had not been secured and one of the whackin' great guns had swung sideways, just as one of the trains was roaring through a little English tunnel. The tunnel had fallen in on the train, flat cars had jumped the rails and tanks were scattered all along the line. The plaintive voice on the telephone asked what orders did I have. I didn't exactly know what orders one issued in such situations, other than perhaps to shoot the OC train on the spot and put him out of his misery.

I poured myself a stiff drink and got in touch with Division HQ to report these happy tidings. A blasphemous AA and QMG at once demanded what charge I proposed to lay against the errant commander of the train. "Well, we might charge him with damage to government property," I suggested brightly. "Then, according to King's Regulations and Orders, we could deduct the cost from the officer's pay — it would only take about 600 years for him to pay back British Rail. Or maybe, we could send Spike and his engineers to build them another bloody tunnel."

As it happened, the 1st Armoured Brigade did reach Linney Head on schedule, and early the next day, in the mist and drizzle, we lined up all our beautiful RAM I Canadian tanks, to make their first target run over the rough course. The first squadron started up the gentle grassy slope which lay ahead. They only advanced a hundred yards or so and then, to our amazement, all came to a halt. The newly designed caterpillars, with rubber treads, spun helplessly on the wet grass — with no traction whatever. Obviously, we should never try to fight in the rain. For once our Canadian design did not measure up to British requirements, so it was back to the drawing board for RAM I.

In touching on some of these lighter moments with the 5th Division, I don't wish to imply that we were having any circus. To the contrary. Sammy and Tom Rutherford drove us hard, training from morning till night and often well into the night. In very short order, the division rounded into a highly efficient formation and acquired a fine team spirit.

To break the monotony, every six weeks or so we could get a 48-hour pass and run up to London. There were air raids every night there but, in today's idiom, that was where the action was.

It was about that time or shortly afterward that the first American troops started turning up in London, to add to the mosaic of uniforms and accents. The Free French Forces had rather appropriated Hyde Park corner as a rendezvous. It became known as "shake-hands corner." The American GIs, gobs and marines took over Grosvenor Square and Piccadilly of an evening, where aggressive young ladies walked in the blackout, with either a lit cigarette or white boots to advertise their presence.

In the same way that Canadian troops had been a novelty in London two years before, the Americans were now in the spotlight. Being a beefy well-fed crowd, with their pants all cut too tight across the ass, with their American accents and with far more cigarettes and pay than the other forces, it took a while for them to be accepted. The only problem with the Yanks, according to the limey troops who had been on short rations for a couple of years, was that "they were overfed, overpaid, oversexed and over here."

As Charles Murphy, editor of *Fortune*, put it when the Canadians arrived, "The Englishman expected to welcome another Englishman, or at least a Dominion cousin who would think like an Englishman and respect English ways. Instead he found an incomprehensible North American character who for an Englishman's taste drank too much, bragged too much, had too much money. And even with a good Scottish or Welsh or Yorkshire name he was quite capable of materializing as an Eskimo from Hudson Bay, a Ukrainian from the wheat prairies, a French Canadian from the logging camps, or a Nova Scotian fisherman."

Notwithstanding these differences, the British and the Canadians discovered in proper time that they had much in common. And one circumstance that helped to hasten the understanding was the arrival of the Americans. The British, to their consternation, found that while the Americans had all the peculiarities of the Canadians, in twice the intensity, they were also an entirely different breed of North Americans, with infinitely more complicated ethnic strains. And so for the next few months in the pubs of Britain, the Canadians tried to explain Americans to the British, and the British to the Americans.

On The Lighter Side

Britain in wartime had a peculiar talent for absorbing people, which it did very quickly, almost too quickly as far as all the WAAFS and WRENS were concerned. As soon as you got to London on leave, you headed for the Bank of Montreal where your pay was deposited for you, then to the established Canadian hangouts to see who else was in town.

One night, Canada's legendary little newspaper correspondent, Greg Clark, and I had a happy pub-crawl through the dark streets of the West End, visiting various bottle-clubs. As we groped our way in the blackout and got lost crossing Berkley Square, we sang, appropriately, the popular hit, "A Nightingale Sang in Berkley Square."

"What in hell does a nightingale sound like," I asked Greg, who was a noted naturalist. Greg tried to make a noise like a nightingale but it didn't quite come off. Well he would do a whippoorwill call for me, which he did.

From the far side of the square, through the darkness, came an incredulous American voice, "Jesus Christ, a whippoorwill over here." Greg was triumphant.

As Greg kept popping up in various battles over the next few years, I might here explain that he had also served in the trenches, all through World War I, as adjutant of the regiment commanded by Victor Sifton. In the mud at Passchendaele, due to his short stature, a large sergeant had to carry him piggy-back into the attack. With a fine knowledge of King's Regulations and Orders, he was renowned for his skill in defending every rascal in the unit who came up on orders or court martial. He had also won an MC for bravery in action.

On another 48-hour leave in London, I was with some friends at The 400, a club where they kept a private bottle of whiskey for you. I mentioned that I was looking forward to my next leave, when I would be due for five full days. I had no idea how to spend that amount of time. It would be interesting to get over to Ireland, I speculated. But there were

105

restrictions against Canadian troops visiting Ireland, except on "compassionate grounds" or where one had near relatives. Unfortunately, I had no close relations in the Emerald Isle.

To my surprise, back at the brigade a few weeks later, I received a letter from Ireland. "My dear Nephew... We are delighted you are planning to visit us... We look forward to your arrival... Your loving aunt... Mrs. Flynn."

Who was Mrs. Flynn? I hadn't a clue but it might be worth a try. I attached the letter from my "loving aunt" to an application for my next leave to go to Ireland. It worked, and shortly afterward I was on a night boat crossing the Channel to Belfast.

The little ship was crowded, largely with Irish lads serving in the British Army or Royal Navy and, like myself, headed for some leave. It was odd that most of these boys in British uniforms were from the neutral south of Ireland and were against the "bloody Brits," though they saw nothing incongruous in their serving in British units.

With a real threat of German U-boats in the Channel and the ship's bar open all night, we spent the time in drinking and lively debate, and didn't bother about bed.

If they were happy to fight the Germans I asked, why were they also content to let the German embassy operate freely in Dublin? Reportedly, the German U-boat warfare in British waters was directed by the Dublin embassy. While on their leave, why didn't they just shoot the German ambassador, I asked. He might in fact be responsible for torpedoing the RN ships they served in.

After a few drinks, I rather warmed to the subject and began to promote the idea. We could slip across the border, get a Bren gun and shoot the bastard; then, in a fast car, race back across the border. It would cause an international incident, rupture diplomatic relations with Germany; the south of Ireland would then be in the war and the U-boat warfare disrupted. After all, our job was to shoot Germans, and the guards at the Irish border would likely help our getaway.

I thought I had the whole scheme organized but by morning, on the cold docks of Belfast, and with our wonderful hangovers, the project was rather forgotten. It seemed more practical to check into the Queen's Hotel, have a hot bath and fall into bed.

I might mention that some years after the war, the noted Irish writer, Shane Leslie, told me it would have been a sad mistake to shoot the German ambassador, as British Intelligence found his mail and wireless messages very valuable. They had broken the German code and didn't want him dead. Indeed, they would likely have shot me had we bumped him off.

About noon I was awakened by a telephone call at the hotel. It was Mrs. Flynn. "What are you doing in a hotel?" she demanded. "You are supposed to be staying with us."

I gathered my thoughts. "Mrs. Flynn, you don't know who I am and I don't know who you are. I was delighted to get your letter. It was most kind of you but I have no intention of imposing on your hospitality." In fact, I had only brought a sweater, some flannel bags and a good pair of boots with me. I had it in mind that I would take a little private walking tour by myself through some of the little villages and up to the Mountains of Mourne, which I had heard about.

She would have none of it. Finally, it was agreed I would spend Sunday at her home and then leave on my route march Monday morning. The next day her husband, a professor at Queen's University, picked me up and drove me out Malone Road to play golf on Malone Golf Course. (I had always believed all the Malones came from the south.)

Chasing a flock of sheep out of the way before we drove off at each tee, we enjoyed a very pleasant game. Seemingly, the sheep were used to keep the grass down on the fairways.

Mrs. Flynn was an older woman but full of energy, and a warm hostess. In her comfortable home, she gave us an excellent dinner, teaching me how to make crepe suzettes in the process.

As I sat with the professor before a blazing fire, sipping Irish whiskey that night, I noticed the portrait on the piano of a good-looking young man. Amazingly, I knew his face. It was their son, they explained. "What unit is he in?" I asked. "I am certain I have seen him some place."

They both smiled. He was an actor they said; his name was Errol, yes, the movie star. Then I got the rest of the story. They felt badly about their own son . . . a marvellous, handsome chap, a great athlete and horseman before he hit Hollywood. "Women destroyed our boy," the older man said sadly. "He should be in the army, not chasing girls in Hollywood."

Mrs. Flynn, it seemed, belonged to some women's committee for war work and, amongst other activities, organized some sort of hospitality scheme for young soldiers on leave. Someone from The 400 Club in London had sent her my name.

On the Monday morning, in my best marching boots and with only a haversack, I took a little train from Belfast, with no idea where I was going. For the next several days, I did some good walking along the Irish coast, stopping at small pubs and visiting the Mountains of Mourne. Here I sent a letter, postmarked "the Mountains of Mourne," off to an old friend in Canada, Billy Patterson, once Premier of Saskatchewan.

Back in the thirties in the Depression years, while I was with the *Leader-Post* in Regina, I had enjoyed the odd drink with Billy. On such occasions, he had felt compelled to sing his favourite song, "Where the Mountains of Mourne Run Down to the Sea." The problem had been to make him stop singing.

SEVEN

Back To The Infantry

WORLD SCENE

*Japanese naval defeat at Midway — Rommel captures
Tobruk — Monty to command 8th Army. Heavy
Canadian losses in Dieppe raid. Australians halt
Japanese in New Guinea. Canadian forces in England
grow impatient. Demands for action also raised in
Ottawa. Stalin calls on Allies for second front.*

It was just about the time I started to feel I had mastered something of the mysteries of armoured warfare and had fully converted from infantry to tanks, that I received orders to rejoin the 1st Infantry Division, then deployed on the coast between Seaford, Eastbourne and Hastings, as brigade major of the 2nd Brigade, commanded by Chris Vokes. The brigade included my earlier regiment, the Princess Patricias. Chris Vokes, a Permanent Force officer, was a fine fighting brigade commander, or as Monty was to say later, "a good plain cook." He was also a very old friend from Regina days.

It was not until later that I learned that the 1st Division was expected to see action before too long and Chris had asked for my posting as his Brigade Major, over the strenuous objections of Tommy Rutherford.

It was rather like coming home when I joined the 2nd Brigade HQ. I was able to see many old friends I had known in Canada, before being seconded to Ralston's office. The Brigade HQ was situated on the outskirts of Eastbourne, and the "Shiny 2nd Brigade," from the standpoint of training and efficiency, was rated tops in the Canadian Army. It had formerly had such distinguished commanders as General Perks, VC, and General Potts.

Few infantry divisions have had the good fortune to benefit from two solid years of such extensive battle training before seeing action, as did our 1st Division. They had embarked for France just before the collapse at Dunkirk and some units had also started off for Spitzbergen, but in each case they were withdrawn at the last moment.

Regardless of this long period of training and months of guarding the invasion coast of Britain, training was still kept up at a furious pace, with dozens of special courses and exercises every month. It was a delight to see a division operate with such smooth efficiency, but it was also a tough routine I found, with 30-mile route marches in full battle order and running over the cold downs in the dark each morning before breakfast. While it was a painful period in some ways, it was certainly more satisfying than a desk job back in Ottawa.

Occupying forward defence positions along the most critical coastal area, we were subjected to repeated "stand to's" and false alarms. The stretch of beach known as Pevensey Flats had been the traditional landing point for invaders of Britain throughout history. It was here that William the Conqueror and his Norman Knights had stormed ashore. Nearby was the site of the great Battle of Hastings, and the ruins of Pevensey Castle still marked the site of the first Norman fortress.

As the weeks went by, we came to know every country lane and hamlet in the area, even in the dark. Over the downs was the home where Rudyard Kipling had once lived. Close by was the little village of West Dean, where Jack Dunfee, a former world champion race car driver, and his gorgeous actress wife lived. Jack, one of the famous Bentley Boys, held many racing records at Monte Carlo and Brooklands. He was prominent in the theatrical business at that time and was widely known at all the best restaurants in London, as well as in the fashionable country homes.

The movie star Benita Hume had left Ronald Colman for Jack, just before the war, but Jack had then run off and married Sandra, who had starred with Jack Benny in the Hollywood movie, *Artists and Models*. She was selected for her role as "the world's most beautiful blonde" according to the leading artists of the day . . . and she lived up to her billing.

Because of the heavy air raids on London, Jack insisted that Sandra remain in safety at West Dean, where he had a small farm. This did not suit Sandra, who complained that more German bombs fell around the farm than at their mews in London. The reason for Jack's insistence was that he was likely chasing some bit of fluff in the city, said Sandra.

Curiously enough, Sandra was quite right about all the German bombs landing around their farm. For security purposes, I couldn't tell her the reason. The fact was, the entire coast section was designated at that time as the number one target area for the expected German invasion. Beaches had been mined and all railway areas, bridges, oil depots and so forth had been secretly wired for demolition and mass evacuation. Secret headquarters and fire control positions had been dug deep beneath some of the lovely gardens, quite unknown to the owners.

One moonlit night, just as I was to descend into a dark cavern beneath a gentle English garden to check a telephone circuit, I spotted a few lines of poetry engraved around the base of a little fountain, something about "the song of the bird in the morning, the smell of the rose at night — you are nearer God's heart in a garden than anywhere else on earth."

Inspecting all the infernal explosives and wiring, hidden just a few feet below that garden in order to blow the entire countryside to hell and spray blazing oil on invaders, it didn't seem to me that the garden was really very close to God's heart just then.

Unknown to Jack Dunfee, his farm was the particular pride of the camouflage boys and was used as a clever decoy to draw the German bombers away from the city of Eastbourne. With electric wires strung through hedges and country lanes, and with shaded green and red lights visible only from above, the farm at night would have the appearance of city streets and traffic lights to German pilots.

I could not explain this to Dunfee, but I did suggest that he let Sandra get to town occasionally. Indeed, simply for her own protection, I invited her up to dinner in London myself once when I had a spare 48-hour leave. For some odd reason, I found myself very popular with all the officers in the dining room when we came in for dinner and dancing at the Dorchester.

Even then, in the fall of 1942, the possibility of a German invasion could not be ignored, and every so often a false alarm would be raised by some lonely outpost at Beachey Head, Birling Gap or Friston. Peering out over the Channel in the dark of night, a worried corporal would be convinced he saw the black shadows of enemy assault craft approaching the beaches. At other times the RAF would get the "colours of the night" mixed up with their emergency identification signals, used when one of our own damaged bombers was trying to get back to England.

These colours were changed each night and might be red over green over green or some other such sequence which, by chance, might be the same combination of colours to be fired that night from Verey pistols to signify a German landing. In such instances, our entire brigade group would be routed out of bed on a minute's notice and go roaring off in the dark to battle stations.

There were several memorable snafus and trying moments. One evening we received a triple confirmation of an enemy landing — from our own outpost, from the RAF fighter station at Friston, and from the local coast guard station. The question was whether to take the serious risk of delay — in blowing up roads, bridges, railways and food depots — or wait for a further check. Fortunately, we waited till we received a negative report from an officer patrol.

Every so often a great sea mine would be washed ashore on the nearby coast, to go off with a mighty bang when it hit a pier, or to get stranded in the barbed wire on the beaches, near some built-up area. This entailed a dirty job for the bomb disposal boys.

In one lucky incident, however, the first German magnetic mine got washed ashore. The Admiralty was desperately anxious that the great gadget should not blow up till they discovered how it operated. None of the bomb disposal engineers knew how to defuse it, and my recollection is that they hoisted it up on a tank transporter and drove it through heavily populated areas around London, to a place where they could work on it. Quite by accident they discovered the right screw to take out first.

Nearly every day at that period, the German air force created a distraction, which bothered the mayor and corporation of Eastbourne as well as all the local citizenry. Around noon, three German Focke-Wulf fighter bombers would come racing in from the sea at wave-top level, avoiding detection by radar or spotters. The flyers would select some gap in the cliffs or valley, which cut through the high downs, to follow inland. Then circling around at low level, doubtless to take photographs, they would race back across the Channel, always dropping three or four bombs on Eastbourne as they went. The streets would be crowded at the noon hour and there were casualties nearly every day.

Invariably, the bombers would be halfway back to France before the AA guns of our coast artillery could be swung into action. As for the forward fighter stations of the RAF, they also proved useless in intercepting the raiders. Air patrolling produced no results and crews could not be scrambled quickly enough, when the enemy was spotted.

Because our brigade was in command of that sector of the coast, the city fathers laid their complaints at our door. Chris Vokes had a short temper and did not take kindly to the critics. Each day his lunch would be ruined when he heard three or four planes go racing overhead — then the crunch as more bombs hit Eastbourne. Red-faced and blasphemous, he would race outside to see the Boche raiders departing unscathed, homeward bound for their own lunch. Then he would grab the telephone and give both the AA people and the RAF station hell.

After several weeks of brooding over this situation, Chris came to a decision. "If the bloody RAF and gunners can't knock them down, we'll have the infantry take over the job," he roared.

Accordingly, the next day he called out every Bren gunner in the brigade and posted them on rooftops, in trees and in water towers — in fact, any place where a field of fire was possible. He had each magazine loaded alternatively with armour piercing, incendiary, tracer, and regular ammunition. Each gunner was issued a haversack ration and was told he was to remain up in his tower or tree during all daylight hours, till we shot the bastards down.

Several days went by but no Germans, and we were looking a bit stupid in the eyes of the local RAF chaps, who would provoke Chris by politely asking each day about our shooting.

As a last resort, Chris had the four padres in the brigade paraded before him. He explained the situation and pointed out that our lads were all getting browned off and hungry sitting up in trees. It was now up to the padres, Chris said. He wanted some co-operative praying. They were to get down on their knees and ask God to send us some Germans . . . and damned quickly. Did they understand their orders? Well, march out and get on with it.*

Sure enough the very next day our game worked. A couple of German planes came roaring over from back of the downs and some 150 Bren guns fired off all at once. The Jerry was only a few hundred feet up and going full out when he was hit. His plane went down immediately, ploughing its nose deep in the ground.

Chris and I grabbed a jeep and raced to the spot. The smoking tail end of the plane was protruding from the ground, the forward fuselage completely buried. Then I noticed the pilot's arm protruding from the wreck. While it seemed impossible that the pilot could have survived, I bent over and took hold of the arm to see if there was any pulse. The arm came off in my hand. We went back to the mess and had a drink.

That evening Chris had great satisfaction in telephoning the RAF station that we were coming over for a drink — on them — and we were prepared to give a short lecture on anti-aircraft tactics. Needless to say, the PPCLI, the Seaforths and the Edmontons all claimed credit for the kill.

Nearly every day that winter there was some small tragedy or human drama enacted along the invasion coast, some daring rescue by the coast guards, dogfights between the RAF and the Luftwaffe, someone blown up on the mine fields along the beaches, a motorcycle despatch rider killed on a night convoy or a children's schoolhouse hit by a bomb. Working with the local Home Guard, the Canadians gave whatever aid was possible, but there was a growing restlessness among our troops that it was time we saw some real action for a change instead of the endless training.

There are two particular incidents which remain in my mind from that period. One night a badly battered RAF bomber, with several of its crew wounded, made a gallant effort, on its return from a raid on Germany, to reach the British coast. We had been notified by the forward airfield at Friston that the plane was in trouble. It was losing altitude fast and would have to crash-land on the coast, so we alerted all our night outposts.

* At the time of the Battle of the Bulge, near Bastogne, nearly two years later, General Patton is recorded as having employed his U.S. Army padres in a similar role, to get him a break in the flying weather for fighter support.

Tragically, the plane crashed in the ocean only a hundred feet short of the pier at Eastbourne. For a short time the plane remained afloat and the wireless kept operating. The situation was serious. The crew was badly smashed up and the plane was sinking fast, but it was impossible to reach them in the dark. That whole section of the beach had been heavily mined and strung with barbed wire. The pier itself had been sealed off, wired and booby-trapped against any German invasion or commando raid.

We worked frantically with the coast guard to get a lifeboat round to them or work our way out through the mines and along the pier, but it all proved useless in the short time available. The bomber, with its wounded crew, sank beneath the waves before we could help. Breakfast wasn't very cheery that morning.

On another evening, word was received by Jack Dunfee that his younger brother, Geoffrey, a night fighter in the RAF, had been shot down. Like his two older brothers, Jack and Clive Dunfee, Geoffrey had been a race driver before the war. He had been stationed at a nearby airfield and frequently visited the little farm at West Dean, which he owned jointly with Jack and Sandra. He had a German shepherd dog which he took everywhere with him, even up in his fighter plane in the early days of the war.

When he had been switched over to a newer model of aircraft, however, there was no room for his pet dog, which had to be left on the ground. Each time that Geoffrey took off on a mission, the dog would sit faithfully beside the air strip waiting for his master's return. When Geoffrey's plane failed to return one morning, the dog continued to wait. It would not accept any food and could not be coaxed away from its vigil. After several days, the station called Sandra to come and get him. She was the only other person the dog would obey.

The Dieppe Raid

Our 1st Division troops were not the only Canadians who were getting restless as they trained endlessly in south-east England, eating NAAFI sausages and Spam. Back in Canada, Ralston and the Canadian government were beginning to wonder when we would see action. Although Canada had placed no restriction on how the Canadian forces overseas were to be employed, we had stipulated that they were to be used as formations with a Canadian identity, not broken up simply as reinforcements for Imperial or British regiments. Our units had been freely offered for operations in France, or Norway, or coastal raids, but the British had urged their retention in England, as the main strike force in South East Command, to guard the invasion coast.

Our only real action or combat had been the disastrous raid in August 1942 at Dieppe by the 2nd Division, commanded by General Ham Roberts. There has been much controversy about this costly raid by the Canadians, not only regarding its purpose and its execution, but also concerning what was achieved. Allegedly, it was to be a deliberate test of a frontal assault on a built-up port area, to provide information and experience for the subsequent Allied invasion of the continent. It was to test out weapons and engineering techniques on an enemy beach and to destroy enemy wireless installations. Again, it was reported as merely a diversionary raid to put the German defences off base and hold German divisions in France.

After the event, when the heavy Canadian casualties (900 killed and more than 2,000 taken prisoner) were announced, the gossip merchants had it that there had been a serious breach of security before the raid. The Germans had been alerted and were waiting for us. The air cover plan had been badly executed and there had been no pre-bombing of targets by RAF, or too little bombardment of defences by the navy. Again, the whole plan had been faulty and not based on the latest intelligence reports.

Supposedly, the original planning was bad and had been done by Monty when he held South East Command, before leaving to take over the 8th Army in Italy. The operation had been first contemplated many months earlier and was supposed to be carried out by British troops, but had been rejected by some of the English commanders as being too full of faults, and then shelved till it was suddenly dusted off quickly for the Canadians, with no time to develop a better plan.

Supposedly, Ham Roberts and some of the senior Canadian staff officers, when they studied the plan, considered it to be badly drawn, but they felt they had to accept the risk rather than appear faint-hearted by rejecting the operation, particularly as they were looking for action of some sort.

After the war, charges were made that Admiral Mountbatten, at that time head of Combined Operations, or General Paget of Home Forces, McNaughton or perhaps Alanbrooke, the British CIGS, was to blame for approving the plan, known to be faulty.

There have been volumes of detailed reports, both official and otherwise, as well as some excellent eye-witness accounts published about Dieppe. With a few minor discrepancies, they all undoubtedly give a fairly clear picture of what actually transpired. However, major contradictions still persist over the real purpose of the operation, as well as the planning aspects and their approval.

At the time, our division had been alerted to pick up and assist survivors of the raid as they made their way back to the various small ports along the south-east coast.

We welcomed home with cigarettes, tea and hot soup these relays of stragglers from their hopeless heroism, and obediently filled in the pages of official questionnaires with which we had been provided. What were the lessons of Dieppe? It must be demonstrated that the raid was a calculated practice run for the ultimate invasion.

Their glorious victory, except that of the spirit, unachieved, there were some valuable lessons at that. A Sten gun becomes useless when soaked with sea water, as particles of sand jam the mechanism. Unless engineers can land first to demolish sea walls, tanks become stationary targets on a beach. But these were merely side benefits to the real but costly sacrifices of Dieppe.

In the following weeks, I checked out many aspects of the operation with senior friends at both Combined-Ops and the War Office and talked to many of those who had been directly involved either in the planning or in the actual operations. Among those I spoke to was Lord Lovat, who had commanded one of the attached commando groups.

Following the war, when contradictory stories began to circulate about the purpose of and background to the raid, I made a point of discussing the subject further with such people as Monty, Field Marshal Alanbrooke, General McNaughton, General Crerar and Ralston.

It would be presumptuous to pretend I could provide the definitive answers to all the questions about Dieppe, but the following comment, based on the above considerable research, may be of interest.

While the Dieppe raid was vitally important and made a valuable contribution to the Allied grand strategy at a critical time, its purpose was certainly not merely to test German coastal defences or our assault landing techniques for the subsequent invasion of Normandy. These were the official reasons announced at the time and widely accepted after the war till the publication of *Bodyguard of Lies* by Anthony Cave Brown in 1973, where a much different story is told.

The real purpose of the raid was deception, to make the Germans believe a full scale invasion was intended, to hold more German divisions in France and so take the pressure off the hard pressed Russian armies. Secondly, it was in direct response to the incessant demands of both Washington and Moscow for a second front as early as 1942.

Both President Roosevelt and General Marshall, the U.S. Chief of Staff, were convinced that Russia was on the point of collapse. They were confident and adamant that the invasion of France must be undertaken that year. Towards this end Marshall had directed Eisenhower, his then unknown Chief of the War Plans Division, to prepare an invasion plan code name Sledgehammer, which Roosevelt approved.

Though Eisenhower had no battle experience and the U.S. could only contribute three raw infantry divisions, and two armoured divisions, towards an initial assault, Marshall firmly believed that a cross Channel invasion could succeed against the twenty-five experienced German divisions, then located in France. Nearly all the naval support for the assault would have to be furnished by Britain, as well as a large portion of the air support. He could not grasp how thinly Britain was already stretched in securing her home defences, in the Mediterranean, in North Africa and the middle east in keeping the vital sea lanes open and facing Japanese pressures in the far east.

Both Churchill and Alanbrooke realized that such a foolhardy adventure could only result in total disaster. A bitter argument developed between the Allies. At one point the American chiefs threatened to pull their forces entirely out of Europe and concentrate all their efforts in the Pacific to first defeat Japan, if they didn't get their way.

Churchill vainly tried to win the Americans over to his strategy, of first wearing down the Germans and dispersing their forces by threatening them from every flank, in Norway, France, Italy and the Balkans, until the Allied armies were strong enough to strike effectively at the weak points. In the American view this was simply "pinprick" warfare.

Unable to sell his strategy to the Americans, Churchill compromised by offering to make a raid on the French Coast and through deception, threaten simultaneous attacks in Norway and in the Persian Gulf, while the U.S. undertook a landing in North Africa. This was reluctantly agreed to by the U.S. (By building up Allied strength in the Mediterranean, Churchill still hoped to attack through the Balkans ahead of the Russians.)

To implement this program Churchill had Combined Operations headed by Mountbatten, dust off a previously rejected British plan, code named Rutter, for a raid on Dieppe. Various Canadian units were also issued with winter clothing and given ski instruction to simulate preparations for an attack in Norway.

114

The Rutter plan, renamed Jubilee, was hastily revamped and despite many weaknesses both in security and adequate air and naval support, was handed to the 2nd Canadian Division for immediate action. Though a courageous sacrifice and doomed from the outset, Dieppe did prevent Hitler from withdrawing divisions from France at that time, which might have ensured a German victory against Russia.

In discussions with Field Marshal Alanbrooke some years after the war, he commented that while Dieppe achieved its purpose in holding German divisions away from the Russian front, it finally brought home to the Americans, the realities and problems of launching a second front and brought an end to their naive demands for a premature invasion. A shocked Eisenhower also revised his rather casual ideas about Operation Sledgehammer.

Alanbrooke further recorded after the war that the RAF suffered equally heavy losses at that time for the same purpose, in deception raids on the coast of France, losing nearly a thousand pilots and aircraft in these missions.

As recorded by Monty in his memoirs, when he learned that the plan was to be altered and rescheduled he wrote to General Paget, C-in-C Home Forces, recommending that because of security, "the plan should be considered cancelled for all time"; if a raid was essential, a different target should be selected.

More Waiting

Although latrine gossip held that further actions were in the offing for the Canadians, the weeks went by and the endless training continued. In November 1942 came the news of Monty's great victory at El Alamein, then reports that the horror at Stalingrad had come to an end and the exhausted German divisions were now being encircled by strong Russian forces. But still the impatient Canadians were held in England.

As though to keep us occupied, selected Canadian officers were sent on a series of special courses that winter. For myself, there was first an army-air co-op course at Old Sarum for several weeks, then later an air-liaison course at the RAF fighter station at Biggin Hill.

At the Old Sarum course, the joining instructions stipulated that officers would not bring their army servants, as batman service would be supplied by the RAF. It was a cold and desolate encampment and we were accommodated in rows of corrugated Nissen huts, miles from the nearest town.

Our chief instructor was a mad RAF type who wore a kilt below his regulation battle-dress blouse. To have some sport with us foot sloggers, the flying instructors would take us zooming all over the sky in little reconnaissance planes, skimming the tops off haystacks and then getting us lost in the clouds. Then when we had lost all sense of direction, we would be handed a map and told to orient ourselves and identify obscure features on the ground.

I was perished with the cold the first night I crawled into the little cell which had been assigned to me in one of the tin huts. The room furnishings consisted of a small iron bedstead, on which you spread your bed roll, a small chest of four drawers, a little table, one chair and a miniature coal stove but no coal.

Eventually, wearing long underwear and several sweaters as I shivered inside my bed roll, I managed to get off to sleep.

In the morning, to my amazement, I awoke to find a cheery fire blazing in the little stove and a saucy young woman, in WAAF uniform, serving me a cup of hot tea in bed, as she got busy polishing my boots. The world took on an entirely different hue. I had never heard of batwomen before.

For a second I forgot that I was at a British station, and instead of preserving the proper aplomb or indifference of a field officer, I demanded, "How long have the RAF had this cosy deal organized?" As I got shaved with the hot water produced by the little cockney girl, I carried on some light banter with her. This, as I was to discover later, was a grave mistake.

I was the only Canadian on that particular course, and for the first day I rather got the frigid treatment from the limey officers. One of the English officers, however, seemed to be a bit friendly and have a little life in him, so I suggested that he join me in grabbing a bus into the nearby town for supper in a pub and a look at the local cinema.

He was quite agreeable, so we had a pleasant evening in the town. The following morning, when I awoke in the Nissen hut, I could see my breath in the air. There was no fire in the stove, no cup of tea and no saucy WAAF to cheer the morning.

After shaving in cold water, I staggered over to a ghastly breakfast in the mess and then to my first lecture. About an hour later a runner from the adjutant's office arrived at the classroom. Major Malone was to report to his office forthwith.

The adjutant was a fat, frozen-faced fellow with a walrus moustache. I was not invited to take a seat.

In a very superior tone, he began, "About this incident in your quarters last evening . . . "

"What incident?" I demanded in some heat.

"Hah!" sniffed the fat boy. "Kindly explain this if you please," and he handed me two charge sheets. Seemingly, two of the young WAAF batwomen had been placed on charge at twenty hundred hours the previous evening for being drunk and causing a disturbance at hut number 86 — my room.

My assertion that I knew nothing whatever about all this nonsense was greeted with scepticism. Obviously, he did not believe me . . . you never know what these colonial officers might be up to, he implied.

But luck was on my side. I had an alibi, a witness, the English officer who had gone into town with me. We had not returned to camp till after midnight. I could tell the fat boy to stuff it.

Later that day I learned that yesterday had been payday for the other ranks, and my little batwoman and a pal had tied one on someplace, then came reeling and singing back into camp and started banging on the door of my room, shouting out, "Good old 86." Apparently, my light morning banter the previous day had won me some new friends.

Regardless of my ironclad alibi, for the duration of that course I detected a rather smug and doubting attitude among the British officers in the mess. Each time I arrived for meals, I caught the glance of some officer indicating, yes, that's the Canadian chap in 86, you know.

The moral was quite obvious. If you suddenly find a little cockney WAAF in your bedroom some morning, for God's sake ignore her and, above all, no friendly banter.

Biggin Hill was a main fighter station, and each night after dinner there would be a rush into the projection room by the young pilots to see the combat films of the day's fighting against the Luftwaffe. Movie cameras attached to the guns on each plane were activated when the firing started. It was only when the film was developed and studied that official recognition would be granted for a kill. These pictures of air battles were certainly dramatic, but I was more interested in studying the intense faces of the young flyers in the audience. For the most part, these boys were still in their early twenties; it gave you a very odd feeling night after night watching these films of planes exploding, while sitting beside lads, scarcely out of their teens, who had survived the dogfights you were watching.

One fresh-faced young boy, in particular, caught my attention. In one week he had scored three hits. At the same time he was taking a lot of ragging from his pals in the mess. Apparently a dance was to be held in the mess, but his girl friend couldn't come. She was still attending a girls' boarding school nearby and the headmistress wouldn't let her out for the dance. The young pilot's pals had pinched his photograph of the young lady. She still wore a school uniform and her hair in pigtails, while her 19-year-old boy friend was coolly flying his Spitfire each day in a life-and-death battle in the clouds.

Several times I watched another frequent drama, enacted by a young girl who operated "button B." In an emergency, when one of our planes or pilots had been shot up in the air, the pilot would, as a last resort, push Button B, which signified he was in bad trouble, couldn't land, had lost direction, was blinded or his instruments were destroyed.

When the red emergency signal lit up on the board at central control, this young WAAF officer would try to establish voice contact with the pilot. Then she would call in wireless stations, perhaps in Bristol and Dover, to work out a fix on the plane so she could give the pilot his location and height. Then would come the tense period of trying to talk the wounded pilot down and direct him to the nearest air strip, which she had alerted. Sometimes she won, but frequently she lost and had the bitter experience of hearing a pilot's final words as he crashed at sea or exploded in flames. She was a pretty girl and, like most of the pilots, also very young. Following Dunkirk, the youth of Britain had certainly proved they could meet the real challenge when it came.

At these various air courses I was taught some elementary aspects of navigation and flying with dual controls, as well as operating a Link trainer. Contrary to the theories of Bomber Harris and other air marshals at that time, I was never under any illusion that the war could be decided by bombing and air power alone. The victory would have to be won by tanks, infantry and field artillery, supported and transported by the air force and navy. I would be happier fighting on the ground. The real benefits from these courses was in learning how to call in bombing raids on enemy targets or close fighter support for infantry attacks, and in understanding the necessary wireless procedures in working through air-tentacles.

Then they started shipping us off to commando and survival courses in Scotland, followed by combined-ops planning with the Royal Navy at places like Troon and Largs.

Of all these special courses, the combined-ops planning school with the RN was by far the most interesting. In this field, the Brits certainly knew their stuff, after centuries of experience as a naval power and supporting expeditionary forces across all the oceans of the world. It was a delight to work with these old navy types in Scotland, and without question they taught the U.S. Army as well as ourselves all the essentials of both the "long sea voyage," and the "short sea trip."

As a problem, you would be told to work out the loading sequence and landing schedules covering an entire divisional or brigade group consisting of units of all arms, infantry, armour field artillery, engineers and recce regiments, as well as all their supporting depots and supply columns.

The loading sequence was to be carried out in accordance with available dock space at scattered ports and arrival times of troop trains and vehicle convoys.

All the various units would then have to be dispersed and loaded on perhaps 40 or 50 great ships on a tactical basis, according to speeds of different ships in various convoys. Each unit was to be split up between two or more different ships, so that if one was torpedoed or sunk there would be sufficient elements of the army unit on another ship, capable of carrying out its tactical mission with sufficient vehicles, ammunition, rations and so forth.

For the assault on the beaches, the ships must each be loaded in a reverse order, so that the bulldozers or light AA guns, which might be required first, came out of the holds first. Operating in mixed planning teams, with British, American and Canadian staff officers, we would sweat through all-night sessions fitting all the hundreds of pieces into their right niche and sequence. Our completed plans would then be submitted to a team of RN instructors or umpires. Sadly we would then watch these old boys gently torpedo our masses of calculations. They would show us how we had placed a Bren carrier or medium artillery piece into a ship's hold, where the winches weren't heavy enough to hoist it out again or it was too wide for the hatch.

The RN had scale models of every transport ship afloat, together with deck and hold charts showing the accurate dimensions, sizes of hatches and lifting power of winches. Every ship was different. As well, you must have a substitute plan to be adopted when some of the expected shipping could not rendezvous in time.

The navy was then just starting to phase in scores of all the new type of small landing craft, such as LCMs, LCAs and LCIs, with beach ramps and so forth, which had just been developed by U.S. shipbuilders in Florida. These fast-moving small craft were designed to off-load the great liners and transports from anchorages about seven miles off a beach and then, under fire, make a run to shore.

Assault Exercises

It was a few weeks after the combined-ops planning course that we received orders to move our entire brigade, together with the 3rd Field Regiment and, also under command, portions of our Divisional Engineers, Support Battalion, Recce Regiment, Service Corps and so forth — a total of 16 units all told — from Eastbourne in Sussex to the general area of Inveraray in Scotland, by rail and road convoy, for a major assault landing exercise. Vehicles were to be at light scale only, the balance of heavy vehicles and stores to be left in Sussex.

In retrospect, this realistic exercise, employing both large ships and many landing craft, should have been the tip-off that some real action was in the works. But there had been so many false starts before that we saw it simply as another of the endless training exercises.

It was a wet cold day as we marched from the nearby station into the shabby little port of Inveraray, which lies at the base of misty Scottish mountains and is dominated by the grim castle of the Duke of Argyle. We were billeted in long rows of Nissen huts, scattered through the Duke's forest and up the adjoining glens.

The Seaforths, one of the regiments in our brigade, had "mistakenly" brought along their fine pipe band. So the evening of our arrival, I directed their CO to have his Canadian pipers, in kilts, march up to the historic Scottish castle and play retreat at sundown. They made a brave showing and, as the old Duke was in residence at the time, we rather expected that he would make an appearance — as is the custom — to request the final number and take a salute. But the miserable old boy just ignored us.

The reaction of the impoverished villagers, when they saw the kilts and heard the pipes, was quite different. They tumbled out of their poor little homes along the dockside and gave us a tremendous cheer. Each night thereafter we had retreat played in the town square and forgot the Duke and his castle. Most of the little homes in the town, which were owned by the Duke, were in bad repair, and we gathered that the old boy was none too popular with his tenants.

For some reason, Scotland and her people have always been popular with Canadian soldiers. When Canadian soldiers had a 10-day leave coming up, they could request a free travel warrant to any place in the British Isles, except Ireland. Invariably, the great majority always headed for Scotland, where they seemed to feel a bit more at home. This was not due to any particular Scottish ancestry, as the preference was the same by Canadians of Ukrainian, Polish, Dutch, Czech or French backgrounds. Possibly our troops found the Scots more open. While rather blunt, they seemed more friendly and with more genuine warmth than the reserved English in the south.

Each day our units were kept busy learning how to waterproof vehicles, how to load them on great ships, trans-ship them at sea into landing craft and then drive them, through several feet of waves, to remote beaches. The infantry would be embarked at night into great transport ships and taken out to sea about eight miles. Then just before daybreak the men, loaded down in full battle order, including grenades and extra bandoliers of ammunition around their necks, would climb down long scrambling nets, hung from the tall sides of the ships, and into scores of small assault craft which rose and fell dangerously alongside in the heavy ocean swell.

One raw cold morning, just at dawn when our flotilla of small landing craft went racing in formation toward the rocky shores of Scotland from several miles out, one of the loaded LCMs, just off our port bow, suddenly disappeared before our eyes.

The heavy pounding of the sea had smashed open the front landing ramp of the boat so that it became a virtual scoop. Driven by its powerful engines, the boat simply made a dive to the bottom, with its cargo of a Bren carrier and lorry-load of ammunition. The troops were thrown into the cold water and some went down with the armour-plated craft.

119

Instantly, I grabbed the wireless set and "in clear" called ship's control for rescue craft. On all these exercises we were trained to use a complicated code in every wireless transmission. As Brigade Major, I was expected to carry three different coding machines tied to a strap about my neck. These small metal machines were adjusted to codes which changed each day. Separate machines were required for three different links: G, A&Q, and RN. You twisted a series of little rollers to work out your message — all very complicated and time consuming.

As minutes were vital, if the men remaining afloat were to be saved, I hadn't wasted time fiddling with any code machine. A number of the men were saved, but this indiscretion of mine on the wireless resulted in a severe rocket for me from the War Office.

Seemingly, all wireless broadcasts were monitored and my Canadian voice talking in clear had been picked up and traced. The reprimand pointed out that an enemy intercept could determine that a Canadian division was carrying out major assault exercises off the coast of Scotland. I was at fault no doubt, but at least several lives had been saved.

An American division was carrying out similar assault exercises in the same area and we would take turns using the available shipping. Also with us was a small but very keen team of American civilians, who went racing about all over the ships, seemingly without any control whatever and completely ignoring all naval and military practices. We discovered that they were the boys from Florida who had designed and built all the new types of assault craft and had enthusiastically come over on their own to work with the troops "to make damn sure their boats worked." In point of fact, several of them, including the manager of the boat company, even sailed with us some months later to watch the boats perform on the Sicily invasion . . . which they did superbly.

To my surprise, one day at Inveraray I received an invitation to tea at the castle from the old Duke of Argyle. As I recall the visit, the great hall of the castle looked like an enormous old armoury. In rows all along the wall were hundreds of pikes, swords, muskets and spears, apparently the equipment for his entire clan in years gone by. At the village pub later, one of the locals assured me that after a highland raid of old, against the MacDonalds, the Dukes of Argyle always had to gather up the weapons afterward, so that their own clansmen would not be tempted to use them against the castle some day.

After tea with the Duke, he very kindly gave me a tour of his castle and told me something of the old feuds between the Campbells and MacDonalds, and of the sinking of a great Spanish galleon off the little harbour at the time of the Armada.

But then he got down to the business at hand. Apparently, he was concerned about the possible behaviour of our Canadian troops. The Americans had been very bad, he complained. He had a great forest, in which every tree was numbered and recorded according to variety and age.

A small metal tag showing a serial number and the Argyle crest was embedded in the bark on every tree. These the American GIs had removed by the score for souvenirs, and they had also chopped down several of the trees. Then when the Duke had summoned the general commanding the U.S. division to register his complaint, the general had not only treated the matter very lightly but, on leaving the castle, himself pinched the Duke's favourite bonnet, which was hanging from a thumb stick near the door, as a souvenir for himself. Of course, I assured the Duke, Canadian soldiers would never be guilty of such behaviour.

I could perhaps have told him about a letter which was received by General Price Montague, the senior Canadian officer at Canadian Military HQ in London, from a Scottish woman. In her letter, the woman explained that a Canadian, Private McSnook, had stayed at her home on his last leave, and as a result, she and her daughter were both pregnant. McSnook had also borrowed their bicycle, and what she wanted to know was where in hell was the bicycle. As an illustration of his varied wartime problems, Price kept this letter framed and hung on the wall of his office.

Travelling back and forth from London to Glasgow on the overnight train for all these Scottish exercises and courses, you tried to catch a seat on the ghost train, a secret unscheduled run which left each night from a hidden siding back of the regular terminal. This secret run was for security purposes. If an enemy agent saw a covey of RN captains and admirals, generals or merchant skippers all catching a train for Glasgow on a particular date, he could determine pretty closely that a convoy or task force was due to sail from Scottish ports and so alert U-boat packs in the North Atlantic.

On the ghost train you had a sleeping compartment and got a good night's rest. That is, if your trip was considered top priority and you were lucky enough to get a security travel warrant from Movement Control. I had travelled in this style once or twice when I had been Staff Secretary to the Minister.

For normal trips on the regular overnight train, common infantry types like myself and even colonels sat up all night in a shabby old carriage under austerity conditions. The one or two sleeping cars on the train were reserved for major generals, admirals or cabinet ministers, and such exalted beings.

After a long, cold drive in an open jeep from Troon one night, I arrived at the Glasgow railway station about an hour before train time. Not looking forward to sitting up all night on the train, I started to wander over to the bar in the Central Hotel to fortify myself for the ordeal. Crossing the blacked-out terminal, I noted a kiosk at which a small queue of senior officers had formed. As I suspected, this was where the privileged sleeping compartment reservations were picked up.

On the basis that anything was worth a try, I fell in at the end of the line, turned up the collar of my trench coat and tried to assume the look and manners of a full general. Perhaps my rank badges wouldn't show in the dark. After all, it was war.

As the girl at the wicket handed out each compartment ticket, she ticked a name off a list she had in front of her. When my turn came I quickly spotted a name that had not been crossed off, and in a gruff voice barked, "General Davidson. Have you got my reservation?" Obligingly, the young lady crossed out the name Davidson and handed me a compartment ticket. With this piece of luck I quickly vanished in the dark and made for the bar in the Central Hotel.

Sitting in the bar drowning their sorrows as they also waited for the train to depart, were two old Canadian friends, Majors Alan Embury of Regina and Jim Armstrong from Toronto.

As I joined them for a whisky, I listened to their bellyaches about having to sit up all night. I offered my sympathies but made no mention of my private compartment until just a few minutes before departure time. After glancing at my watch, I casually observed that I thought I would get into my compartment now and tuck into bed before the train pulled out.

They refused to believe that I had a compartment until I showed them my precious green ticket. "How in hell did you rate that?" they demanded. "Very simple," I replied. "I just went up and asked for it. I am surprised that you've been sitting here all this time without even trying."

With that, they both went bolting out the door for the little wicket in the station, while I slipped quietly on to the train, ducked into my compartment and bolted the door. Just as the train was due to pull out, there came a heavy knocking on the compartment door. I ignored the pounding for a bit, then in a great parade ground voice I roared, "Stop that goddamned row. Get away from that door; I'm trying to sleep."

The pounding continued, as some excited railway official tried to explain that there had been a mistake. As long as the pounding went on, I continued to roar blasphemies like an enraged general. Finally, the noise died down. Presumably, other accommodations had been found for the real General Davidson. I was home free . . . or so I thought.

The train had been rattling along for 20 minutes or more when I made the fatal decision just to wander through the tourist-class carriages to gloat and say good night to my pals before I turned in. The moment I opened the door, two great bulking forms came crashing into my compartment. Embury grabbed the little berth and Armstrong got the pillow and blankets. After a fruitless struggle, I had to sleep on the floor with my great coat pulled over me. Embury had always proved to be a difficult fellow.

A Date With a Spy

There was a bonus that went with these trips to various courses: nearly all the train connections had to be made through London. With proper planning, you could usually wangle a night or two in London, coming or going, if you had any pay left.

I was fortunate in having many friends in London and could always be sure of finding a good party at such places as the Bagatelle, the Hungaria, or Cafe de Paris, before it got hit with a bomb one night, tragically killing several of my pals, including Phil Seagram.

During one 48-hour stop in London, I had the intriguing experience of meeting a beautiful female spy named Solange Malifaitre. She was in the uniform of the Free French Forces, and it was not until later that I learned of her espionage activities. Though I checked with several of my M1-5 contacts after the war, I never did discover her real name. My staff officer's notebook of that period gives her phone number as GROS-1358.

When I arrived in London on that trip, I telephoned my friend Brigadier Pat Kelly, the Paymaster General (a useful friend to have when your pay records got mucked up). Pat was a handsome old boy with his silver hair and gold tabs. He had a bright eye for the girls and knew London well, as he had held the same job in World War I.

Pat gave me a great welcome, insisting that we meet together that evening at the Hungaria, his favourite restaurant.

We were halfway through our dinner that night, listening to the czymballum and drinking Bull's Blood, when the headwaiter came to our table and whispered something in Pat's ear. Pat looked a little flustered, excused himself and left the table, I assumed, to take a telephone call.

As the minutes went by and Pat did not return, I began to look about the restaurant. Over on the stairway leading down into the restaurant, I spotted Pat carrying on a very animated conversation with a stunning doll in a French uniform. The doll was obviously in a temper and Pat was clearly on the defensive in their heated debate.

Always ready to assist a pal in difficulties, I walked over to join them.

"Here, you mustn't talk to my dear old grey-haired friend like that," I gently chided the young lady.

"Fiche-moi la paix," Solange snapped at me, and continued to blast Kelly in broken English. Eventually, when we got her cooled down, she came over to our table and ordered some cognac, which surprisingly Kelly was able to command.

It seemed that Kelly had made a date with Solange that same night, also at the Hungaria, which he had completely forgotten when I called him. For some reason she allowed herself to become upset when she arrived to see Kelly halfway through his dinner, without her.

Again, to help Kelly out of a difficult situation, I suggested that Solange should have dinner with me the following night. "I would not stand her up as Kelly had done," I joked. We could go to Kempinsky's on Swallow Street, which was open all night, and we could dance to Crazy George, an excellent pianist who was a wartime exile from Vienna. After a bit more abuse for Kelly, she accepted my date, had her dinner and left.

The next evening at Kempinsky's, our dinner proceeded happily for a bit and then Solange excused herself to go to the ladies' room.

Glancing about the room a few minutes later, I happened to see that instead of going to the ladies' room she was making a telephone call at a booth near the door. Later, as we danced, and she would turn quickly on the dance floor, I got the very clear impression that she was trying to avoid being seen by someone. Subsequently, she ducked out again during the evening to make more telephone calls. She seemed very preoccupied about something, certainly not myself.

Recognizing this, I called it an early evening and caught a taxi for her back to her hotel and said a polite good night.

A few weeks later, back at our brigade headquarters near Eastbourne, I was reading the Sunday newspapers one morning when my eye caught a small item: Three German agents, posing as members of the Free French Forces in London, together with their female accomplice, Solange Malifaitre, had been convicted of espionage and executed in the Tower.

This rather braced my ideas a bit about taking unknown young ladies to dinner. The next time I saw Kelly in London, I made an observation about the nice girl friends he had and suggested he might give me a little warning next time. Kelly confessed that he had been equally astounded with the news and allowed that he really didn't know much about Solange either, except that he had met her through some RN commander at the Admiralty.

Despite these London and Scottish diversions and an endless variety of special courses and training exercises, the Canadian Army in England was becoming very bored by the end of 1942. The demand was growing: "When the hell are we going to see some fighting?" This same demand for action was also being raised in Canada, not only by the press and the public but also by Ralston and his cabinet colleagues. The situation was starting to loom as a political scandal and threaten the government in Ottawa.

Official requests that the Canadian Army should be used in an active role had actually been made several times, not only at the War Office level in Britain but also direct to Churchill himself. McNaughton was being blamed in some measure for the delay.

There were two factors operating against Canada's request for action. Britain was quite happy to see the Canadian Army, with its fully integrated structure and command, remain in England for the eventual cross-Channel invasion of France. Whether or not the Canadian Army was ever seriously considered for a role in Operation Torch, the landing in North Africa, is not entirely clear. The British, however, were becoming sensitive at that time to an unfair slur being made by German propaganda and Lord Haw Haw, that England was fighting all her battles with Empire troops, such as the Australians, New Zealanders, South Africans and Indian divisions. Added to this was the desire, for purposes of morale and propaganda, to have the North African landing appear an exclusively American operation, even to the extent of putting some British troops in U.S. uniforms. Hitler and his command staff harboured the belief that the British would wish to keep the Americans out of the Mediterranean. They would be surprised and shaken to hear that a landing operation on such a scale as Torch could be developed so quickly by the U.S. forces.

Secondly, General McNaughton held the view that Canadian formations should be employed only as a complete army, under his own control, not split up in brigade or divisional groups as components of other armies in scattered theatres.

With his bold and widely quoted phrase, that the Canadian Army formed "a dagger pointed at the heart of Berlin," McNaughton's ambition understandably was to lead the Canadian Army when the great invasion came. Indeed, press speculation that he might be chosen as Allied commander for all the Allied land forces for Normandy had not been dismissed from McNaughton's thoughts. This would hardly be a prospect, however, if the Canadian Army became dispersed beforehand.

There are several conflicting reports regarding the ultimate decision to employ Canadian troops for Operation Husky, the invasion of Sicily. Supposedly, the proposal originated with the British War Office, which made the request to General McNaughton. McNaughton was subsequently reported as arguing that he was not against Canadian forces being employed "where and when they can make the best contribution to winning the war," but he still argued that the army should be employed as a whole.

From my talks with both Ralston and Field Marshal Alanbrooke after the war, the following facts are abundantly clear.

As early as the fall of 1942, when it became apparent that a German invasion of Britain was no longer a serious prospect, Ralston pressed for the early employment of Canadian divisions so that they could gain actual battle experience. He was greatly concerned about the risk of committing our entire army into the critical assault in Normandy with not one of our divisions having had previous battle experience.

In October 1942, Ralston sent a formal request to British authorities that Canadian troops be given an active role in some theatre. As I recall the message, shown to me by Ralston, it read, "Canadian government considers it imperative that Canadian troops now in England be employed in an active theatre of operation before the end of the year."

Then, when the news of the American invasion of North Africa was released, Ralston, who was in England, immediately asked the British government why Canadian forces were not included. It was at this time that the British explained that Torch was intended primarily as a diversionary operation, and that it was important for the attack to appear entirely a U.S. Army operation. As Churchill stated in the British House of Commons, "Neither militarily nor politically are we directly controlling the course of events in the North African invasion."

After the war, claims were made that General McNaughton had tried to have Canadian units used in North Africa. If this were the case, certainly it was not known in Ottawa or discussed with Ralston. All the evidence would indicate that McNaughton strongly resisted the employment of any of our divisions separately.

McNaughton consistently argued, both with Ralston and with General Kenneth Stuart, the Canadian Chief of Staff, that there was no need to worry about the morale of Canadian soldiers in England, or about gaining battle experience before the Normandy invasion. In this view, McNaughton was clearly out of touch with his field formations. While he was able to occupy his interests and activities with the design of special equipment and scientific experiments, his troops were fed up to the teeth marching back and forth across Surrey and Sussex. Though recognized as the best trained and equipped army of the Allied forces in Europe, they were tired hearing of British, Australian and American battles. They wanted action themselves. They resented the odd taunts in the village pubs about "God's Gift to the Girls of Sussex" or that the war would be over before the Canadians ever fired a shot in anger.

It was in April 1943 that McNaughton finally received a direct request from General Alan Brooke,* the British CIGS, for a Canadian division to participate in the Sicily invasion. He transmitted this request to Ottawa, where it was immediately approved, and McNaughton seemingly accepted the decision with good grace, perhaps not realizing Ralston's hand in the matter.

Before giving some account of the Sicily operation, there is a further matter concerning General McNaughton during the pre-Husky period, which has importance in understanding McNaughton's subsequent actions. It also helps illustrate his relations with the British chiefs, prior to being relieved of his command the next year.

The following incident was related to me shortly after the war by Lieutenant-General Price Montague, who throughout the war held the appointment of Senior Canadian Officer Overseas at Canadian Military HQ in London. Except for purely operational matters and internal administration within our field formations, all Canadian Army matters in England, in respect to training camps, records, pay, legal aspects, accommodation, discipline and so forth, came under General Montague's HQ. All army communications with Ottawa in theory went through his hands. He was also responsible for liaison with the War Office and the British government on all military matters. On non-military subjects, his

---

*Later, Field Marshal Viscount Alanbrooke.

liaison was with Vincent Massey, Canada's High Commissioner, who occupied an adjoining building in Trafalgar Square.

As was the case with Argyle House, the Canadian Military HQ in World War I, CMHQ and Price Montague were viciously criticized at times by many individuals serving in field formations. It was traditional in the army that someone back down the line must be blamed when things went wrong with pay, promotions, rations, leaves or whatever. The buck was usually passed to "those bastards back at CMHQ," who became the butt of most bellyaching, whether warranted or not.

The truth is that Price had to carry out a very difficult and thankless role which did, at times, require some pretty skillful footwork and a fine political hand. Although I had many rows myself with Price and his staff during the war years, we remained good friends, and in retrospect I can't think of anyone who could have better handled this difficult assignment. Price had served overseas in World War I. He knew all the fine points of the game and had the old soldier's skill in handling awkward situations.

In many areas, such as leasing of buildings, damage to property, supply contracts and review of courts martial, Montague exercised a special authority on behalf of the Canadian government. At rare times, when McNaughton took a few days' leave or had to be absent from his Army HQ at Leatherhead for conferences, Montague would drive down from London every few days or so to sign any essential orders or documents.

On one particular occasion, McNaughton disappeared completely for nearly a week. Supposedly, he had gone to have a few days' rest on the estate of an English tycoon friend. Some emergency arose and a call was put through to the country estate but McNaughton was not there. Nothing was known of his whereabouts. General Montague came down from London immediately and a search was started for McNaughton.

In checking through McNaughton's office papers for some clue, a sealed envelope was discovered marked, SECRET — To Be Opened in an Emergency. Montague tore open the packet, to discover a complete set of operational orders covering the deployment and initial moves to be taken by the Canadian Army in the event of a German invasion. According to the story, as told to me by Montague, these orders were completely different from the instructions laid down by the higher British authority of South East Command and Home Forces, covering counter-invasion operations. A secret foreword explained that McNaughton had no confidence in the British plans and dispositions or in the British commanders. Regardless of the circumstances, if the invasion of Britain started in his absence from HQ, the Canadian Army would act independently of the British and would at once occupy the new positions outlined in his own orders, carrying out roles McNaughton had determined, contrary to the British operation orders.

This seemed quite incredible, but Montague, in a private conversation, assured me it was the actual situation. He was very disturbed at his discovery, but as the threat of invasion seemed pretty well past, Montague took no action in the matter at the time, nor did he bring up the subject with either McNaughton or the War Office, which would have caused a frightful row. It no longer seemed important. The matter is, however, important now, toward understanding the actions taken a year later to have McNaughton removed. Even at that early stage, both Brooke, the British CIGS, and General Paget of Home Forces, quite unknown to the

Canadian authorities, had begun to have doubts about McNaughton's abilities as a field commander.

When McNaughton finally turned up, back at his HQ, a few days later, it was learned that he had gone off secretly by himself to take part in a three-day exercise with a Canadian infantry regiment, to prove that he was physically fit and capable of doing a 30-mile march in full battle order. No one on his staff had been told where he was going or what he proposed to do.

Canada House

One further association must be appreciated to bring the future picture into focus: the relationship between the senior Canadians in England at that time and the British authorities. Vincent Massey, our High Commissioner in London at that time, although ably representing Canada in a very demanding wartime responsibility, was not without his vanity. He also suffered at times from petty jealousies. Frequently his nose was out of joint when the limelight focussed on General McNaughton and he was forced into the shadows. It was either McNaughton or Montague who accompanied the King and Queen on their inspections of the Canadian troops, and who appeared at great official functions and banquets, resplendent in their uniforms and medals.

Massey was also resentful of Montague's authority from the Defence Department, to negotiate directly with British government departments. His endless desire to have his picture in the London newspapers was a matter of some amusement in Fleet Street.

Several times he lobbied Ottawa to have his stature raised to cabinet rank. (For a period during World War I, a Canadian cabinet minister had been resident in London, sitting in on Empire conferences and speaking for the Canadian government.) When his requests were turned down, Vincent then thought he should have a military aide in uniform to accompany him in official circles. His nominee for this appointment was my friend, Captain Campbell Moody, a polished and attractive young officer then serving on Montague's staff at CMHQ. Prior to the war, Moody had been in the New York office of the Bank of Montreal. He knew his way about in both business and social circles and was adept at handling difficult situations.

After much wrangling Vincent achieved his desire, but to his chagrin it was ordered that while Moody would be made available on loan from the army to External Affairs, he must wear civies while carrying out this civilian assignment. Moody proved an excellent aide for Massey, smoothing over many troubles and also serving as press secretary at Canada House.

While difficulties seldom showed on the surface, there were times when frictions between McNaughton, Montague and Massey produced some heat on all sides, particularly during visits to England by Ralston, Howe, Prime Minister King and other officials from Ottawa, who tended to deal directly with the service chiefs rather than through Canada House. Massey undoubtedly had a difficult role to play.

Mrs. Massey, in contrast, was completely devoid of any vanities or pretensions. She was a very generous and kindly woman who went flat out to help and work with the thousands of young Canadian men and women in the services who passed through London during the war. Under her supervision the Masseys' country estate became a convalescent home for hundreds of wounded Canadians upon their discharge from hospital. In London, she helped organize men's canteens, club rooms and a junior officers' lunch club where she herself, with a group of women volunteers, served up the meals every day. She also operated with a group of delightful old dowagers in London in organizing dances at the Grosvenor House for young officers on leave; here they could meet some English girls, other than the regiment of prostitutes on Piccadilly.

EIGHT

Action At Last

WORLD SCENE

*October 23, 1944. A turning point in the war as
Montgomery's 8th Army victorious at El Alamein —
African Corps retreats — American and British troops
land in Algeria and French Morocco. France scuttles
battle fleet at Toulon. U-boat warfare in Atlantic
intensifies. Churchill and Roosevelt meet at
Casablanca, demand "Unconditional Surrender."
German troops surrender at Stalingrad. Rostov and
Karkov recaptured by Russian troops. German
resistance ends in North Africa. Canadian troops to
see action at last.*

Nothing appeared unusual one morning when Chris Vokes, our brigade commander, stuck his nose into my office at our HQ, near Eastbourne, and mentioned that he was going up to London for a couple of days. The units in the brigade were to carry on with their routine training programs — no special events were scheduled — and I was to take charge while Chris was away. Had I been a bit more suspicious, I might have been alert that something was up from Chris's clear direction that I was not to inform the COs of the units in the brigade that he was absent. As for the brigade staff, he would simply be on a short leave.

I thought little about Chris's leave till three days later, when he telephoned me mysteriously from London. I was to ask no questions but was to report to London myself by 1000 hours, the next morning. I was to go to the Bank of Montreal to get some money, a normal procedure for Canadian officers arriving in London on leave. All officers' pay was deposited there.

Someone would meet me at the bank and give me further instructions. That was all Chris would tell me. I was not to inform the unit COs that I would be away as well. Sammy McLean, our staff captain, could sign any necessary orders during my absence. Presumably, the other officers on the staff would assume that Chris and I were taking advantage of a dull period for a brief toot in town together . . . not an unreasonable assumption.

Arriving in London rather puzzled, I first checked into my regular flat at Old St. James's House, 7 Park Place, and then wandered over to the bank when it opened. As I began writing out a cheque, an officer I had not seen before sauntered over and quietly gave me my next instructions. I was to go back to my flat, remove brigade patches and Canada shoulder titles from my uniform, then take a taxi and head toward Norfolk House, an insurance building in St. James's Square. The taxi should not go straight to the building but should drop me off three or four blocks away. I was to walk the remaining distance. With all this mystery, I suddenly understood that something real was afoot.

129

Since the war, an historic plaque has been placed on the side of Norfolk House, recording that this building served as the secret Allied Planning HQ during World War II.

For the next three weeks, together with other selected officers of the 1st Division as well as staff officers from the navy, air force, combined-ops and the marine commandos, I would be working all day and long into the night, completing detailed plans for the invasion of Sicily.

The security was extremely tight. Half the staff were working on totally different plans, for an invasion elsewhere on the continent — a cover plan. No one knew which plan was the real one, which was the cover. We each received a coloured identification card, indicating to the guards on the doors which part of the building each officer could enter. From the coloured markings, an officer would also know to whom he could or could not talk about his work. There could be no comparing of notes between sections. Some officers would know the exact size and composition of the forces to be moved and deployed, but not the actual destination or identify of units. Other officers would know one of the target areas — either the real one or the cover area — and have maps and aerial photographs to plan the deployment of troops and support services, but they would not know the exact date.

Every office had a double baize door. The outer one had to be closed before the second could be opened, to avoid any chance of someone in the hallway seeing a wall map or chart, or hearing any words of conversation. The windows were heavily draped with baize cloth to prevent any view from outside buildings.

That first morning I was briefed by a senior British officer from combined-ops. I was to be in charge of planning for the 2nd Brigade group which, together with our three infantry battalions, the Patricias, the Seaforth Highlanders and the Edmonton Regiment, was to include 12 other units: the 39th Field Regiment RCA, a battery of light AA artillery, engineers, the 50th and 51st British Marine Commandos, and so forth.

I was then told that our divisional commander, General Harry Salmon, had been killed when his plane was shot down the previous day, while he was flying out for a conference in Cairo with General Montgomery of the 8th Army.

No one had yet been appointed to replace him, but my brigade commander, Chris Vokes, together with the GI of the division, Lieutenant-Colonel George Kitching, had just left by plane that morning to cover for the Canadians at the Cairo conference.

There was a brief security flap due to the possibility that General Salmon might have been carrying written details of Operation Husky when his plane crashed, but these fears proved unfounded. Whether true or not I can't confirm, but a story circulated that an Intelligence study of this plane crash provided some of the ideas for the subsequent ruse to mislead the Germans in the "Man Who Never Was" incident. In that scenario, a body dressed in a British officer's uniform was dropped in the ocean, where the currents would bring it to shore to be recovered by the Germans. The uniform and despatch case carried by the officer were partly burned, creating the idea of a plane crashing. The fake orders carried in the briefcase, when fished from the ocean, succeeded in misleading the Germans.*

I did not know for certain whether the plans I was to work on at Norfolk House were for the actual operation or the cover plan, but it was quite clear that, after the long period of inactivity, this was the real thing for our division.

I was to be in charge of drawing up plans and operation orders for the 2nd Infantry Brigade, covering the movement to Scotland of our brigade together with all its attached units and the carrying out of an "embarkation for a 'long sea voyage' for an assault landing on an enemy held coast." The planning would be of considerable complexity. Some 92 ships, exclusive of escort vessels and RN support craft, would be employed for our division alone. An American division, embarked from the U.S., would join us at sea, together with British divisions sailing from Cairo and various North African ports. The combined convoys would rendezvous at night and then make a run in the dark for the shores of Sicily. We would be employing, for the first time, all the newly designed U.S. assault landing craft, in ferrying our troops from the big ships to the beaches in assault formation. Under command, on our immediate left, would be two Royal Marine Commando units to deal with enemy coast defence guns sited on cliffs rising from our beach. Further to our left would be the 1st U.S. Infantry Division. On our brigade right would be the 1st Canadian Infantry Brigade, with British units further to the right.

Complicating the landing would be the fact that our assault troops would have to be supplied across open beaches, as no harbour installations were to be captured in the early stages. The overall plan called for simultaneous assaults in the areas of Palermo and Catania, an alteration on the original concept.

Loading of the great convoy called for exact tactical planning so that, in the dark, first priority equipment and supplies would reach the beaches in correct sequence. Both loading and operational plans had to allow for the contingency that some of our ships might be sunk before reaching the anchorage area; the assault program *had* to proceed.

Provision was also to be made for split convoys; ships of different speeds would sail on schedules which would bring them all together in the target area at the correct time and in the correct sequence.

Needless to say, at the briefing I was a trifle awed when I realized that, in the absence of Chris Vokes, I was to have the responsibility of drawing up the 2nd Brigade plans and orders. I was a mere major then — and 1st and 3rd Brigade plans would be co-ordinated by Brigadier-General Howard Graham and Brigadier-General Howard Penhale, respectively, both of whom had seen active service in World War I.

Throwing divisions, corps and even entire armies gaily about in Staff College exercises had been great fun and games — but this one, I realized, was not a game.

It would not be possible to record all the problems and late night conferences that followed in the next few weeks at Norfolk House, as we worked long hours under heavy pressure, with endless changes made to

*Details for this deception are given in *The Man Who Never Was*, by Lieutenant-Colonel Ewen Montagu, and also form the basis of the novel *Operation Heartbreak*, by Duff Cooper.

loading schedules and equipment switched to minimum scales for various units. Detailed studies of recent air photographs and new ship allocations meant ongoing revisions in our plans.

To meet this workload, most of the officers, like myself, adopted a routine of having a short lunch and shower at the Royal Automobile Club, which was nearby, then breaking again for a snack about 6 p.m., and then working right through till midnight or later, when we would go to some all-night club for dinner and a few drinks before rolling into bed.

Major Dick Danby of Vancouver, who was a divisional staff officer at the time, frequently joined me for a late supper at either Kempinsky's or the Liaison Club, which was upstairs off one of the arcades on Piccadilly. Two incidents remain in my memory of that period. Although quite minor, they tell something of London's wartime picture.

At Kempinsky's restaurant, the excellent pianist, named George, played all night long. Whatever the customers wished, he would play — from ragtime to arias from Grand Opera, which he would also sing with gusto. Frequently he would pick up the pretty little cigarette girl, seat her on the top of the grand piano and then dramatically sing passionate love songs to her. The 16-year-old youngster, with her cheery little face, was a great favourite of all the patrons. One night, George asked for silence and announced the engagement of the youngster to a blushing young RAF officer. There was great cheering and congratulations from all around the room, and champagne was ordered for the young couple.

A week later, I was at Kempinsky's again and noted that the little girl in her fluffy skirt and tights was missing. The room somehow seemed more subdued. George had lost his bounce and sparkle. The young pilot, the girl's fiancé, had been shot down two nights after the engagement party. The little match girl never came back to Kempinsky's — they didn't know where she had gone.

At the Liaison Club one evening when a heavy air raid was in progress, Dick Danby and I arrived for a late bite of supper well after midnight. There was never a menu, just a single hot dish which you ordered while you had a drink at the little bar, then took to a table. There was an elderly little civilian at the bar when Dick and I gave our order. When our drinks were served, he very politely asked if we would have the drinks on him. We thanked him but pleasantly refused the offer. He insisted, however, so we agreed — if he would have the next one on us.

The building was shaken at intervals by nearby bomb blasts, before our plates of supper arrived. By then we were on friendly terms with the man, but wondered what he was doing out at that hour.

When we left the bar to find a spot for our plates, the little Englishman pressed us to come over to his table and meet his wife. To our amazement he steered us over to a table in the corner, where he introduced us to a delightful old girl who was sitting there, quite unconcerned about the crash of bombs and heavy crumps of AA guns.

They were a very jovial, well-spoken old couple and we had a pleasant supper together and several rounds of drinks. We didn't ask any questions, but around two in the morning decided to get off to our beds. The little man then insisted that he drive us to our billets. We felt certain he must be a bit drunk — there would be no chance of finding a taxi in the dark at that hour while an air raid was on. Oh no, he said, he had his own car. "The old boy's really corked," I whispered to Dick. "We will have to see that they get home somehow." Civilians couldn't get patrol coupons for driving about at night; and even if he had a car we couldn't let him drive it, with fire trucks and air-raid wardens racing about between the rubble.

We jollied the old couple along down the elevator into the dark, where we were amazed to find a limousine and a chauffeur waiting for our new-found friends. We prevailed on the driver to drop the old couple off first, to see them safely home; then we were driven to our own billets in style. When we had said good-bye to the old boy, he asked us to join him for dinner at the Savoy on the following Thursday evening.

When Thursday rolled around, Danby and I were both inclined to ignore the invitation, feeling quite certain that our new friend would have forgotten all about his invitation. Still, we didn't wish to see the old boy stood-up, so we decided to wander down to the Savoy for a drink, just in case. If he didn't show we could go on for supper by ourselves. But our elderly Liaison Club friends were waiting for us and gave us a tremendous dinner, complete with champagne, brandy and cigars.

Our host, we discovered, was a Mr. James F. Stewart, who was head of Imperial Chemicals or something. Despite his age the British government had co-opted him for the duration of the war, to take charge of some munitions and supply division of the War Department, and he had to be in London every day. His children were all grown up and away.

Rather than sit by herself in the country, Mrs. Stewart had decided to stay in London despite the air raids, simply to be with her husband who, like ourselves, worked late into the evening at his war job. Then instead of listening to the bombs fall each night alone in her apartment, she would join her husband for a late supper at one of the all-night clubs with the young people in the services.

One made strange and chance friendships in wartime London. It was Britain at her best. Gone was the normal peacetime reserve and aloofness. In the common threat and shared dangers, there was a new friendliness. People were able to exchange a cheery word and make new friends . . . even with Canadians, Americans and Poles. It was a Britain all veterans remember.

As our invasion plans started to take final shape, it was suddenly announced that the next day General Alan Brooke, the CIGS himself, together with Lord Louis Mountbatten, head of combined-ops, and other war lords, would visit Norfolk House, at which time each of the brigade plans would be presented by their respective commanders for vetting and approval or otherwise. I was even more shaken to be told that my presentation would be the first, to be followed by Graham's and Penhale's.

The momentous day arrived and I tried to appear relaxed and full of confidence as I stepped up on the dais, before enlarged maps and air photos, to face several rows of hard-faced admirals and frigid generals.

I must now confess that the lessons from the Staff College, which seemed rather useless at the time, carried me through the ordeal. When I sat down not a word of comment was offered, not a question was asked. Perhaps my presentation had been so frightful that it was beyond or beneath comment by the gods. Graham was called next and then Pen.

I was wondering whether perhaps I should do the decent thing and go out and quietly shoot myself, when the director of operational planning took the floor and announced that the plans for 2nd Brigade were approved without change. I had an extra whisky that night at the "Haywire" Club.

There was one serious problem, however, about our landing plans, which caused us a great deal of worry. The air photographs clearly showed a long sand bar, just off our beach about a hundred yards from shore. The marine maps indicated that the depth of water over the bar at the time of landing would be only four-and-one-half feet. Unhappily, the draft or clearance of the small LCAs and LCMs required to ferry our troops ashore, was also four-and-one-half feet. Could the naval charts be trusted? Was there possibly only a three- or four-foot clearance over the sand bar? Would all our landing craft become stranded a hundred yards off shore and become sitting ducks when dawn broke?

More charts were called for and more air photos were taken, but no one could give us assurance that the depth would be at least four-and-one-half feet. So important was this point, it was decided that a British submarine would be sent out immediately to check the beach. It would surface at night, put some men in a rubber dinghy, and they would do an actual measurement. The men would then hide out on the beach till the following evening, when the sub would return to take them off.

The men would wear simple seamen's dark sweaters and bags showing no RN identification. If by bad luck they were captured, their cover story would be that they were survivors of a recently torpedoed merchant ship.

Several nights later the survey crew was landed by the sub off the shores of Sicily, but that was the end of them. For several nights following, the sub returned for the men, but they never showed. We were back where we started with our problem, and the seamen were likely prisoners; would this blow security? Would they be forced to talk?

It was then that some scientific bloke or professor was sent over to us from the War Office. He brought with him special viewers, calipers and other measuring instruments and went to work on our photographs. By determining the height of the photo plane, the wind direction, the distance between waves over the sand bar, and so forth, he came up with the surprising but absolute assurance that there would be precisely four-and-one-half feet of water over the bar at the time of our landing. We thought he was just a bit mad, but who was to contradict him? We had to take it on trust.

It should be recorded that during the event, when our LCMs did race in the dark toward the Sicily beaches, a few of them bumped lightly as they scraped over the bar. The old boy was dead right.

At last all the hundreds of operation orders, maps, scale models for briefing troops and supply schedules for every unit were completed at Norfolk House. They were packaged up for delivery under guard to each ship in the great convoy, then to be assembled in Scotland. These sealed orders would only be opened and distributed when the ships were 48 hours at sea. Then each battalion, right down to platoon levels, would be carefully briefed as to its exact role in the assault. Every service unit, vehicle repair depot, casualty clearing station and engineer section would be shown on the maps and models exactly what was expected.

Meanwhile, all our units were already secretly on the move to Scotland, by rail and road, along with their equipment. The move out of

Sussex for security reasons was at night with very little advance warning, except to key personnel. Not even tradesmen's accounts in nearby towns were to be settled before departure. They would be cleared up by the Acton records' office, some time later. New troops would occupy our old brigade billets and areas at Pevensey, Polegate, Eastbourne and Seaford. To the locals, it would simply appear as a normal relief for an exercise.

While I had been responsible for drawing up the complex movement orders for Scotland, the entire responsibility for co-ordinating the actual move of our brigade group was, in the absence of both Chris Vokes and myself, carried out by three bright young men on our Brigade HQ: Jim McMullen of Vancouver, John Brophy of Winnipeg and Freddy Reesor of Edmonton. They did an amazing job. Everyone, together with his equipment, arrived at the right areas in Scotland: Inveraray, Hamilton, Gourock or wherever. Tragically, both McMullen and Brophy would be killed in action during the Italian campaign.

To ensure that nothing had been overlooked, it was planned to carry out a final 48-hour assault exercise just before we sailed. Orders for this exercise, based as closely as possible on the actual Husky operation, had been drawn up simultaneously at Norfolk House. Every unit would embark on the same ships it would use for the real invasion, as well as landing from the same type of craft and in the proper formations. Each platoon commander and lorry driver would get to know the boat crews he had to work with and the routine for clearing the beaches on landing.

While these moves to Scotland were in progress, Chris Vokes and George Kitching arrived back from Cairo, after an unscheduled, emergency stopover in Portugal. Portugal being a neutral country, the men had been forced to hide their head gear and take any badges off their raincoats, as they had no civy clothes with them. After they spent two days wearing raincoats and trying to look like civilians, the British embassy was able to get them on a civilian plane back to England. At this time, it was also announced that my long-time friend, Guy Simonds, had been appointed to command the division, to replace Harry Salmon.

After tidying up the final details at Norfolk House, Chris and I caught a train back to Eastbourne, to pick up the rest of our belongings and close out our old headquarters. We would then make the run to Scotland on the Sunday night train, to arrive in time for the final brigade exercise.

En route to Eastbourne, Chris filled me in on his meetings in Cairo and briefed me about the form with Monty and the 8th Army, which we would be joining shortly.

Amongst other oddities, they had practically done away with all written orders in the 8th Army. Everything was done verbally at O-Groups, with only brief chinagraph notes made on the map boards and map traces supplied by Intelligence sections. In the matter of dress while fighting, Monty and his 8th Army officers had gone completely informal — everything from neck scarves, used when needed to prevent breathing sand and dust, to corduroy bags, sweaters, odd head gear, long Arab sheepskin coats or U.S. Air Force jackets. For the feet, the fashion was suede desert boots or "brothel creepers," as they were called.

It all followed the old tradition of the English gentleman at war. In peacetime, protocol and correct dress were everything for the regular British officer. But, as explained in a brief manual issued by Debret's Peerage, war is not treated quite so seriously. It dictates a more sporting approach . . . rather like a grouse shoot. The rules of dress are rather forgotten. The officer wears his most comfortable clothes and adopts his most casual manner.

All this was rather distressing news, as the only costumes Chris and I would have for the dusty roads and heat of Sicily would be our regulation army-issue shorts and bush shirts. The next day being Sunday, there would be no chance of any shopping before going to the embarkation areas in Scotland. We would clearly look like the new boys at school when we joined the fabled 8th Army.

It took all Sunday morning to clear out the paper and records at our old HQ, turn over to the new brigade the traces of the mine fields on beaches and other essential data. As for our own personal gear, the trick was to divide everything up into duplicate kit bags, one of which would go with us, the other to follow on a supply convoy due in Sicily on D + 30. The object was that if your original kit got bashed up or lost on the landing, a complete refill might be available in 30 days' time. The duplicate kit bag would contain all the essentials — a second razor, tooth brush, carton of cigarettes, bottle of whisky, plus a fresh shirt and fresh underwear. A very wise precaution, as it turned out.

Having completed all these details, with an hour or two to spare before our train left Eastbourne, I got in a jeep and drove over to the little village of West Dean to have a farewell drink with Jack and Sandra Dunfee. They had become fast friends during my Sussex posting, and while I could not tell them I was leaving, I was anxious to thank them for their hospitality.

While enjoying a drink with them, I suddenly had a thought. "Jack, you don't happen to have a spare pair of corduroy bags?" I asked. Indeed he did, and without knowing the reason for my enquiry he was quite ready to loan them to me. He brought them down . . . but it was no go. They were miles too big for me. At this, Sandra said she had a new pair she would gladly lend me if urgent, and she produced a lovely pair of tailored bags made of pale fawn corduroy. The only problem was that, being made for a girl, there was no fly; instead, they had a sort of buttoned-up flap in front. I hesitated for a moment but then, what the hell; no one would notice. Besides, this was the only chance I had of getting some bags before we sailed. I accepted Sandra's kind offer and took them along.

For some strange reason it seems that fashion has always been important on the battlefield: the cloaks and plumes of the Crusaders under King Richard, the lace and silver buckles of Prince Rupert's Cavaliers. In World War I, it was the fashion for commanders to lead their troops over the top in trench raids, nonchalantly armed with only a swagger stick or cane.

The equivalent style for officers in the Desert Rats and other formations in the 8th Army at that time was a horse tail switch, hanging from a thong on the wrist and indolently used to brush away the flies and other insects. These switches were particularly in evidence in the midst of heavy enemy shelling, or when one went casually forward to check out a brewed up tank that had run into "a spot of bother." Despite the unorthodox fashion and flair of the 8th Army, most of the fads had a very practical application and had counterparts in the dress of Rommel's Africa corps.

136

Off the Ayrshire coast, the big exercise came off in great style. With a cold wind blowing in the North Sea, thousands of Canadian troops, weighed down with full battle equipment, extra bandoliers of ammunition and grenades, clambered down huge scrambling nets in the dark. Leaping into hundreds of small landing craft bouncing about in the heavy sea, the troops made for the rough coast of Scotland, eight miles away.

Then, wading through the salt water shallows, we made brave rushes across the beaches, followed by a tactical advance inland in the bitterly cold morning. We climbed over the moors and glens for hours in wet battle dress, and I still don't understand why the entire division didn't wind up with pneumonia.

When we finally occupied a defensive position, about noon, and tried to get some warmth back in our limbs, I noticed that my long-time friend Alan Embury, 2 i/c of the Saskatoon Light Infantry, our support battalion, was missing. He had been attached to our Brigade HQ as an observer officer for the exercise. Alan, a lawyer in civilian life, was wise in the ways of the army and had read all the King's Regulations and Orders.

Coming ashore with me in an LCM, he had insisted on wearing his great coat and muffler, as well as bringing along his batman, and taking his bed roll, folding camp bed and other such comforts of home. He was adamant on the point that his orders were "to observe," not participate or get wet and sleep on the ground. Knowing the impossibility of winning any argument with Embury, I put up with his nonsense.

When our assault craft had grounded about 25 yards off shore in the dark, Embury had waited till everyone else had jumped off and the boat was lighter, then ordered the midshipman to take the boat closer into shore for him. He carefully placed his bed roll and other comforts on his batman's head, and then, holding up the skirt of his great coat, he started to tippy-toe to the dry beach.

Seemingly the tides, currents or underground streams can cause irregularities in a beach. Whatever it was, Embury and his batman, complete with bed roll, after walking a few steps, simply sank out of sight in the cold water.

Once I had seen them crawl safely up on the shale, dripping wet, I had got on with the imaginary war. But now that our defensive positions were secured several miles inland, I felt I should roust out Embury. Who knows? We might have to call up some supporting four-inch mortar fire to defend our positions at night.

A short distance ahead of our position, tucked away in a little glen — supposedly in enemy hands — was a small Scottish village. Following my suspicions, I took a saunter over to the little collection of houses. As I suspected, Embury, following procedures covered in the military manuals, had formally billeted himself on the natives, giving the householder a correctly drawn memo of requisition. He had also managed to requisition a bottle of whisky. Having drunk this, to ward off any chill, he had taken off all his wet clothes and gotten into bed with his muffler tied around his tummy for some strange reason.

When I had shaken him awake he explained, in all particulars, a paragraph from a new army pamphlet he had just received, *Care of Troops in the Desert*. According to this pamphlet, although it might be very hot during the day in desert areas, it could be extremely cold at night; one should be very careful to wrap up warmly before going to

137

sleep. Special care should be given to the kidneys because if they got cold, one could catch beri beri or jaundice or something equally horrible. The only dry garment Embury had was his muffler, so obviously it had to be worn around his kidneys. I might add in passing that the warning of jaundice proved to be entirely valid in the months ahead.

Another body which had been missing when I had established wireless contact with all units once we were ashore, was that of the CO of the Royal Marine Commandos. When I had called in code on the wireless for "Sunray to set," I had been able to raise only a cockney seaman who gave me some double talk about Sunray not being available, or not being able to speak.

Finally, I caught up to the boss marine commando and explained to him, in no uncertain terms, that when HQ called Sunray to the set, we expected to speak to him or, if he were dead, then to whatever officer had taken his place — not some bloody naval rating.

The dashing marine CO loftily advised me that in the Royal Marines, as in the Royal Navy, officers did not waffle on the wireless. Signals were always transmitted for them by signal ratings. Their officers didn't even understand wireless procedure.

In that case, I observed, he had better get busy and learn wireless procedure in the next 24 hours — because while he was under command of an infantry brigade, he would damn well speak on the blower when he was called. I didn't care to run the risk of units shooting each other up in the dark just because he didn't understand wireless transmission in code.

He listened to me, but I didn't feel my remarks had quite gotten through to him.

"Oh, don't worry old boy, I'll keep in touch with you on the beach," he said as he left.

By the time this exercise was over, with both equipment personnel and live ammunition divided up into assault and light-scale echelons and all vehicles being re-waterproofed for landing in salt water, it was now obvious to everyone that a real show was in the offing. Though none of the units yet knew our actual destination, all concentration areas were sealed off. With the issue of shorts and bush shirts, however, the guessing was the Mediterranean, either Sardinia or even Yugoslavia.

A Farewell Visitor

The final night of our exercise an officer, wearing a waterproof turned up at the collar, his head jutting forward and his hands in his coat pockets, made his way through the dark to our Tac HQ, which was established in a bluff of trees. As he drew near, I was surprised to see that it was General Andy McNaughton, our Canadian Army Commander. There were no formalities about his arrival. He spoke quietly, saying he just wished to know how our exercise had gone. We sat down together on the ground, and he listened carefully while I reviewed several of our difficulties, such as making wireless contact with the marine commando units and marching in wet battle dress. Clearly he had come to say good-bye to the 1st Division as it left his army command and to wish us well.

It was the division he had commanded himself and taken overseas early in the war. While he had opposed any breaking up of his command, he was genuinely anxious to see us do well when we joined Monty's 8th

Army. He showed no bitterness. He had been assured that after the experience of the Sicily landing, the division would be returning to rejoin his command in time for the Normandy invasion.

The following day our new divisional commander, Guy Simonds, arrived at our brigade to carry out a personal inspection of the units. Guy had a pretty cold and intimidating manner, and Chris Vokes was a trifle concerned about how Jefferson, who was commanding the Edmonton Regiment, would stand up under Guy's brittle inspection. Not that Jefferson wasn't competent — quite the reverse — but he had a retiring, soft-spoken manner and took a bit of knowing. Like the men under his command, our brigade staff had come to recognize that Jefferson was well endowed with a combination of determination, ability and a great deal of common sense. He could be relied on absolutely.

Chris sent word down to Jeff at the Edmontons to take a double whisky and speak out when Simonds came to inspect his outfit. The inspection did not go well, however, and on his return to Brigade HQ, Simonds was adamant that not only should Jefferson be removed before the assault, but so also should the COs of two other units in our brigade group: a Major Welch, commanding an anti-tank battery, and one other CO, whose name escapes me.

Both Chris and I argued strongly against these last-minute changes. Bringing in new COs who had not been through the training exercises with their troops was too risky. Besides, these three men were surely entitled to a fair show before being condemned.

Guy remained unmoved, but with great credit Chris, in his blunt manner, stuck with his point. Finally he elicited from Simonds a grudging consent that the three COs should be given their chance in action. If in the first week they didn't stack up, Chris would undertake to fire them himself. As it happened, Simonds' snap judgment proved to be completely wrong. Once in action, Jefferson quickly proved to be one of the best COs in the division and subsequently won a DSO and promotion to brigadier.

Welch, when he got into action, showed us how to shoot up German tanks by moving his guns up with the advance guard, and quickly earned for himself the title of "Tiger" Welch.

The night before the final embarkation, all our units decided to throw farewell parties, and Chris and I received pressing invitations to all the different messes. Obviously, it was our duty to cover as many as possible. Taking a safe driver with us, we covered the glens and highlands, attending all the parties we could. The evening ended for us at the Seaforths' mess, where everyone was dancing eightsome reels and "strip the willow" in their kilts, to the howl of the bagpipes.

No sooner had we arrived than we were divested of our battle dress, adorned in kilts, and propelled into the whirling dances. My particular problem lay in the fact that I have always found Scotland in the early spring perishingly cold, and was wearing some marvellous long Canadian underwear beneath my battle dress. I did my best to roll up the legs of the underwear beneath my kilt, but it required only a couple of swings and turns and they dropped to my ankles. In part, this was due to the vigour of the dancing, as the Seaforths had managed to locate a fine, healthy crew of Scottish WRENS at a nearby naval station. They were all buxom lasses, used to rowing dorries out to the lighthouses in the Irish Sea. After nearly being swung clear through the walls of the dance hall a dozen times by several of the women, who were clearly in finer physical shape than ourselves, I began to think that they should be the ones to assault the shores of Sicily. Either by Divine guidance or the luck of Irish origins, both Vokes and I somehow or other managed to find our beds that evening and to embark in good order the next morning on HMS *Circassia*.

Operation Husky

After the many weeks of long and exhausting hours at Norfolk House, then the pressures of the move to Scotland, with a full-scale landing exercise, it was a relief to climb into my narrow bunk on the *Circassia* for a decent sleep at last. No more last-minute changes could be made; the die was cast and wireless silence had been ordered.

As luck would have it, I found myself appointed OC of the ship. Happily, this job does not involve one in any way in the operation of the ship itself. The OC ship, however, was responsible for working out rotating meal schedules on board as well as all discipline, boat drills, exercise periods and so forth, for the thousands of troops jammed between decks. While one group would do PT on deck, another crowd would be feeding, while a third group would be receiving a detailed operational briefing, with air photographs, from their own officers. A fourth group, waiting their turn to get up on deck, would spend the time in crowded passageways and holds, shooting crap or playing poker.

Fortunately, after the first day at sea I was able to off-load much of this work onto the shoulders of our able staff captain, Sammy McLean of Montreal, and to duty officers appointed by each of the various units. I then relaxed to enjoy the cruise, while watching, with fascination, the forming up of our enormous convoy at sea, complete with battleships, destroyers, corvettes and even a couple of submarines as escorts — a staggering spectacle.

The plot was that our convoy, which could not be concealed, was to head for Malta, simulating the regular monthly Malta convoy. The Malta convoys were regularly attacked by both German U-boats and torpedo bombers from Nazi bases in Italy and the south of France. Our real destination, it was hoped, would not be discovered. Other, similar convoys from New York, Malta and Cairo, Tripoli, Algiers and elsewhere in North Africa were to join us in the dark, someplace south of Malta; at this time the long line of ships, with their escorts, would carry out a marvellous counter march or pirouette, and head for the beaches of Sicily, through some mine fields. Thank God, I didn't have to be involved with any aspects of that great production.

The flag ship for the actual assault on the beaches was the *Hilary*. She would serve as a combined army and naval HQ afloat for the first 48 hours of the attack, with direct communication with the assault battalions and the Beach Master, till a Tactical Division HQ could be safely established ashore. Support fire would come from the battleship flotilla leaders of the assault boats, as well as from the RAF air cover.

General Simonds and a portion of his divisional staff were embarked on the *Hilary*. Our own ship, the *Circassia*, which was equipped and organized as an assault landing ship, was the convoy leader for Force V; her skipper, Commodore Sir David Bone, was responsible for co-ordinating the movement of troopships and merchant supply ships until we reached the anchorage area off the Sicily coast.

About the second day at sea, when my own ship job was fairly sorted out, a ship's orderly came to my cabin with an invitation to join Sir David for a pre-dinner drink in his cabin. With all his convoy responsibilities, I had rather expected to find the commodore a great burly seadog of middle age, with a well-tailored beard. To the contrary; he was a short, elderly, soft-spoken man, with several rows of faded medal ribbons on his double-breasted reefer.

To my further surprise, I learned that he was a brother of my old friend James Bone, editor of the Manchester *Guardian*. Like Jim, he had a kindly twinkle in his eye and talked with a Scot's accent in short, abrupt sentences. As we sipped a whisky, I found it hard to convince myself that this was the man responsible for all the complex shipping manoeuvres needed to land us at H-hour on the right beach in the dark.

Very gently, I touched on the importance of hitting the right beach, so that we could get a bearing on Pachino airfield and link up properly with the Americans on our left. I also enquired about a new mine field, which had been detected in the latest air photos, just before we sailed.

"Oh, the army's always concerned about hitting the proper beach," the old boy replied. "Don't worry, we'll land you right on the target."

After a further taste of the whisky, he continued. "The Scots Greys got all steamed up once, about landing their horses. They tried to lower them with slings, into the landing barges, but the waves tossed the barges about so badly, they broke all the horses' legs. We had to show them how to do it. We just dropped the horses overboard and they swam to shore."

It was an interesting yarn, but obviously he was talking about World War I, when cavalry was still in fashion. "Were you commanding a ship then at the landings in Gallipoli, Sir?" I asked. "No, no, it was during the Boer War," he replied, in very matter of fact tones. "I had a sailing ship, of course, in those days."

At this point, I really did begin to worry. I thought of all the complexities of our forthcoming landing of waterproofed tanks, Bren carriers, great artillery pieces and hundreds of loaded lorries, over open beaches and much of this dependent upon a skipper who had unbelievably commanded a sailing ship in the days of the Boer War. In the words of Admiral of the Fleet, Sir A. B. Cunningham, Allied Naval Commander in the Mediterranean, "this would be the greatest seaborne attack that has so far taken place in history."

My fears proved quite unnecessary, but at this point a few words about Sir David are in order. Between wars he sailed the seven seas as commodore of the Anchor Line, from which service he was immediately recalled by the Admiralty when each war broke out. In his sailing days he had been a long-time friend of the author Joseph Conrad and was familiar with ports in all quarters of the globe. In World War I he commanded various ships.*

I was to see the commodore many times again during the war, in the harbours of Manila, Algiers and Naples.

Sir David's ship was well known to the Allied troops of many countries, as both an assault landing craft and troop transport. The *Circassia*, at

---

*The story of these adventures are recorded in Sir David's excellent books, *Landfall at Sunset*, *The Brass Bounder*, and *Merchantman Re-armed*, some editions being illustrated by his equally distinguished brother, Sir Muirhead Bone, a member of the Royal Academy and official Admiralty artist.

various times during the war, carried British, Canadian, American, Dutch, Polish, Indian, Russian and French soldiers, and Japanese and German prisoners. Apart from the landings in Sicily and Calabria, Sir David landed Americans for Operation Torch, American rangers at Anzio, and French forces for Operation Bigot. He had delivered troops and supplies, often unescorted, to Singapore and Manila, had made the run to Odessa, and had sailed up the river to Saigon in Indochina. There was little that this merchant seaman didn't know about the sea. His career at sea dated back to 1890 and covered the days of the square riggers, when he served as mate in rounding the Horn.

Whenever I saw his ship in port, I would send out a signal inviting him to shore for dinner with me. But my invitations were always rejected. His reply was always the same: "Come aboard and dine with me. Only mean and miserable people live on land." The sea had always been his home. He had little love for the land or for landlubbers.

Various times later, in naval circles, I heard him referred to as "the only skipper who boarded his ship by wireless." To disguise my ignorance, I refrained from ever asking him the meaning of this curious label. The story, however, is related in one of his books.

In World War I, while commanding a large troopship sailing from Marseilles, loaded with troops for the Dardenelles, his ship had been torpedoed and sunk. Before sinking beneath the waves, Sir David had managed to get all the troops and all but a dozen of his ship's crew safely off in lifeboats and rafts. His ship was then making her final plunge, stern first, into the depths. At this point, the commander of a small destroyer swung the stern of his ship beneath the upturned prow of the trooper, and the remaining crew were able to scramble off with ropes and drop to the deck of the destroyer, leaving Sir David still on his bridge, directing operations.

Then, as the troopship slid below the waves, the suction dragged the destroyer alongside, and her wireless mast briefly brushed the bridge of the sinking ship — "like the finger of God," to use Bone's own words. In that brief moment, Sir David seized the wireless mast and was slung clear — hanging high in the air, but saved.

When he was finally "beached" about 1947, he retired to share a cottage with his brother Jim, who had also retired, from the *Guardian*, in the village of Tilford, in Surrey. I made a pilgrimage to see them both in Surrey several times before they died, at great ages. A young housekeeper was taking care of them. On my last visit, just before leaving I took the young housekeeper aside and asked her how it was going. "Don't worry," she said. "They get difficult at times, but I'll see them both out." She did.

NINE

Sicily — D-Day

WORLD SCENE
*RAF Squadron bombs Rhur Valley dams — U-boat
crisis in Atlantic overcome. U.S. forces drive Japanese
troops from Alaskan island of Attu. Malta fights for
survival against heavy German air raids — Canadian
troops join Monty's 8th Army.*

As our great convoy approached Gibraltar we encountered some real heat at last. Under the blistering sun, the troops lost no time in stripping off their kit to catch a tan, with memories of Canadian summers seemingly ages ago.

Before the day was out, an order had to be issued to prevent cases of serious sunburn. With a blistered back, it would be impossible to pack heavy loads of kit and equipment ashore. Benefitting from similar experiences on troop movements to the Middle East, the order read that any man unable to carry a pack due to sunburn would be charged with willfully making himself unfit for action.

In the cool of the evening, I decided it was about time to sport my newly acquired corduroy bags. There were many envious glances and I felt quite superior, until Chris, with his customary tact, said, "those look like women's pants." Outraged at such an ill-mannered suggestion, I assured him that this was the latest design for desert operations. I don't think Chris ever discovered where I got them.

On a more sober note, we came under several heavy attacks by torpedo bombers of the German Luftwaffe shortly after we cleared the Straits. We had issued incendiary and tracer ammunition for all the automatic weapons on the ship, and they all joined in the curtain of fire put up by AA guns of the ships in the convoy.

I don't think we got any of the German planes, but the intense fire did succeed in driving off the attacks. Three of our ships, the *Devis*, *St. Essylt* and the *City of Venice*, were sunk. The other ships were forbidden to break convoy or halt to pick up survivors. There wasn't much gaiety in the mess halls that night, as we speculated as to which of our pals we had left swimming in the ocean.

As a precaution, I had taken with me, written out in my own code and symbols, a rough breakdown of the cargoes of both equipment and personnel on each ship. We had lost some of our 25-pounders, some anti-tank guns, and all of our wireless vehicles. This meant we would be entirely dependent on the small pack wireless sets we carried ashore, to keep in touch with our units for some weeks, till our wireless vehicles could be replaced.

Well, there was nothing I could do about it at this stage. We would have to worry about replacements after the landing.

I was aware that our division was being detached from the Canadian Army only on a temporary basis, to get battle experience with the veteran 8th British Army, primarily on the insistence of Canada's Defence Minister, Ralston. The main Allied thrust across the Channel was not to be launched till next year. We were to return to England as assault troops for that invasion.

But as Colonel Ralston confided to me later, there were other considerations in his mind at that time. He was haunted by the risk of having the entire Canadian Army launched across the beaches of Normandy, without any real battle experience. From his experience in World War I, he knew this was too great a gamble, regardless of McNaughton's dreams. Further, he was nagged by the possibility that Germany might suddenly collapse or capitulate, and the war would end with our highly trained army never having fired a shot, an army for which he was responsible to Parliament and the nation.

Although it was true that, up till that time, the Canadian Army could only record such discouraging diversions as Hong Kong and Dieppe and guard duties in the south coast of England, Bermuda, Newfoundland and Kiska, nevertheless our national stature was never higher in world terms. Our contribution in the air with the RAF, the RCAF and the vast Empire Air Training Scheme was widely recognized. At sea, the Canadian Navy had come of age overnight and, together with the Royal Navy, carried a full share in keeping the vital convoys moving across the Atlantic, to supply not only Britain but also the Middle East and Russia. Britons had not forgotten, that after the fall of France, their only effective ally for a time had been Canada.

But now the picture would change. The enormous resources of the United States in manpower and munitions were starting to pour into Europe and the Pacific theatres of war. Although Canada's early and whole-hearted contribution to the war effort had been vital at the most critical point, its importance now would start to wane.

What I was not aware of, as I walked the deck of the *Circassia* during those few peaceful and sunny days, was the fact that the British High Command, after careful assessment and trials, had reluctantly come to the conclusion that Canada's Army Commander, General McNaughton, despite his great capacity for research, science and dedication, was not fit to command in battle. It was not only the great snafu during the ill-fated training exercise Spartan in south-east England that determined this, but the realization that McNaughton's scientific mind, for some reason, did not seem to respond well to sudden changes or crises. In the eyes of the British he seemed preoccupied with new gadgets, experimental equipment and novel developments in tank and artillery techniques. Instead of concentrating on his job as a field commander, he was devoting much of his time to scientific research. It was the view of both General Paget, his immediate superior, as well as Brooke and his colleagues at the War Office, that McNaughton could not do justice to his command.

But this was not realized in Ottawa at that time, either by Ralston or other government officials. The War Office understandably was somewhat diffident in conveying this critical opinion to the Canadian government, or directly to McNaughton himself. Greatly appreciative of Canada's contribution to the war effort, the War Office hesitated to raise an issue of such national sensitivity. Certainly Canada had the right to appoint whomever she wished to command her army, but such was the British opinion of McNaughton's abilities that they decided they would never risk having British formations serve under his command in actual operations.

At this same time, the first inklings of another critical situation began to surface. This was a problem which a year later would mushroom into a full-blown political crisis and seriously threaten the life of Canada's wartime Liberal government. Manpower and the supply of reinforcements for our combat units were the issues. In creating an entire army structure, as well as our large commitments with the RCAF and navy, had Canadian defence planners perhaps over-reached themselves? Were the anticipated wastage (casualty) rates realistic? Could we keep our formations up to strength without conscription?

Each time Defence HQ in Ottawa sought approval from Parliament for additional units and formations, the military chiefs had been closely examined on the manpower aspects. Always the cabinet had been assured that sufficient recruits could be found — without conscription — for full war establishments, as well as our battle reinforcements. Even the ad hoc units General McNaughton had created overseas, solely on his own authority, had been provided for in their calculations. Even so, as recruiting figures started to slow down across the nation, Prime Minister King and several of his cabinet colleagues, mindful of the conscription troubles in World War I, began to have doubts. Mackenzie King had given clear assurances to Quebec against compulsory overseas service, and Air Minister Chubby Power had pledged his home province that he would resign from the cabinet if conscription was ever brought in.

Fears on this issue continued ever present in King's mind. He knew it was political dynamite.

The time for relaxed speculation on the *Circassia*, however, was all too brief. On July 9 our great convoy of ships started to join formation with sister convoys as we approached Malta. As far as we could see on all sides, the armadas from the United States, and from Alexandria and other North African ports, came over the horizon, together with battle cruisers and flotillas of destroyers.

With this great concentration, unfortunately, also came bad weather. In naval terms it was a "moderate gale" with wind force 7, which churned up enormous waves. The smaller craft — the LCIs, corvettes and little minesweepers — could be seen tossing about wildly. For minutes at a time they would simply disappear from view, as they crashed down into the troughs between the great surging seas.

If these mountainous waves continued till morning, it would be virtually impossible to land troops and equipment across the open beaches at Pachino. Conferences were held and urgent signals were exchanged between ships. Our plans did not provide for any cancellation or delays at this late stage. In the dark it would be a nightmare trying to alter or reverse the convoy patterns.

Shortly after sunset the wind seemed to die off a bit. The naval chiefs gave a qualified forecast, that the worst of the blow would be over by morning. Still it was not an encouraging prospect to the thousands of troops, as they peered out into the dark at the heaving waves. Then came the final word . . . the show was on, regardless of weather. There was also a last minute report of a new enemy mine field off the beaches. Our air reconnaissance had not detected it earlier and we had no plans for sweeping it in advance. Our force commander decided to take the risk, and he ordered his own ship to lead the way through the dangerous waters. If landings were found to be impossible, he would send up three red rockets about midnight, which would call off the whole show.

My own job on the landing was to go ashore with the early assault waves, just before first light and, with a small party, establish our advance Brigade HQ in the bridgehead. As my brigade commander, Chris Vokes, would have to remain afloat as acting divisional commander, until Guy Simonds had established a tactical HQ on shore, this meant I would have control of our brigade group for the first few critical hours of the landing.

It was this responsibility that concerned me the most as I gathered my small group together about 3 a.m. To go with me in the LCM were Sammy McLean, our staff captain; Norman Pope, the intelligence officer; the CO of our defence platoon, together with several of his men; two or three signallers with the portable wireless; Manser, my driver batman; and a few others.

It was only at this point that I started to consider seriously the fact that now, after endless courses in all forms of combat, every type of training in weaponry and field tactics, I could in the next few hours be involved in actual battle.

As I was to discover in the months ahead, nearly everyone cherished some myth or conviction as he went into action. Some nursed a good luck charm. Some simply considered themselves invulnerable to enemy fire. Tragically there were a few who walked quietly into battle with the firm conviction or premonition of death. Certainly, everyone experienced tension and carried hidden fears of some sort as we waited those last few hours. How would we behave and act when the fighting started? We had long been accustomed to the heavy air raids on London, but now it was our job to kill.

Curiously enough, though I never felt very brave when it came to fighting, I did not seem to fear getting bashed about or shot up. My great worry was that, under fire, I might find myself suddenly paralysed with fright and do something stupid, fail to give the right order, make some frightful mistake in an emergency, or otherwise fail in my responsibilities. As for the chances of getting killed, it just couldn't happen. I could accept the chance of being wounded, but I was absolutely convinced I would not get killed. Fortunately this illogical obsession stayed with me through each campaign which lay ahead, in Sicily, Italy, Normandy, north-west Europe, and the Pacific.

The commander of our defence platoon came up to McLean and myself on the deck and saluted. He reported our small boatload all present and correct, then asked what weapons I proposed to carry when we waded ashore. I hadn't given the matter much thought, but on reflection I realized that my pistol was not particularly adequate to the occasion. He suggested we might find a sub-machine gun appropriate. After debating the matter briefly, Sammy and I both opted for a simple 303 service rifle and a couple of grenades. Not that I hadn't qualified with every make of machine gun from the old Lewis and Vickers to the Thompson and Sten, but when it came right down to the wire, the rifle seemed more reliable.

Then all the troops started strapping on their equipment. We checked the final minutes on our watches and the first serials clambered down the scaling nets into the assault landing craft. At that point, the balloon went up. The two monitors with their 15-inch naval guns fired first. Unseen, but close beside us in the dark, HMS *Roberts* and her sister ship sent salvo after salvo crashing through the night with huge blasts of flame. The noise was deafening and the blast of the great guns almost tore the shirts from our backs.

With this curtain raiser, the whole performance got underway and the guns of all cruisers and destroyers started to speak across the water. Bomber squadrons from North Africa suddenly roared overhead, and in a matter of moments we heard their bombs dropping on Pachino airfield and other shore installations. As promised, the RAF set the water tower alight on the enemy airfield, which in the dark gave an accurate bearing for the landing craft heading for the beaches, seven miles away.

Exactly as we had rehearsed, the Tanoy or loudspeaker system on the *Circassia* called up each boatload in order, and the men swung over the sides of the big ship, down to their proper landing craft that came along in ordered sequence. Then our own serial number was called. Just before swinging over the side, I remembered our commodore, Sir David, and I quickly ran up to the bridge to say good-bye. Even in that short time on the *Circassia*, I had formed a great respect and affection for this gallant 70-year-old mariner.

Above his trousers in the warm night, he was wearing only his pyjama top, which fluttered wildly in the breeze with each blast of the great naval guns beside us. Using the night binoculars slung around his neck, he followed each flotilla of landing craft as it formed up behind the pilot boat, before heading into the dark. Giving his orders quietly, Sir David was completely absorbed in his duties.

Above the roar, I shouted my good-byes and shook his hand, then I raced back to join my landing party. I was already over the rail and partway down the net, when Sir David came running down from his bridge. Seemingly, he had just realized I was off. Reaching over the side of the ship, he managed to open the flaps on my haversack and stuff into it a bottle of whisky. "Be sure to send me word how it goes," he shouted.

The tension held high as our LCM, commanded by a 17-year-old midshipman, made its run-in through the darkness. We could see the beaches ahead, lit up with explosions every few seconds. Remembering all the blood-and-guts indoctrination of the battle courses, we were quite prepared to do our stuff. I had brave visions of dashing madly up the beach through the mines and barbed wire, dodging machine gun bullets, but it was all rather a letdown.

There was some scattered enemy firing but thankfully there were few casualties. We did get wet wading ashore. A few phosphorus flares and Very lights lit up the scene. The assistant beach masters seemed to be running in circles for a while, locating exits off the beach in the dark, but that was it. Rather a letdown.

We could hear some firing off to our right, and shortly afterward the distant strain of the Seaforth bagpipes could be heard, confirming that Bert Hoffmeister and his Highlanders from Vancouver were safely ashore.

In the interest of conserving the last ounce of weight in the initial assault, definite orders had been issued that bagpipes would not go ashore. Nonetheless, they made a very happy sound that morning. Later I learned that due to some skill by the Highland hands of old David Bone, the pipes got loaded in some wrong boxes . . . "by accident."

Optimistically, back in Scotland, Chris Vokes and I, working over an aerial photograph of the Pachino area, had selected the exact spot where we wanted to establish our first brigade command post and where he would rendezvous with me, as soon as his job as stand-by division commander was finished.

On the photograph, we had identified a small path leading off the beach between a curious series of rows, which then led into a well-defined trail that ran inland about half a mile to a small farm building.

We had joked about such precise planning, as we realized the odds of hitting the beach at that exact spot in the dark were less than a hundred to one. I took a compass bearing, however, from the spot on the map to the water tower down the coast at Pachino airfield. Just in case.

Amazingly, we did locate the exact path when we landed, and the curious rows in the air photo turned out to be rows of grapevines.

When our small group reached the farm building, we discovered five or six Italian soldiers holed up. They gave us little trouble and quickly surrendered. It took only a few minutes on the wireless to contact our units and confirm our position. All reports were good. Enemy opposition had been slight and our own casualties very limited.

As soon as it was daylight, some of our beaches and forward positions were attacked by enemy fighter planes, which screamed in at low altitudes. An advance party of Divisional Tac HQ, which had just landed in an amphibious DUKW, got hit badly. An old friend, Gussy Dyer, Brigade Major RCA, had his leg shot off in one of the attacks.

No sooner had we located a command post than prisoners started to arrive, sent in to brigade for interrogation by Intelligence. We really weren't ready for them, so after giving them a fast check-over I had the few members of our defence platoon march them back to the beach, where the poor beach commander said a prisoner of war cage would be established. I had broken my watch in the landing, so when our Intelligence officer was searching and questioning the prisoners, I had him requisition the best looking timepiece he could locate for me under the definition of spoils of war for operational necessity.

Under command of our brigade for the actual landing were the 50th and 51st Royal Marine Commandos. The mission of the two marine commando units was to land on the left flank of the Seaforths and silence the enemy shore batteries, which were sited on the high escarpment in that area just back of the shore line.

It was essential in the assault that we maintain close contact by wireless with these two raiding parties, and I was concerned that, in the dark and confusion, we might by accident shoot each other up.

The marine commander had treated the whole matter very casually in Scotland. He hadn't directly rejected our instructions about the wireless, but he off-handedly replied, "We'll keep in touch old boy — don't worry."

He was as good as his word. As it happened, they didn't use the wireless set at all. After taking the enemy gun positions by surprise, they had shot most of the gun crews and chucked the remainder off the cliff.

Shortly after daylight, I was surprised to see the marine commander, Brigadier Laycock, come driving up to our command post in a little

Italian car. He gave me a cheery wave of the hand. "Told you we'd keep in direct touch," he said, as he reported his mission accomplished.

We hadn't been established very long before Chris, together with a few more of our HQ personnel, came striding up the path, full of steam and energy.

In very short order, once the forward units had gathered themselves together, we started to move inland again under a blazing sun. A few pockets of enemy resistance delayed our advance briefly in some sections, but our troops pushed rapidly forward.

Before the landing, all our officers and NCOs had been impressed with the need to enlarge our beachhead rapidly and regardless of casualties. The essential in any assault landing is to secure sufficient depth in the bridgehead — to ensure that the beaches are not under direct or observed enemy fire, and that the larger ships can move into close anchorage to off-load more troops, ammunition and heavy equipment. In the early stages, it is largely a race as to whether the invading forces, with the element of surprise and mobility, can build up faster than the enemy, who has all the advantages of roads, railways and fixed defences in concentrating his strength. As was the case in the Gallipoli landings in World War I and repeated in World War II at Salerno, the great fault was the failure to drive inland fast enough and far enough to protect the landing beaches.

We had been warned that after the first rush ashore, the tendency was for everyone to go to ground and dig in too quickly. Even a delay of a few hours gave the enemy time to rush up reserves and concentrate his areas of fire and defence.

With this in mind, we had set our D-Day objectives at eight miles inland and were determined to reach these lines at all cost that first day. We had little or no transport ashore at that stage, so it was marching for everyone across the dusty Sicilian countryside, dotted with poor little farms and the odd olive orchard.

About four in the afternoon, our HQ group called a halt for a brief rest. Chris and I got out our maps to check our position. To our surprise, we were some 17 miles in from the beaches.

Then, for the first time, we both relaxed for a moment. We could hardly believe our good fortune. We were already twice as far inland as we had hoped and all our units were moving well. To celebrate, Chris and I, despite the heat, took a good whack at Sir David's bottle, then sent a personal wireless message, as promised, back to the old commodore on the *Circassia*.

Shortly afterward, we received an order from Division. Seemingly, when the large transport ships started to move in closer to shore, they had come under fire from a lone enemy coastal gun. It had not been recorded on our maps, provided by Intelligence, and, consequently, had been missed by both commandos and our mop-up patrols. We were ordered to send a platoon all the way back to the beaches to deal with it.

We alerted a platoon of the Seaforths and called for the platoon commander to report to our command post to be briefed on the gun location and his mission. It meant another 17-mile march in the heat, but it couldn't be helped. To give the platoon some fire support, we also called for a single tank from the tank brigade to rendezvous with them in the target area.

149

The young Seaforth subaltern arrived and was given his orders. He accepted them without complaint and started off to pick up his men and begin the long march back in the dust. As he moved away, I noticed that he seemed to be limping slightly. I called him back and asked if his feet were OK. He insisted that everything was fine, but I had my suspicions and ordered him to take off his boots. He protested but obeyed. His socks were soaked in blood from several enormous blisters. He had not been able to change into dry socks, which all ranks carried ashore to prevent the salty sea water from burning their feet.

He couldn't march in that condition, but he objected strongly when I suggested his platoon be replaced. We resolved the matter by having his feet greased up and getting the tank to pick up some of his men and himself, to ride back on the turret. We had no other vehicles forward at the time. It should be added that they cleaned out the enemy gun position in good order.

Details of the subsequent Canadian advance through Sicily in the weeks ahead have been recorded in various official reports, so I shall not attempt to give a history of the campaign but simply offer a few random comments and personal reactions.

The 51st Highland Division, forming part of the 30th Corps along with ourselves, had landed beside us on our right flank, just east of Pachino. To the north of their beaches, 13 British corps, supported by an airborne drop, made a landing near Syracuse and very quickly captured that port.

On other beaches some 35 miles west of our landings, the U.S. 7th Army had assaulted with the 45th U.S. Division and further west had landed at Gela and Icata.

The initial assaults were successful at all points. There was little opposition from the surprised Italian coast defence forces and only a few limited counterattacks for the first couple of days on our front. The Americans faced some heavier going at Gela.

The main German forces (the Hermann Goering Panzer Division and 15th Panzer Grenadier Division, later reinforced by the 29th Panzer Grenadiers and 1st Parachute Division) were concentrated further inland, but within a few days these crack formations were committed against us. The opposition had begun to stiffen.

Our 30th Corps was ordered to drive across the island to the north coast, with the 51st Highland Division directed via Adrano, near Mount Etna, while our Canadian division was given the line Modica, Ragusa, Caltagirone, Valguanera and Leonforte.

There is a curious transformation which takes place in an army or division when it is first committed to battle, almost unnoticed at the time and rather difficult to explain in precise terms. There is a sense of drawing together. This was certainly the case when our division joined the 8th Army with all its diverse regiments — Polish, Indian, New Zealand, Scottish and Canadian. There was an instant fraternity or comradeship, brought about no doubt by shared dangers and hardships.

Within each division, brigade and regiment, there grows a conviction that your particular regiment or brigade is the best. In this, our 2nd Brigade — tagged the Shiney 2nd Brigade back in World War I — was no exception. There was a deserved pride and self confidence in the brigade group when it landed on the Sicily beaches. Morale couldn't have been higher. Then, as our units, the Patricias, the Seaforths and the Edmontons, sorted themselves out tactically under fire and looked to each other for support, confidence increased with each operation.

Perhaps the best description of this phenomenon is recorded in Farley Mowat's book, *The Regiment*, which tells the story of the "Hasty Pees" (Hastings and Prince Edward Regiment), which served in Sicily as part of the 1st Canadian Division. He describes very accurately the regimental spirit of comradeship, which develops in action but simply doesn't exist on Civvy Street. When a man is wounded, in trouble, or needs help, his instinctive reaction is how to get back to his own unit, his friends — in effect, his home.

Whether he considers his CO a bastard or whether his company includes some first-rate rascals and bums (as most companies do), it is his family.

Conceding some bias but having subsequent experiences in other formations in other theatres, it is still my belief that our 1st Division at that time was likely the best trained and best co-ordinated Canadian division to see action. Not that our 3rd Division in Normandy — or indeed any of our other formations — need to take a back seat to any of the Allied forces, but the Red Patch of the 1st Division came to signify something extra in battle.

Guy Simonds, commander of the Division, was unquestionably the ablest field commander produced by Canada during the war. He maintained an icy exterior at all times, and though respected for his professional ability, courage and brilliance, had very few close friends. His sense of humour was very restricted and dry, and he spoke with the clipped Camberley accent. His decisions were often harsh and brutal when dealing with incompetence or failure. When he removed an officer from command, as he did on a number of occasions, even in the middle of battle, he was seemingly devoid of any personal feelings, past friendships or indeed humanity itself. Some of his firings were considered unfair and unwarranted, and for this reason he certainly created enemies, but few would criticize his ability to command in action.

He had been a professional soldier all his life and from his earliest student days at Royal Military College, had firmly resolved to some day command Canada's military forces.

He achieved his ambition and he deserved it. Early in the war, he noticeably patterned himself on Monty, with many of his abrupt mannerisms and his method of issuing orders.

Subsequently, at a very young age, he held acting command of the entire Canadian Army during many, if not most, of our important battles in north-west Europe. Following the war, he also reached his goal of being Chief of General Staff in Ottawa.

(It is fair to record that his great abilities in field command were not in evidence in his peacetime appointment in the postwar years. The skills required in combat, where the commander's authority is absolute, do not serve well in dealing direct with political chiefs and cabinet ministers. Guy had little diplomacy about him. He could not temporize or conciliate to achieve an objective. When he was overruled by constituted civilian authority, his only recourse seemingly was to plan a rigid defence and immediate counterattack. History repeated itself, in that what serves in war seldom succeeds in peace.)

Chris Vokes, commander of the 2nd Brigade, was also a professional soldier, but in a far different mould than Simonds. A powerful, rough and hot-tempered Irish Canadian, Chris had little of Simonds' polished expertise or sophistication in staff planning. Like Simonds, he could also be brutal and unfeeling at times and was also feared by many a junior officer. With it all, however, he was a more understanding character and deep down had a warm and emotional streak. He had a great personal bull-like courage and was indeed a superb fighting brigade commander. Despite his bad outbursts of temper at times, he also had a broad touch of rowdy humour about him. He was not immune from the odd error in judgment, but was able to recognize it when he cooled down. This was recognized by those who served under him, and he was accorded a degree of affection not granted to Simonds. He was also what was known as a good two-fisted drinker.

I knew and understood Chris better than most, and over many years developed a sincere affection for him, with all his seeming roughness of character. Our friendship dated back to prewar days, when he was a captain and district engineer officer at HQ, MD 10, in Regina.

Other colourful Canadian characters in Sicily and Italy at that time were Brigadier Geoff Walsh, CRE; Brigadier Bruce Matthews, CRA; Brigadier Wyman of the tank brigade; Major Malim Harding and Lieutenant-Colonel George Kitching at Divisional HQ, and the "great operator" Pres Gilbride, the DAQMG. They made a great team and all succeeded to higher commands as the war progressed. In action, they demonstrated a superb skill in improvisation and, when necessary, could show a fine disregard of the text books and staff college procedures.

Gilbride was the prince of scroungers, in keeping our supplies moving up to the front line. At one period, indeed, he purloined and operated as his private line a section of the Italian railway system running up the Adriatic coast. Whether he really understood much about military formalities we never knew, but he certainly knew his way around the 8th Army.

Acting on the theory that cigarettes attracted enemy snipers at night in the forward areas, Chris Vokes took to chewing great wads of Dutch snoose or snuff. He sported a rather pirate appearance and selected the most villainous-looking NCO, a roughneck named Sailor, to accompany him everywhere as his combined bodyguard, driver and orderly. They made a fearsome pair, roaring about the forward area.

Just before leaving Sussex, Chris had published in Brigade Orders a prohibition against shaving the upper lip ... applicable to all ranks. It was a harmless gag which produced a monster moustache-growing contest, and everyone went along with the nonsense. Chris gave as his reason that, as it was no longer necessary to attract the girls in Britain, everyone should look as fierce as possible now to scare the hell out of the enemy.

For the first few days of the Sicily landing, we had only a handful of officers to man our command post, so at night I set up a duty watch. Apart from the defence platoon, each of the officers would take a spell at the W/T set while the others would stretch out on the ground to get a few hours' sleep. I had just completed my own watch one night and then groped through the darkness to wake Sammy McLean to take over. I called and prodded his recumbent form several times, but there was no response. A bit peeved and aching for some shut-eye myself, I gave him a couple of gentle kicks on the butt with my boot. Still no answer;

something was wrong. Shining a flashlight on his face, I got an instant shock. His whole face was puffed up like a football, his eyes were mere slits, his other features also unrecognizable, and he was quite unconscious. When we failed to bring him to, I called for a jeep and had him rushed back to the beach area for evacuation to a hospital ship. It was a week before he rejoined us, looking very washed out.

A week before the landing, the MOs had started all ranks on a routine of four or five mepacrine tablets a day, to guard against malaria. Sammy had been violently allergic to the stuff and it was lucky that we tried to wake him when we did.

My earliest recollection of Guy Simonds those first few days ashore was when he suddenly turned up at our command post in a scout car, driven by a cheery-faced young tank officer named Stafford. As yet there was no divisional HQ established ashore. Guy seemed to be just swanning about on his own for a look-see. The odd shell from an enemy 88 was coming our way, so Chris, Guy and I worked our way to some higher ground, to see if we could spot where the fire was coming from. Guy had stepped off to the side a bit, to get a better view with his binoculars, when another shell crashed down, seemingly on the exact spot where Guy was standing. When the dust and debris settled, Chris and I rushed over. Guy was still standing, unhurt and quite unconcerned. He made a few quiet comments and then started off to another sector. Perhaps it was a bit of bravado, but it was rather impressive, nevertheless.

Later in the day I ran into Guy again and suggested he should bunk in with us for the night, in a small olive orchard. He refused my invitation, saying he had some rations with him in the scout car. When he was tired, he and Stafford would find a place to stretch out under a tree someplace.

Our division was very fortunate in having a gradual baptism to fire. The fighting was not too heavy for the first few days. Units might be held up for a few hours by an enemy position, but once a company could bring down a concentration of mortar and Bren gun fire, the enemy slowly withdrew. No set piece attacks were required.

There was some initial reaction when our troops first saw some of their pals killed and wounded, but a hardened disregard soon developed, almost too much so. Once we had a few more vehicles, forwarded up from the beaches to move up supplies and ammunition, we started to advance more rapidly.

I was following along in a jeep behind one of our advancing companies, when Simonds came forward to check the situation. As we drove along together through a shattered village, we came upon the body of a Canadian soldier who had been killed only an hour or so earlier, with the advance guard. In the blazing sun his corpse, all swollen and bloated, was bursting out of his bush shirt.

In battle order, other members of the regiment filed along the road, past the body, simply ignoring it. Simonds was furious. Climbing out of his jeep, he halted the line of men moving forward and gave them all one hell of a blast, telling them, in no uncertain terms, that the least respect they could show was to take a few minutes to dig some earth over their comrade's body, to shelter it from the heat.

Privately, I had rather prided myself in being able to remain fairly collected and unmoved in an emergency. The first time I saw men killed, however, I was rather disabused of any such notion.

I had been watching a young subaltern, together with half a dozen of his men, advance in extended order toward a bluff. Ahead I saw them suddenly all go to ground at the same instant. At first it seemed that the officer had given the order to take cover. Gradually, however, it dawned on me they had all been cut down with shrapnel from a mortar bomb. I ran forward at once.

Rolling the young officer over on his back, I saw the rips in his shirt where the pieces of shrapnel had cut into him. Pulling his shirt open, I saw where his chest had been torn and laid back in half a dozen places. Blood was oozing out of the ragged holes in his chest wall. He was conscious, but I knew there was nothing I could do except pull the shirt back over the fatal wounds . . . perhaps he wouldn't see them. He coughed a bit and asked me to prop him up. I realized that the blood would soon flood his lung cavity, so it would make little difference. When I propped his back up against a tree, he asked me to take care of the others . . . but could he have a cigarette first? I lit one for him and placed it between his lips, then went on to the next man. The waist of his trousers was soaked red with blood. I got his web belt undone and undid the buttons of his trousers . . . his intestines had been ripped wide open. I went to the next man — his elbow had been completely shattered. I was able to get a shell dressing wrapped about the pieces and tied it on the best I could.

Other observers had come up to join me and we got a signal back for a jeep ambulance. I glanced back at the young officer. He had taken only a couple of puffs on the cigarette and then slipped away . . . without a whimper.

When I saw the survivors safely on their way to the rear in the jeep, I had the feeling that I had done everything possible, calmly and efficiently. I then started the sad job of recording the details of the dead men from the identity discs hung around their necks. All went well until I tried to write down the names and regimental numbers. It was impossible. My hand could hardly hold the pencil much less write a word, it was shaking so badly.

An incident of a happier nature during those first days in Sicily still remains in my thoughts. One evening just at dusk, we suddenly seemed to lose contact with the enemy all along our front. Neither of our two forward battalions could report the enemy positions. Their forward patrols had pressed well ahead but the enemy had just vanished. By dark we still hadn't a clue about where the enemy had gone.

Chris ordered the Seaforths to send out an officer patrol to re-establish some contact again, without delay. Major Budge Bell Irving of the Seaforths took on the mission. He was told to report direct to Brigade HQ as soon as he could make any contact whatever. Off he went, with two or three men on foot, into the darkness. We waited impatiently all through the long hours of the night, hoping for some report but not a single sausage. As dawn started to break, we began to fear he was lost or taken prisoner.

To our relief and amazement, shortly after daylight Budge and his lads came driving happily along the road in a German armoured car. Throughout the brigade, Budge was always considered to be just a wee bit mad.

It seems that his patrol had come across the enemy armoured car in the darkness, with its German crew lying sound asleep around it. The patrol had quietly done-in the German crew and wheeled away in the armoured car.

Instead of reporting back at once on their contact, they had then set out for a little holiday tour about the enemy area for the next few hours. Though Chris blasted Budge with a royal rocket for not observing orders, he was secretly very happy at the outcome. (At the time of this writing, Budge is serving as Lieutenant-Governor of British Columbia.)

About this same time, our brigade had the good fortune to bag a complete battery of Italian horse artillery. The horses and mules, as spoils of war, posed a little problem. We decided to turn them over to some of the poor farmers in the area. As several of the chargers were really fine animals, however, and we were still badly short on transport, Chris had the happy thought that we should perhaps make use of them for a bit.

The following day, with the horses well groomed, the saddles and equipment all polished, and the halter ropes pipe clayed, Chris and I rode off on a visit to each regimental HQ, to the obvious surprise and delight of all observers. Sad to relate, these saddle horses were reluctantly handed over a few days later, to a nearby farmer.

Our first link-up with the American forces, which had landed to the west of us, occurred at the small town of Ragusa. Late in the day, orders were received for our brigade to push ahead rapidly through Ragusa and up the twisting mountainous road leading north toward Grammichele. We issued our movement orders without delay, but it was dark by the time our forward convoys started to swing up the road out of town.

Soon afterward, other vehicles started to mix in with our convoys. In the dark, with no lights showing, some time went by before our forward echelons realized they were getting all tangled up with an American convoy, which was also trying to use the narrow road. Eventually, a provost sergeant on a motorcycle got back to me about the confusion. I worked my way forward, up the tangled mixture of U.S. and Canadian vehicles, till at last I contacted a rather heated U.S. officer.

He explained that his division had been ordered up the road and had priority on right-of-way. I contested this proposition, and after a short debate, we both sent orders down the line to halt the convoys, as the snarl-up was getting hopeless and becoming a good target for any enemy attacks.

The U.S. officer and I each got on the blower to our respective divisional headquarters to determine just who did have the right-of-way. There was no room for both on the single track road in the dark.

Our divisions, in turn, had to pass the question higher on up the line for clarification. While we waited, the general of the U.S. division came up and joined us. Eventually, the word came down from "God" — the Canadian mission took priority and was to have right-of-way. That was fine, but we wondered just how in hell we could sort out all these hundreds of vehicles in the dark on such a narrow twisting road.

While the U.S. general was not too happy about the decision, he accepted the order with good grace.

"Give me thirty minutes," he declared, "and I'll get all our boys cleared out of the way for you." It looked impossible, but he was as good as his word. With great speed and efficiency, he worked all their vehicles out of our way. This miracle of traffic control certainly improved our estimate of the U.S. Army, the new boys.

It was largely a war of movement throughout Sicily and, in order to keep our little Tac HQ up with the advancing units, we often had to move our location two or three times in a day.

It was well after midnight on one move, when I decided to swing our three or four HQ vehicles off the road into a small field for the rest of the night, so our men could get a few hours' sleep and some breakfast in the morning.

We had come to learn, the hard way, the skill of the retreating Germans in booby-trapping likely crossings, buildings and vehicle areas. Small fields leading off the narrow roads — likely parking areas, we discovered — were frequently sown with land mines. The mines were often connected together with innocent-looking old strands of fence wire, which could get tangled up in the lorry wheels or be pulled out of the way by the unsuspecting. Then, all the local scenery would take off into the sky.

The pioneer NCO came back, after checking the field I had selected, and reported it safe. In fact there were some other troops already asleep in there ahead of us. Behind the low stone wall, in the dark, I could see the curled-up forms of half a dozen other men sleeping, so I gave the order to make camp.

We settled down quickly for some needed sleep in the remaining hours of darkness. The drivers and W/T operators, taking their blankets, joined those already asleep near the wall and curled up beside them.

When daylight dawned, there came some yells and loud profanity. Our boys discovered that they had been snuggled up alongside half a dozen dead Germans for the night.

General Achille d'Havet

One of the highlights of the campaign for myself was the capture, or rather the surrender, of the Italian general commanding our sector of the coast, Major-General Achille d'Havet of the 206th Coastal Division, who also had part of the 54th Napoli Division under his command. By chance I played a principal role in the little drama.

Since the war, there have been various conflicting accounts written about this. The following CP news story filed by war correspondent Ross Munro, who was present at the time, is entirely accurate.

> Modica, 15 miles northwest of Ispica, gave up as the Canadians were preparing to strike it and here the Canucks captured their first Italian general — Gen. Achille d'Havet, commander of 206th coastal division which was supposed to defend the coast where the Canadians landed.
>
> With the Canadian attack imminent, the general asked for terms and was told "unconditional surrender." He accepted and Maj. Dick Malone, of Winnipeg, went into Modica to arrange the capitulation. They came away with the general and his staff and took them to the Canadian general.
>
> I was at headquarters when the Italian general and his party arrived. Wearing shorts and a bush shirt, the Canadian general received them in his headquarters under the trees.
>
> The Italian told him a few things about his defeated division and asked if he could retain his revolver as a gesture of military honour. Permission was granted — but the general's ammunition was taken away from him first.

We were aware that HQ of the Italian coastal command was located on Modica and our intelligence reports indicated that the town was strongly garrisoned. In consequence, when our own troops approached the town, Chris decided that we should organize a full battalion attack with some preliminary artillery support from the 3rd Field Regiment before the actual assault.

He left me at the command post to relay orders to the Patricias; then he departed for the artillery area to co-ordinate their fire program, which he planned to get started in 40 minutes' time. I was to advise the infantry accordingly.

Quite a number of civilian refugees had started to make their way out of the town, coming along the road to our HQ location.

Our intelligence officer, Norman Pope, was herding them away, though detaining the odd one for questioning. I was busy on the wireless set when he brought in one very excited Italian civilian, who spoke a little English, saying I should listen to what the man had to say, as it seemed important.

The Italian civilian claimed he was an *avvocato*, a lawyer, and that the military garrison in the town wished to surrender. He pleaded with me not to have the town shelled, as many women and children would be killed. He kept insisting that the Italian garrison and their commander wished to surrender. I doubted his statement and demanded, if that were the case, why didn't they send out an officer with the offer . . . why did they send him . . . why should I believe him . . . it could be a trap.

The urgency of his appeal finally convinced me that his claim was worth investigating. Certainly there had been a surprising absence of enemy activity in the past hour. On the basis that the *avvocato* would accompany me, both as surety and interpreter, I decided to go into the town myself under a white flag and check his story, though I realized we could get shot up in the process.

After sending an immediate message to Vokes at the Arty O-Pip, to report my intention and requesting him to delay the Arty bombardment, I set out in a jeep, accompanied only by my driver and the lawyer. At the top of the jeep's wireless antenna I tied a large white handkerchief, silently praying it would be seen in time by the enemy.

We descended into a small valley, then drove openly up the winding road into the town without a single shot being fired at us. About a mile out of the town, we encountered Lieutenant-Colonel Booth of the tank regiment, off to the side of the road in a scout car. He was making a recce of the defences. I told him what was afoot, and asked him to hold his position and keep me covered in case things went wrong and I needed support to get back. Then we found our way to the centre of the little town, where I was astonished to see rows of Italian soldiers formed up in the market square. On the ground beside each man was either a small bundle or a shabby suitcase of personal belongings, which would be needed in a POW camp.

The lawyer guided me to a modern headquarters building. On the way in, I thought what a bloody fool I was to trust him. Here I was accompanied only by a driver and armed with only a pistol. The sentries at the door made no effort to halt me. I was met by a naval aide who spoke English; he showed me into a nicely decorated ante room, then went to announce me to his general.

I walked up and down the waiting room for several minutes, then the sailor returned to ask if I was or was not a general. If I was not, he explained, his general could hardly surrender to me. I was a little annoyed at this and said that I represented my general, and that if they were going to surrender they had better make up their minds darn quickly. He was a little hurt to discover I was a mere major, but away he went to the general again.

After I had resumed my wait for a few more minutes, the thought suddenly struck me that there was something wrong about this picture. We were supposed to be the conquerors, but I was being left to cool my heels in a waiting room. The general was likely taking the time to destroy his operational maps and codes.

Trying to look tough then, I burst open the door and waved my pistol at the startled-looking group of Italian officers. My Italian was just sufficient to shout at them, *"Arrenditarvi unconditionale . . .* come with me." And away we all marched, the general, the chief of staff, the mayor of the town, the naval aide and several others.

In General d'Havet's office I had noted the operational maps covering all the walls and the piles of papers on the desks, which could be very valuable regarding enemy defence positions. I could not just go off and leave them unguarded. There was only my driver available, so I posted him at the door with his Bren gun, telling him to let no one enter and to remain there till some of our people arrived. He looked just a trifle wide-eyed when he realized I was abandoning him, but he only gulped and replied, "Yes, Sir."

This posed a transportation problem. We couldn't all get in my jeep and I was now without a driver. After some discussion, it was decided that we should take the general's Fiat and his driver. We all jammed in, the general, myself and the naval attache sitting in the back seat, so I could keep an eye on things.

I had taken the precaution of removing the general's pennant from the little flag staff on the car radiator and replaced it with my rather dirty white handkerchief. I was not anxious to be shot up on the return run by our own people.

We drove off without hindrance past the long lines of Italian soldiers and headed for Guy Simonds' command post.

Outside the town we stopped again briefly to give the story to Booth, who was in position on the side of the road, and to tell him where we were going. I also told him about the lone driver I had left on guard at the HQ and suggested he try to get some people in quickly, to give him support. We next ran into the British corps commander, who had come forward to see what was up; my message to Chris had been quickly relayed on to him.

He agreed that I should continue on and turn d'Havet over to Guy Simonds, together with his orders to Guy to get his people cracking on past Modica, without delay.

As we drove on, it suddenly dawned on me that the general and his officers still had their pistols belted about their waists. This didn't seem quite correct, so I asked them to hand them over. They all objected to this idea. For a moment, being outnumbered five to one, I wondered how far I should press the issue. Certainly I couldn't march them all up to Simonds carrying loaded pistols, so I stopped the car.

Then the naval attache explained. The general considered that, as his troops had fought with valour, they should be entitled to turn over their pistols, with honour, to a general of equal rank. It all seemed rather silly but finally I agreed they could keep their guns if they emptied the chambers first and handed all the cartridges over to me. Everyone was happy then, so we pushed along.

Glancing at the general, I was surprised to note among his medal ribbons a British DSO. I asked, through the interpreter, about this seeming discrepancy and received the general's reply that the Duke of Devonshire had awarded him the gong personally in World War I. The humour of the whole situation then started to reach me, and I made the crack that the general seemed to have chosen the wrong side this time. The general did not think this very funny.

Reaching our divisional HQ, I sent one of the ADCs off to dig up Guy and get him prepared to receive a formal surrender . . . our first enemy general of the war. In a few moments, Guy appeared, pulling a beret on his head.

All went well, everyone saluted and the general formally turned his empty pistol over to Guy. Guy talked to him briefly, then had him and his staff officers sent on back to Corps for interrogation by the Intelligence boys.

During the drive back, I had passed an envious eye over the Italian Fiat. It was well fitted up with special equipment, a far more luxurious bus than our jeeps . . . and even jeeps were in short supply.

If I could get it away fast before Guy got any fancy notions, it could come in pretty handy back at 2CIB and would be absolutely ideal for the brigade major.

With this plot in mind I tried to slip unobtrusively away, but Guy was too quick for me. After returning my salute, he sauntered idly along after me to the car, which he circled in a slow inspection.

Being fully aware of my intentions, he took his time. Finally, he paused in front of the hood. Then, without a trace of a smile, he slowly unscrewed the little silver flag staff from the radiator cap.

"I think I can use this," he said. That was all. The car was mine, and I lost no time sorting out the gears and driving off to dangle my prize before old Chris. (General d'Havet's pennant, I might add, was safely in my pocket and not noticed by Guy. I still have it as a memento of the event.)

Sad to relate, several weeks later, after I had been wounded and evacuated, my driver, Manser, who tried to guard my loot till I got back from hospital, had to jettison the car over a cliff one black night. Seemingly, the gears or clutch burned out on a narrow mountain road and the Fiat blocked the whole brigade convoy. Despite Manser's protests, the provosts simply ordered him to shove it over the edge into space.

Several confused accounts of the surrender at Modica surfaced after the event and found their way into various monthly war diaries. In one version it was reported that two other officers accompanied me into the town, which was certainly not the case. Several different units, in the confusion, each claimed that their patrols were first into the town and took all the Italians prisoners.

Certainly patrols of several units would have pushed on into the town after the surrender, as all opposition had ceased. Finding the entire garrison ready to parade off to a POW cage and seeing none of our own people about, they would conclude that they were accepting the garrison's surrender. In fact they were in one sense, as the lone driver I had left at the HQ building could hardly have moved the entire garrison out by himself while still safeguarding the enemy HQ records.

Which of these patrols was the first to enter Modica after my own visit to the Italian HQ, I can't say. But certain it is that General d'Havet had long since gone and been formally turned over to Simonds, before they arrived on the scene.

In recording that the fighting was relatively light for the Allied forces in the early days of Sicily, I do not wish to imply that it was easy going all the way. There were many sharp engagements with the Hermann Goering Division, along tortuous rocky roads; and the Germans were experts in delaying tactics, with ambushes, demolitions and mine fields, dominated by machine guns and 88s.

The heat and dust also made the going heavy as the 1st Division attacked one enemy position after another and successively captured the towns of Vizini, Grammichele, Caltagirone, Piazza Amerina, Valguarnera, Assaro, Leonforte, Agira and Regalbuto. The division then linked up with the British to assist them in the final thrust of the campaign through Adrano; this led to the joining up of the British and American troops in the capture of Messina, to end the campaign.

The hardest fighting centred around the towns of Assaro and Leonforte, and Agira. At Assaro, the Hastings and Prince Edward Regiment distinguished itself by a perilous scaling of a steep mountain face at night, to outflank and surprise the German 15th Panzer Grenadiers defending the town. It was a bold and dangerous move but it paid off, despite heavy casualties under repeated German counterattacks. The Canadian CO, Lieutenant-Colonel B. A. Sutcliff, was killed in the operation. A long-time friend, Major Lord Tweedsmuir, took over command. His father had been Governor General of Canada.

At Leonforte, the Edmontons fought their way across a ravine into the town, just at nightfall, and got themselves badly bogged down in some ferocious hand-to-hand street fighting. All their companies were committed in the melee. They were able to hang on till morning, when a strong rescue or supporting attack was launched by the PPCLI and several squadrons of tanks, which cleared out the Germans.

Regiments of both the 1st and 2nd Brigades, and the Three Rivers (Tank) Regiment, took a heavy pounding in the capture of Agira. The RCR, Three Rivers, 48th Highlanders and Hasty Pees all got repulsed, with heavy losses, on the first try. Ralph Crowe, C.O. of the RCR's, was killed shortly afterwards at Nissoria. The Patricias, Seaforths and Edmontons went in on the next phase to complete the job.

I must confess that until the Sicily campaign, I had secretly nursed some serious worries, heresy perhaps, that when we got into action all our complex field services — ordnance, medical, army service corps, field workshops and so forth — would just collapse in a marvellous snafu.

On paper, during the training exercises and staff college battles, it looked dandy. A man for every job and everything provided for in the orders. I also knew that they had recruited some very able and experienced men from industry, whom I had known before the war.

Nevertheless, my private doubts remained. It was all very well when our divisions first were concentrated in Canada and later deployed in south-east England; we could go tearing off along well kept roads for a few days or a week, setting up temporary camps in the forests, owned by

△
December 27, 1941, Canadian leaders
leaving the White House in
Washington, D.C. after meeting with
President Roosevelt and Prime
Minister Winston Churchill. Left to
right: Canadian Minister to
Washington, Leighton McCarthy;
Prime Minister W. L. MacKenzie King;
Minister of National Defense, Col. J. L.
Ralston; Minister for Air, C. G.
Power; Minister of Naval Services,
A. L. MacDonald.

◁ Shortly after Dunkirk, Col. J. L.
Ralston, Vincent Massey and the
author at No. 10 Downing Street in
London, planning with British officials
to expand the Canadian war effort.

Brig. General Chris Vokes and author inspecting German fighter-bomber shot down in Sussex by Bren-gunners of the 2nd Canadian Infantry Brigade.

1st Armoured Brigade staff being introduced to King George VI during an inspection at Frencham Common, Surrey. Left to right: Maj. Gen. E. W. Sansom; Queen Elizabeth; King George VI; Brig. Gen. "Tommy" Rutherford; Maj. Chas. Turnbull; the author; Capt. Pelham Reid.

△
A church service held at First Canadian Army. Left to right: C. D. Howe; Lieut. Gen. A. G. L. McNaughton; Col. J. L. Ralston; Maj. Gen. P. Montague; Maj. Gen. E. W. Sansom.

◁
Newsmen aboard one of the convoy ships that took part in the invasion of Sicily. Left to right: Ross Munro; Peter Strusberg; L. S. B. Shapiro.

△
Gen. Montgomery, C-in-C 8th Army, standing on a "duck" while speaking to Canadian troops shortly after the assault landing at Pachino in Sicily, July 1943.

◁ The 12th Calgary Tank Regiment advances through the ruins of Regalbuto in Sicily in 1943 as the 1st Canadian Division moves toward Mount Etna.

Gen. A. G. L. McNaughton, Commander of 1st Canadian Army, addresses
Canadian troops in Sicily.

Col. J. L. Ralston visits Lieut. Gen. H. D. G. Crerar at HQ 1st Canadian
Corps while at Taormina in Sicily.

Princess Patricia's Canadian Light Infantry and 2nd Canadian Infantry Brigade troops leave a tank-landing ship at Reggio, Italy, Sept. 3, 1943.

Gen. Montgomery carrying his famous umbrella and wearing his corduroy bags, shows his collection of canaries and love birds to Col. J. L. Ralston during his visit to Monty's Tactical Headquarters on the Adriatic coast of Italy.

Canadian Army Photo

After accepting the surrender of the 206th Italian Coastal Division, the author delivers the Italian commander, Gen. Achille D'Aveti DSO, together with his Italian Naval Advisor, to formally hand over his unloaded pistol to Maj. Gen. Guy Simonds, GOC 1st Canadian Division.

The author greets Col. J. L. Ralston at Foggia, Italy before escorting him to Gen. Montgomery's TAC HQ at Vasto, Italy.

Canadian Army Photo

△
The author, on his way to join Montgomery's TAC HQ as Canadian Liaison Officer in Italy, being welcomed back from hospital in North Africa by Greg Clark.

Canadian Army Photo

Herbie, the cartoon character made famous in the Canadian troops daily newspaper the *Maple Leaf*, was created by cartoonist Bing Coughlin of the 4th Princess Louise Dragoon Guards during the Italian Campaign.

I told ya so, ya put the gears in backwards!

You scram! There aint room fer three here.

Picture or no picture, I'm not runnin' past that open space again fer no photographer.

friendly landowners and farmers . . . the rations and petrol came up, even the mail. In the odd traffic accident, any injured were quickly whisked away down a fast highway to a nice modern and sanitary hospital. The vehicle would be towed to the Aldershot area, where permanent workshops and enormous parts depots were available. Sometimes during exercises, the umpires would declare a number of men dead or wounded. A tag would be put round their necks and they would have to lie down to act out the part . . . not in any mud hole of course, or under a shattered building or burning tank. No real bullets or shells were flying. On paper, there was always enough morphine, ambulances could always use nice highways, and bridges hadn't really been blown up.

As for rations, the RCASC on exercises could send back our "B" Echelon vehicles loaded with our full draw of meat, bread, etc., and the petrol lorries were fully loaded with high grade fuel. But we knew that they were really drawing on a big civilian bakery and large oil storage depots just a few miles back along the highway.

What in hell really happened I wondered when a hundred or more real casualties had to be hauled out of the mud, in action, with bridges and roads blown up and no way to evacuate them. Could the light aid detachments and REME people really patch up hundreds of vehicles when a huge convoy was shelled or shot up from the air . . . and when they had no local hydro installation to plug into?

What happened when supply convoys didn't get through at all, or got lost, or when half their vehicles were damaged and they were reduced to about 40 per cent "runners"?

The whole set-up seemed pure theory and would, I feared, prove quite mad and hopeless under modern battle conditions. I raised this happy speculation in the early training periods several times with some of my many friends in Ordnance, RCASC, REME, Medical Corps and such, but was always told to butt out, and to leave that end of the game up to them. The bloody system would work out OK, they knew what they were doing, and besides — thank God — it wasn't my business.

Confession is good for the soul, so I now freely admit that to my utter surprise I discovered, within the first few days of our landing, that the entire set-up fell quickly into place. Even though we had landed at assault scale — that is, with only a limited number of vehicles and stores — it all worked superbly.

All my old friends on the service side of the game, Eric Elwood, Culver Riley, Shelford, Red Curry, Gilbride, Fleury and a host of others, had been quite correct when they assured me that their people could deliver when the time came. In the months ahead, with great drive and initiative, the services more than honoured their claims. Sometimes it meant creating mule-pack trains to get supplies forward under fire, across almost impossible mountain trails, to keep our forward troops supplied.

One of the most sobering realities of war came when we saw for the first time the straggling lines of poor refugees, making their way back along the roads from the battlefront. No longer was it just a clip from a movie newsreel. With their homes shattered and burnt, these bewildered old women and children straggled pathetically along the mountain trails, past our convoys of tanks and army lorries. Some leading a goat or a donkey, some carrying babies, they sought only food and shelter. Day after day this became a familiar sight all through Sicily and Italy. It would be the same through France and Belgium, and later Japan. Often it would be necessary to herd them forcibly off the roads to keep our military traffic moving.

The troops would toss any spare rations they had to the ragged little children, begging — with their big brown eyes — for *biscotti*. What did these poor little people know of politics, of Hitler's ambitions, of fascism, or even of democracy, for that matter?

Nearly always they walked barefooted. Shoes were a luxury. As the colder weather approached, Canadian troops were outraged when they first discovered that frequently the bodies of their dead comrades were being dug up for their boots. Gradually for the Canadians, war assumed an image even more despairing than the bombed-out areas of Britain.

My own career in Sicily approached a sad and inglorious finish just as our division reached Leonforte, then ended with a dramatic bang.

We anticipated that the Germans would make a determined effort to hold Leonforte. It was fairly easy going on the advance march, however, till the town came in sight across a long valley a mile or two ahead. One of our units reported that its forward companies had the town in view. They considered that a set-piece assault on a battalion scale, with full artillery support, would be required. Accordingly, a halt was called so a reconnaissance could be carried out and a plan developed. Chris agreed that I should go forward and take a first-hand look at the scenery.

Our ships having been torpedoed back near Gibraltar, our brigade was still forced to operate without many of its vehicles. Indeed, it was subsequently claimed that during the whole campaign, the Canadians had marched on their flat feet further than any other division in the 8th Army . . . and our brigade staff was no exception.

At this stage, the 1st Brigade, a bit better off than ourselves for vehicles, had been drawn back in reserve for a few days' rest. Their commander, Brigadier Graham, had a personal Bren gun carrier, equipped with wireless, in which he went charging about.

It would be ideal for my recce, and with the W/T set I could get early information back to Chris, which could speed things up. Accordingly, I got Howard Graham on the blower and asked if he would lend me the carrier for a few hours. He would not need it in reserve.

He generously sent the carrier forward, complete with driver, spare driver and W/T operator. As back-up to the wireless, I had one of our own despatch riders follow us on a motorcycle — and off we went to see the layout, first hand.

Working our way forward we reached one of the leading platoons. The young lieutenant had his men under cover on the brow of a hill, overlooking the valley. On the far side could be seen Leonforte. A small river wandered through the valley, which was crossed by a single bridge. Except for the odd round from enemy gun positions, everything seemed pretty quiet.

To launch our attack on the town, the little bridge was essential if we hoped to bring up any anti-tank guns or mortar carriers for support. From what we could see through our glasses, the bridge was quite intact.

With our past experience this should have been a warning to me; the Germans had blown virtually every bridge on their retreat so far.

When I discovered that the lieutenant hadn't attempted to get a patrol down to the bridge, to see if it was mined or wired for demolition, I was a bit short with him. We should grab it before it was too late. On my orders, he started a section down the valley across the open space.

Then it struck me that in the Bren carrier, I could whip down across the open stretch faster than his section and with greater security. Time was of the essence if we were to get to the bridge before the Germans blew it.

So I gave the order and away we went in the carrier. I was aware that the approach to a bridge was a likely location for enemy land mines, but the purpose seemed to justify some risk.

Just as we were about a hundred yards from the bridge, we hit it . . . a double Teller mine. The blast hurled the carrier into the air, twisting its armour plating out of all recognition.

Before I lost consciousness, I was fully aware of hurtling through the air, realizing what had happened and then hitting the ground again with a great force.

How long I lay unconscious on my face I don't know, but it can only have been for a few minutes. Slowly, I grasped that I had been hurt, and then I was vaguely conscious that machine gun bullets were kicking up the dust on the road around me. The roadside ditch was only a few feet away and I tried to roll into it. Despite all my efforts, I couldn't get my body to move; my legs simply would not respond. A few feet ahead of me on the road was, I could hazily make out, a round object about the size of a football. It was red and wet. With horror, I slowly recognized that it was the head of one of my drivers, with the scalp and flesh torn off. Could it be that the reason I could not move myself was that my own legs had been blown off? I moved one hand down to feel and grabbed something wet and sticky. I brought my hand back to look and found I was grasping what looked like raw liver. More convinced than ever that either my legs were gone or my guts ripped open, I made another effort with my arms to roll myself over into the ditch. Finally I succeeded, but I have little recollection what happened next.

I was told that the section following behind was able to reach me before too long and get me loaded off on a jeep, back to an improvised casualty clearing station in the ruins of a bombed-out church in Caltigirone.

The other occupants of the carrier had all been killed and the despatch rider, who had been following too close behind on his motorcycle, had ploughed into the wreckage and wound up with a broken shoulder.

I would like to think the reason I wasn't killed with the others in the jeep was due to good luck or providence, which I felt certain went everywhere with me during the war, but the evidence was that it was a sandbag which saved my life. As a precaution against mines, it was the practice to lay filled sandbags on the floor of carriers and other combat vehicles where possible. For the next couple of weeks, as I recovered in a field hospital, I kept scratching out grains of sand which had been blasted into my back and scalp.

Sicily was over as far as I was concerned. According to the official records, it was a great victory. Enemy losses were estimated at 250,000 killed, wounded and prisoners, 65,000 of them German. Total Allied losses had been some 31,000. Of these, Canadians killed and wounded had been 2,434, not as heavy as we had expected. On the credit side, the 1st Canadian Division had come through its baptism of fire well. It had operated smoothly and had gained valuable experience. The Red Patch established in World War I continued its proud tradition.

For myself, I had gained confidence in the knowledge that in action I did not panic or become paralysed with fear and was able to handle my job with some intelligence. With a luck that was to remain with me throughout the war years, I had survived the first of many close calls.

163

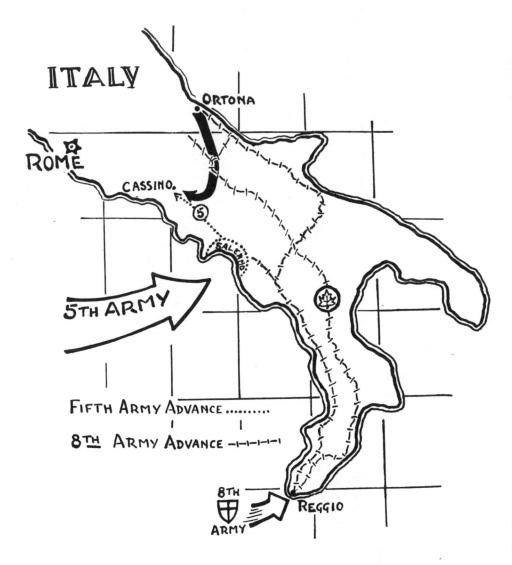

ITALY

ROME

ORTONA

CASSINO. F.

⑤

SALERNO

5TH ARMY

FIFTH ARMY ADVANCE ....

8TH ARMY ADVANCE -I-I-I-I-I

8TH
ARMY

REGGIO

Sketch map of Italy showing the relative advances of the British 8th Army under General Montgomery and the US Fifth Army under General Mark Clark.

TEN
Hospital And Italy Invasion

WORLD SCENE
Mussolini impeached — Marshal Badoglio takes over
as President of Fascist Grand Council. Sicily captured
by Allies. Canadians to remain in 8th Army for
diversionary landing in Italy. Churchill and Roosevelt
meet in Quebec City to plan 1944 invasion of France —
Plans approved and command decided for Normandy.

During the next few weeks while I recovered in a British field hospital in North Africa, many changes, quite unknown to me, were afoot regarding the Canadian Army, its higher command and its future employment. New situations had arisen, and top level decisions had been made in Ottawa, London and Algiers regarding General McNaughton and the future role of the 1st Division. In addition, a first-class row had developed between General McNaughton and Monty.

I recall regaining consciousness again in a shattered little church in Caltagirone, which served as a casualty clearing station. For a time I was vaguely conscious of what went on around me, then slowly realized that I was quite deaf. Even when a doctor tried shouting at me, I couldn't hear a word.

There was still no movement whatever in my legs. When I felt to see if I still had them, the pain in my upper body became unbearable. Through the haze, I recognized Bev Leach, a young Canadian doctor I had met at many good parties in Regina some eight years earlier. In some fear I demanded to know whether I would be crippled and deaf for the rest of my life. Even scribbling his reply on a scrap of paper, Bev could tell me nothing. I would have to be evacuated to a field hospital in North Africa for examination and x-ray. Before accepting a hypodermic-needle, I received Bev's assurance that he would try to have me evacuated to a Canadian hospital if possible. This request he scribbled on the tag tied around my neck.

Along with a score of other wounded, I was flown in a converted transport plane, first to Tunis and then, the following day, to a large British tented hospital in the desert, near Maison Blanche, an old French Foreign Legion encampment some miles out of Algiers.

It was a big field hospital, with rows and rows of marquee tents serving as wards for many hundreds of wounded, nearly all of them British. There was no running water in the wards, no sanitation. Deep open ditches, which served as latrines, had been dug outside each tent. Every few feet a short post had been erected for the men to hold on to, no seats whatever being provided. In the heat of the day, with every patient suffering violent dysentery, the stench was appalling. Hordes of flies added to the misery. They settled on the food the moment it was served, coming in droves direct from the outdoor toilets. At night there were mosquito nets to pull over the hospital cots, which did provide some temporary relief until the next call of nature came. Four times a day, every patient was given eight sulpha tablets, which he washed down with gulps of highly chlorinated, tepid water. They had little if any effect on the dysentery.

All the orderlies were what the British called wogs and the Americans Ay-rabs. They were filthy dirty and wore their loose native dress as they dispensed the bedpans and food. During the day they tried to peddle hard-boiled eggs brought to the tents by itinerant Arabs from nearby camps, riding or dragging tiny little donkeys with top-heavy loads.

The cheerful little limey nurses bustled about doing their best, but the odds were against them. The entire scene conjured up tales of Florence Nightingale and the horrors of military hospitals in the Crimean War. As to the morale of the patients, suffering continuous dysentery, apart from shrapnel wounds, fractures, missing limbs, and surgery of all kinds, the reader will be left to his own imagination.

In the same tent ward as myself, there were mostly junior officers, some with bad shrapnel wounds but most of them with broken bones and amputated limbs. Four or five of them were survivors of the glider landing operations in Sicily where, in the darkness, many of the gliders had come down in the ocean or crashed off course on shore.

The second morning in hospital, all the nurses started rushing about in great agitation and fear, putting everything shipshape for the CO's weekly inspection. We all did anything we could to help — trying to get shaved out of tin cups of cold water, making up our beds — before the great man arrived.

Whether he was a good doctor or not I can't say, but he certainly knew little about camp organization or sanitation. He was a typical frozen-faced regular officer, with clipped speech, a superior manner, and an air of complete indifference to both his staff and his patients.

Everyone was ordered to stand to attention at the end of his cot. As I still had no use of my legs, I was exempted from this exercise. But all the others, regardless of considerable pain in many cases, were obliged to remain at attention for an interminable period, awaiting the CO's arrival. Maybe this was acceptable with the Brits, but to Canadian eyes it seemed the ultimate in stupidity.

We were all subjected to a rather snotty survey by the CO and his adjutant, while the little nurses quaked in their shoes. Then came the customary question, "Are there any complaints?"

I was still in a pretty black mood with both myself and the whole bloody war at that stage. As senior officer in the ward, therefore, I spoke out, demanding why these men were obliged to stand at attention for half an hour when they should either be in bed or allowed to go urgently to the latrines.

There was a complete silence for several minutes. The nurses looked bug-eyed in horror and disbelief at my seeming audacity.

Very coldly, the CO came over to my bed and picked up my medical chart.

"A Canadian," he sniffed. "They always give trouble." With that he, his adjutant and the matron marched stiffly out of the tent, making no attempt whatever to answer my question. I could see that I had clearly invited some future troubles for myself.

For several depressing days I went through a series of tests and x-rays, which meant painful trips from tent to tent, carried on a stretcher or in a jeep. I was assured my full hearing would soon return. Both eardrums had been burst in the explosion, but they would heal by themselves. The back and tail of my spine were the problems. The muscles and nerves had been badly torn, but happily my spine seemed intact. Only time would tell about the back. There were also a few cracked ribs, but all in all I had been lucky to come out alive. There was talk for a while of shipping me back to the U.K. or Canada, and at the time, feeling pretty low, I was almost ready to go. I had had all I wanted of war. Fortunately, the higherups decided to wait for a while and see what use I got of my legs.

In retrospect, I went through the usual transition period of most casualty cases — several days of feeling sorry for yourself, then starting to wonder how things were going at the brigade without you, followed by a feeling of shame at ever having thought of going home and leaving the job to your pals. Then, as things started to pick up and news of the campaign began to trickle through, there came a determination to get out of the lousy hospital and back to your unit as soon as you could wangle it.

As each day passed, the nerve fibres in my back started to mend and I regained a bit more response from my legs. Despite considerable pain I was able to stand up once more. Before long, I was able to get about slowly, with the use of crutches and a wheelchair. Then, like everyone else in the field hospital, I was soon laid low with a violent attack of dysentery.

One morning an orderly came to our tent with an order that the OC of the hospital wished to see me. It was a long haul across the sand in a wheelchair to the administration building, but I duly reported, attired in a cotton dressing gown and canvas sandals; not a very military figure.

It was a very formal meeting. The British CO informed me that because I was the senior Canadian in the hospital, he wished to record that he and his staff were considerably browned off with the behaviour of their Canadian patients. Until then I had not been aware that there were any other Canadian soldiers in the camp. The British colonel then went on to relate all the sins and outrages committed by a dozen or more wounded Canadian other ranks who were located at the far end of the encampment. There were formal charges against all of them he said, and then handed me a stack of charge sheets.

I looked them over. They were serious offences, all right, but I had trouble keeping a straight face. In one instance, four or five of the wounded Canadians had managed to slip out of their tents at night and catch convoys into Algiers. On their return to camp, they had slipped down into the darkness of a nearby gully to finish off a few more bottles of Algerian wine.

Unhappily, the CO had been making some rounds that night and, hearing rowdy voices in the dark, had called out, "What are you men doing down there?" In reply, a Canadian soldier had shouted, to wit, "aw go f--- yourself."

The other charges were all similar in nature. Certainly contrary to "good order and military discipline," I agreed.

Granted permission to talk to the culprits, I had an orderly push my wheelchair to the far end of the camp, where the Canadians' tent was located. They were nearly all from the Edmontons, one of the regiments in my own brigade, a pretty tough crowd but fine soldiers in battle.

They recognized me at once and were quite prepared to accept my comment on their behaviour. Asked what they thought they were doing, they all had the same reply. They hated the lousy camp and simply wanted to get back to their regiment. I pointed out that on their present course, they would likely end up in a military prison and never see their unit again. After some further words, I got their assurance for good behaviour till I could see what I could do for them.

Returning to the OC of the hospital, I asked how long it would be before the men could be moved out of the hospital. I had heard that a Canadian field hospital was now set up in Phillipville. Could they be transferred? "It was an outrage that British authorities should have to put up with such scandalous behaviour," I said.

Though most of the Canadians had been cut up pretty badly with shrapnel, the British CO said he would gladly ship them out at once.

"Our Canadian authorities should certainly deal with such crimes," I assured him. "If he would just let me have all those charge sheets, I would see that the papers were sent along to the proper Canadian command and the men dealt with severely."

Happily my suggestion was accepted. The Canadians all left in lorries the next day for Phillipville. Somehow or other, the charge sheets I obtained got lost en route.

The problem of getting out of the hospital myself was not easy. There was still talk about evacuating me to England. A young nurse gave me physiotherapy treatments each day on my legs and back, which did some good, but I was down to 125 pounds, due to dysentery. I became convinced that recovery from the dysentery would only be possible if I escaped from the filth of the hospital, and that I would surely die if I remained.

In talking to the little physiotherapist, I gathered that she had a boyfriend in the RAF whom she was able to see every second night, when a convoy of petrol lorries made a halt at Maison Blanche. He was, in fact, the young officer in charge of the convoy, which delivered fuel regularly to various air fields under cover of darkness.

After some coaxing, the nurse agreed to help me with an escape plan. The next night that the petrol convoy halted, she would arrange with her boyfriend that the tail boards on one of the lorries be left down, so that I could hoist myself in without being seen in the darkness. Then he would drop me off at some point where I might hitch a ride to a Canadian reinforcement or holding unit, reportedly now functioning along the coast somewhere toward Phillipville.

The real problem was that I had virtually no clothes or kit. Everything, even my boots, had been blasted off me when the double Teller mine exploded. Only a fragment, the thick waistband of my army shorts, had survived, together with the pockets attached to the waistband. By great good fortune, cleverly sewn in the waistband were several thousands of French African franc notes, issued to some of us as escape money — should we be taken prisoner — prior to the assault.

Beyond this my sole possession consisted of a little bag distributed to us in hospital as a gift from some Red Cross ladies in Brazil ... a godsend to all of us. It contained a safety razor, some soap, a toothbrush, writing pad, pencil and a few other useful oddments. Blessings on the ladies' aid in Brazil.

I was able to snitch a bush shirt and a pair of issue shorts from another patient, but had to set forth without any headgear or rank badges, and with only canvas bedroom slippers on my feet.

I ducked out under the tent when the convoy arrived and was hoisting myself into the lorry when the little English nurse appeared out of the darkness and slipped a half-bottle of whisky into my hands — the entire monthly NAAFI allowance for herself and her tent mate. It proved a lifesaver in the cold night drive along the coast.

After the painful next few days, during which I hitch-hiked up the coast, telling implausible stories, I had the good luck of spotting a vehicle with Canadian Army markings, and I managed to flag down the driver. While he seemed to doubt my story, he agreed to drive me to the Canadian reinforcement camp, which was indeed now operating, in a cork forest near Phillipville.

On arrival, I duly reported myself in to the commandant, a Colonel Hedley Basher, whom I knew slightly. He recognized me but expressed surprise when I told him I had been properly passed by a medical board and discharged from hospital to return to my brigade. He couldn't understand how I had been discharged without uniform or kit, or why I didn't have any papers or discharge certificate. I assured him it would all arrive in due course. "Just the usual army red tape," I said.

Colonel Basher was of the old school, a strict disciplinarian who knew the Manual of Military Law backward and permitted no laxity whatever in regulations. I would not be permitted to rejoin the 1st Division in the field until some written orders were received from above, and my medical records and discharge papers had arrived from the British hospital. Meanwhile, I was to draw some proper kit from stores. He would find some useful duties for me while I waited. He also pointed out that my former appointment as brigade major of 2nd Brigade had been filled after I was wounded. Instructions would be required about some new posting for me.

Still feeling pretty shaky, I didn't try to argue with him for fear he would see through my pose of everything fine and fit. Quite obviously for me his program was just not on. He would wait till Doomsday before any discharge papers arrived . . . they didn't exist.

A brother officer from my regiment, the Queen's Own Rifles, was also in the camp, in transit to some new appointment. He generously donated a spare cap he had, with the proper QOR badge and a few other items, to make me look a bit more respectable.

In addition, he passed on the current gossip that the 1st Division would not be returning to the U.K. as originally planned, now that the Sicilian campaign was over. Instead they would be jumping off soon on some new operations, likely an invasion of Italian Corsica, he thought. In Italy, Mussolini had been dumped by the Fascist Grand Council, and Marshal Badoglio was now the boss there.

In addition, he understood that General McNaughton, the Canadian Army Commander, was in the theatre someplace, having come from the U.K. to visit his 1st Division.

Quite clearly, my course was to get back to the division before they went cracking off in some new direction. Chris Vokes or Guy Simonds, the divisional commander, would find a job for me fast enough. Once I was in the forward area, the paper work could be sorted out either

169

through the "Black network" at the MS Branch, or through the confusion of a paper barrage and the "fog of war."

The following day in the transit officers' mess, I noted two young RCAF pilots, which seemed odd, so I engaged them in casual conversation to discover what they were about. General McNaughton was indeed in the theatre; in fact, over in Sicily right then. They had piloted him out from England. The next day they were to fly over to an air field at Malta and wait there till McNaughton was ready to fly back to England.

Later that day, when Part II orders were posted, I noticed that I was to preside as president of a court martial in Phillipville in two weeks' time. Colonel Basher clearly anticipated that I would be with him for some while. When the two RCAF pilots took off next morning for Malta with McNaughton's plane, they had a stowaway aboard.

After hanging around Valetta harbour for a day or so, I managed to get a lift on an American transport plane to Syracuse in Sicily.

An Exciting Job

It was some months later before I learned something of the background to McNaughton's visit to Sicily and the strained relationship between him and Monty at that time. Several conflicting versions of this episode have been published, as well as numerous denials. The facts, however, are now pretty clear. After the war, my talks with both Field Marshal Alexander and Montgomery confirmed the following scenario.

Ralston, Canada's Minister of Defence, had overridden McNaughton's wishes that Canadian forces be employed in battle solely as a complete army. McNaughton had reluctantly agreed that our 1st Division and an army tank brigade could be separated from his army and used for the Sicily invasion, to gain battle experience, then be brought back to England to rejoin his army for the Normandy invasion.

The 1st Division had only been in action with Montgomery's 8th Army in Sicily a day or so when General McNaughton announced that he wished to visit the formation. He cleared his trip with both the War Office and General Eisenhower, then Commander-in-Chief in the Mediterranean; however, when Eisenhower's HQ notified General Alexander of the impending visit and requested that the 8th Army be advised, there was an immediate blow-up by Monty. On no account did he want McNaughton sticking his oar into things when the Canadians were getting their first baptism of fire. Guy Simonds, the divisional commander, was also experiencing his first command in action. As since recorded, Monty did indeed tell Alexander that if McNaughton set foot on the island without his approval, he would place him under arrest — though he was quite prepared to have McNaughton visit the Canadians later, when they had settled-in a bit.

Alexander supported Monty in this, though he was a bit more diplomatic in passing along Monty's response, saying simply that permission to visit the battle area was not granted.

McNaughton was, of course, furious, seeing this refusal as an affront to Canada — a denial of our right as a separate nation — as well as a direct personal slap at himself. Commenting later on the matter, General Alexander said, "It was unfortunate that General McNaughton's visit came when the Canadian division was deeply involved in its first battle against a formidable foe . . . a visit at this time by such an important person would have caused extra work and some embarrassment."

By curious chance, I suddenly found myself projected unexpectedly into the centre of this row. When I landed in Syracuse, I set off at once for the Canadian supply depot, in the hope of locating some form of transportation to our forward area. Not wishing to be too visible or invite embarrassing questions, I was nosing quietly around the transport pool when I ran directly into General McNaughton. He recognized me at once and asked how I was feeling.

I had last seen him some months earlier, during an assault landing exercise off the coast of Scotland. Now, he was surprised to see me out of hospital so soon — he had heard of my misfortune with the Teller mine and the death of the other members of the carrier crew. In response to his concern, I assured him I was quite fit again for duty. (In point of fact, during my brief stop in Malta I had been able to purchase a wide canvas surgical belt, which I could strap up tight underneath my bush shirt. With this hidden support it was possible for me to stand erect.)

McNaughton talked to me briefly about various aspects of the campaign, then asked what job I was going back to. I confessed that this was rather uncertain at the moment, but I was sure there would be a job waiting for me. McNaughton paused for a moment, as he turned something over in his mind. "How would you like to go to General Montgomery's tactical HQ as Canadian liaison officer?" he asked. "You might be able to help our relationship with the British HQ . . . protect our Canadian interests a bit . . . keep General Montgomery more closely in touch with any 1st Division problems."

At that time I still knew nothing about his row with Monty. What job would be available for me back at 1st Division, was indeed uncertain. Being a personal LO to Monty at Tac HQ 8th Army could be pretty exciting.

It should be explained that in his desert campaign, Monty had reversed the practice whereby army commanders remained with their main HQs in some town miles behind the actual battle area. Instead, Monty maintained a very small operational or "Tac" HQ, consisting of only a few younger staff officers, well forward on a mobile basis, where he could be in direct contact with the combat formations each day.

Apart from allowing closer control of the battle, this procedure saved the commander from becoming bogged down in all administrative details and enormous paperwork necessary at the main headquarters of any army.

With only his own personal caravan, a mess lorry and a few wireless vehicles, Monty could move his centre of operation very rapidly to any part of the battlefield, from day to day, as required.

When necessary, his very able and popular Chief of Staff, General Francis de Guingand, or his chief engineer, his artillery commander, or his chief intelligence officer, Colonel Bill Williams, could come forward to Tac HQ — for conferences, briefings or O-Groups.

The only permanent staff stationed at Tac HQ with Monty consisted of a couple of junior staff officers, two or three ADCs and three or four liaison officers. The LOs were Monty's eyes and ears in keeping in daily touch with the battle.

Ronald Lewin, one of Monty's biographers, has recorded that Monty was most discriminating, as a commander as well as a person, in his selection of these liaison officers. He gave them wide-ranging authority, and also one of the most difficult and dangerous jobs in the battle area. Each day he demanded that the LOs go as far forward as possible to the most active sector of the fighting, to make contact with the lead infantry companies, scout-car patrol or armoured squadrons, so that they could obtain for him a clear, first-hand report of the battle areas before nightfall.

Sir Winston Churchill in his memoirs, recording one of his visits to Monty's Tac HQ, described this system of daily operational intelligence. He tells how these three or four LOs, like homing pigeons, returned from their dangerous mission by late afternoon to give Monty "the form," independent of the official and routine "sit reps," which came in later.

The responsibility of Monty's liaison officers was widely appreciated throughout the battle zone, and unit commanders gave them all the help possible and whatever transport was available, land, sea or air.

Writing in his own memoirs after the war, Monty described the LOs in the following terms: "They were young officers of character, initiative and courage; they had seen much fighting and were able to report accurately on battle situations. It was dangerous work, some were wounded and some were killed. They were a gallant band of knights."

The prospect of joining Tac HQ seemed pretty attractive, though McNaughton did warn me that I would have an added responsibility: to ensure some degree of harmony between Monty and the Canadian authorities, despite Monty's many foibles and difficult temperament.

McNaughton reasoned that my previous experience as staff secretary to Defence Minister Ralston, together with my knowledge and personal contacts with many of the senior British and Canadian commanders, would be of considerable help in the assignment.

It didn't take me long to make up my mind. Before the day was out I had my joining instructions. I was to be issued a jeep from the ordnance depot, pick up my batman-driver, Rifleman Manser, together with my bed roll, at 2nd Brigade HQ, and then report myself ready for duty to Monty in Taormina. Monty's Tac HQ was presently located there in Lady Hulton's villa, which had been occupied only a few weeks earlier by the Germans. It was fortunate that I had been able to wangle a new jeep in Syracuse. On our dusty drive to Taormina, Manser, with great apologies, explained how he had lost my precious Italian general's car.

During my conversation with McNaughton, he confirmed that the Canadian troops in Sicily would not be returning to England just yet. Additional intelligence was that the 1st Division would be taking part in an Italian invasion in just a few days' time.

I was not aware then, however, that Ralston and Stuart had visited McNaughton in London toward the end of July and had strongly urged that the Canadian forces in the Mediterranean be built up to corps strength, complete with its own Corps HQ and with the addition of our 5th Armoured Division.

For McNaughton, such a move as this would shatter any dreams he had of leading a complete and autonomous Canadian Army for the invasion of France. It would be a bitter pill to swallow after the assurances he had received about the return of 1st Division. The final decision to establish a Canadian corps in Italy was made only at the end of August, through an exchange between Churchill and Mackenzie King.

On The Home Front

While these sudden changes in my own fortunes were being effected by McNaughton, another situation of far greater drama and importance was unfolding, between Ottawa and the War Office in London, concerning McNaughton himself. Unknown to either McNaughton or myself at the time, a drastic turning point was approaching in McNaughton's army career. Again I would be involved, though to a lesser degree.

In the Canadian mind, McNaughton, with his brilliant scientific record, was seen as a potential leader of the Allied forces when Europe would be invaded. If the well-equipped Canadian Army, assembled under his command in England, was to be, in McNaughton's own words, "a dagger pointed at the heart of Berlin," it was accepted that the dagger would be directed by the hands of McNaughton. The stature of McNaughton never loomed larger than it did at the time of his visit to Sicily.

It was McNaughton's genius which had mechanized our army and introduced new artillery techniques. It was McNaughton who was continually testing scientific weapons and procedures.

Behind the scenes, however, some grave doubts had arisen at the War Office and in the minds of Britain's military chiefs as to McNaughton's ability as a field commander — his actual capacity to direct armies in battle.

Their fears regarding McNaughton's capacity as a commander peaked following a large-scale army exercise named Spartan. For the exercise, McNaughton commanded the attacking force; his army was to test its skill in breaking out of a beachhead. Although not fully trained in such large-scale manoeuvres, Canada's 2nd Corps, which included one of our armoured divisions, was employed in the exercise. Its performance was poor. There were breakdowns in communication and in supply and movement control.

It was widely rumoured at the time that Army HQ, during some periods of the exercise, had lost control and did not even know where some of their divisions were located. Whatever the truth of this allegation, it was certainly not a good performance in the eyes of the War Office; rightly or wrongly, much of the blame had privately been directed at McNaughton.

Understandably, due to national sensitivities the British chiefs were hesitant about expressing their doubts to Ottawa, where they realized McNaughton was revered almost as a god.

Subsequently, McNaughton charged, indeed became obsessed with the idea, that the British generals were simply out to get him. This, he believed, was partly through jealousy and partly due to ancient grudges and disputes between himself and Brooke, dating back to World War I.

In the months to follow, McNaughton began to see almost everyone as his enemy. He next became convinced that it was Monty who was out to get him; then it was Canada's Minister of Defence, Ralston. Later he felt that he had been sabotaged for political reasons at home and that other Canadian commanders were in on a plot to destroy him.

During that summer, one version had it, the question of McNaughton's ability was first raised with Canadian authorities in an Allied war conference in Washington. Here it was alleged that Brooke told Canada's representative at the meeting, General Maurice Pope, that McNaughton had not come up to expectations in exercise Spartan. He had become too far removed from his troops. The story went that Brooke made this comment in the knowledge that Pope would report the information to his bosses in Ottawa, the CGS General Stuart and Defence Minister Ralston.

Certainly Canada would be within her rights if Ottawa decided that McNaughton must remain. It would not be a happy situation, however, for either McNaughton or the British Army group commander under whose authority he would have to serve. But if confidence was lacking at the command level, and concerning McNaughton's individuality and strong will, for the general to remain would simply invite disaster.

During my period in hospital, I had been rather out of touch with such developments, both operationally and politically, but, briefly, that was the picture when I started off for Taormina.

It was a strange feeling, now, driving along the main roads in Sicily and not having to worry about mines or how far ahead the patrols were. One could take a minute to look at the scenery along the way. And what a God-forsaken scene it was! Dust everywhere, except in the clumps of tropical vegetation that grew in strips along the base of the mountains. It was startling to see how quickly the scars and litter of war had started to disappear, though the campaign had wound up only a few weeks before. "Brewed up" vehicles along the roads had already been collected into salvage dumps, and newly erected wooden bridges were starting to replace the precious Bailey equipment.

As I turned in from the coast road and wound up the steep hairpin turns, it was easy to see why Taormina was famed as a honeymoon resort. The little village clings tightly to the jagged mountainside and from the top seems actually to overhang the blue water hundreds of feet below. In the background Mount Etna, rising up into the clouds, provided a background for this living watercolour. Only a few weeks before, General Rommel had used these villas for his command headquarters. Now Monty was the boss man of the estate, and in a few months the site would next become the home of General Crerar and Canadian Corps Headquarters, on their way to join Monty in Italy.

My arrival and reception at Tac 8th Army were neither happy nor auspicious. I was covered with layers of Sicilian dust, with the sweltering drive from Syracuse via the 2nd Brigade. I had seen Monty many times before, but only from a respectful distance, when he had visited our Canadian units in Sicily and also in south-east command back in England. Following his great victory at Alamein and the defeat of General Rommel in North Africa, Monty had become a legendary figure or, as one writer put it, the "mascot" of the 8th Army.

On arrival I was first greeted by a dark-haired young major, Dick Vernon, who despite a fairly dashing desert get up — including corduroy slacks and red suede desert boots — was, like myself, from a black button regiment. He eyed my disreputable kit and dirty appearance in a most superior manner, and in an incredulous tone said, "Oh, so you are the new Canuck . . . well, you had better come and see Master." I gathered that "Master" meant Monty, so ignoring the studied reception, I followed the major on up to the villa.

The odd, studious-looking lieutenant colonel lounging in the ante room gave us only a casual glance as we entered, then went on reading a sheaf of papers. While Dick Vernon went into Monty's office, I wandered aimlessly about the room thinking how damn rude these English officers could be — not even a "hello" or "have a chair" from this washed-out looking colonel. He had thin, mousy hair brushed over to one side of his head and wore large spectacles which accentuated his thin face and pale blue eyes. I was later to learn that this was Monty's intelligence expert, Bill Williams, a former Oxford don, who was rated at that time to be the best informed man on German army tactics and formations.

But here came Dick again. Monty would see me now. I came to attention in front of Monty's desk and gave my version of a smart salute. While I explained who I was, Monty said not a word but looked at me closely for a minute. Then abruptly waving his hand at me with a motion that indicated I should leave, he said, "You're dirty, go away, go away and wash your face, then I will talk to you." That was the end of the interview. I was furious, but there was nothing else to be done, so I turned and left the office.

While I found a room and tried to make myself presentable and dump my gear someplace, I managed to cool down a bit. Certainly I needed a wash very badly, but even drinking water had been scarce on the way up from Syracuse.

In this charming villa, they seemed to have forgotten that most of their 8th Army had fleas, and that baths were non-existent.

I rationalized, however, that regardless of provocation, my job was to build a happy bond with the Brits. It was a wise decision. Before many days passed and I got on with my duties, I found that Monty was for the most part both pleasant and considerate when dealing with members of his personal staff. He had a clipped dry sense of humour and, at dinner time, encouraged a bit of banter around the table. He enjoyed making small bets with his officers when they were bold enough to predict the outcome of some current activity or sporting event. He managed to win most of those bets, and we paid off in cash. Others have recorded that when he lost, Monty often paid off the small amounts by cheque, knowing the cheques might not be cashed — his autograph being more valuable than the face amount of the cheque. This may be so, but I can't say; I was always careful not to win.

As time went on, I was able to establish a considerable degree of confidence and frankness in my often touchy dealings with Monty, on matters of Canadian concern. This was to prove of great value later, particularly during subsequent campaigns in Normandy and north-west Europe.

My first assignment was another D-Day assault landing with our Canadian division. Two days after I reported to Monty, the Canadians together with the British were to land in the toe of Italy, near Reggio di Calabria. I was to go in with the leading brigade in the early hours of the morning. After spending D-Day in the bridgehead, contacting various formations and getting an exact picture of developments, I was then to make my way, by whatever means possible, back across the Straits of Messina. The purpose was to ensure that before dark, Monty received a first-hand report on the landings. For his own use on D-Day, Monty had arranged for the loan, from the Royal Navy, of a motor torpedo boat. He proposed to cruise up and down offshore to view that side of the picture, treating the MTB as his private yacht.

As I was to discover later, the British-Canadian landings in the toe of Italy were intended only as a feint, for the purpose of drawing German divisions down from the north of Italy. Our landing was to create the impression that the entire 8th Army was being employed — that this was the main assault. Immediately afterward, the 5th Army, consisting of two corps, one American and one British, were to effect the main landing farther north at Salerno and, it was hoped, cut off German divisions which had come south.

Although shipping had been allocated to take the Canadians back to England as soon as the campaign in Sicily ended, Monty had asked that the Canadians remain in the 8th Army long enough to carry out the landing at Reggio. The Canadian authorities had agreed that our troops could be employed "for limited operations in toe of Italy," before returning to the U.K.

Monty explained to me that he felt some of the British regiments in the 8th Army, who would also be returning for the 2nd Front and had been away from home a long time, should have priority on this shipping. It would mean more to these men, getting home before Christmas, than it would to the Canadians, going back to England.

He also briefed me with the intelligence that secret negotiations were going on with the new Italian government. The Italians were prepared to surrender, once the major Allied landing at Salerno had been made. Then with the Allied forces to support them, Italy would give us assistance in clearing the Germans out of the country.

Our 3rd Brigade, commanded by Brigadier Howard Penhale, was to lead the Canadian assault this time at Reggio, with 1st and 2nd Brigade to follow. I found my way to Penhale's HQ the afternoon before the landing.

Pen gave me a warm welcome back from hospital and at once arranged that I would go in with one of his leading infantry companies on an LSI (landing ship infantry) for the assault. An LSI is rather larger than an LCM or LCA which all have front-end ramps to lower when they strike the beach. The LSI has a deeper draft and, consequently, runs aground in somewhat deeper water offshore. When this happens, gangways on each side of the ship drop down, so that the troops can dash down into the waves. At that late stage, there was no way Pen could phase in a jeep or motorcycle for me on any of the landing craft, but I assured him I would be able to shift for myself once ashore and find some means of getting back across the Straits of Messina the next evening to report to Monty.

Pen then outlined on a map his dispositions, objectives and lines of attack. In order that I could get an up-to-the-minute picture before returning to Sicily in the late afternoon, we arranged to meet at the proposed site of his forward HQ, a park just on the outskirts of Reggio.

I stayed with Pen till midnight, then found my way in the dark to the LSI, where one of the infantry companies was already loading. Shortly after 4 a.m., the preliminary bombardment opened up across the Straits with massed artillery. Joining in were all our available heavy and medium guns, together with some medium and heavy artillery borrowed from the U.S. 7th Army, as well as big naval guns from a score of battleships and cruisers. It was a pretty terrifying spectacle: thousands of shells, directed at the defences of Reggio, screaming through the night.

Dawn was just breaking as our landing craft grounded about 50 yards offshore. Already, some elements of the beach brick (beach control teams) were getting established along the shore. Several Bofors anti-aircraft guns were being pulled into position to deal with German planes, which would certainly arrive with the dawn to shoot up and bomb the landing areas.

It was still half light as I lined up to go down the narrow gangway, which had been lowered as soon as the ship grounded. Above the roar of the naval bombardment, I suddenly heard the scream of a low flying plane. It appeared at rooftop level, a German Focke-Wulf fighter bomber, flying parallel to the beach, with all machine guns firing. It made directly for our ship, dropping a single bomb as it passed overhead.

Grabbing the ship's rail, I quickly clambered over the side and dropped about six feet into the shallow water. As I made this undignified departure, I saw the bomb strike the forward deck of our LSI. For a couple of minutes I played submarine, trying to submerge in the shallow water, waiting for the explosion. But nothing happened. Seemingly, the bomb had crashed straight through the deck and also the hull below, and buried itself in the sand without detonating. Possibly it had been dropped at too low an altitude. Whatever the reason, I counted myself lucky as I sloshed up on the beach.

A fast survey of the beach showed all was going well. Vehicles and men were being shuttled quickly ashore in good order. Engineers were already opening vehicle exits from the beach, and naval ratings were setting up control points and signal centres.

Then came the German plane again, sweeping the beach with its machine guns. A few yards ahead of me was a newly dug slit trench, and I dived for it. The owner of the trench landed on top of me a split second later. He was not very gracious when we were able to climb out safely again, and his army boots had not helped my back very much. However, I thanked him for the temporary accommodation, then pushed off while he was still muttering about our lack of air cover.

Other than a few odd shots from the direction of the town, there was no sign of enemy infantry fire on the beach. Only an occasional shell from some German 88 battery positions in the hills beyond the city opposed our landing, along with a few enemy planes. I made for the town on foot, joining up with an infantry patrol. They anticipated some house-to-house fighting as we penetrated the built-up area, so we moved cautiously for a while. It was soon apparent, however, that the German forces had withdrawn back into the hills.

There was a lot of rubble in the streets but much less damage from our artillery than I had imagined. We had tried to concentrate on defence positions rather than civilian areas. The people of the town soon started to appear. The women looked scared and scurried about gathering up belongings. Conversely, the men seemed almost happy to see us and were quite ready to talk.

The big surprise came when several Italians demanded to know when the big American landing was to take place up north. Even among our own troops, security had been very tight about Operation Avalanche (U.S. 5th Army landing at Salerno), due in a few days' time. If the shopkeepers of Reggio knew so much about it, I wondered, just how much did the Germans know of our plans to cut off their divisions here in the south.

As the forward infantry made their way through the town and pushed into the hills after the retreating Germans, I caught a ride in a Bren carrier to see what I could find out about the German positions back in the hills.

Moving up one of the narrow roads, we first came across an odd parade of men in assorted rags of uniforms. They were liberated prisoners of war, our own people — British, Canadian, American and many other nationalities. Once our landing was secured, the Italian guards at the POW camp had opened the camp gates and disappeared. There were cheers, tears and handshakes all around, as the freed prisoners crowded around us to ask news of the war, our landing and the whereabouts of their regiments.

Of particular interest to me were two young British engineers. Just prior to the Sicily invasion, a submarine had dropped them at sea one night, off the Pachino beaches. Their task had been to check the depth of water over the sandbars offshore, for the landing on our assault craft. They were to work at night, then hide out on the shore till dark the next night, when the submarine would pick them up again. Unhappily, they were captured before completing their mission.

On capture they, together with other members of their small team, had been repeatedly interrogated separately by enemy intelligence officers. These two men had managed to stick with their story, but they did not know if the other members of their team had survived the ordeal. What they wanted to learn now was, had their teammates been able to hold out, or had they cracked under the pressure and revealed their purpose and location of our landing. The two engineers were happy when we were able to assure them our landings at Pachino had achieved surprise and had gone well.

Other than giving them a few cigarettes and directing the sorry-looking column on back toward our beach installations, there was little we could do for the men. As we got further up into the hills, our party started to come under a bit of small-arms and mortar fire from some German rear guard positions. I remained long enough to plot some of the enemy positions on my map and then hit back for my four o'clock rendezvous with Penhale at the park.

Luckily I was able to catch a ride on an amphibious DUKW, which had ferried some troops ashore and was returning to the beaches.

Penhale had his small Tac HQ set up under some trees in the park: a wireless vehicle, a small lorry, a couple of jeeps, and DRs on motorcycles. His driver was making some Compo tea when I arrived, so I gratefully accepted Pen's offer to share a mug. We then got together to mark up our map boards and share what information we had gathered.

Suddenly there were several bursts of machine gun fire from some bushes behind us. We both dived at once under a nearby jeep and grabbed for our pistols. We could only surmise that some German patrol had infiltrated back toward the beaches or had not been mopped up when the park was cleared by our infantry. As we tried to sort out the picture and plan a strategic withdrawal, another few bursts of small-arms fire cut through the leaves on the nearby trees. Then one of our own sergeants came smiling out of the bush with his sub-machine gun.

With a broad grin on his face, he reported that he had just shot a leopard and saved us from its attack. At first we thought the man was simply off his rocker, but he proved correct. Apparently the heavy naval shelling the previous night had smashed some cages in the local zoo, and several terrified animals had escaped. We subsequently learned that the leopard had mauled a child very badly and had slashed a few local Calabrians.

Back in Sicily that evening, after presenting Monty with a pretty clear picture of the Canadian positions and their build-up program, I recounted our surprising encounter with the leopard. (In his memoirs after the war, Monty recorded that we were attacked by a puma. I recollect that it was a leopard.)

Each day I was given a new assignment visiting various sections of the front, according to where the action was. Most frequently I was to keep Monty in touch with our Canadian forces, but as the 8th Army fought its way up through the mountains and along the shores of the Adriatic, I was employed to work with both army corps and each of the divisions. Some days I would be sent to the forward positions of the Indian division. Another day, it would be the New Zealanders, or the French African Goums, or the 78th British Division. On several occasions I travelled across the mountains, to contact U.S. forces in Mark Clark's 5th Army on the west coast of Italy. I soon learned how to get quickly about the battle areas, either driving my own jeep or catching rides with various units. At times it would be a scout car or a tank; at other times, a navy patrol boat up the coast, when bridges had been blow. I resorted at times — as I had when working as staff secretary for Ralston early in the war — to the use of faked orders. When the situation called for a lift by plane or priority over a bridge under construction, I was able to produce transport requisitions forged on Monty's authority. The big thing was to get accurate, first-hand information back to Monty without delay. Any means justified this end.

As advertised, being in on the action each day made the job pretty exciting, though rather exhausting at times. While a regiment or brigade might have a solid stretch of action for a couple of weeks, they would be pulled back into reserve every so often to rest up and refit. Our job did not have any rest periods, but we did have one advantage: each night we returned from the battlefront for a hot meal and a sleep — though Monty made all his staff bed down outdoors, even in the snow. Whether he thought this would keep us fit or whether it was to demonstrate that his HQ was not going soft, I can't say. However, I had no complaints. I enjoyed being in the know about operations, and each day brought new adventures.

Very quickly I came to know all the divisional and brigade commanders in the 8th Army, as well as their staffs, and many of the regimental commanders. In addition, I was able to keep closely in touch with old pals back at 1st Canadian Division, many of whom envied my job and freedom of action.

One might imagine that a subordinate commander would be suspicious or resent an army LO snooping about his forward positions and then reporting back direct to the big boss, but quite the reverse was true. I was always given a kindly and helpful reception by any of the corps, divisional, brigade or unit commanders. They co-operated in marking up my map board, telling me their exact situation and voicing any serious complaints. They knew that information through normal channels, relayed back through various HQs, could be delayed and perhaps become garbled or edited en route. They found it reassuring that Monty would have a clear picture of their exact situation first hand, before the day was out.

The English officers at Tac, while pleasant and polite, were inclined to keep their distance a bit for the first week or so. When they thawed out, I found them to be a cheery and enthusiastic crowd. Dick Vernon acted as G II Ops; then there were three young ADCs during that period: Johnnie Henderson, Noel Chavasse and John Postin. The other liaison officers were Barham and Duckworth. Harry Llewellyn and one or two others, who worked for Monty's Chief of Staff, Freddie de Guingand, out of Main Army HQ, used to visit us from time to time. Other frequent visitors from Main Army were Bill Williams, Monty's intelligence chief; Miles Graham on the Q side; Belchem on Ops; and the corps commanders, Brian Horrocks and Miles Dempsey. This constituted Monty's highly efficient command group. Though quite aware of Monty's peculiarities and odd personality, they also recognized his great professional ability as a field commander and they formed a very loyal and dedicated team.

Brian Horrocks summed up the picture pretty well some years after the war, when he was being interviewed on a television show. Asked about Monty, he paused for several seconds, then replied: "If there is ever another war, I would travel a long way to serve under Monty again. But in time of peace, I would go twice as far to avoid him."

My own relationship with Monty developed slowly but firmly. Our short briefing and report sessions each day were on a pretty formal basis. I was continually amazed at how well Monty kept himself informed about everything in his army, even down to regimental levels. The morale and clothing of his soldiers, the problems of an artillery battery in getting ammunition or spare parts, the evacuation of wounded, the ration issues — all were matters of concern to him.

When I brought back my reports from the forward areas each day, he expected precise and complete details. I discovered very early, that in answering his questions it was much wiser simply to say I didn't know, rather than to take even an educated guess at any answer. On one occasion, when I had outlined for him the company positions to be occupied at night by one of the battalions, he demanded to know where B Company HQ were situated. I indicated a small cutting which showed on the map and said I thought it was in about there. Quite wrong, Monty snapped; it's over on the other side of the brigade. He was entirely correct I found, when I checked the next day.

Monty did not drink or smoke and his habit was to retire early to bed, regardless of the battle situation or any operational crisis. One night, when a surprise enemy counterattack had penetrated the front some distance, one of the formation commanders got on the line to an ADC at Tac HQ and insisted that Monty should be wakened and informed of the situation. He overrode the ADC's protest that on Monty's orders, he was never to be disturbed once he had retired. Accordingly, the ADC woke Monty and explained how far the Germans had reached.

After hearing the report, Monty sharply replied: "Well, he knows the Germans shouldn't be there. Tell him to kick them out but don't bother me about it in the middle of the night." With this, Monty went back to sleep.

The many stories about Monty's odd behaviour at times, his rudeness, misplaced humour and supreme confidence became legends* throughout the war years.

In respect to smoking, Monty insisted that all cigarettes be extinguished before he entered a room for a conference, to hold a briefing or to issue orders. On one occasion when he had been visiting a U.S. area, the American general had been showing Monty about his sector. At the end of the tiring tour, the two men got into Monty's car to drive back to headquarters. The American general politely enquired as to whether Monty would object to his smoking. "Not at all," replied Monty. Only after the American general had dug out a packet of cigarettes and was about to light one, did Monty add, "but not in my car."

On another occasion, when Wendell Willkie paid a visit to Tac, Monty was deliberately rude to his distinguished American visitor. Unaware of Monty's objection to smoking during meals, Willkie lit up a Camel between each course and blew smoke about the table. This was too much for Monty, who finally rose from his seat, turned his chair about so that his back was to Willkie, and then, for the balance of the meal, carried on a conversation with the man sitting on his other side.

Conversely, when Monty toured the forward areas himself in his open touring car, he would always take a large supply of cigarettes and hand out packages whenever he stopped to talk to the troops slugging up the mountains or through the mud. He used an open car with his pennant flying in front, and sat alone, in the back seat, wearing his distinctive beret. He considered it important that he be seen and identified frequently in the forward areas by the troops; they should realize that he knew about the conditions under which they were fighting.

This was undoubtedly a carry-over from World War I. Monty, in talking about the trench warfare and mud of the previous world war, when he was a junior officer, told us that generals, with one or two exceptions, were seldom seen in the forward areas. Most of their time was spent at their billets in comfortable chateaux, miles behind the lines, where they had little concept of the conditions of their men in the mud. Understandably, the situation resulted in resentment among the combat troops.

Curiously, Monty was capable of great kindness and consideration at times to his juniors and subordinate commanders. On more than one occasion to my knowledge, when Monty noted that an officer was showing the effects of the day-to-day pressures, he would ensure that the man was given some leave, though the officer himself was unaware of Master's intervention.

When on occasion I was delayed on my way back to Tac, perhaps due to a blown bridge, a convoy held up by enemy shelling or simply miles of mud, Monty would delay dinner long enough for me to wash up and have a quick drink before we sat down.

He followed the British Army custom in his mess, that except for the normal courtesies toward a senior, all officers, regardless of rank, spoke

* Prior to the publication of *Missing from the Record*, I had, as a courtesy, sent Monty the galley proofs of those sections dealing primarily with himself. The extracts included a number of anecdotes touching on some of his outrageous behaviour and bad manners at time.

I did not ask him to edit or verify any of these incidents but did request that he advise me, before publication, if there were any serious errors. Some days later, I received these sections, marked up with a red pencil, back from Monty. He made no changes in any of the operational or strategic accounts, but he had crossed out a number of the stories about his often arrogant and inexcusable behaviour. Written in the margin were such comments as "this simply didn't happen." Clearly, there were a few incidents he wished to forget. As none of these items was essential to my book, I did make a few of the deletions requested, but kept the censored pages as a souvenir.

and conducted themselves on an equal footing. Frequently Monty would hold forth on some pet theory regarding key battles in history, or perhaps offer his own interpretation of the Scriptures, subjects on which he was well versed.

He saw both God and Jesus in somewhat military terms. He held that the concept of Jesus being meek and mild was quite in error. To back his claim, he would refer to Christ overturning the tables of the money changers. Similarly, it was "The Lord mighty in battle" who gave us the victories. Almost without exception, Monty had a biblical quotation in the special orders of the day he issued at times of major operations.

One classic Monty story ran as follows: As the final battles of the war were launched, Freddie de Guingand emerged from Monty's caravan with Master's draft of his final order of the day. Someone asked Freddie how Monty was feeling about it all. Freddie was quoted as saying, "Oh, he feels very cocky about everything. He hasn't called on God for any help whatever this time."

Another theory that Monty expounded to us was how the Bible demonstrated the need for a vigorous training program to win wars. In illustration, he would relate how Moses led the starving Israelites out of bondage into the desert, a rabble, slave population. At first they had to dodge about and avoid any warlike Arab tribes in the desert, but then, after a hardening 40-year training period in the wilderness, they were able to march victoriously against all opposition.

It was, I believe, Alan Moorehead who, in commenting on Monty's personality, very aptly quoted G. K. Chesterton: " . . . of old, the Puritan in war was certainly the Puritan at his best. It was the Puritan in peace that no Christian could be expected to stand."

One evening in the mess when Monty had dismissed out of hand the fighting capacity of the Italian forces, I could not resist the temptation to remind him that the Roman legions had once conquered Britain and imposed their rule on his country for some three hundred years.

"Ah, but those were quite different Italians then," Monty replied. In those days, he claimed, all the real fighting men were sent away to conquer foreign countries. It was dangerous to keep these troublesome fellows anywhere near Rome. Then, because Rome was short of manpower for domestic chores, they imported tens of thousands of docile slaves. They were the ones who subsequently populated much of the country, as the ladies of Rome also suffered from the shortage of true Roman manhood.

During the brief period that our Tac HQ was located at Taormina in Sicily, there was a minor incident which provided some passing amusement. The villa which we occupied had been the property of Lady Hulton. With the liberation of Sicily, her London property agents immediately got on the job, and our little mess received from them an invoice covering Lady Hulton's stock of wine and tableware, which had disappeared. These items, however, had disappeared prior to our occupation. After an ad hoc committee of our mess discussed the demand, we despatched a formal reply stating that the request for compensation should be directed to the previous tenants. The previous tenants had been German General Rommel and his staff.

ELEVEN

The Race To Save Salerno

WORLD SCENE

*8th Army strikes north. British and U.S. forces launch
main assault at Salerno — Italy surrenders. Germans
seize Rome, also Italian fleet. German divisions drive
to wipe out Salerno beachhead. Mussolini freed by
German paratroops. Italy, though largely occupied by
Nazi forces, declares war on Germany. King's Italy
established at Taranto.*

The 8th Army, despite some German rear guard action, blown bridges
and mine fields, rapidly pushed into the mountains north of Reggio, as far
as Spromonte. To speed things up the Canadians were ordered to send a
flying combat group down to the Adriatic side and up the Coast Road to
Catanzaro, and then to capture Crotone. Meanwhile, the 5th British
Division was moving up to the west coast, parallelling the Canadian
advance. Although the German rear guard offered serious resistance at
some points, to delay our advance, it was obvious that the Nazi divisions
were withdrawing to the north.

The 8th Army assault had been planned as a feint only, and consequently our units had been committed with limited scales of equipment and
transport. We were hard pressed at first to maintain our rate of advance
through the twisting mountain roads, and frequently vehicles had to be
pooled to support the leading columns.

The larger American 5th Army landing at Salerno to the north was
carried out on the 9th of September to cut off the retreating German
divisions in the south and to capture the port of Naples.

The plan was that when the main 5th Army landing went in, Mussolini
was to be impeached and arrested. The new Italian government, under
Marshal Badoglio, would then surrender, attempt to seize Rome and
subsequently support Eisenhower's forces in neutralizing German units
in Italy.

These plans had been developed in secret negotiations carried on
through Bedel Smith, Eisenhower's Chief of Staff, after Italy's General
Castellano had secretly contacted the British embassy in Madrid.

The surrender document had been secretly signed in Sicily as early as
September 3, the day our own landing went in at Reggio, but the
announcement was to be delayed until the Salerno assault went in.

Unhappily, things did not work out as planned. Led by Marshal Badoglio,
the Fascist Grand Council had arrested Mussolini and smuggled him
away in an ambulance to a prison hide-out. A day ahead, the German
command had wind of what was afoot. They moved quickly to seal off
Rome and disarm the Italian militia just before the Salerno landing.

Then things went badly for the 5th Army assault at Salerno. Because of
U.S. insistence, many of the naval landing craft had been returned
needlessly to the U.K., to aid in the build-up for the Normandy assault,

which was not due until the following spring. As a result the 5th Army build-up on the beaches was dangerously impeded. In addition, the leading units failed to realize from the very start the importance of driving inland at all costs, to safeguard the beaches from direct enemy fire. Our larger transport ships had therefore to remain anchored some miles out to sea. This also slowed the rate of build-up ashore.

In contrast, mobile German divisions, with the benefit of highway transport, quickly encircled the lodgement area and pinned down the Allied forces. For a few weeks it was touch and go; would the 5th Army be driven back into the sea?

At this point in the campaign, General Alexander, then in command of all the land forces, sent Monty a signal ordering the 8th Army to push north as fast as possible, thus to relieve the Salerno beachhead.

For two weeks the landings at Salerno remained in serious danger. In Berlin, Dr. Goebbels confidently noted in his diary that the German general staff believed it could hurl the 5th Army back into the ocean.

Here was perhaps the first illustration of the Americans' distrust of, or failure to grasp, Britain's historic strategy in respect to naval power and the use of a flexible sea-based army in attacking continental Europe. Britain had long understood the value of employing minimum force over a wide circumference to tie down enemy forces.

Obsessed with the concept of an early major assault across the Channel, followed by a massive land battle, the Americans failed to see the real importance of operations in the Mediterranean.

As convincingly described by British historian Sir Arthur Bryant,* the Americans did not appreciate the extent to which Allied operations in Sicily, Italy and Yugoslavia would compel Hitler to divert his divisions away from the eastern front, where Russian divisions were collapsing before his panzer armies. Nor did the Americans recognize the manner in which such operations would draw German divisions from the Normandy coast.

In consequence, the American chiefs of staff had curtailed the number of assault landing craft and aircraft carriers which could be employed in the Mediterranean theatre. Instead of landing in greater force closer to Rome, the 5th Army landing was limited both in scale and mobility.

A defeat at Salerno would have been a major setback for the Allies at that time. As it was, the operations in Italy succeeded in drawing some 40 Axis divisions away from other fronts at a critical period. The majority of the German fighter air force also had to be stationed in western Europe, which gave the Russians a much needed air superiority.

In addition, Tito's uprising in Yugoslavia, as well as partisan threats in Greece and Albania, were encouraged. Had Hitler been able to use on the Russian front some of his divisions tied down in Italy — 15 or 20, it has been estimated — it could have been decisive.

Monty immediately sent the 5th British Division pushing up the west coastal road, and the 1st Canadian Division went cracking off inland to capture Castrovillari and then Potenza. Plans were also made for further 8th Army troops to be landed at Bari. In short, what was intended as only a feint by the 8th Army had now become a full-scale dash to save the Salerno beachhead further north.

*See *Triumph in the West*, by Sir Arthur Bryant.

There were two great obstacles: a shortage of vehicles, and a proper scale of administrative services required to extend our supply lines several hundred miles through the mountains, against growing German resistance. Every bridge was blown, every river approach was mined.

Our engineers performed miracles in temporarily bridging the enormous chasms to get our troops and equipment across. Bridges spanning great defiles and valleys had been dynamited, and the tangled wreckage dropped to river beds hundreds of feet below. Our Bailey bridging equipment was used up in the first few days. Operating often under direct fire, our engineers improvised every stratagem to keep things moving. Sometimes they would blast down both sides of the cliffs to fill the river bed temporarily, and then bulldoze a crossing over the rubble. Again at night, they would take assault boats down to the ocean and ferry winches and other equipment across the mouth of the river, then fight their way back on the far bank to build new footings for timber bridges.

When all else failed, the engineers would hook steel cables onto scout cars, carriers and anti-tank guns; then, with winches, they would lower them down the cliff face to river beds. Here the cables would be unhooked, and winches or tow trucks on the far bank would yank the vehicles and guns through the river and up the far heights.

This could be a pretty hairy adventure for the drivers of such vehicles, as I discovered several times myself when, while clinging to the steering wheel, I had my own jeep winched across a deep valley.

With an all-out effort, the Canadians were able to reach Potenza just a few hours before the 1st German Parachute Division was able to reinforce the town.

At this stage, the 8th Army had completely outrun its supply columns. Mule trains were being established to carry rations and munitions into hills for our advancing troops.

But our objective had been achieved. The Germans launched their final counterattacks on the Salerno beachhead on September 12 and 13, but they were held by the 5th Army, backed by tremendous naval fire from battleships moved in close to shore. Then, with the developing pressure from the advancing 8th Army on their southern flank and from the rear, the Germans were forced to withdraw. Salerno had been saved.

Monty was never very popular with Americans, and after the war some statements appeared in the U.S., claiming that Monty had been slow to act, and that his advance to save Salerno had been delayed needlessly. Subsequently, when some articles of mine appeared in the *Saturday Evening Post*, telling the real story, my remarks were immediately challenged by several U.S. Army officers and a senior editor of a news magazine. To answer these critics, I simply referred them to their own official records, the daily Sit Reps from Italy which were still available at the Pentagon.

The fact was that in a period of 17 days, on short notice, the 8th Army, with only two divisions ashore, advanced some 200 miles (400 road miles), fighting across a difficult mountainous country devoid of proper roads, to relieve Salerno. This was a role that had not been planned for in advance, or even anticipated. Short of vehicles and with a reduced scale of support, weapons and supplies, the achievement was of a very high order and quite unequalled during the rest of the campaign. The nature of the terrain strongly favoured the defence, and the Germans fought savagely from every strong point.

185

Once Monty's left flank joined up with the 5th Army bridgehead and the Canadians on the right pressed farther north, the Germans were forced to withdraw to prevent being cut off. Breaking out of their bridgehead, the U.S. 5th Army quickly headed north to capture Naples, with its important harbour.

The 5th Corps then came under Monty's command and, with other units of the 8th Army, raced to capture the large air fields at Foggia. With these air strips, our bombers could strike at enemy industrial centres in the north, as well as across into the Balkans.

The Canadians next drove inland to capture Campobasso and then struck east to the shores of the Adriatic. Turning northward then, up the coast roads to Vasto and Termoli, they encountered stiffening German resistance at every river crossing and mountaintop. There was no word whatever as to when the Canadians would be moved back to the U.K. for the Normandy invasion.

This decision would undoubtedly be made at the War Office level in London in consultation with Canadian Military Headquarters (CMHQ) and Ottawa. Nevertheless, as senior canadian officer in the field, Guy Simonds felt a bit uneasy about the situation. Although the Canadians had been placed fully under command of the British 8th Army, Guy still bore a degree of direct responsibility to Canadian authority. His terms of reference had been very concise: that his Canadian units could be employed "for limited operations in the toe of Italy," before return to the U.K.

We were now well up the leg of Italy. Further operations were being planned. The idea that our landing was only to be a feint had long since been forgotten. We were now part of a full-scale campaign, the Canadians forming part of a front that stretched clear across Italy. There was no talk whatever of any return to England now.

To the contrary, it started to look like a long stay in Italy for the Canadian 1st Division and Army Tank Brigade. A leave centre was set up in Campobasso, depots for equipment and supplies were being built up, and more Canadian reinforcements were coming forward through Phillipville.

Following a long talk with Guy about the situation, I raised the question formally, at his request, with Monty.

Monty was unable to throw any light on the problem. He had no exact information as to when the Canadians were to leave his command.

"Tell Simonds not to worry," he instructed. "The Canadians were doing well. As long as they continue to win their battles, Simonds doesn't need to worry about exceeding his authority."

Another issue about that period which caused some Canadian concern was in respect to a shipload of Canadian vehicles that arrived in Naples' harbour. This priority shipment had been speeded up by Ralston to replace the various vehicles and guns which had been lost when our three transport ships had been torpedoed just past Gibraltar.

The Canadians, however, were not notified that the much needed vehicles had arrived. By chance, while I was handling some business for Monty back in Bari, I noticed that quite a few of the British rear units had suddenly acquired a lot of brand new Canadian-made jeeps and lorries.

It seemed rather odd that the limey maintenance units should be so well equipped with the new four-wheel-drive Canadian vehicles when the Canadian combat units, struggling through mountains and muddy valleys, were having trouble moving their ammunition up.

All the British brass hats in the maintenance area seemed to have snaffled off nice new Canadian vehicles for themselves. I was given the usual red tape explanation at first when I tried to make some enquiries, but I soon got to the bottom of the mystery. Apparently when the three shiploads of Canadian vehicles had arrived, the members of the British dock operating unit had simply parcelled them out among their friends. It was the old army game of grabbing what you can without asking too many questions.

After long months of desert warfare and the mined roads of Sicily, the entire 8th Army was desperately short of vehicles. The runners we did have were badly worn jobs, patched up from cannibalized parts by field ordnance and REME detachments.

A first-class row now developed and Simonds asked me to clear the matter at once, direct with Monty. I presented our case as forcefully as I could to Master, saying that these vehicles had been pinched behind the Canadians' backs, while they were busy fighting Germans. I tactfully did not mention that the Canadians were now mad enough to do their fighting with the rear units back in Naples.

Monty took the matter in hand and investigated my report without delay. He then proposed a solution. The essential vehicles would all be rounded up and sent forward. He acknowledged that they had been sent by Canada to bring our own units up to scale again.

But what about the British fighting units, Monty enquired. At present they are far worse off for lorries, jeeps and carriers than are the Canadians. Would your people be happy with their own units all up to scale but knowing that a British regiment fighting beside them is 30 per cent or more short of vehicles to bring up their rations and ammunition? He made his point. Without reference back to London or Ottawa, all the new Canadian vehicles would be shared with the British, wherever the need was greatest.

More often than not, the Canadian Army Tank Brigade found itself under command of a British division, to support the British attacks. Week after week, as the fighting went on, the Canadians became more absorbed into Monty's 8th Army. Like the New Zealand, Indian and Australian troops before them, the Canadians took pride in being part of Monty's victorious army, with its Crusader Cross insignia. At the same time, their own fighting achievements soon gave the Canadians a pride in themselves and a reputation with the other divisions. With a curious magic, Monty instilled in his men a confidence in their own abilities and an absolute faith in his leadership.

As early as possible, once a regiment came under his command, Monty would arrange to have all ranks gathered together for his visit. He would position himself where he could be seen, perhaps on the back of a lorry or on a hillock. Then, informally, he would tell the men to break ranks and gather about him. With his hands clutched behind his back and his head thrust forward, he would speak to them:

"I have come here to have a look at you and so you can have a good look at me. We are going to see a lot of each other ... have some adventures together and win victories. You can't be a great general unless you win victories — and I intend to continue as a great general. Any time I commit you to battle, you can be quite certain you are going to win. My reputation means something to me — I can't afford to have any defeats. I

187

won't order you into any battle unless I know you can win — so don't worry about that. Now where are all you chaps from? (Shouts from the troops.) Where do the best soldiers come from? (More shouts from the troops.) Oh, I *thought* all the best soldiers came from western Canada." And so it went each time, with minor variations.

Watching the men's faces, one was always impressed with how this rather simple, rather arrogant message went over. While Monty may have given great offence to those outside his family, there was no doubting the bond of faith and loyalty he created with his own men. They accepted him absolutely as both leader and mascot. His idiosyncrasies, brusk manner and brittle humour, they seemed to understand and relish. Certainly they trusted and believed in him.

New Battle Lines

As soon as the Italian surrender on September 8, 1943, had been announced, the Germans reacted quickly to establish strong defences covering all the approaches to Rome. Then when the 8th Army had relieved the Salerno beachhead, crack German divisions were moved down from the north. They established a series of strong defensive lines stretching across Italy. Consequently, our advance was now slowed considerably. Each day the enemy resistance stiffened and the fighting became more fierce.

It is not possible now to recall all the various missions Monty entrusted me with during this period in Italy, but a few trips of particular interest do remain fresh in my memory.

On several occasions as I scouted forward each day to contact the leading units, I found myself involved in German counterattacks or, thanks to the twisting mountain roads, by accident got ahead of our own troops and had to make an inglorious retreat for cover, as fast as my jeep would travel.

Manser, who had become indispensable to me as both driver and batman, did not find life too happy at Tac. There were subtle differences in the relationship between officers and other ranks in the English Army, as compared with Canadian formations. Whenever circumstances allowed, therefore, I took him with me in the jeep. We always carried such items as sand tracks, a few grenades and a Tommy gun, as well as a wooden box of rations, Compo tea, tins of M&V, some vino and whatever else Manser could scrounge, in case we had to bunk down somewhere on the road overnight.

On one occasion we had, on orders, remained in a forward area till after dark, to discover how a certain night attack against an enemy position developed. Leaving Manser with the jeep back down the road, I had gone forward on foot with one of the company HQs, "to pick up the form," as Monty termed it. With this mission accomplished, I rejoined Manser and we set off to drive home in the dark along the narrow mountain road. At some point we must have taken a wrong turn. It was never too easy in that part of the country to maintain direction at night, because of the way in which all the roads twisted through the mountains. There was a glimmer of moonlight, but the stars were completely clouded over. After nearly an hour of winding through a deep valley, we realized that we were hopelessly lost. The question was whether to lie up till daylight, or try to find a high point of land in order to locate ourselves on the map or gain some general directions.

Then, suddenly, a darkened convoy of military vehicles came down the road toward us. We felt our worries were over. Manser was driving as the convoy passed us in the dark. I strained my eyes, trying to recognize some of our divisional or unit markings on the vehicles. Halfway past the convoy, I noticed, with horror, swastikas on several of the lorries — and then came a couple of Volkswagens. Clearly, we had wandered back of the German lines.

"Don't bother looking," I told Manser, "and don't try to speed up. Just keep on moving." By a miracle we got by in the dark without being detected, but we still had no idea where we were.

Unless we could find our way back to our own lines before daylight, we would likely end up in the bag. We kept on moving till we reached a road on some high ground, where we stopped to try to get our bearings. The roads twisted and turned so much, a compass was almost useless. Finally deciding to take every turn bearing left, we started off again, with me driving and Manser now with our Tommy gun cocked for action.

As dawn started to break in the distance, I caught a glimmer of the ocean on our left as we topped the crest of a hill. We were heading south, all right. Then through the half light, a road barricade suddenly loomed round a bend, only a few dozen yards ahead. There were some German guards lounging on the roadside. I told Manser not to fire unless he had to, and pushed the accelerator down to the floor. We went crashing through the barricade before the guards could collect their wits, and were round the next bend before they could fire.

A few miles further on, we reached some of our own patrols. They were suspicious of us at first, but when we identified ourselves they directed us back to the coastal road leading to Termoli.

Where exactly we had been, I had no idea. So I didn't bother trying to explain to Monty at breakfast, other than regretting that I had been delayed a bit on the way back.

On another occasion, an English LO and I had been detailed to cover a large-scale river crossing. Our instructions had been to remain in the bridgehead throughout the day to see how our build-up was going and also to observe the progress of the engineers in building some bridges for our vehicles and armour to cross.

The river flowed through a wide and deep ravine. The Germans held the high bank of the far side, and in considerable strength. We managed to get across the river with the forward infantry units, but getting back across the river later in the day was quite another matter.

Our assault units had not been able to drive the enemy back from the far crest, and the Germans had kept up a fierce fire all day with mortars, machine guns and 88s. Our people were pretty well pinned to the ground and our engineers had been able to do little about building bridges. Finally after dark, I rendezvoused with the other LO, and we bagged a lift in an inflatable boat, back across the fast flowing river.

Parallelling the river on our near side, back about 200 yards or so from the bank, was a roadway. The German artillery and mortars had the road registered for night fire and kept up a steady bombardment all night long. Several times we made a run to cross the roadway and climb the steep hills behind, but no luck. On one of our forays in the dark, we encountered the opening of a big drain pipe or culvert, which ran a long way back and then under the road. There was a good depth of hard road surfacing above the drain, so we decided to try our luck at crawling under the roadway. We groped our way along the pipe, sloshing through the muddy water as far as we could go. The exit was blocked by a heavy metal grating which refused to budge. We were both tired, cold, hungry, and soaked through. There was nothing to do but to crawl back again. Regaining the entrance, we peered out at an awesome sight: flares and tracers lit up the sky, and shrapnel was flying about in all directions. The game was just not on. Back we went into our sewer pipe and spent the rest of the night there, perched on a couple of iron braces, with the dirty water up to our knees. One of the most unpleasant nights of my life.

Between the crashes and roars overhead, we speculated during the night as to what sort of blow-out we would have if we ever managed to get out of the filth and back to London on leave together. As it happened, we never did manage to get together in London; a few weeks later my partner was posted back to the Staff College at Quetta in India.

Several days after this drain pipe episode, when the PBI, with some artillery support, had driven the enemy back from the heights on the far bank, our engineers, with amazing skill and energy, got five or six temporary bridges erected, despite some enemy shelling.

A week or so after these bridges were completed, we were hit by a tremendous rain storm.

That morning while we were grabbing some breakfast at Tac, a sad Sit-Rep came in over the HQ wireless. The river had turned into a raging torrent. Unbelievably the water had risen about 15 feet overnight, and every one of our precious bridges had been washed away.

With virtually no anti-tank guns or armour to give close support, our forward infantry were now cut off from any supply of ammunition, rations and petrol.

Monty read the report quietly and made no comment. After breakfast, he told one of his ADCs that he wished to see the senior corps engineer officer at tea that afternoon. When this unfortunate officer arrived and had finished his tea at Tac that afternoon, Monty casually raised the matter of the bridges.

"Tell me, General," he asked, "how many bridges did we build across the river?" When given the answer, he then enquired as to how many were now operating. He adopted a rather surprised attitude when the corps engineer explained that none was now operational . . . that during the night the river had surprisingly — in only a few hours — risen over 15 feet and the bridges had been washed out. Most unusual.

"Do you mean to say that a week after our troops had secured the river crossing, we haven't a single bridge in operation?" Monty demanded. "You say the rise in the river was quite unusual?"

Monty then reached for a small Italian geography book he had placed by his chair. "This is a child's school book," he said. "It states that it is not unusual at this time of year for rivers to rise over 16 feet in this area. Every Italian school child knows that — why didn't you? You're sacked." Monty stood up. The tea party was over.

I was then called for and ordered to have Brigadier Geoff Walsh, chief engineer for the Canadian division, report to Master as soon as possible.

When Geoff arrived, he was handed the job of rebuilding the bridges at once, which he did in fast order.

During my period with Monty in Italy and my subsequent association with him in north-west Europe, I witnessed several incidents such as this, where an officer was sacked on the spot when Monty considered him incompetent or negligent, or when Monty felt his own intentions were being deliberately thwarted.

At Main Army HQ there was a small group of LOs headed by Major Harry Llewellyn (later Sir Harry Llewellyn, a horseman of some note who won an Olympic gold medal for Britain after the war). They reported to Freddie de Guingand, Monty's Chief of Staff, as well as to David Belchem, the BGS (Ops). There was a certain amount of rivalry between us over being the first to get battle reports back to our respective bosses. Obviously de Guingand never liked it when Monty had information before it reached his ears.

Harry visited us frequently at Tac and we were all on excellent terms. The race to beat each other carried a rather sporting flavour. Later in north-west Europe, Harry didn't seem to be around Monty's Tac HQ very often. I wondered vaguely about this till some years after the war, when I read Harry's explanation in his book, *Passports to Life*. Seemingly, when he was detailed to recce a site for Monty's HQ in Normandy, he had roused Master's ire by telling him why he could not have this or that desired location — because the places were needed for some other installation.

When Harry reported back to his immediate boss, de Guingand, he was informed of a signal just received from Monty — Llewellyn was not to go to Monty's Tac HQ again.

The morning that Monty had learned of the Sangro bridge disaster, he instructed me to see how the Canadians were getting along on the far side. He made no suggestion as to how I should get across the river this time. The river banks were no longer under direct enemy fire, but there was a fast current running now and the river had swollen several times in size.

The first thought was that I could get the sappers on the bridge sites to raft me across in some way, but then I had a happy inspiration. Since the landings back at Reggio, Monty had appropriated a DUKW (an amphibious vehicle commonly called a duck) for his personal pool of cars. He had used it once or twice for a recce when we had moved up the Adriatic coast, but had pretty well forgotten about it in recent weeks.

I waited till I saw Monty climb into his usual open touring car that morning to leave for the forward area, then went over and borrowed his DUKW for my expedition across the river.

The river current proved too strong for the DUKW, so I had to drive down to the ocean where we were able to cruise across the mouth of the river.

I was back at Tac again that afternoon for an hour or so before Monty sent for me; apparently he thought I had not been able to make the crossing. Joining him in his map caravan, I pointed out all the Canadian positions and reported what the brigade commander was currently planning.

"Oh, you did get across," said Monty. "How did you go?"

I knew that Monty objected to people using any of his vehicles, whether or not he wished to use them, so I had hoped he wouldn't ask this question. I replied very casually that I had used the duck and quickly went on pointing out more positions on the map.

Monty made no further comment till I had completed my report. As I left the caravan he called me back.

"Tomorrow I would like you to get me a report from the brigade on the left. See what their form is.

"And oh," he added, "how do you propose getting over the river this time?"

"Well, I thought I might use the duck again," I replied.

There was a gleam in Monty's eye. "Oh, no. That is *my* duck. I shall be using it myself tomorrow."

I felt quite certain that he never thought of using the duck till I had reminded him of its existence.

I was perhaps lucky to escape to fate of Harry Llewellyn. Indeed, I was fortunate during my entire association with Monty, not only during the war years but also after the war when he was at NATO and the War Office. I never had a serious run-in with him or received any of his lethal rockets. There were times when I had to present and argue a Canadian position a bit strongly and offer advice which ran contrary to his own wishes, but he was never rude or held any resentment. He was usually pretty formal with me, though in the mess or during personal visits he could be both considerate and even entertaining with his dry repartee.

Unforgivable

Perhaps one of the worst instances of Monty's rudeness concerned U.S. General Mark Clark. Without any advance notice, in mid-September the general drove over from the other side of Italy to pay a courtesy visit to Monty. Presumably it was to thank Monty for his assistance at Salerno, but this was never really known, as Monty simply refused to see him.

When Clark arrived at Tac, John Henderson, Monty's ADC, went to Monty's caravan to announce the U.S. general. Monty was possibly peeved about a story circulated in the U.S. that he had been slow in coming to Clark's relief.

Henderson was nonplussed when Monty said he didn't care to see Clark. "What shall I tell him?" Henderson asked. "Tell him what you want . . . tell him I am out," Monty replied indifferently. Clark, who was standing just outside and could not help but overhear this conversation, departed without comment.

Not long after this, General Eisenhower called an O-Group conference for his army commanders at a certain map reference point. Monty was rather taken by surprise when he arrived for the conference and discovered the map reference point happened to be the location of Mark Clark's HQ.

To rub it in a bit, Clark greeted Monty at once and with every courtesy. The perfect host.

Unhappily, Monty never quite grasped the harm he did to Anglo-U.S. relations, or the penalty we would ultimately pay for his thoughtless indiscretions. It all really started when the U.S. forces under Patton first arrived in North Africa. Certainly the Yanks, the new boys in the theatre, were a bit cocky and made many mistakes. But instead of playing the diplomat, Monty could not refrain from talking down to them and ragging them with a bit of his British dry wit. This was neither understood nor appreciated by the U.S. generals, who greatly resented his air of superiority.

The much publicized bet with the Americans in North Africa, which Monty won by reaching Sfax by April 15, appeared to Monty as simply a bit of fun. The wager was a U.S. flying fortress from Eisenhower for Monty's personal use. Monty foolishly demanded payment in full, even though the matter was bound to have repercussions in Washington. The Americans paid up but they didn't forget.

Monty could not appreciate that once Ike was placed in overall command, he would have to come to terms with the Americans. Even later in north-west Europe, when the number of U.S. divisions far outnumbered the British, Monty still failed to reconcile himself to this situation.

On a happier note, there was a celebration at Tac on the first anniversary of the Battle of Alamein. Tac was located then in the Foggia area, near the small Italian village of Lucera. Each of us in the mess was made responsible for some part of the preparations. My job was to provide some fresh meat, either liberated or bartered. Someone else was to look after the music, another the wine, another the entertainment and so forth.

Fresh meat was almost non-existent, but on one of my sorties through an abandoned farm area, I managed to capture a small sheep. I had grabbed one which seemed to be of adequate size for our small mess, but by the time Danny, the cook, stripped off all the wool, it was only the size of a large cat. So I had to go back and chase up another one.

I have forgotten his name, but one officer allegedly composed songs for London musicals before the war. He came up with several ditties, among them, "Our Merry Mobile Bath."

This was inspired by an elaborate Italian bathtub we carted about on one of the HQ lorries. It had been expropriated from a bombed-out old palazzo. The tub would be set up periodically in an olive orchard, with the bottom drain plugged up. Then a bucket brigade from a handy well or stream and using jerry cans, would fill it for some multiple bathing to remove the dirt and fleas. The man having the last turn didn't come out very clean.

Three or four local Italian musicians were located in Lucera, whom we billed as the "Lucera Swingsters." Included with the group was an elderly chap who played the piano well and also spoke English. He claimed that many years before he had been a pianist in Paul Whiteman's band in New York and had come back to his old home in Lucera to retire. He brought along with him his little nine-year-old granddaughter. She was a shy little waif with big brown eyes and she wore a ragged little cotton dress. Her bare feet were muddy and she seemed very forlorn as she timidly asked for *biscotti*.

We had liberated a super grand piano from some place and had it set up in an olive orchard, together with a small platform. There was lots of vino, so it was a great evening. Our pianist was excellent and we kept him going till a late hour under the moonlight, with requests for old favourites, barrack-room songs and such current wartime melodies as "Lili Marlene" and "La Vie en Rose."

I have always enjoyed music, and there was a rather haunting refrain I had often heard the local Italian women singing as they washed our shirts in the river. I hummed the melody for our pianist and he knew it at once. No, he didn't think I could get any records of it or any sheet music. It was

193

just a folk tune here in Calabria. He would play it for me. He went over and lifted his little granddaughter and stood her up with her muddy bare feet on top of the piano. In the moonlight she sang for us; *"Mamma, sola per te la mia canzone vola..."* It was beautifully done, and she was rewarded with great applause and a couple of chocolate bars. Before the old pianist left, I had him scribble out the words and bars of music for "Mamma."

Several times after the war I tried to interest some of my various musical friends to play the melody for me, but they said I didn't have the right number of flats or sharps or something. Then one day I read in an English newspaper that the great Italian tenor Gili, in his farewell concert in London, had included in his program the folk tune "Mamma." From then on the song was an instant success. It made the hit parade in America and versions of it were recorded by countless singers, ranging from Connie Francis in Las Vegas to boy soprano Heide in Germany. My musical friends may listen the next time I tell them I have a good tune.

King's Italy

Many complications soon arose when the Fascist Grand Council deposed Mussolini and sued for peace. In legal jargon, Italy then joined the Allied cause as a "co-belligerent," whatever that meant. In reality, the Germans at once seized control of the northern part of Italy, and a crack team of German paratroopers rescued Mussolini from his secret mountaintop imprisonment. While the Germans had thus established military control over the major part of Italy, there was confusion about civilian authority in Calabria and the south.

As each area was liberated in the south, town majors were appointed by the army and AMGOT officers (Allied Military Government) were set up in control of major centres. Technically, when these areas no longer remained within the combat zone, they were to revert to the civilian control of our new Italian ally. The trouble here was that no elected or effective Italian government remained in existence once Germany sealed off Rome and rounded up former members of the Grand Council.

In these circumstances, it was determined that AFHQ in Algiers would simply appoint a temporary civilian government till the whole of the country was liberated. To avoid untold political squabbling, it was first decided to establish a presidential type of administration with the presidency being offered to Benedetto Croce, the famous and much respected Italian philosopher and historian. Because of his age, the old man turned down the job. I had the good fortune to meet this fine gentleman before I left Italy, and was much impressed with his wise views on this troubled world.

Finally it was decided to bring back the King of Italy, to serve as a rallying point and establish what was known as "King's Italy," with a temporary capital near Taranto.

There was much infiltrating from the north through our lines. The escapees included some of our own airmen who had been captured, former Italian officials, and senior Italian soldiers. Often they were aided by local Italian farmers who knew all the mountain trails. The legendary Popski, one of our own behind-the-lines experts, was also instrumental in organizing many of the escapees. The Germans took advantage of this situation by frequently infiltrating some of their agents through our lines in the guise of civilian escapees. Their mission would be to signal back intelligence regarding troop movements and to spot artillery targets such as storage depots and HQ locations.

Our own Provost Corps established a network of checkpoints to round up and screen all the refugees, and extra security precautions were established around our HQ locations. Monty's Tac HQ was always pretty well concealed. We avoided using any office buildings or houses. Just our few lorries and caravans would usually be hidden in a bluff of trees several hundred yards off the main road of advance. Our own and any visitors' vehicles were kept camouflaged and always some distance away from the camp proper. There were no signs or arrows designating the HQ, other than a small metal standard, topped with a small crusader's cross and the numerals 35. This standard stuck at the side of the road alone would mark the foot path leading to our camp. Convoys and marching troops would pass it all day without realizing its meaning. Commanders, staff officers and despatch riders were, of course, in the know — but woe betide them if they ever tried to park their own vehicles too close to the little compound.

One day the Provost Corps, screening the refugees escaping through the lines, managed to pick up a pretty hot prisoner. He had been secretary of the Fascist Grand Council and had been present at its final meetings after Mussolini was toppled.

We were still pretty much in the dark about just what was happening at a political level up north. This man could give us the story, and I was at once detailed to escort him back to Taranto for interrogation.

He was glad to get away from the Germans and was no danger to us in any way, so I set off alone with him in my jeep, for the long drive back along the Adriatic coast. It was slow going because of endless army convoys and blown bridges. There was lots of time to talk. He spoke good English and told me his whole story.

Some earlier yarns about Italy during the war, told to me by an Italian-American friend, Frank Gervasi, a top feature writer for *Collier's* magazine, came to my mind as we drove south. During the first years of the war, before the United States joined in, Frank had been sent to Italy to negotiate for the publishing rights on Count Ciano's famous diary.* Besides being foreign minister, Ciano was also Mussolini's son-in-law.

Frank Gervasi had not succeeded in his mission, but on his return he had regalled me with lurid stories about his highlife in Rome with the Fascist hierarchy. He claimed to have slept with the wives of several of the prominent Fascist officials. This I found a bit hard to believe, so I questioned my prisoner about it — about one titled lady in particular. "Oh yes," said my prisoner, "everyone in Rome slept with her." And then he added to the story.

As we were unable to get through to Taranto that night, I decided we should stop over at Bari. Taking my prisoner into the Albergo Imperiale, Bari's largest hotel, I went to the reception desk and demanded a double room for the night.

The dapper Italian receptionist was all courtesy and smiles but sorrowfully regretted that he had no vacancies. None of my arguments,

*Count Ciano's diary revealing many Axis secrets and recording the relationship between Hitler and Mussolini was published several years after the war, when Mussolini was dead.

protests or threats to call the town major could change his mind. He was full of apologies but the answer was *niente*. My prisoner, standing behind me, smiled slightly as he listened to my protests. He then stepped forward, clapped his hands together loudly and let go a great torrent of abuse in Italian. I couldn't catch many of his words, except his order that the hotel manager be paraded at once. In a matter of seconds we had the best suite in the hotel. The Fascist authority had not been forgotten. The fact that I wore the uniform of the victorious army meant nothing, while the words of my civilian prisoner brought instant action.

It took most of us a while to understand fully the Calabrians. Unless you were smart, they simply absorbed you and happily swindled you at every turn. You could be furious with them but it was also hard not to like them or to withstand their infectious humour and instant emotions.

As Croce was to explain to me later, the Calabrians, through many centuries and countless occupations, had learned to live with and absorb their conquerors. Gradually the conquered always won out.

Timberwolf

It was after we had started to drive up the Adriatic coast toward Termoli and Vasto that Monty asked me, casually at dinner one night, if I knew the meaning of the code word Timberwolf. Apparently the word had appeared in a signal received from Canadian Military HQ in London. He didn't understand it, and he asked me to see what I could find out about it, either at 1st Division or back at 2nd Canadian Echelon in Naples.

A day or two elapsed before we discovered that it designated an operation whereby the 5th Canadian Armoured Division, together with a complete Corps HQ staff under General Crerar, were en route from England to Italy, to join Monty's 8th Army. It still seems incredible that Monty wouldn't have been advised of this in advance, but such was the case. There had been some slip-up in communication.

Understandably, Monty was put out. "Why wouldn't they ask me first if they were needed," he asked. To begin with, because of the mountainous type of warfare, he didn't need more tanks. The 8th Army presently had more armour than it could deploy. Similarly another Corps HQ was redundant, for each of the existing Corps HQ could easily administer one or two more divisions if required.

On making some private enquiries through Canadian channels and through AFHQ in Algiers, I was able to piece the picture together a bit for Monty.

Apparently, the proposal to send out a Canadian armoured division and Corps HQ had originated in Ottawa and had been agreed to by the War Office, once it was known that the 1st Canadian Division would not be returning immediately to the U.K. The 1st Division had acquitted itself well and gained much battle experience. The thought was that some Canadian armoured units should also get battle experience, and that one of our Corps HQs should gain some knowledge of operational control.

When I explained these purposes to Monty, he soon came to accept the situation and helpfully started to plan how these new formations could be worked into his operations.

His first concern was the additional Corps HQ under Crerar. Crerar had never commanded in the field before, even on a regimental or brigade level. Monty's proposal, therefore, was that he should first take over acting command of the experienced 1st Canadian Division, for a month, with its well-integrated staff, to get the feel of things before tackling a corps responsibility with his entirely green staff. To provide this opportunity for Crerar, Monty suggested that I try to work out an arrangement where Chris Vokes, who was temporarily commanding the 1st Division, should go on leave for a blow-out for several weeks, while Crerar took over this veteran division. Chris had not had any leave since before the Sicily landing. Guy Simonds was on the sick list, and Chris had taken over his heavy responsibilities for the past couple of weeks. Meanwhile, all the elements of Crerar's Canadian Corps HQ could be assembled back in Sicily. The 5th Armoured Division would be concentrated in the Caserta area, carrying out a few exercises before being brought forward into action.

Guy Simonds, when released from hospital, would take over command of the 5th Division, for armoured experience. Chris would be appointed to command the 1st Division full time when he returned from leave. Crerar, having gained some experience in battle command, could then return to his Corps HQ, which Monty would make operational, placing the 1st Canadian Division and one or two experienced British divisions under Crerar's command till he got the feel of things.

This program, carefully thought out by Monty, was very much in the Canadian interest — but it never got off the ground. Crerar flew out a few days ahead to see Monty, and he simply refused to play. He took the position that Vokes did not need any leave. Also, he would not step down, even for a couple of weeks, to command a division. He insisted that he should remain in command of his Corps HQ until it could be made operational, and accordingly, he moved with his large HQ staff to Taormina in Sicily. This was simply a matter of pride on Crerar's part. As far as Monty was concerned, it was a needless irritant.

No sooner had Crerar established himself in Sicily than he shot off a signal to Monty's Chief of Staff, de Guingand in Italy, advising that, as he would be visiting Italy frequently, he was shipping his personal caravan, staff car and jeep, complete with drivers and batman, to be kept and maintained at Army HQ for his personal use. This posed an awkward situation at Main HQ. Apart from the bother of having to drag these extra vehicles about for Crerar's convenience, nobody relished the idea of having a spare corps commander hanging about, expecting all the courtesies and attention due his rank. Besides, any such arrangement would certainly require advance approval by Master.

As soon as I heard of the project, I sent a message to Crerar saying the vehicles would not be welcome and diplomatically warning him off, but to no avail. The vehicles arrived and Monty was furious.

A few days later a signal from Crerar reached the Tac HQ, ordering me to meet him the next day with a staff car at Foggia airfield and to escort him to see Monty at Tac. On reading the signal Monty became very chilly and pointed out to me that I was on his staff, not Crerar's. My orders, he said, came from him not Crerar, and I was to point this out very clearly to Crerar. Yes, I was to go to Foggia, meet Crerar and tell him this — and also to tell him that Monty didn't wish to see him at that time. When he did want to see him, he would send for him; meanwhile, he was to remain at Taormina. This was not a happy assignment but there was no way out of it. Crerar was now under Monty's command, so off I went.

While Crerar knew the army book backwards, he was very much the Permanent Force Staff College officer. He was very exact on the administrative side and a stickler for correct procedures and protocol. I knew Crerar fairly well, as I had worked under him for a time in Ottawa when he was Chief of the General Staff. We had also both accompanied Ralston on his mission to see Churchill early in the war. He was not a broadgauge man and seemed always to be caught up in the narrow technicalities of his appointment. Throughout the entire war, I suspect, Crerar nursed a lingering contempt for the civilian or militia soldier.

Regardless of any personal views, my job was to ensure, as far as possible, a happy relationship between Monty and the Canadian command. Some real diplomacy was now called for, but Crerar didn't give me a chance.

As he stepped down from his aircraft at Foggia, he acknowledged my formal salute with the briefest of greetings.

"Where is the staff car?" he demanded. As soon as the car swung up, he climbed into the back seat and shut the door. Obviously I was to ride in front with the driver.

"Take me to Tac Army HQ," he ordered, and away we drove. We had only driven a mile or so when I realized there was no easy out; I would have to tackle things head on. I couldn't let Crerar just walk into disaster. Tapping the driver's arm, I told him to pull over to the side of the road. Crerar demanded to know why we were stopping but I ignored him, telling the driver to get out and walk up the road a bit — to have a cigarette. I would call him when he was needed.

Not wishing to seem too brutal, I took an informal approach and came right out with it.

"Harry, Monty says he won't see you and I don't know how to tell you any other way." He was stunned for several minutes. The Camberley composure evaporated. "Well, what do I do now?" he asked.

For the next few minutes I tried to explain Monty's attitude and peculiarities, assuring Crerar that he could count on Monty's full support but shouldn't try to crowd him. My recommendation was that Crerar should simply swing over and have an informal visit with Chris Vokes at 1st Division, to give some reason for his trip, and then to return to his own HQ at Taormina and await Monty's orders. Meanwhile, I would return to Tac and tell Monty that he quite understood, didn't wish to be in the way and would simply make a courtesy call on Chris before returning to Sicily.

Happily, Crerar accepted my advice. Monty did not pursue the matter further but got busy with de Guingand, planning how the new Canadian division and Crerar's HQ could be integrated and brought into action as quickly and smoothly as possible.

Guy Simonds was posted to command the 5th Division and Monty outlined certain training exercises the division was to carry out, preliminary to its first operational attack. Alternative arrangements were worked out for Chris Vokes and Bruce Matthews, at 1st Division, to get some leave in Cairo, and plans were advanced toward sorting out an active role for Crerar's HQ.

Crerar had a passion for formal written orders and would not leave the paper war alone. Through years of soldiering in the regular army, it had become a disease with him. The real blow-up came very quickly, just after Guy Simonds returned from hospital and took command of the 5th Division concentrated near Caserta.

On the operational side, Guy received orders directly from Monty, in respect to special armoured exercises preparatory to going into action. On the administrative side, Guy's division answered temporarily to 2nd Echelon HQ in Naples, on which he was based for supplies and equipment. Guy then started to get a third set of contradictory orders from Crerar in Taormina, directing that he submit written copies of all returns, parade states, daily training syllabi, and so on. Guy, who had less use for paper than even Monty, blew at once. To begin with, he wasn't under Crerar's command — and he registered this point by a very curt signal to Taormina. Consequently, a first-class row developed between the two Canadian commanders before Monty got wind of it at Tac.

Occupied with attacks to crack the stiff German defences, Monty became exasperated with Crerar's nonsense. I was ordered to take a plane and fly at once back to Taormina and tell Crerar he was to stop issuing orders to units not under his command; on no account was he to issue any more directives to Simonds until the 5th Division came under his command. After seeing Crerar, I was to fly over to Caserta and see Guy, tell him to cool down, just get on with his orders from Monty and ignore any orders to the contrary.

It was a very bumpy flight in the little aircraft to Taormina, and I had been running a bit thin ever since the hospital period and dysentery in North Africa. It must have shown when I reported to Crerar, for he first asked how I was feeling. Would the message wait till after dinner, perhaps? Why don't you stretch out for an hour, take time to clean up a bit? Then we can talk after dinner.

His offer was simply too good to refuse . . . to stretch out on a real bed, with a roof overhead, then a bath with hot water. At Tac, Monty insisted that all his staff sleep outdoors on the ground, in bed rolls, even when it snowed. You managed a shave from a tin of warm water in the morning. For my own part, Manser would wake me with a dipper full of hot Compo tea, half of which I drank but the other half used for shaving. I remember, with thanks, Crerar's kindness to me on that occasion.

Clean and refreshed, I went down to the mess ante room just before dinner. Crerar had not yet arrived but, to my surprise, waiting for him was a Medical Corps brigadier whom I recognized at once. It was a Dr. Fred Van Nostrand, an old friend, whom I had last seen many years before in Toronto. He was an older man and had seen service in World War I. He now held the appointment of Chief Psychiatric Advisor to the Canadian Army, he explained. Happy to see each other again, we reminisced for a few minutes. Then I asked what on earth he was doing all the way out here. Fred first checked to ensure that the mess waiter had left the room. Then, to my astonishment, he confided that Crerar had summoned him from London to come out and certify that Guy Simonds was insane. I was thunderstruck, but Fred assured me this was the true purpose of his trip. He was to proceed the next day to Simonds' HQ in Italy to observe and examine him.

Our conversation was cut short by Crerar's arrival, and we went in to dinner. There was an exchange of news about London and the battlefront in Italy for a while, then Crerar brought up the subject of Simonds. He had become mental, Crerar insisted, had been released from hospital too soon . . . was suffering some form of nervous breakdown . . . was quite irrational . . . was now sending insane replies in response to Crerar's signals. I simply listened and wondered how I could best relay Monty's orders to Crerar after dinner.

It was an unpleasant job but Monty's orders were duly delivered, when I was alone with Crerar after dinner. There is little of benefit to the bearer of bad news, and I fear my stock with Crerar suffered a bit further when I had finished. Crerar heard me out but made no comment whatever. My plane couldn't take off till next morning. He would see that I was given an early call.

Before turning in, I went along to Fred's room and gave him the picture as best I could. He had no means of transportation to Italy, so asked if he could catch a ride in the plane with me to Simonds' HQ in the morning.

Landing near Naples the next day, we caught a ride together to 5th Division HQ. Guy was away visiting one of his brigades but had been notified in advance of our visit. He would be back in time for dinner and wished us to join him at his "A" mess.

During dinner, Guy was his usual alert, rather crisp and formal self. He was pleased at the training progress being made by his new division, and wanted to know the news from the front and future plans. Then he brought up the subject of Crerar. The man was "quite bonkers" he assured us . . . had gone off his rocker . . . should be in an institution . . . was sending insane signals all over the place. Fred and I exchanged glances over the table but offered no comment. Guy was an old friend of many years' standing, so it was not so surprising that he spoke so frankly. He, of course, had no inkling as to the purpose of Fred's visit, but no doubt relied on the respect of a doctor for confidences. Certainly Guy became a bit high-strung during battles but, without doubt, he possessed one of the sharpest military minds in the Canadian Army.

After dinner, aside to Fred I asked what he was going to do about the situation. He smiled and threw up his hands. "I am going back to London as fast as I can get there," he said. "This isn't a problem for me."

I never did learn how Fred wiggled out of this situation, but after a private chat with Guy, I returned to Tac the next day and reported my mission accomplished.

Fortunately, my trip seemed to have achieved its purpose, as the pressures from Crerar eased off. It was fortunate, particularly in Crerar's own interest, as quite unknown to Crerar, Monty, or myself at that time, the great decision regarding Crerar's future command of the Canadian Army would rest with Monty before many weeks had passed.

Slugging Up The Coast

As we pushed our way up the coast of Italy, the weather deteriorated rapidly and the German defences grew stronger and the fighting fiercer. Every mountaintop village became a German fortress and the countryside a morass, wherever tanks or heavy vehicles churned up the sand. Series of four-wheel-drive jeeps all chained together had to be used to bring ammunition forward through the mud to the artillery positions. As Monty commented at the time, it now became apparent why Caesar always "went into winter quarters" when the winter rains and mud arrived.

Supplies for our infantry units in the mountains often had to be carried by mule train. Casualties increased, but step by step the 8th Army moved forward, crossing endless rivers with steep banks and with all bridges blown — the Feltrino Valley, the Moro, the Arielli — through the Bernhardt line, the capture of Termoli — and on toward the Sangro River — Ortona and the Gustav line. The Allied purpose to contain as many German divisions as possible in Italy was being achieved, but at heavy cost. Facing the 8th Army, Kessclring's forces included an elite paratroop division, the 90th Panzer Grenadiers, the 16th and 26th Panzers and the 65th Infantry Division.

My daily liaison trips across the front varied from day to day, according to the action. Apart from Canadian operations, I also came to know the 8th Indian Division, the New Zealanders, the Irish Brigade, the French African Goums, and the Polish troops in action.

Among the many memories of that period which remain fresh is the one of a heart-rending night on the road with a small convoy of ambulances operated by a group of American volunteers. They were all of them conscientious objectors, sincere in their beliefs. Refusing the U.S. draft, these young men at the outbreak of war had volunteered as ambulance drivers. They had been in front line action long before the American forces landed in North Africa.

I was on the coastal road from Vasto to Termoli and, like the small convoy of U.S. ambulances, was held up for hours in a mile-long column of army vehicles. A bridge had washed out ahead and no detour was possible in the mud. The ground on either side of the road was a quagmire. It was a pitch black night and bitterly cold. The hours passed as the endless column waited for the engineers to construct a temporary bridge.

To keep the blood circulating, I got out of my jeep and started to walk back along the dark column. As I approached the half-dozen ambulances, I could hear the wounded men inside moaning dreadfully and shrieking. They had all been badly smashed about by machine guns and shrapnel from German mortars and were headed back to a casualty clearing station. They had been held up so long on the road that all the supplies of morphine had run out. I talked to the young American lad in charge but there was simply nothing further that could be done for them. I stayed working with them till dawn, trying to make the wounded a bit more comfortable on their cramped stretchers, adjusting bandages and mopping up blood in the dark. The screams of the wounded men and the dedication of the ambulance boys remained in my mind a long time. It changed my views considerably about conscientious objectors. They had been serving in battle before Pearl Harbor.

My visits to the Indian Division were always of interest, particularly the operations of the Gurkha regiments. Fighting over the high ridges and steep valleys, they taught the 8th Army a lot about mountain warfare, night patrols and handling ammunition mule trains under fire.

On one occasion, a veteran British regiment failed in three separate attacks to capture a small Italian town perched high up in the hills. The job was then turned over to the Gurkhas, who took the town with a single company in a night attack, scaling the slopes quietly and using their kukris.

They held the town against repeated German counterattacks for two days. The Germans then managed to work three great Tiger tanks with flame throwers up into the town in the darkness. It was something entirely new for the Gurkhas. They had never seen flame throwers before, and when the Tigers rumbled through the streets, scorching every building with huge blasts of flame, the Gurkhas had to take the back door out. With their fighting reputation at stake, they retook the town a few days later. Monty sent me over to report on this second attack, a brave and rather bloody performance.

I was always puzzled about a ritual I saw performed several times by Sikh regiments. High up in the mountains on a plateau covered with snow, hundreds of Sikhs, bare to the waist in the bitter cold, would be sitting on their haunches in long rows as though on parade. They would all rub themselves with snow and then, very deliberately, start winding their long turbans about their heads. Whether this was a religious performance or a form of morning PT, I don't know, but it was a rather striking scene to encounter suddenly on an Italian battlefield.

It was also during this period that I came to know the legendary guerilla fighter Popski, of Popski's Private Army. Before the war, Popski was a businessman in Cairo. When the desert campaign started, he formed a small band of guerillas to raise hell behind the enemy lines with small night raids, sabotage, helping prisoners to escape, stirring up the local peasants, grabbing intelligence about enemy movements, or what have you.

It was alleged that he had changed his name to Popski and took up his adventurous underground activities, primarily due to marital problems. Be that as it may, he was certainly courageous, passionate and slightly mad. He would come back through the lines every so often, sometimes to guide escaping prisoners, bring intelligence or obtain weapons and explosives. To avoid being picked up by our own provosts and to avoid unwanted curiosity, he and his men, when back in our own area, would discard their scruffy civilian or native garb and don regulation battle dress. To complete the disguise, they required some form of regimental shoulder title to sew onto their battle jackets. In the same way that the Princess Patricias Canadian Light Infantry carried the letters PPCLI on their sleeves, the insignia PPA (Popski's Private Army) was adopted. It was not according to any approved dress regulation, but it served its purpose.

Popski would often be behind enemy lines for weeks on end, but on his return trips always checked in with our Intelligence people at Main Army HQ and, at times, reported direct to Monty. We were instructed to give him all the help we could and, as far as possible, whatever materials he asked for to carry out his work. He was a carefree soul, enjoyed a drink and amused us when he turned up and recounted his current exploits. He usually demanded more tommy guns, ammunition, hand grenades, explosives, and tobacco and foreign currency with which to bribe people.

The most effective merchandise was tobacco, but it was far too dangerous for him to carry Allied brands of cigarettes. On several occasions, I had Manser and some of the other drivers stay up at night slitting with razor blades the paper wrappers off cartons of "Victory V" and "C in C" issue cigarettes, to meet one of Popski's rush orders.

When Popski was operating with the partisans across the Adriatic from us, we frequently arranged some air drops for him. On one memorable occasion, he turned up and demanded the use of a small aircraft to fly him across the Adriatic for some important reason.

A young captain by the name of Stafford undertook the mission. He was not a regular air force pilot, but he did have his pilot's wings for small artillery spotting aircraft. When Stafford returned from the flight, he recounted a hair-raising adventure. When they took off in the small plane, Popski was carrying a sackful of hand grenades. Seemingly, he had teed up a small band of partisans to attack a German wireless post. This involved charging up a hill with little cover, but Popski had promised his boys some direct bombing support.

According to Stafford, he didn't realize that he was on a bombing mission till the very last moment, when at the zero hour Popski told him to circle down low over the enemy position. At this point some coloured rockets went off and Popski, pulling back the cowling, started dropping hand grenades over the side.

The little plane was completely unarmed, so when enemy tracers started flying upward, Stafford headed for home over the Adriatic as fast as he could go, damning Popski all the way. Popski, however, was delighted; he had seen his partisans swarm up the hill as soon as his grenades started to explode.

In his memoirs after the war, Popski related how after a few drinks one evening, while visiting the HQ of the 1st Canadian Division in Italy, he engaged in a friendly wrestling match with the divisional commander. Popski never concerned himself too much about rank and perhaps he might have had an extra drink or so, but the record should be corrected. It was not the general he wrestled on that occasion but the senior divisional staff officer, at the time Malim Harding of Toronto.

Another colourful character at that period was Pres Gilbride, the A&Q of 1st Division. In army jargon, Pres was known as an operator, and he had a touch of imagination. Among his many responsibilities was the horrendous task of transporting tons of supplies each day by motor convoy along the muddy coastal road, to each of the forward brigade areas. He noted that a bombed Italian railway line ran from Bari all the way up the coast to Ortona and beyond.

In short order, he located a few railway engines which were still working, and, together with some former CPR men from the various regiments, put the line in operation once more to haul freight for the Canadians. The divisional engineers gave a hand in repairing the bombed rail line, and Gilbride's Railway began to make history.

It may now be recorded that after the railway had been in operation for a few weeks, a couple of enterprising souls conceived the idea of converting one of the engines into a sort of armoured train and taking a run further up the line into German-held territory. A machine gun was mounted on the cow catcher and off they went up the line, with the idea of shooting up a few Jerries. It was not an authorized trip and there were some questions asked when the engine, after many hours, failed to return.

There was a telegraph key in the nearby little station and the telegraph line still seemed to be operating. One of our signallers tapped out a message, hopefully for some Italian operator behind the German front. "Questo il treno Inglese?" the message read. In due course, a reply came over the wire: "Il treno Inglese boum boum." That was the last we ever heard of our armoured engine.

On rare occasions my duties would take me back on a quick visit to Naples, usually in connection with supply difficulties. Located here was the Canadian 2nd Ech HQ, under Brigadier Warwick Beament, together with various other British and U.S. Admin. services for both the 8th and 5th Armies. By luck, I managed to get into Naples the day it was liberated by the U.S. forces. In honour of the liberation, the Italians staged a gala but unrehearsed performance that night of the opera *Madame Butterfly*, at the famed San Carlo Opera House. It was an hilarious evening. Many of the stage arrangements went wrong but the singing was stupendous, with countless encores demanded by the shouting Italians. Like the rest of the audience that night, I acquired a new species of fleas from the padded plush seats.

On another of my trips back to Naples, I checked in at the office of the town major, to get a ticket assigning a room for the night at one of the designated transit hotels. (The farther back one got from the front, the greater the amount of red tape.) I was given a room slip but told I would have to share the room with a Colonel Philip Astley, a British Guards' officer who had just arrived from London. At the hotel, I met the colonel, a tall, strikingly handsome man in a beautifully tailored uniform. He was a pleasant chap and had a good bottle of whisky in his haversack. After a few drinks, we decided to have dinner together at the Officers' Club, where he told me he had to report to 8th Army Main HQ the next day but hadn't found any means of getting there. As I had a station wagon and was driving myself back the next day, I offered a lift. I would be going right by Main HQ, which was located near Termoli.

While scanning the notice boards and troop's newspapers at the Officers' Club to see what entertainment might be available, we read that the glamorous movie star Madeleine Carroll had arrived in Naples to put on a show. Gossip had it that she had flown out with some RAF air marshal.

Quite casually, my new acquaintance mentioned that he had once been married to her. This seemed interesting but he made no further mention of the matter, nor did he suggest that we might see where she was performing. After we had finished his whisky back at the hotel and were about to turn in, he said he was going down to the lobby for a minute to see if he could find out where Madeleine was staying . . . might try to see if he could get through to her by telephone to say hello.

When I awoke in the morning, Astley's bed had not been slept in. I asked no questions when he turned up after breakfast, looking a bit the worse for wear.

Leaving Naples, we took the road up to Campobasso, from where I intended to swing east down the coast road. It was a bad trip. First we encountered miles of mud and, as the steering gear of the station wagon was faulty, I had trouble keeping out of the ditch. It took us several hours to reach Campobasso and then we ran into heavy snow. We debated about trying to struggle on through the mountainous roads down to the coast and decided it was worth the try. Once we got out off the high ground, it should be easier going.

About 10 miles out of Campobasso, we started to run into heavy snow drifts. I had had considerable experience driving through snow in western Canada, but with the crooked steering it was simply no go. As we repeatedly dug ourselves out, it started to get dark and our spare petrol was used up. The only building in sight was a burned-out little farm house. We trudged over to it, to discover the roof had caved in. A little farther off we located a low shed. It was a chicken house, the floor covered with chicken droppings and ancient feathers. However, the roof was sound and the walls intact, so we decided to bunk in there where we could stretch out till daylight keeping warm with the help of a small field cooker which I carried in the wagon.

It was a cold, grim scene in the morning when we struggled awake to brew up some Compo tea. The handsome colonel of the previous day had disappeared. Without a shave, and with his uniform, like my own, now crumpled, the marks of Whitehall and the West End had vanished entirely. Moreover, we discovered that we were both infested with chicken lice. As we dusted the feathers and chicken droppings from our kit, I wondered just what thoughts went through his mind when he compared these sleeping arrangements with those of the previous night. After all, it was war.

The question of winter uniforms had continued to haunt the 8th Army until well into November. Week after week we were assured that the warm clothing was on its way ... that supplies had arrived at the base ordnance depot ... that stocks would be available within the week at every brigade. But nothing came to protect the men from the cold mountain winds.

Gilbride did manage to negotiate a loan of some extra blankets from the U.S. Army for the Canadians. Unlike British issue blankets, the U.S. ones were khaki in colour, almost the same shade as our regulation battle dress. It didn't take the boys in the Edmonton Regiment long to discover that these blankets could be quickly cut up and sewn into very serviceable parkas, similar to those used in the Canadian north. The parka fad spread like wildfire throughout the Canadian divisions. Officers and men alike all started to have their extra U.S. blankets cut up and converted into khaki parkas, complete with hood, despite the howls from Main Army HQ. Eventually Monty was brought into the act, and I was told to see the divisional commander and order him to have this destruction of military property halted at once. All unit COs were to reprimand their men and ensure that the price of the blanket was stopped from the pay of any man who had stitched up a parka.

As I was delivering this order to Guy Simonds at his HQ, I saw the OC of the Recce Regiment, arriving in his jeep to see Guy, wearing one of the condemned blanket parkas himself. He was a good friend and I tried to warn him off, but he walked right into it. The usual smile dropped from the colonel's face, as Guy proceeded to tear a strip off him for setting a bad example to his men. Obeying orders, the colonel subsequently paraded all his men, relayed his orders and recorded that the price of a blanket would be stopped from his own pay, too.

Monty's patience was by now exhausted over the procrastination back at AFHQ over deliveries of winter uniforms. Despite his repeated demands, none of the serge battle dress arrived. After breakfast one morning, he finally had a signal sent to Force HQ, telling a senior supply officer back in Algiers that he wished to see him.

When the officer duly arrived at Tac, Monty greeted him with disarming courtesy. Then after tea, Monty said, "Ah, come over into my caravan, where we can have a chat."

There was no sound of raised voices or any altercation within the caravan, but when the door opened, the visiting officer staggered out white in the face, obviously very distraught. As Johnny Henderson, Monty's ADC, commented, he looked as if he was going to burst into tears. He brushed aside Johnny's offer to call his car and strode silently to the car park.

Shortly afterward, Monty, clad in his customary grey sweater and corduroy bags, came bouncing out of the caravan.

"Well, what did that man look like?" he demanded, beating his chest with both fists. "What did he have to say?"

"He didn't seem to want to talk," Johnny volunteered.

"Oh well, he must talk ... get on the phone to Main Army HQ right away. Tell them to strike now while the iron's hot ... demand all the stores we need."

Exactly what happened in the caravan we never determined, but all the winter clothing which had been delayed for weeks, suddenly started to arrive the next day by air lift.

Ralston's Visit

It was while our Tac HQ was still located near Termoli that a signal came over the ACV wireless one day addressed to me from my former boss, Canada's Minister of Defence, Ralston. Monty handed it to me without a word, after breakfast. According to staff duty etiquette, it should not have been addressed directly to me.

The signal was to advise me of Ralston's imminent arrival in Italy and requested that I meet him with a staff car at Foggia air fields, to take him to Tac, as he wished to see General Montgomery and visit the Canadian troops.

When I had finished reading the message, Monty very coldly demanded to know who Ralston was — and why Ralston presumed to give orders to me, while I was on his personal staff. This caught me a bit by surprise, so I played for time. I explained quietly that Ralston was Canada's senior Minister of Defence and had been one of my former chiefs.

"Oh, a politician?" Monty snorted. "I haven't much use for them. I don't like to see them out here at all. I suppose he will have to visit the Canadian division, but I don't care to see him."

There was dead silence for a few seconds. Here was something that had to be faced even if it risked my job. During the past few months I had established a fairly good relationship with Monty, so I spoke frankly.

"Sir, I don't think you can refuse to see him. He represents our Canadian government."

I then went on to point out that Ralston was equivalent to Britain's Secretary of State for War. There would be serious repercussions in Ottawa and Whitehall if he refused to meet Ralston. Ralston had given up his law practice and joined the government when war was declared. During the previous war, he had commanded a regiment in action, with considerable distinction.

Monty fixed me thoughtfully with cold blue eyes for several seconds.

"Well, I suppose I will have to see him," Monty concluded. "Bring him up for tea at four on Wednesday; I will give him an hour. He will have to leave right afterward. I can't put him up over night."

This was something, but not entirely satisfactory as far as I was concerned. After the meeting it would mean I would have to drive

Ralston in the dark over twisting mountain roads in the forward area to reach the Canadian area for the night.

I was determined that there must not be another McNaughton-style incident, so I dropped in at Main Army HQ at the first opportunity, to have a word with Freddie de Guingand, Monty's Chief of Staff. He agreed to do what he could for me.

When I met Ralston at Foggia and started our long drive to Tac, I briefed him as well as I could, urging him not to be put off by Monty's curt behaviour or seeming ill manners at times. In every respect, I assured him, he would find Monty the complete professional, a hard realist in matters of war. He might speak bluntly but he was fully aware of Canadian interests and sensitivities. Furthermore, when in action, he was respected and trusted by the Canadian troops who fought under his command. During our drive Ralston did not tell me the real purpose of his visit, but he did confide that General McNaughton, Commander of the Canadian Army, was to be replaced in the near future.

At Monty's invitation I joined them at tea, and it came off in good style. Afterward, Monty invited the Colonel over to his caravan for a private chat, which lasted till after seven in the evening. Meanwhile, I had been standing by with a car. Then, surprisingly, Monty opened the door of his caravan and called for one of his ADCs. Colonel Ralston was staying the night with him, he announced; the guest caravan was to be made up. Quite obviously they had hit it off well together. Indeed, the next morning they continued their talks and it was noon before we got on the road to visit the Canadian formations.

Ralston gave me the gist of his conversations with Monty while we drove to 1st Division HQ, and then on my return to Tac Monty gave me his version of their talks. Ralston informed Monty in confidence that McNaughton would be resigning his command shortly. This was the first Monty had heard of it. Stories were subsequently circulated that Monty had a hand in McNaughton being fired, but this was certainly not the situation. Back in South East Command, Monty had always felt that McNaughton allowed himself to get far too involved in gadgets and research instead of learning how to handle an army in the field. It was also known in limited circles that Monty had refused to let McNaughton visit the 1st Division in the middle of the Sicilian campaign, but I can record that McNaughton's removal came as a complete surprise to Monty.

The exact steps and the real circumstances leading to McNaughton's resignation I did not learn myself till much later. As there has been much confusion about this dramatic development and many conflicting versions published after the war, it will be dealt with in some detail later in my story.

At that time, although there had been no official confirmation, rumours were rife that Monty was to be appointed to command the land forces for the Second Front, when the invasion of France was launched. General Paget was also thought to be in the running, as well as General Morgan, then charged with planning the operation, Overlord as it was called. Both the U.S. Chief of Staff General Marshall and the British Chief of Staff General Brooke were known to be candidates for the job of Supreme Commander.

When Ralston explained to me that one of the main reasons for his visit to Italy was to discuss with Monty who should replace McNaughton to command the Canadian Army, I put two and two together. Ralston obviously knew then that Monty was to command the Second Front, and it was important that the Canadian Army Commander was acceptable to Monty.

In his private talks with Monty, Ralston had suggested that Crerar might be the best replacement for McNaughton. Monty questioned this simply on the basis of Crerar's lack of command experience in the field. That Crerar had repeatedly brushed Monty the wrong way ever since his arrival in Italy, however, was not mentioned. Ralston then asked about the suitability of Simonds for the appointment. Monty agreed that Simonds had indeed demonstrated great ability in handling the 1st Division in action and was perhaps the most promising Canadian commander. He considered Simonds, in fact, the best operational commander we had at that time.

On balance though, Monty felt that Simonds was still pretty young and lacking in mature judgment for such heavy responsibilities. He still had something to learn about handling subordinate commanders, many of whom were older than himself. There had been an awkward situation at an O Group back in Sicily, when Monty had to intervene personally, in a row that developed between Simonds and one of the brigade commanders. Being overly keen, Simonds had been rather inclined to tell the brigadier how to run his brigade. The brigadier had publicly demanded to know whether he or Simonds was supposed to be running the brigade. Though Monty was never accused of exercising much tact, he certainly used some diplomatic skill on that occasion to smooth matters and offer Simonds some timely advice.

Monty also appreciated the importance of having a Canadian command the Canadian Army. If a British officer was appointed, it would go down very badly in Canada. As it was, the Canadian public would be none too happy about McNaughton's retirement.

At the conclusion of their talks, it was agreed that Monty would give General Crerar an early chance to command his corps in action in Italy, and would keep Ralston posted about whether he considered Crerar capable of commanding an army.

Following this visit with Monty, Ralston spent the next several days seeing various Canadian units along the front and visiting casualty clearing stations, talking to the wounded. It was not just a sightseeing tour; Ralston knew the grim business of war only too well. He was determined to see conditions for himself and to ensure that the troops were getting every support from the home front.

Subsequently, he held meetings with the supply and administrative chiefs back at 2nd Ech and then with Crerar and his staff at Corps HQ. Ralston next called a press conference of all the Canadian war correspondents in the theatre. From my prewar newspaper days, I knew most of the Canadian correspondents; Ross Munro, Ralph Allen, Lionel Shapiro, Fred Griffin, Wally Reyburn, Doug Amaron, Bill Stewart, Matthew Halton, JAM Cook, Maurice Western, Greg Clark; Bert Wemp, Marcel Ouirnet, Charles Lynch, Gerald Clark, Shalto Watt, Peter Stursberg, Bill Boss, and Dick Sandburn. Many were old friends. Ralston, however, did not ask me to attend the conference with him. He spoke to them alone. Afterward, I gathered the conference had been rather in the nature of a "beef" session, with complaints from everyone.

Other than through letters from home, the Canadian troops got little news from Canada. We saw the occasional outdated English newspaper and, on rare occasions, the British and U.S. troops' newspapers, *The 8th Army News* and *The Stars and Stripes*. We were not aware that there had been a lot of critical news stories in the papers at home, by warcos complaining about press facilities, poor wireless transmission, censorship squabbles and delays, their lack of transportation and accommodation, and no regular briefing in the field by army authorities.

Further complicating their problems, were inter-service and inter-allied rivalries, plus the fact that many of the correspondents had little knowledge of military matters themselves or knew how an army operated. In particular, they resented their stories being censored by British censor officers.

Consequently, the government in Ottawa was subjected to heavy opposition attack and was embarrassed when Canadian newspapers published war stories from the correspondents complaining endlessly about lack of proper news facilities and their difficulties in getting accurate reports.

It was on our drive back to Naples, for his farewell meeting with Crerar, that Ralston told me about this situation. He concluded by telling me that the warcos had made a request that I should be put in charge of the press operations again for a short period, with sufficient authority to reorganize the whole set-up. They had argued that because I had been responsible early in the war for reorganizing the army press services in Canada, I should tackle a similar job here in Italy. They pointed out the advantages I had in dealing direct with Monty, knowing all the commanders and also the day-to-day operations of the 8th Army.

This was also the wish of Ottawa, Ralston continued. It was one of the other subjects he had discussed during his private talks with Monty. Monty, he said, had agreed, though he had originally planned that I should return with him to England when he took command of 21st Army Group for the Normandy invasion. He felt I should continue my liaison role for him when the Second Front was launched.

"What about it," Ralston demanded. "It will only be for a short period. We also want you to get a Canadian Army newspaper started over here, the same as the Americans and British have. You know the Canadian Press people in Canada," he reasoned. "Gil Purcell and Joe Clark back there assure me that if you take the job, they will see that you get a proper wire service each day, sports stories and scores, national news, politics, comic strips . . . whatever you want."

In a large measure the complaints of the warcos were entirely justified. No proper provision had been made for them in the theatre. The Canadian officer in charge had not been given sufficient authority to deal with their many problems. He had meekly accepted the direction of Allied Force HQ — that he must remain in Algiers and not visit the combat areas, without approval. He had resigned himself to this situation and consequently had little idea about or control over what went on in Italy. In addition, he did not have the necessary backing to obtain the vehicles and equipment essential for the front line warcos and transmission services.

Ralston's proposals caught me entirely by surprise and they were not particularly to my liking. It was all very flattering, but my present job was both interesting and exciting and I hated any thought of giving it up, particularly if there was any chance of returning with Monty when he went to command the invasion of France.

At Tac HQ, of course, there had been great speculation, even a private lottery, as to which members of his staff Monty would take back with him for the Second Front. Freddie de Guingand, Bill Williams and Belchem were of course front runners, as well as one or two of the ADCs, but the betting on the LOs and Ops officers was not too heavy. Obviously there was much heavy fighting still ahead for the 8th Army in Italy, but the major action and excitement would come in France, when the cross-Channel assault was launched. If at all possible, I didn't wish to miss this historic event.

I did, however, recognize that with my knowledge of Canadian newspapers and editors, together with my army experience, I could likely do much toward sorting out the problems Ralston recounted. But it would be a thankless job. Warcos, though able reporters, were by nature individualists, inclined to bellyache and stir up problems. There would be, of course, the handful of prima donnas who could never be satisfied — and their endless squabbles about priorities, censorship and transmission. There would also be some senior officers caught up in their own authority, trying to order correspondents around and tell them what they should or should not write. Some generals still imaged they had both the authority and responsibility for censoring a despatch, just because it was critical.

Thousands of miles from Ottawa, I would no longer have the backing of the Minister's Office. Much as I might wish to help Ralston with his problem, it was not a tempting assignment and I was quite frank in telling him so.

I started to elaborate the many reasons why I did not want the job, but Ralston cut me short. "Are you going to start horse-trading again as to how you will serve in the army?" We both smiled; I had heard that before. "Think it over and let me have your answer in the morning. I want you to do it." He then told me to draw up a list of all my objections and he would see what might be done to counter them.

There was an additional responsibility he wished me to take on. As he explained it, when any controversial issue flared up in the battle area, some CO sounded off about government policy, or some major snafu occurred, the government and defence chiefs in Ottawa always read about it first in the daily newspapers. They had no exact details or direct information to go on when questions were asked in the House the same day the news story appeared. It would often be a week later before any official reports reached the government through normal army channels.

The reason for this was simply that a warco could file a story via a high-speed wireless station in Naples, which would roll off the presses in Canada a few hours later. Official army reports on such situations had to be processed through Division to Corps, from Corps to Army, to AFHQ in Algiers, from there either to CMHQ or to the War Office in London and then relayed back to Ottawa. As a result the government repeatedly found itself under fire and in the impossible position of being unable either to confirm or deny news reports, sometimes for a period of days.

Part of the new job, Ralston explained, would be the responsibility of advising his office direct in any emergency situation or critical development in the field, which was likely to hit the papers in Canada before the official reports were received by the Department in Ottawa.

"Are you suggesting that I simply by-pass the Corps commander, Crerar, Monty, Alexander and everyone else on any blow up or policy squabble and report direct to Ottawa? I am a serving officer," I reminded him. "I have to report and take my orders directly from the commanders here in the field."

Ralston brushed this objection aside. "It will only be in emergency situations," he said. "Only dealing with the press aspects. I will formally clear this; it is most important."

That night in Naples I sat up for several hours as Ralston had asked, considering his proposition and drafting up, in memo form, all the various reasons why I did not wish to tackle this rather impossible job. It would simply be asking for trouble.

The following day, Ralston took my memo and demolished it point by point. As to the existing restrictions on the movement of correspondents to and from the theatre and within the Canadian Army area, I could have full authority to let them go where and when they wished. No longer would they be controlled from AFHQ in Algiers. I could establish a press HQ in the field and simply have an LO represent me in Algiers. I could draw sufficient jeeps to keep the correspondents independently mobile. A proper establishment — drivers, cook, conducting officers, despatch riders, transport officer and so forth — could be organized with an adjutant and QM to draw proper rations and supplies. I could establish a main press camp, as well as forward press camps as warranted, to provide a proper base for both the correspondents and newspaper staff. There would be a film unit and photo units, and a transmission officer. I would be given some Canadian press censors as soon as they could be trained, to work with army intelligence and the Ops Branch at whatever level I chose, so that Canadian warcos would not have to submit their copy to British censors.

I had raised the matter of possible interference by senior officers and a correspondent's responsibility to report events as he saw them, subject only to operational security. On this point Ralston assured me that on purely press matters, I would have absolute authority. He would see that I had this in writing before he left.

By the time he got through with my memo, I had hardly a leg to stand on. About a daily newspaper for the troops, I asked who would be responsible for editorial policy. Would it be a free press or an Army-dictated sheet? Would the editor have a free hand or have to take orders from every senior officer who took objection to what was published? What about the troops' letters to the editor, perhaps complaining of rations or various services? Would we be free to publish them?

It would have to be entirely a troops newspaper, I argued. If the troops ever got the idea it was just an official propaganda sheet, echoing the official views of the top brass, it would be doomed before it got started. Some of these factors had not entered Ralston's thinking before and we debated the difficulties for some time.

Finally I got agreement. If I started a daily paper there would be no interference whatever with the editors on press matters or editorial policy. There could be no charges that the paper was propaganda or government controlled. I would be free to draw up my own editorial policy, the style of the newspaper, the news content, whether or not it carried letters to the editor, pin-up pictures or whatever. The editors would answer only to me. This was a pretty tough demand for Ralston to swallow, but I convinced him it was the only safe approach.

Higher authority could register any complaints with me, fire me if they wished, but would not attempt to direct, discipline or interfere in any way with my editors. I agreed to draft a written editorial policy for the editors to follow and let Ralston see it in advance. If he didn't approve, he needn't give me the job. On any other basis the government could be accused of political purposes.

Another point which caused some debate, was my comment that all too frequently press officers were put under pressure by commanders who were overly concerned with their own press coverage, and tried to cast press officers rather in the role of personal press agents. While not stated in my memo, this objection was primarily directed toward Crerar who felt the correspondents should always report his speeches and remarks in full, as well as include pictures of himself on every possible occasion, whether or not of any news value. This was a delicate point for Ralston, who knew exactly what I was getting at. Crerar was, after all, the senior Canadian officer in the theatre.

The other points of my memo were all of a similar nature. Ralston put my memo in his pocket and asked that I join him for dinner that evening with General Crerar and General Beament, commander of 2nd Ech in Naples.

There were several other senior officers at the dinner, and when the meal was over, Ralston outlined steps he proposed to initiate in Ottawa as a result of his visit to Italy. Then to my surprise he brought up the subject of myself, and the press problems, saying he wished me to tidy up these difficulties as soon as Monty left for England. He went on to tell about the troops' newspaper he wanted started and concluded by saying he proposed giving me complete authority on all press matters in the theatre, as well as direct access to his own office in Ottawa, when necessary. There was no comment whatever from either Crerar or Beament. After a pause, Ralston continued. "Malone has raised a number of objections about why he doesn't wish to tackle the job." Then to my embarrassment, he read aloud my private memo.

"I don't see any reason why all these objections can't be countered. It is important to see that our press facilities are put in order without delay. Both the British and Americans make proper provision for war correspondents, newspapers and psychological warfare in the field. We must do the same." He then turned to Crerar and Beament: "You will both I know want to give Malone all the support he needs in this." Again there was a few seconds of silence, then both generals, after a few questions, agreed with the colonel's conclusions. Their agreement, however, did not seem overly enthusiastic, particularly over the bit about my direct access to Ottawa when necessary. There was nothing else for it but to take on the job for Ralston, with no further bickering.

True to his word, Ralston, before he left the next day, gave me a written directive covering both my responsibilities and authority, duly signed by himself and initialled by both Crerar and Beament. He also arranged that I should draw, on my own signature, whatever money I required from the field cashier to get a daily newspaper published for the Canadian forces.

To remove any fears of Crerar and Beament that I might try to operate behind their backs, I undertook to keep them posted whenever I felt it necessary to report to or deal direct with Ottawa on press matters. It was also agreed that I would take up my new duties when Monty left for England, then slated for the end of the year, just a few weeks off. With these arrangements decided, Ralston then volunteered that if I made a good job of it and got matters in shape before the invasion of France, he would ensure that I got back in time for Operation Overlord, and there would be a job waiting for me.

When I returned to Tac, I reported these developments to Monty. He agreed fully with the decisions, and when he had read Ralston's written directive he countersigned it as well, so there could be no misunderstanding on the rather unorthodox arrangements.

In passing, I might add that while I carried this written directive signed by Ralston, Crerar and Monty throughout the rest of the war, I seldom had recourse to reporting direct to Ottawa, except when I was later posted to MacArthur's HQ in the Pacific, and I was careful never to abuse this privilege. There were a few occasions in Italy and north-west Europe when I did contact Ralston's office direct on urgent issues, but for the most part any direct reports to Ottawa went through Joe Clark, then director of PR for all three services, who sat in on all meetings of the Chief of Staffs Committee. Merely the fact that I carried such written authority, however, made it possible to resolve the majority of press squabbles and foul ups on the spot. Curiously enough the direct contact with Ottawa worked largely in reverse, as the majority of such exchanges and requests were initiated from the Ottawa end.

1943 Draws To A Close

The weeks prior to Christmas saw some of the fiercest fighting during the entire Italian campaign, particularly for the Canadians. Under appalling weather, units of the 1st Division, commanded by Chris Vokes, fought their way through mountain roads deep with snow and across valleys swimming in mud. By desperate effort the Morrow River was crossed, San Leonardo and Casa Berardi captured. Then as Christmas Day approached, the Edmontons and the Seaforths launched a joint attack on the coastal town of Ortona. Here the house-by-house defence by the German Panzer units called for an entire week of costly street fighting and demolition before the town was captured.

During that month of bitter fighting, every regiment in the division shared the burden and sacrifice. The battle casualties suffered by the division amounted to 176 officers and 2,163 other ranks in those few weeks alone. With the capture of Ortona, the Canadian strength was exhausted and a halt was called.

Monty's Tac HQ at the time was located just back of the battle area on some high ground near the little town of Fossacesia. Members of Monty's small staff still slept out in the open each night and frequently had to shake the snow off themselves and their bed rolls when they awoke at sunrise. The breezy English officers at Tac held the mad assumption that being from Canada I relished and enjoyed this polar bear existence. They could not have been in greater error.

After one particularly perishing night, a fellow LO named Barham and I billeted ourselves in a small broken-down farm hut or, in Canadian terms, an old shack. Aided by the ever-faithful Manser, we closed up most of the cracks in the hut, got some wood cartons for flooring and some potato sacks to cover the entrance. Getting away with this great luxury for one night, we were encouraged the next day to design a small heater, fashioned from an old oil drum. Some nearby sappers obligingly cut a hole in one side of the drum and supplied us with some tins to serve as a chimney. Life took on meaning once more. Unhappily, several others of the staff, seeing our success, began to follow suit. Then came disaster. Monty's cold blue eyes detected this evidence of softness and depravity, and back we went to the cold ground and the winter blizzards. The accommodation for his personal staff was to be no better than that of any infantry platoon in action, he reminded us. I refrained from suggesting that from my own personal knowledge, the majority of Canadian soldiers at that time in the mountains, had enough initiative each night to scrounge or rustle up far more comfortable sleeping arrangements than his own staff enjoyed.

On most days I made my regular tour of the Canadian area, but it was heavy going trying to reach all the forward positions in the mud and snow. It was clearly apparent that our major drive was over for the winter. Apart from weather conditions, our supply position was critical. Often the ammunition, rations and petrol had to be manhandled up miles of mountain trails and the wounded carried back on stretchers through mud where vehicles couldn't operate.

On a few occasions when things were critical with the 78th Division operating further inland on the left flank, I was sent over to check the situation with the New Zealand and Indian units. Their objective was Orsogna, but the going was impossible for them against the German hilltop defences. In many ways their conditions were worse than the Canadians'. Some of their men had died of the cold and their supply situation was acute.

Sometimes, partly to kid Chris Vokes and also have him press ahead, Monty would have me ask Chris why the 1st Division didn't straighten out their front line a bit in the mountains. What was delaying him? This would enrage Chris, who would roar at me through his great red moustache. "You tell Monty if he would get to hell up here and see the bloody mud he has stuck us in, he'd know damn well why we can't move faster."

On other occasions, Monty would have me take his 8th Army Tac HQ road sign and set it up about a mile forward of Chris's Divisional HQ. Invariably Chris would call me and demand to know what Monty's road sign was doing away up there. "Oh, Monty's moving his HQ up there tomorrow," I would assure Chris. That always produced action. Chris would burn everyone's tail that night and have everything moving by morning.

About this same period, true to his word, Monty made preparations to commit some units of the 5th Canadian Armoured Division into battle and also move some elements of Crerar's Corps HQ over from Sicily toward an operational role.

Once more Crerar managed to put his foot in it. During his unofficial visits to 1st Division when it was fighting through the mud and mountains, he had been shocked at the casual manner of dress adopted by all ranks. The Canadians had adopted the easygoing style of Monty and his desert veterans — the officers wearing sweaters over their bush shirts or under their open-neck battle dress and at times desert boots, while the other men had quickly learned to use whatever came handy to keep warm or camouflage themselves from the enemy. In addition, following the practice originated by the 8th Army in the desert, Canadian drivers had painted names of girl friends and slogans on their tanks and vehicles.

Greatly offended, Crerar issued a directive to all Canadian COs, whether under his command or not, stating that as senior Canadian officer in the field, he did not approve of such informal dress and practice, and henceforth all commanders were to ensure that their men were correctly dressed at all times and names were to be removed from vehicles. They were to remember that they must uphold the reputation of the Canadian Army in appearance.

The effect of this order on men who had been in continuous action for many months, and were presently struggling through miles of mud under fire, and were covered with fleas and at times short on rations, needs no explanation. It became a subject of laughter throughout the 8th Army. To further aggravate the situation, a few weeks later Crerar issued a 16-page movement order, complete with map traces, start line, order of march, provost details and feeding arrangements, covering the movements of portions of his HQ to the mainland, all according to Staff College standards.

He did not appreciate that paper had virtually been eliminated in the 8th Army since Monty took command in the desert. Even movement and battle orders for entire divisions were now simply a matter of verbal orders issued briefly at O Groups, with a few essential times and localities noted on map boards. All units had become accustomed to move on short notice according to set procedures without any written orders. Unfortunately, on the distribution list of his order, for "information," Crerar included practically every formation HQ in the army. It became almost a collector's item, passed around in amazement that so much paper was required by the new corps to move a few HQ vehicles about in the Admin. area.

In an effort to retrieve the situation, I flew back to Taormina again and tactfully tried offering a little advice. Crerar listened but didn't agree or seem to understand, as he at once produced the draft of another long memorandum he was preparing, on the subject of troop morale and the importance of all Canadian commanders to forbid any bellyaching or complaints in the ranks. He seemed oblivious of the fact that throughout history, for men in battle, bellyaching is traditional . . . bellyaching about the delays, rations, the mail, the QM or whatever else comes to mind.

He became very touchy when I tried to talk him out of it, again reminding me that he, as corps commander, carried a heavy responsibility and authority regarding all Canadians in the theatre. All I could do was have him eliminate some of the histrionics and more ludicrous passages before he issued it. The great production of paper did, however, start to slow down very quickly.

Although there had been no official announcements and no date set, it was now widely known that Monty would soon be leaving his legendary 8th Army. Notification of his new appointment for Operation Overlord finally arrived from the War Office, a day or two before Christmas. At Tac a Christmas dinner was planned rather as a farewell to Master.

It was late on December 23 when I left the Canadian area to return to Tac, and the roads were appalling. I was driving the staff car with the faulty steering gear, and in the dark, with the mud, it was impossible to keep the vehicle on the road. There were endless holdups at river crossings but I was determined to reach Tac for the farewell celebration. I did manage to reach the coast road about four in the morning, but then my luck ran out. The car slithered down a steep bank and gently rolled over. I was too tired even to scramble out. Shutting off the ignition, I went to sleep in the upturned car. When I awoke many hours later, stiff and half frozen, to greet the happy morn, I found little to be joyful about. When I finally got winched out and reached Tac, the party was long over.

I did, however, have a few farewell words with Monty. He wished me well in my new duties, asked that I keep in touch and contact him as soon as I returned to England. General Sir Oliver Leese, a guards officer, was to replace Monty in command of 8th Army and Lieutenant-Colonel, The Lord (John) Tweedsmuir, was to take over my job as Canadian liaison officer in Italy. Tweedsmuir had joined the Canadian Army and rose to command the Hasty Pees. Like myself he had been wounded in Sicily, subsequent to leading a spectacular attack at Assoro. We were old friends and I was glad to hear that he would be my replacement at Tac.

On the arrival of General Leese, changes soon became apparent at Tac. Regulation tin Nissen huts were erected under cover of the olive trees, gravel paths were laid through the mud by the engineers, and the car park was surfaced. Winter lines were being established. I was still packing my own gear when John Tweedsmuir arrived. He was enthusiastic about his new job and the opportunity and freedom he knew I had enjoyed, swanning over the battle area each day to keep up with the changing action.

I did not disillusion him, but quite obviously Tac was not going to be moving anywhere for a while. Some weary months of winter were ahead before any major attacks could be launched again.

It was a sad business saying good-bye to all my friends and driving away from Tac for the last time. We had shared many dramas and comedies together. Danny, the cook, gave us a great box of mess extras to load in the station wagon. Manser, however, was happy we were heading back to a Canadian environment once more. He had served cheerfully while at Tac, but he had never really adjusted to the life of the other ranks at a limey HQ, where class distinctions were always apparent.

TWELVE
Press Problems

WORLD SCENE
*U.S. forces invade Solomon Islands in Pacific.
Russians recapture Kiev. Canadians cross Sangro and
Moro Rivers in Italy. Encounter savage house-to-house
fighting in Ortona. General Eisenhower named to
command Normandy invasion. Retirement of General
McNaughton announced. Canadians capture Ortona.
Russian advance into Poland. Allies establish new
beachhead at Anzio, south of Rome. Japanese attack
India.*

In his biography of Greg Clark, Jock Carroll records that "the invasion of
Sicily and Italy created the greatest concentration of Canadian war
correspondents since the beginning of the war. It was also to bring into
focus the problems of Allied joint operations, inter-service rivalries and
press and communications difficulties. For these reasons, Lt. Col. Dick
Malone was to be placed in charge . . . "

This much of Jock's account is quite correct, but his further comment
certainly requires some explanation. Jock records that on taking on my
new responsibilities, I requisitioned "one of the largest whorehouses in
Naples as an officers' mess." This report is only partially correct, and I
did prevail on Jock to insert the word "unwittingly" in his story before it
rolled off the presses.

To keep the story straight, as soon as I took over I felt it essential to
close down the press offices back in Algiers and set up a proper base HQ
in Naples, closer to the front, where I could bring together under one
roof all the odd pieces of my new command: warcos, conducting officers,
signal personnel, cameramen, and so forth. With this base established, a
forward press camp, just back of the battle areas, was opened; here, the
warcos could make daily visits to the units in action, get accurate
operational briefing at corps, divisional or brigade levels, and have copy
relayed by despatch riders. Then at the wireless transmission centre near
Bari, a Canadian officer, Roy Beamish, supervised transmission and
ensured that Canadian copy was given top priority.

In addition to providing transit accommodation for warcos coming to
and from the theatre, the Naples base was also to provide initial
accommodation for the personnel required to produce the new army
newspaper. Essential requirements at the Naples base, I felt, were lots of
bedrooms and bathrooms, so that correspondents could come back to
Naples from time to time to delouse themselves and get a hot bath and a
few proper meals.

Toward this end, I ordered the sergeant major to locate a building with
lots of bedrooms and bathrooms. Before the day was out he came back
with much double talk, about troubles with the town major, the local
billeting officer, and so forth, regarding my order. Not holding with such

217

red tape and regulations, which immediately took over in the rear areas once they were liberated, I told the CSM to ignore all the nonsense. Just go to the *Carabiniere,* explain what was needed, then move in. I would fight the red tape afterward.

Later that day when the CSM took me over to see our new base HQ, it did seem a bit unusual to find a building in Naples with a good mess area and 25 or 30 separate bedrooms, each with a separate bathroom. I approved the CSM's location immediately. The local occupants were ordered out and we moved in.

The next day Emilio, the owner of the building, asked to see me. He explained that he had formerly been head chef at Shepeards Hotel in Cairo, and he produced a big photo of some 20 or more chefs all in white uniforms, himself in the centre, to substantiate his claim. His proposition was that he should remain to cook for us and at the same time be able to keep an eye on his property.

This seemed a reasonable proposition as army cooks did, at times, leave a little to be desired, so I agreed. Cheered by my acceptance, he then suggested that his sister Maria should also be allowed to remain; she could do the laundry. That also sounded reasonable, but I put my foot down when Emilio then suggested that his cousin Luigi should also stay and make himself useful.

Arrangements were made to draw army rations, and Emilio was ordered to produce a full course meal that same evening. Word was sent out that I expected all the warcos and conducting officers to move in, get cleaned up and sit down to a proper mess dinner.

Greg Clark, intrigued when word of this sudden change in press matters reached him, celebrated with a few drinks and bought some fish down in the harbour area, so that Emilio could make his favourite bouillabaisse. Rather carried away then with the whole idea, Greg secretly recruited a dozen itinerant musicians and one-legged street beggars from the Via Chiaia, to come and play their squeeze boxes and fiddles for the dinner.

The early part of the dinner was a great success. Everyone was cleaned up, and Emilio's meal, concocted out of army rations, was magnificent: a moulded cold salmon, superb spaghetti, corned beef quite unrecognizable under an Italian sauce, and some excellent vino. Then when Greg threw open the doors to disclose his beggars' symphony, the evening started to get out of hand. Greg was in his element. To restore order, I ultimately told Greg to consider himself under arrest and confine himself to his room. Nonetheless, it proved a happy evening to inaugurate a change in press operations.

A day or so later I became puzzled over the fact that every bedroom was equipped with a bidet. A few local enquiries confirmed my suspicions. However, the accommodation suited our requirements, so I kept a straight face and just ignored all the clever jibes of my friends.

There was one other feature of those billets about which I also remained silent. Making a quick inspection of the new quarters one morning, I went into the kitchen to compliment Maria on the excellent spaghetti she produced for every meal. I was astonished to see her down on the floor on her knees. Spread in front of her was a great sheet of dough, made from our flour ration. As I watched, she took the large comb from her hair and drew it across the rolled dough to fashion the long strings of spaghetti, which she later put out on the dusty rooftop to dry. Then returning the comb to her jet black hair, she went on with her business. When the warcos and conducting officers continued to praise Maria's spaghetti, I kept my own counsel.

The next step was a trip to Algiers to close out our press operations there. Eisenhower's staff was unhappy about this, but our senior press officer at AFHQ and his office staff were serving no useful purpose whatever, so far removed from the battle zone. Here my letter of authority served its purpose. I agreed to have a liaison officer to keep me advised and represent me at AFHQ for any Allied or joint press conferences; as well, I would fly back from time to time during any emergency.

While at AFHQ, I also secured agreement to process Canadian copy direct from the field, employ our own Canadian censors, arrange our own transmission procedures and move correspondents to and from Italy without checking in and out through Algiers.

Two other matters were also dealt with in Algiers. I had received advice from Ottawa that there were five or six Canadian young women wandering loose somewhere around North Africa. My orders were to round them up and ship them home. This was easier said than done, as they were fully enjoying their adventures.

Seemingly, about a year earlier these girls had been secretly recruited by someone in our Department of External Affairs and shipped quietly out to North Africa ahead of the American landings. This had been possible because during the war, Canada never severed her diplomatic relations with Vichy, France. The idea was that these girls would be fluent in French and do a bit of propaganda broadcasting over the French African radio stations.

What they accomplished, I was never able to discover. Of the three I was able to locate, two had heavy French-Canadian accents and the other, surprisingly, was an attractive young lady I had once skated with in a skating carnival many years before in Regina. She could go a long way on her looks, but I couldn't believe that her high school French would be very convincing to a French African audience. I duly ordered them home to Canada and arranged air transportation. But as they were, strictly speaking, not subject to military discipline, and as I have never been too successful in dealing with females, my orders did not seem to have much effect. Several months later I gathered they were still running about North Africa, some of them working for the U.S. Army special services or something.

My other project was to contact and co-ordinate Canadian interests in the theatre with Canada's General Vanier, at that time in Algiers and serving in a dual capacity as Minister to the exiled Allied governments in North Africa, and as military liaison officer for General de Gaulle's HQ.

I located Vanier in a nice villa on the outskirts of the city, where he gave me an excellent dinner. Relations between de Gaulle's Free French Forces and the French Forces in North Africa under Admiral Darlan, Vanier explained, were still very cool. The officer corps in French Africa rather regarded de Gaulle as a deserter. At Roosevelt's insistence, de Gaulle had not been advised of or consulted on the U.S. landings in North Africa. Because of de Gaulle's dictatorial attitude, the Americans had determined to collaborate with Darlan, the Vichy government's representative in Africa.

The Americans considered that Darlan would be more helpful in gaining French African support for their landing; de Gaulle's participation in the operation, they argued, would incite the French garrisons to oppose the Allied landings. The U.S. also contended that intelligence reports indicated that Britain was bitterly hated in North Africa. Consequently, it was implied that the North African landing was exclusively American.

This rejection of de Gaulle and recognition of Darlan by the U.S. caused much embarrassment to both Canada and Britain. Churchill in London felt obliged to announce in the British House that the U.S. "was responsible for all political arrangements there," though sometime later it became known that a proportionately large participation in the landing had been British Army, Navy and Air Force, some troops wearing the U.S. uniforms.

At the time Roosevelt gave a public explanation for his actions; the arrangement with Darlan was "a temporary expedient justified by the stress of battle."*

Subsequently, General Giraud, who had been quietly taken to North Africa in a British submarine, was appointed Chief of all French Forces in Africa, with Darlan's consent.

As will be recalled, following a conference in Algiers in June 1943, de Gaulle and Giraud announced the formation of a French Committee of National Liberation, of which they would be co-chairmen.

On December 24, 1943, just prior to my visit to Algiers, Darlan had been assassinated and Giraud had been appointed High Commissioner for French Africa.

As Vanier explained all these complicated political factors, I realized just how sensitive his own position was at that time. We also exchanged information on the military situation.

He was particularly anxious to have my views on how Canadian interests might temporarily best be served, in the event of a sudden German collapse or surrender and before any armistice or peace provisions could be implemented and put in place. I gathered from his remarks that in the event of a sudden collapse in France, he would be assuming, temporarily at least, the responsibilities of our Canadian embassy in Paris.

I had some limited knowledge about the general Overlord planning in London, which did give some consideration for such contingencies as a sudden collapse in Europe prior to any assault, followed by an immediate occupation, or a successful assault landing followed by a short campaign, then surrender and occupation. In either event, I suggested, a period of military control would have to remain in force at least till the Germans had all been disarmed and some form of civilian authority reconstituted in each country.

It was Vanier's understanding that in such circumstances, I would have the initial responsibility of co-ordinating matters of press, censorship,

---

* An indication of Roosevelt's distrust and dislike of de Gaulle, at that time, is revealed in Roosevelt's letter to his son John, telling him about the Casablanca meetings.

"It was realy a great success and only General de Gaulle was a thoroughly bad boy. The day he arrived, he thought he was Joan of Arc and the following day he insisted he was Georges Clemenceau. Winston and I decided to get him and [General] Giraud to come to Casablanca and to hold a shotgun wedding. I produced the bridegroom from Algiers but Winston had to make three tries before he could get the bride."

220

publicity and political communications in liberated Europe, insofar as Canadian interests were involved. He asked me to think these matters through and let him have my ideas on how they could be provided for in an emergency. This was all news to me, but I agreed to draft out some rough plan and let him have it, without delay, for clearance in Ottawa. We also agreed to keep in touch on future developments.

As I was leaving, Vanier confided that he would be accompanying General de Gaulle when the Free French Forces landed in France and a new government was established in Paris.

Not overly impressed with what I had seen of the Free French Forces to date, or of the initial performance of the 1st French Brigade, which had been committed to operations with the 5th Army in Italy, I jokingly quipped that we would be waiting in Paris for him and General de Gaulle when they arrived. I had not intended to be flip in any way, but as events developed, my comment was not particularly tactful or timely.

The Army Newspaper

I was back in Italy a few days later and, with Ralston's memo in my possession, it did not take long to get press services operating efficiently, with rear and forward press camps each complete with camp commandant, transport sergeant, cooks, and so forth. Even though accommodation in the forward area was still primitive, the new arrangements were greatly welcomed by the warcos. I was also able to scrounge two portable gas-operated electric generators to provide some light for writing at night.

The next step was to get the daily army newspaper started. After considering various names, I decided it should be called *The Maple Leaf,* a name with a distinctive Canadian flavour. Subsequently, I was able to establish other editions of *The Maple Leaf* in Normandy, Belgium, Germany and England. As the paper proved popular and established a great reputation for itself during the war, I arranged with Ralston, after V-J Day, to have the title registered in the name of the Canadian Army as the exclusive owner of the copyright.

The first copies of *The Maple Leaf,* complete with CP news from Canada, news pictures, cartoons and pin-ups, were rolling off the presses in Naples in a matter of days.

The story is perhaps best summarized in a *Maple Leaf* souvenir booklet, issued the following year in Holland.

> Within six days of the go-ahead signal the first *Maple Leaf* was born at Presse il Mattino in Naples. Ever since that day the Canadian Corps with the 8th Army has been getting its daily newspaper.
>
> But it wasn't all done with a snap of the fingers. The problems of bringing the newspaper into the world were numerous. The first was to locate a press and overcome the difficulties of operating Italian machinery. Paper had to be borrowed or stolen. There was none for sale. There were electric power failures, bridges washed out on the supply route, and even a threatened libel suit. Papers had to be flown each day up to the Sangro River. Sometimes 'ducks' were used to make deliveries to the boys on the Adriatic side. It wasn't all beer and skittles!

Today there is a Maple Leaf sign, hanging in front of Presse Avanti in Rome, and the now familiar tabloid size daily is part and parcel of the Canadian Army. As one soldier in Holland put it, there are three M's in the soldier's life — Meals, Mail and *Maple Leaf*.

In the souvenir booklet, to remove any doubts in the minds of the troops, regarding editorial freedom, I wrote the following editorial comment:

Not only did the higher Army Command and the Canadian Government recognize the need for such a newspaper; they also accepted wholeheartedly the principle that the paper should be entirely independent of official control or editorial direction by the authorities. In the past it had been feared that an unrestricted press was risky procedure in a military set-up, founded and nurtured on discipline. The *Maple Leaf* has demonstrated that the troops can run a free press without invalidating their discipline or their loyalty.

There was only one brief flutter in the *Maple Leaf*'s career of unrestricted editorial freedom (apart from security censorship). This came in Italy early in 1944 when General Sir Oliver Leese took command of the 8th Army; he prepared a personal message to all troops in the 8th Army, and he forwarded a copy of this message to the *Maple Leaf*. Attached was an instruction: 'The Army Commander DIRECTS that the following message be published in The Maple Leaf.' Although the *Maple Leaf* was anxious to publish Sir Oliver's message, the Army Commander's use of the word 'DIRECTS' raised a rather fine point. The crisis did not last long, as 15 minutes later another signal was received as follows: 'Amending previous signal the Army Commander DESIRES not DIRECTS . . .' Well, that was different. Sir Oliver Leese had corrected his own error, and the *Maple Leaf* continued its independence.

Generals, heads of services and senior officers everywhere have, like all other readers of the *Maple Leaf*, exercised their right of protest and criticism from time to time, but this is a privilege also enjoyed by the rawest reinforcement private in the theatre.

The distribution system of the paper was not difficult to work out. Whenever a unit was moved, it had to draw rations daily; so it was arranged to leave bundles of papers, on a scale of one copy per three men, to go forward with the rations, in B Echelon vehicles.

The heads of the various services — ordnance, medical, pay, QM and so forth — were all horrified at first at the thought of the *Maple Leaf* publishing letters to the editor, with the troops free to air their complaints. As it happened, these letters soon came to be welcomed and were must reading for the service heads each day. The correspondence gave the supply people early warning on where problems existed.

In order to safeguard the freedom of the new baby, and to retain overall control, I held the title of editor-in-chief myself; but a full-time editor was appointed to manage the day-to-day operations. Searching for an experienced man, I was told that a reinforcement officer, Captain Doug MacFarlane, who had some editorial experience with a Toronto newspaper, had recently arrived at Corps HQ in Sicily. He came over from Sicily for an interview, and I put him on the job immediately.

Captain Placide Labelle of Montreal took on the job of assistant editor; Lieutenant Fred Whitcombe became business and circulation manager.

All the warcos agreed to make their copy available in the theatre. Sergeants Rutsey and Powell joined the news staff, and by great luck we located a top-flight cartoonist, Bing Coughlin from the PLDG regiment, who subsequently created the famous Herbie cartoon series.

Once all the pieces were in place, I was able to divide my time among the various press camps and HQs in the forward area, with periodic trips taken to the base in Naples and the *Maple Leaf* office. On one trip to Naples I saw that an ENSA show for the troops was being put on by a small group of English players, which included the veteran stage stars Hermione Baddeley and comedian Tommy Trinder, and half a dozen young chorus girls.

As Hermione was an old friend, I made a point of catching her show. It was certainly a cheery production, with lively and rather bawdy skits of the London music hall variety. Having a drink with Hermione after the performance, I asked her why the ENSA shows were always given back in the base area. Why didn't she take her show up forward, where the combat troops in the line could enjoy it.

Hermione explained that her troupe would all like to take the show to the front but the authorities wouldn't permit it, saying that they couldn't arrange any proper accommodation, what with all the buildings bombed out.

"If," I asked her, "I can find some billets for your cast and a hall to perform in, will you bring your show up to the Canadian front?" She agreed, with enthusiasm. Visiting the forward area a day or so later, I kept an eye open for a suitable hall and some living quarters which weren't too badly destroyed or already grabbed up for army use.

It was in the small town of Vasto on the Adriatic coast, where we had a forward press camp, that I located something suitable. The windows had been blown out of the building but they could be blacked out, and the roof was still intact. I sent a signal to Hermione back in Naples and had the provosts put a sign on the building, "Out of Bounds for Troops," to help hold it till the theatre party arrived.

All in all, the concert tour proved a grand success. Regiment by regiment, companies were relieved from their bitter winter positions. We got a mobile bath unit to set up shop in Vasto, so that each man was able to dump his dirty, flea-infected clothes, have a hot bath, change into clean underwear and socks, then have a hot meal, followed by the concert. The show was repeated almost hourly each day by Hermione and her company.

The evening the front line tour ended, we felt we should do something to show our appreciation for the players who had worked themselves almost to the point of exhaustion.

Accordingly, I arranged an impromptu reception and midnight supper for them in the little bomb-damaged town library. We rounded up some good vino and some hot food. Our guests, too tired even to take off their costumes and make-up, came over to the library as soon as the curtain fell down on their last performance.

A few younger officers and some of the warcos rounded out the party, which was a great show. Before long a monster poker game started, with thousands of invasion currency lire, francs, and German marks heaped on the table. Much of the money quite worthless, but that made little difference to the players.

Halfway through the party I paused to survey the scene, which should have been recorded on film. In the centre was Hermione still in her tights, her legs crossed, smoking a big cigar and playing poker with a group of junior officers, all young enough to be her sons. Books from the library shelves still lay about the floor, where they had been scattered and torn by the explosion of bombs. The smeared make-up on the weary chorus girls failed to hide their tired young faces.

Also strewn on the floor were pieces of broken plaster busts and statuettes, also hit by the bombing. Socrates, with part of his head missing, looked up from the floor, while gazing at the scene from another corner was the damaged head of Christ. I wondered what they thought of this war and our weird reception in the shattered library, with the sound of gunfire a few miles away. Greg Clark frequently used to ask me, "Do you ever stop and ask yourself just what are you doing here?" It was hard to find a rational answer that night.

A week or so later, while we were still occupying the little library, word reached us that Greg's younger brother, Joe, then in charge of public relations at Defence HQ in Ottawa, was flying over from Ottawa for some meetings with Crerar and myself; en route, he would have a brief visit with Greg.

On his arrival Joe was able to give us the latest news from Canada and tell us of developments at Defence HQ in Ottawa. He also brought, all the way from Canada, a bottle of Seagram's VO for Greg. He confessed that even with baggage limitations on his Atlantic flight, he had started out with three bottles for Greg — but two had been consumed en route, due to operational emergencies.

Joe also confirmed what I had already heard: that General McNaughton had asked to be relieved as Army Commander, on grounds of ill health, shortly after Christmas. Lieutenant General Ken Stuart, the Chief of General Staff in Ottawa, had assumed temporary command of the overseas army, pending the appointment of a new commander. No decision had yet been made about Crerar for this appointment. While Joe did not know all the details, he gathered that trouble was expected over McNaughton's resignation.

A highlight of Joe Clark's visit was his great operatic triumph. Although there was a tremendous bond of affection between them, there had always been an element of competition between Joe and his legendary older brother. Joe was much more outgoing and flamboyant than Greg, and Greg was always a little envious of his brother's drive and forceful personality. While Greg had served with the infantry in the first world war, Joe had transferred to the air force, to go soaring through the skies.

After a long separation, the brothers were overjoyed to see each other again. Both of them were friends of mine of many years' standing, so we sat up well into the night talking, while we finished off the bottle of Seagram's and much of our best reserve vino.

Joe in his youth had been boy soprano in a choir and then, when older, a tenor of some note. Toward midnight, Greg in a nostalgic mood said, "Joe, sing for me again." In his best whisky tenor, Joe swelled up his deep chest and let go at full volume, with an aria from an Italian opera. His voice held in surprising tone and volume to the end of the song. We gave him a great hand and called for more. Enthusiastic about his own performance, Joe rendered another aria, multo fortissimo. At the end of his encore we were about to give him another hand clap, but we were beaten to it. From outside came the sound of loud clapping and the cries of *bis!bis!*

We opened the wooden shutters on the window and went out on the little balcony to see what was up. There in the courtyard below standing in the dark, was a crowd of 50 or more Italians, all cheering for a further encore.

Greg and Joe were both in their element with this magnificent reception from an Italian audience. With the grand gestures of the great artist, Joe at once threw open his arms in the moonlight and started to roar out another Puccini with deep emotion. He proceeded splendidly for a few bars, but then something suddenly went wrong with his voice. The rich and harmonious notes were transformed into a few dry, rasping scratches and wheezes. A little red in the face, Joe paused and smiled apologetically to his audience while he tried lubricating his vocal cords with a glass of vino. He tried again — but the concert was over. Joe's whisky tenor was equal only to a single encore. It had been a spectacular debut and a dramatic farewell, all in the same performance. As though ringing down the final curtain at a Metropolitan Opera performance, Joe retreated back into the upper room of the library and closed the shutters behind him.

It took another bottle of our vino before Joe's spirits were fully restored. When I finally retired to my bed roll in the next room, Greg and Joe were still reminiscing and arguing about how the great Caruso's voice broke years before in Toronto, while singing *Martha*.

Only once after that did I ever hear Joe attempt to sing again. This was back in Naples, where a meeting had been set up to co-ordinate some arrangements with the RAF and U.S. Air Force. Warwick Beament had asked us to dinner at his mess. He had several visiting brass hats as his guests, including the boss Canadian nurse, the formidable Agnes Neil from England. She had come out to see how all her nursing sisters were doing in Italy, at the field hospital and casualty clearing stations, and was outraged to discover that all her little nurses were wearing men's army issue shorts and pants.

The reason for this was very simple. The ship carrying regular nurses' uniforms had been torpedoed off Gibraltar, and we had nothing else to issue the women except men's clothing. Asked if she would rather have her nurses without pants, sister Aggie became pretty austere and formidable. She ranted about proper skirts for her nurses all during the dinner and afterward, in the ante room.

Finally, in an effort to improve the atmosphere, Joe, displaying all his charm, went over to where she was seated. Putting his arms around her, he sang in endearing tones the World War I song, "If You Were the Only Girl in the World." It had no effect whatever; Aggie sat primly erect without a smile. Joe had bombed in his final effort at a musical comeback. The problem of the nurses' pants was not to be resolved by any sentimental song.

Such lighter interludes as these, however, were far from indicative of the grim winter battles being waged along the front, as troops of the 8th Army tried to drive north and crack the Germans' mountain and river defence lines.

Very early in battle, most men are able in some measure to erect about themselves a hard but necessary wall of indifference and insulate themselves against feelings of emotion. It is not entirely callousness; when, day after day, men are being killed and maimed, emotions can be a serious handicap for those in action or under fire.

There are times, however, when a very close friend is suddenly blasted to bits. Then this wall can be badly breached for a brief period and must be rebuilt more solidly.

This was the case when Chris Vokes's younger brother, Freddie, was killed. Freddie had been together with us at all the parties back in Winnipeg, seemingly years ago. Like Chris, he had a short fuse and loved a fight. He had been a courageous and able officer, a pocket edition of Chris. There was a tear in Chris's eye but a hard set to his jaw, as we drove silently back to 1st Division HQ together, after the sad funeral.

Similarly, it was impossible just to brush things aside or remain unmoved when two of the three young liaison officers at 2nd Brigade, who had come ashore with me in the Sicily landings, were subsequently killed in action. Both were officers of tremendous promise. When Chris had been sent out to Cairo and I had to take over his planning job in London, it was these young officers who had organized and controlled the movement of our entire brigade group, some 16 separate units under command, all the way to the various embarkation zones in Scotland.

Later, near Caltagirone in Sicily, I had witnessed one of these LO's suddenly spring into action when our small convoy of vehicles was being shot up by a German antitank gun. He had been in one of the lead vehicles and had passed what appeared to be a derelict or abandoned German gun position off to the side of the road. After he had passed, the German gun crew suddenly emerged from the bushes to begin shooting up our lorries one after another. Without a minute's hesitation, Jim was out of his lorry. Pistol in hand, he quickly organized a few drivers and led a small attack to silence the enemy. Shortly afterward he had returned to his own regiment, the Seaforths, and was killed during an attack.

A few years after the war, while I was on a visit to Vancouver, I thought of calling Jim's parents, simply to tell them a little about their son and our respect for him. I checked first with Bert Hoffmeister, who had commanded the Seaforths at the time. Bert advised me not to call the parents . . . their wound had been very deep. So I simply let it go.

The other LO had been a Patricia officer of great energy and enthusiasm, and a good sense of humour. He was a fine sportsman, and we had rowed and played badminton together in Ottawa and Winnipeg before the war. At the start of the war he had come to me at Fort Osborne barracks as a reinforcement officer.

As we landed in Sicily, he had received a very disturbing letter about family problems at home. He continued to perform his duties well, but some weeks later he asked to be returned to his regiment.

It was later, when I was trying to reorganize the press services around Vasto, that I ran into John's commanding officer. Knowing we were old friends, the CO confided in me that he was very worried about John. He wanted to lead every attack, refused to take any leave or rest, repeatedly exposed himself to enemy fire. He was popular in the regiment, and many of his friends feared he was deliberately trying to get himself killed.

The CO had a suggestion. He knew that John, having a high regard for me, would be ready to tackle any job if he knew I had any real troubles and needed him. The CO also knew I was trying to get a base camp established back in Naples and was looking about for an adjutant to co-ordinate the administration of all my scattered detachments. John could handle this job, and it would get him out of the fighting area, at least for a while. It would give him a chance to rest up and perhaps cool out a bit.

The stratagem worked. John agreed to give me a hand sorting things out, and we arranged a temporary transfer.

But the odds of the game were against us. John reported back to Naples and took hold in grand style, with all his usual energy. Within a week or so I was able to get the odd laugh out of him again, and he began to relax. Shortly afterward, when he was driving at night in convoy, back toward the front, there was a hold up caused by a blown bridge ahead. John got out in the darkness to see what was happening. He was struck by a vehicle coming in the other lane.

Another tragedy at that time concerned a young film and photo officer, whom I had known as a newspaper photographer before the war. He had performed well in both the Sicily and Italian landings and was well-experienced in battle.

About mid January, I was advised of the pending assault landings planned by the 5th Army at Anzio. This attack was launched in the hope of breaking the winter stalemate along Kesselring's Gustav line.

Participating with the U.S. and British divisions in this landing would be some newly formed Ranger units. It would be the first taste of action for these new commando-type units, which had been trained in the U.S. but were half Canadian personnel and half U.S.

Because of the Canadian participation, Ottawa requested that I send a news team and photographer in with the assault. I selected Terry to handle this assignment, taking with him any Canadian warco who wished to cover the event.

The night before Terry was to leave with his little party, several of the other officers mentioned to me that Terry was very depressed . . . was convinced that he would be killed on the assignment. This bothered me; I did not like to think of an officer starting his mission with such an outlook. I sent for Terry and asked him frankly how he felt about the assignment. He was certainly pessimistic and said he was quite sure he would be killed. I couldn't account for his sudden fatalism or why he should be apprehensive over this particular operation, when he had been involved in dozens of equally hazardous jobs.

Failing to reason him out of depression, I finally asked if he wished to be pulled off the job; I could easily substitute one of the other officers. Terry simply wouldn't hear of it . . . he wouldn't be able to live with himself afterward. I could see his point and didn't have the heart to order him off the job. It was just his imagination, a passing thing I felt.

Two days later, I received a signal from the Anzio beachhead. Terry had received a direct hit from a German antitank gun.

Several years after the war on a visit to Ottawa, I ducked down to the cafeteria in the Chateau Laurier one morning for a fast breakfast. Taking my tray, I occupied the first vacant table. As I ate, I noticed that a young woman at another table was watching me closely. After a few minutes she came over and sat down directly opposite me. She remained silent for several minutes, then quietly said, "I am Terry's widow, and you are Dick Malone, aren't you?"

"Did you know," she said, "that Terry wrote to me the night before he left for Anzio telling me he was going to be killed?"

I never finished that breakfast.

An Odd Assignment

One result of having a direct link with Ottawa, was receiving the odd request for handling curious chores. About mid January, while the battle for Ortona was still in the news, I received a request from Ottawa for a piece of wood from the battle zone, suitable for use in making a plaque. There was a War Savings Bond drive on in Canada, and the government wished to award a plaque, carved from the wood, to the province which proportionately sold the greatest number of bonds during the campaign.

The following day, while driving to Ortona, I passed a badly damaged old structure, where a number of shattered oak planks were lying about, so I went over to investigate. It was an old church property, and the local Italian priest told me that this was the crypt of St. Paul; he was the caretaker of the ancient relic.

I had always understood that St. Paul was buried in Rome, but the priest assured me that this was not clearly established. Seemingly, when the vandals overran Rome many centuries before, the bodies of St. Peter and St. Paul had both been secretly removed from Rome and hidden somewhere beyond the Appian Way. While it was now clearly established that the body of St. Peter had been returned afterward, there was still some doubt that the body of St. Paul was now located in the Church Without, on the outskirts of Rome, as presently believed. Thus, the College of Sacred Relics continued to maintain this shrine near Ortona, which had been nearly obliterated by German artillery fire.

When I explained my purpose, the priest readily gave me permission to remove two pieces of the shattered old oak planks. Here, when we were waging a war against the Nazis, it struck me as a great idea to have our plaque made from the crypt of the first Christian missionary to the Gentiles. I took care to obtain from the priest written permission to remove two pieces of the old plank and send them on a plane returning to Canada, together with a letter explaining the background. I imagined they would be turned over to either the Bank of Canada or the Treasury in Ottawa.

Many years after the war, I remembered this incident and wondered where the bits of wood had ended up. I made a few enquiries but could find no trace of them. I still wonder what happened to them. Possibly because of the religious nature of the wood, the government did not wish to risk offending any group or create any problems in the Province of Quebec. For all I know, the bits of wood may still be stored away somewhere in the Bank of Canada.

Normandy Approaches

As the winter months in Italy drew slowly to a close, the organization of the press service was completed. All the pieces were in place and operating smoothly. The *Maple Leaf* was meeting its daily deadlines.

228

Trained Canadian censors were now handling not only Canadian copy but also copy from U.S., British and other Allied correspondents as well.

At main and forward press camps, small but efficient staffs had been developed, together with a proper complement of vehicles to make the camps mobile, and sufficient jeeps to transport warcos and photographers throughout the theatre. Wireless transmission was also going well, and runs from the forward camps by motorcycle despatch riders were operated on a regular daily schedule.

All eyes were now starting to turn toward the English Channel and preparations for the great invasion of France. Crerar's appointment to command the Canadian Army back in England had been announced. Both he and Guy Simonds said their good-byes and returned to join Monty's new 21st Army Group in England. Lieutenant-General E. L. M. Burns was to replace Crerar in Italy.

Some of the veteran warcos also started making their way back to England, while newcomers from Canada arrived to replace them. Accordingly, I reported my own assignment in Italy completed. While I waited for my next orders, following discussions with Crerar and Chris Vokes, I selected a suitable replacement for myself in Italy.

As these changes started to take place, there was a slight feeling of dejection among the veteran Canadian troops in Italy. They sensed that the big Allied assault landings in France could not be far off, when the balance of the Canadian Army would cross the Channel without them. They would be left to batter away uselessly at the mountains of Italy, simply to tie down some German divisions and miss out on the big show. No longer was there any talk of a spectacular drive across the Adriatic and into the Balkans to join hands with the Russians. From these feelings was born the mournful song, "We Are the D-Day Doggers in Far-Off Italy."

Before his departure from Italy, Crerar worked hard to bring together, under command of his Canadian Corps HQ, all the various Canadian formations; the 1st Division, 5th Armoured Division, 1st Army Tank Brigade, and all the associated Canadian service units. He rightly calculated that in the larger picture, Canadian troops in Italy would operate more effectively as a complete family.

This would also remove any differences and jealousies among the 1st Division, the more recently arrived 5th Division, and Corps HQ. Bringing this about required some diplomacy, as well as pressure in high places.

On his departure, Crerar addressed a constructive message to all Canadian troops in Italy, urging them to work together as a family and to maintain the high reputation of the Canadian Army. He also assured them that they would all be returned to join up once more with the rest of the Canadian Army, as soon as details could be worked out.

Finally orders for my own return to England arrived in the form of instructions from both Canadian Military HQ in London and Defence HQ in Ottawa. I was to assume, simultaneously, appointments at Eisenhower's SHAEF HQ in England, at Monty's 21st Army Group HQ and at Crerar's Canadian Army HQ; as well, I would be representing Canadian interests at these levels, in respect to press, censorship and psychological warfare.

In addition, I was to take active command of all the Canadian press units and facilities, war correspondents, censors, broadcasting, film and photo detachments, press camps, and so forth, and of the special units for psychological warfare, such as loudspeaker units on armoured scout cars for broadcasting messages to the enemy.

It was not exactly the job I had wished for, but it would certainly keep me in the centre of the action and get me back to take part in the Normandy invasion.

THIRTEEN
Farewell To Italy

WORLD SCENE
*Massive Allied preparations in England for Normandy
assault. Bitter winter campaign in Italy — Monte
Cassino monastery bombed. U.S. forces in Pacific land
in New Guinea. Japanese driven back in India by
British and Indian troops. Russian forces recapture
Odessa and Sebastopol and break into Romania.
German Army enters Hungary to counter Russian
threat. 1st Canadian Corps becomes operational in
Italy.*

According to the instructions from Ottawa, I would be "C-in-C of all press forces for Canada in the field, both in North West Europe as well as all other theatres."

The next day I packed my gear, not without some regrets, and made a quick farewell visit to each of the press camps and various Canadian HQs. On my circuit I planned to stop overnight at 1st Division HQ to say good-bye to Chris Vokes, as we had shared many adventures together over the years.

It was a nostalgic visit as we shared a bottle of whisky in his caravan after dinner. He was now commanding the division, which had been in continuous action for the better part of a year. In a burst of generosity, to mark our long friendship, he presented me with his treasured, made-to-order commando knife. Very gratifying to me, also, were the many letters and messages from the war correspondents, thanking me for clearing up most of their troubles and restraints and wishing me well.

One distressing factor in my departure was the fact that I could not take Manser with me. Priorities for air transportation were very restricted. He was considerably upset that, after all our trials and tribulations together, we had now reached a parting of the ways. As he said good-bye, he wanted to know if, could he get himself back to England somehow, I would have a job for him someplace. I assured him that there would always be a vacancy for him in any unit I commanded anywhere, but there was just no way I could smuggle him back to the U.K.

I might add that four weeks later, when I was assembling some detachments near Portsmouth for the Normandy landing, a thin, forlorn character in a filthy crumpled uniform came forward and saluted me. It was Manser. He had stowed away on a cargo ship returning to England. How he located me in Portsmouth I never discovered, and never asked. I immediately listed him in Part II orders as, "taken on strength and promoted to corporal."

While waiting over for a day in Naples for my plane priority to come through, I made a point of visiting Bernadetto Croce, the great philosopher. We talked of the frailties and foibles of mankind, of human ambitions and the futility of war. From where we sat, we could see out over the Bay of

231

Naples and, in the distance, Vesuvius, which had suddenly, after many years, started to erupt once more. As Croce remarked, Vesuvius through many centuries had witnessed countless invasions and wars. When the Hitlers and Mussolinis were simply names in some ancient history book, Vesuvius would still be there, marking future centuries with periodic rumbles and fiery protests. The old man told me much about Naples. I had been able to visit Pompeii and other historic sites in the region but asked him if there was anything I should see before I left the next day. He brought out a map and indicated a tiny little lake just a few miles north of the city . . . Lake Aversa. (On my own map, it was shown as Lake Averno.)

This was where Dante wrote his *Inferno*, Croce told me. It was off the usual tourist circuit, but well worth seeing. On the western side of the little lake, I would find a broad tunnel running down into the bowels of the earth to an underground river . . . the River Styx. This was the inspiration, he claimed, for Dante's epic. The little lake was completely round. The surrounding banks, though now overgrown, rose up in a series of terraces where, in times long past, wealthy Calabrians had once built their villas.

Accepting Croce's suggestion, I wangled a jeep that afternoon and, accompanied by another officer, Homer Robinson, set out to visit Lake Averno. It was exactly as Croce described it. We found the tunnel, and guided by electric torches we felt our way down into the depths. The tunnel was quite wide and the stone floor had been worn smooth by a lot of traffic at some point in its history. At a distance into the tunnel, we came to a door or opening on the side, where some steps, carved out of the stone, led down to a small landing beside a small underground stream. It took little imagination to envision the boatman, Charon, bringing his little barge up to the landing to pick up another corpse. The stream was very shallow and our torches lit up its pebbled bottom.

Having gone this far along the road to hell, we could hardly pass up the chance to cross over and see what was on the far side. Stripping off our trousers, we waded across to a small landing on the far side. This led off into a large chamber with a high vaulted ceiling. The stone roof of the cavern was blackened with smoke; the walls looked like a safety deposit vault in a bank, with hundreds of little boxes, all plastered in, row after row. The plaster around some of the compartments had crumbled away over the centuries, and inside we could see small little heaps of dust or ashes, mixed in with a few remnants of charred bone. Clearly, this was some ancient crematorium.

While I have never been able to check the accuracy of Croce's story, his version was that, following the Eastern custom, bodies of the dead all had to be buried or cremated within 24 hours. They were taken down into the cave by the mourners to the little stone platform, from where the ferryman of the dead brought them across to his cremation chamber. Certainly one could easily imagine how Dante, traversing this dark underground cave, might have created his visions of Hades hundreds of years ago.

After leaving Italy, the "exigencies of the service," according to military terminology, directed my activities to the Normandy invasion, the liberations of Paris and Brussels, the bitter campaigns in north-west Europe, and finally to the islands of Guam, Okinawa, the Philippines, and to MacArthur's HQ in the Pacific, followed by an airborne landing in Japan, the surrender ceremony on the USS *Missouri,* and then liberation of the Hong Kong prisoners of war.

Command Problems In Italy

On the further exploits of the 1st Canadian Corps in Italy — its drive to the Pescara line, the switchover to the 5th Army front to join with the Polish forces in the final assault at Monte Cassino before rejoining the Canadian Army in Holland — I can give no first-hand account.

It is possible now, however, to relate for the first time some aspects of General Burns's period of command in Italy, when he took over the 1st Corps from Crerar.

Burns, a professional soldier, was undoubtedly one of Canada's most brilliant and able commanders during the war. In World War I, as a junior officer, he had experienced the mud and horrors of the Somme, Vimy and Passchendaele. I first came to know him at NDHQ in Ottawa. He had served early in the war as General McNaughton's Chief of Staff in England and then returned to Canada as a deputy Chief of General Staff.

Although not generally known at the time, it was Burns who, as early as 1940, first had doubts about McNaughton's capacity to command an army in the field, despite his many other great accomplishments. The very few who were aware of Burns's views then, dismissed them as superficial.

Burns had a very cold and austere personality and was almost devoid of humour. He seldom wasted a word and had little time for small talk in his few personal relationships. As a result, despite his sharp and penetrating mind he enjoyed little popularity among either his superiors or those serving under him.

As Burns recorded after the war, he realized when he took over from Crerar in Italy, that General Leese, the new commander of the 8th Army, wished to have him removed and also wished to have Canada's two excellent divisions, our Army Tank Brigade and our Corps Troops, dispersed to serve in British formations. However, General Ken Stuart, Canada's Chief of Staff in Ottawa, remained firm and refused to accept Leese's demands.

Subsequently, when General McCreary took over from Leese, he bluntly told Burns that he was not satisfied with him as a corps commander. Despite these problems with the British, Burns continued his efforts to hold the Canadian Corps together in Italy. It was his conviction, born in World War I, that Canadian units, when serving together under Canadian command, could achieve more on the offensive than perhaps any other Allied troops.

Subsequently General Stuart told me that when word reached Ottawa of Leese's determination to fire Burns, Stuart flew at once to Italy to tackle Leese. When Leese remained adamant, Stuart spoke very bluntly. Canada would decide who was to command Canadian formations, not the British. The smoke that followed McNaughton's removal had still not subsided in Canada and it wasn't going to be said that the British were able to fire all our generals. Burns must first be given his chance. If he did not perform, certainly Canadian authorities would find a suitable replacement.

At last Leese backed down, but then he began to horse trade. If Burns was not to go, he wanted one of the brigadiers on Burns's staff removed. Leese could not get along with him, either. He also demanded several other concessions. To ensure peace, Stuart agreed to these requests.

Stuart then visited 1st Corps HQ, but mentioned nothing of Leese's demands to Burns. Before leaving, Stuart told Burns that the brigadier on his staff should be returned to the U.K. For what reason, Burns wanted to know; in his judgment the brigadier was doing an excellent job. Stuart refused to go into detail, simply repeating that the brigadier was to be replaced. To Burns's credit, he answered that he would only return the brigadier to the U.K. if he received a direct order. Stuart gave him the order. When the brigadier departed, Burns courageously wrote to Canadian HQ in London, saying that "acting on orders" he was returning the brigadier, who had done an efficient job and performed well in all matters while serving under his command.

In the following few months, Leese gave Burns little support and in various small ways — for example, dealing directly with Burns's subordinate commanders — tried to undermine his position.

Before he left Italy, however, Burns clearly demonstrated not only his own capacity to command in action but also established that the Canadian corps, fighting together against experienced German divisions, made the best showing of any corps in the 8th Army during that period.

Even General Leese was forced ultimately to concede that the Canadian divisions had proven to be the best during his period of army command, and that the Canadian Corps HQ were highly efficient, not only in the direction of Canadian divisions but also in the handling of New Zealand, Indian, British and Greek formations.

Although Burns himself made little comment after the war about these matters, he did record that just before he went out to Italy to take command, he had a chance meeting with Monty in London. At that time Monty made the comment that the additional armour of the 5th Canadian Division was not really required in Italy then, nor was there room for another Corps HQ.

Later, Monty did recognize the importance of these developments, which allowed for battle experience for Canadian units and permitted the withdrawal of British units and key personnel to serve in north-west Europe. It is questionable, however, whether Monty fully appreciated then that in the minds of both Churchill and Brooke, there still remained some hope of convincing their American ally of the strategic importance of building up a force in the Italian theatre: to launch an attack up through the Balkans, for the purpose of securing Trieste, Vienna and Prague ahead of the Russians.

As events transpired, it was many months before I was able to renew acquaintances with the 1st Canadian Corps. By then they had moved up through the south of France to rejoin the other Canadian divisions in Belgium and Holland.

Back For The Great Invasion

On returning to London, I had the good fortune of being able to move back into my old apartment, at Old St. James's House, No. 7 Park Place, just back of the Ritz Hotel.

Despite its Victorian decor, an ancient hydraulic elevator, and the scars of many bombing raids, my accommodation was very convenient and a reasonably good address. Miss Phillips, the manager and the old doorman had given me a warm welcome home from the wars. A bottle of whisky appeared in my sitting room, together with a kit bag full of old gear that I had left behind. This was a godsend; we had been strictly limited on the amount of kit we could take for the Sicily landing, and most of that had been lost when my Bren carrier had been blown up. Miss Phillips, as she had done many times before, took my tunic down to her flat and got busy with her needle to change my 8th Army badges and sew on buttons and new shoulder titles.

First thing in the morning I checked in at Canadian Military HQ on Trafalgar Square, to pay my respects to Price Montague, then Major General in charge of Administration. Until a few months before, Price had been boss man at CMHQ in London, with the title of Senior Combatant Officer. When General McNaughton had "resigned" as Army Commander, however, around Christmas, General Ken Stuart, the Chief of General Staff from Ottawa, had arrived in England, not only to take over McNaughton's job as acting Army Commander but to assume seniority over Montague at CMHQ in London, with the title, Chief of Staff.

Price and I did not always see eye to eye. He was a veteran of World War I and was much my senior, but nevertheless we were good friends. I had known him in Winnipeg, before the war, when he was serving on the bench as Mr. Justice Montague. He talked very frankly to me about developments in Ottawa and the various changes of command in the Canadian Army overseas.

He told me that while McNaughton had not been in good health, and a medical board had recommended a period of complete rest, the fact was that both the British War Office in London, as well as Defence HQ in Ottawa, had forced McNaughton's retirement. They held the conviction that he was "not fit to command the Canadian Army in the field."

McNaughton had apparently been advised, some time previous to his hospitalization, that he would be asked to step down as soon as a suitable replacement could be found. In the meantime there would be no announcement, and he would continue in his present appointment to avoid any speculation within the army or any public controversy at home.

According to Price, when McNaughton had been admitted to hospital he had agreed with Price's suggestion that he should take the opportunity to request that he be relieved of his command "on the grounds of ill health"; this was, indeed, the case. Price had taken the actual letter of request to McNaughton in the hospital. McNaughton signed and the situation for Ottawa was eased although no decision had yet been made about a replacement. Accordingly, Stuart had come over to take command of the army, on an acting basis. This appeared to be the happiest solution at the time, said Price.

While McNaughton might not be competent to command the army in action, Ottawa recognized that he had indeed made an enormous national contribution and was greatly respected.

Unhappily, shortly after his return to Canada, McNaughton, his pride injured and seeing as an enemy anyone who disagreed with him, had given some bitter statements to the press. When a reporter asked him about his condition, he had said there was nothing wrong with his health. Asked to elaborate, he hinted that his return to Canada was simply politics; the reporter should ask Defence Minister Ralston for some explanation. It was a foretaste of troubles to come.

Much of Price's information came to me as a bombshell. It had been McNaughton who first asked me to tackle the job as Monty's Liaison Officer, when he had rowed with Monty in Italy. I was aware that the relationship between the two had always been brittle, ever since their early period of the war together in southern England. But from my talks with Monty, I also knew that he had no hand whatever in McNaughton's removal.

When Ralston had visited Italy shortly before Christmas, I had acted as his guide about the front for several days. Privately, he told both Monty and myself that McNaughton was leaving, and that a replacement would have to be found. I had taken at face value the official announcement: that McNaughton had resigned his command simply for reasons of ill health.

It was some time later that Lieutenant-General Harry Crerar, after a brief spell commanding the Canadian corps in Italy, returned to England and was appointed Canadian Army Commander for the Normandy invasion.

Monty, I knew, still had some reservations about Crerar's ability, but he had endorsed this decision as there did not appear to be any more suitable candidate. He rated Guy Simonds very highly but did not feel he had sufficient experience yet for Army Command. He also recognized and supported the view that Canada's army should be commanded by a Canadian, if at all possible, not an English general.

I was more encouraged to hear from Price about other new appointments. Many of my old friends from Italy had also been brought back to take over important jobs for the new invasion.

From the 1st Division in Italy, Bruce Matthews and George Kitching had both been promoted major generals: Matthews as CRA at Corps, Kitching to command the 4th Armoured Division. Geoff Walsh had been appointed Chief Engineer of the corps, while Jefferson of the Edmonton Regiment and E. L. Booth had both been given brigades for the Normandy assault. Also brought back for the invasion were three veteran British divisions from the 8th Army, the 50th and 51st and the 7th Armoured.

Subsequently, I was to learn that Monty had also brought back from Italy a number of experienced British staff officers from the 8th Army; they had pretty well taken over at 21st Army Group HQ, which was to direct all the land forces during the Normandy invasion.

This, together with the fact that Monty had insisted on very substantial changes in the invasion plans, had caused some hard feelings with General Morgan and his COSSAC staff* who, for the past year, had been working out the very complex plans for the invasion. As Monty's old staff took over, the comment heard was, "the gentlemen went out and the players came in."

I had only been back in London a few days when I received a call from Monty's new temporary HQ at St. Paul's school. Master wanted to see me.

As on many past occasions my appointment was for tea, which allowed time from his busy routine for a quiet chat. I had no idea what he wished to discuss, but I looked forward to seeing him again.

His greeting was relaxed and affable. At first he enquired about my health, my new appointment with the Canadian Army, about events back

*COSSAC: code word for initial invasion plan for Normandy, prepared by Lieutenant-General Morgan on orders from Chiefs of Staff Committee and approved at the Quadrant summit meeting in Quebec, August 1943; forerunner of Operation Overlord.

in Italy and other such trivialities. But I knew him well enough to realize there was some more serious purpose in his call.

Finally, I was given a clue when he casually remarked, "I see that your Prime Minister, Mackenzie King, will be coming to England shortly. You know him, I believe. What kind of a chap is he?"

I explained that Mr. King was certainly not a warlike character, with his short dumpy figure, sparse hair carefully brushed over his bald spot, pince-nez glasses, and high-pitched voice. In the eyes of the troops, he was considered a pacifist. They blamed him for dithering about on the issue of wartime conscription and believed that he had gone to live in the United States during the First War as a draft dodger. The troops had booed him on parade on his last visit.

In practical terms, however, King was also a very able politician. Recognizing his own limitations in rallying the country to war, he had gathered about him some extremely tough and able cabinet ministers, who carried both weight and respect in the country.

"I haven't much use for politicians," Monty commented. "I suppose he will want to visit the Canadian troops while he is here. Will they boo him again?"

"I am rather afraid they will," I replied. "It is rather traditional in the Canadian Army to hate politicians... they are the people the soldier always blamed in the final analysis for most of his daily beefs."

I told him that during the previous war, the Canadian troops had also booed their Prime Minister, Sir Robert Borden, when he attempted to address them on parade. It took a great deal of courage for any Member of Parliament in civy clothes to stand in front of a parade and risk a Bronx cheer.

The few exceptions were people like Ralston, our Minister of Defence, whom the troops knew had commanded a tough regiment in World War I and could speak to them in their own language.

While Monty always pretended to know little about Canada, I came to realize that he was surprisingly well informed on some aspects.

"Politically, your army has always been conservative, I believe. How is it, then, that they continue to vote for Mr. King?"

I was at a loss to explain this phenomenon beyond suggesting that while they saw King simply as a clever politician and didn't trust him, they did trust and recognize the strength of his cabinet, with men like Ralston, Power, Macdonald, Ilsley, T. A. Crerar and Howe.

"King would be an interesting man to meet," Monty remarked. "But being a serving officer and reporting to the War Office and our own minister, I could hardly ask for such a meeting. I am not too popular at the War Office, you know, or with our own politicians. And they don't like us dealing direct with outside politicians."

This was, of course, my cue and the reason for my visit. "But if our Prime Minister asked for a meeting with you, they could hardly object," I suggested. "That would be quite in order."

"Yes, I suppose that is right," Monty agreed.

I at once assured him that I would pass the word along through our High Commissioner's office at Canada House, so that when Mackenzie King arrived in England he would ask to have an informal visit with him. This I did immediately the next day.

Just as I was leaving our meeting, Monty called me back and drew my attention to a number of press clippings speculating that General McNaughton, the Canadian Army Commander, had been fired as a direct result of his differences with Monty and that Monty had demanded his removal.

"All a complete lie, of course," Monty said. "I had no hand in that matter whatever. It's all very mischievous. Stories like that can do me a lot of harm with the Canadian troops and the Canadian public."

I was fully aware that McNaughton's removal came as a complete surprise. I had been with Monty in Italy at the time he was privately told of this pending development by Colonel Ralston, when he visited Tac 8th Army.

I agreed that I would try to have this impression corrected to whatever extent possible when I held my next off-the-record briefing with the Canadian warcos.

It was only after the war that I understood Monty's reference to not being very popular at the War Office at that particular time.

Britain's Chief of the General Staff at the War Office then was General Brooke (later Field Marshal Viscount Alanbrooke). Monty, Brooke and Alexander had all held commands together in the BEF prior to the dramatic British evacuation at Dunkirk, at which time Monty gained a high respect for Brooke. It is believed that he was the only officer from whom Monty would accept a reprimand with any grace.

After the war, Field Marshal Alanbrooke became a director of the Hudson's Bay Company, and during his frequent visits to Canada I enjoyed many pleasant evenings with him, reviewing events of the war years. He confided, during one of our talks, that he had felt obliged to give Monty a terrific rocket when he came back from Italy, regarding his complete insensitivity and bad manners toward our U.S. Allies. Monty was bluntly told that he had been impossible and rude and had failed to appreciate other people's problems. He had made enemies of nearly all the other commanders, and the American generals objected to serving under him. He had scoffed at their opinions and had openly ridiculed them. He had been high-handed and sarcastic when he could have been generous. It had to stop.

Alan Moorehead, the noted war correspondent, commenting on this situation later, took the position that while Monty may have offended many in high places, he also made hundreds of thousands of friends as well; namely, with the men in the ranks and the thousands of workers in the factories.

Certainly Monty did not hold a very high opinion of many U.S. generals, though he did realize the importance of getting on with them. His problem was simply that he did not understand Americans, their reactions or their informal manner. Tragically, he imagined he did understand them and thought they would understand his brusque British approach to military problems.

Although Monty faced a heavy daily schedule during that pre-invasion period and I was on a constant run myself between Southampton and various meetings in the London area, we did have several private meetings at his request.

Late one evening I was again summoned to report to Monty at once. A critical situation had arisen concerning a senior Canadian officer who would be commanding a Canadian formation in the Normandy landings. Though not fully appreciated, at times Monty was very mindful of Canadian interests and repeatedly went out of his way to safeguard them.

Very bluntly he explained to me that this senior Canadian officer had become rather drunk and garrulous in a London restaurant. In a loud voice at the bar, he had, in breach of all security, mentioned both the date and location of the Allied invasion. British security people, alerted by telephone about his behaviour, had immediately picked him up and placed him under arrest. It was, of course, a serious court-martial offence. Monty had been notified at once, as the situation could jeopardize the entire landing.

I was stunned at the news and hardly knew what to suggest, when Monty asked what should be done and how the matter could be kept out of the press. If the officer was charged and court-martialled, he could not command his units in the invasion. To remove him at this late stage would certainly do harm, as he had participated in all the planning and training exercises. Such a sudden departure was bound to raise awkward questions at a sensitive period and might risk security even further. But if any action was taken, it would have to be done now, not some time after D-Day.

My immediate advice was, that from a press and political point of view, neither Monty nor the British authorities should be the ones to take action. They should simply turn the problem over to the Canadian authorities. As to what action Canadian authorities should take, I wanted a little time to think things through and to check with the censorship people to see if anything had already leaked to the press.

After discussing the matter, Monty accepted my suggestion and a call was put in for Crerar at Canadian Army HQ. The following morning, when it appeared that nothing of the incident had reached the press, it was decided that, in the interests of Operation Overlord, no charges would be laid. The officer would be allowed to carry out his role in the invasion rather than risk questions by his sudden replacement at such a critical time. After the invasion phase was successfully completed, the officer would be quietly returned to Canada for other employment, and no charges would be pressed.

About that same period I had another mysterious call from Monty, this one of a somewhat amusing nature. At our meeting, he handed me a blue airmail letter form he had just received from his brother in Canada. "What do you make of that?" Monty demanded. "I don't know what he's talking about."

I read the letter carefully. It was an abject apology from his brother, asking Monty's forgiveness for something he had done. The letter went on to say that he hadn't thought Monty would mind, but he shouldn't have done it without Monty's permission first . . . it was too late to call it off now, and so forth.

"He's quite mad," Monty confided. "I have never told him anything . . . haven't written or cabled him in years. You're from Canada. See if you can find out what all his nonsense is about."

The brother's letter contained a phrase, "your cable received last night gave me an awful shock." This was really the only clue I had to go on, so I checked the next day with the cable censors, where during the war years records were maintained of overseas cables. I had an approximate date to go by, so the matter proved very simple. Sure enough, the censors produced a copy of a cable to Monty's brother on that date, duly signed B. L. Montgomery. This was indeed odd, as Monty was emphatic he had never cabled his brother. Someone, it seemed, was a bit mad.

I subsequently learned that the Red Cross in Vancouver had approached Monty's brother, asking if he had anything of Monty's they could auction off or sell lottery tickets on, to help out in their local fund-raising campaign, "A Salute to Montgomery." In response, his brother had donated Monty's christening mug, which Monty had given him back in 1924.

The Red Cross were delighted and the campaign was well underway, when a furious cable was received from Monty, reading, in part, "... I take the utmost objection to your disposing of my personal property without my permission. Kindly have it returned to me immediately."

At this stage, I quietly backed out of the situation; this was obviously a family matter, not a military or security problem. Later, I gathered that the source of the mystery cable had likely been Monty's mother, who was something of an odd character and didn't get on too well with any of her family. Apparently hearing of the Red Cross donation from some source, the elderly lady had dashed off the cable, signing Monty's name to it.

Several years after the war, when having lunch one day in the Vancouver Club, by odd chance I was introduced to Monty's brother. We talked about the great Field Marshal for several minutes, then the brother commented, "Of course he's quite mad, you know."

Mackenzie King Arrives

It was shortly after Mackenzie King's arrival in London that Monty let me know my message to Vincent Massey's office had borne fruit. King was to drive down to Monty's country hideout for a private meeting. Trum Warren, Monty's Canadian ADC, would take him down in a staff car, with no fanfare or publicity.

As it happened, General Crerar, the new Canadian Army Commander, learned of the visit in advance and simply invited himself, at the last minute, to join the Prime Minister for the visit. There was little Warren could do but hope for the best.

When the little party arrived, Monty was at the door to greet them. Surprised at seeing Crerar with the PM, he wasted not a moment in dismissing him. Telling Crerar it was the Prime Minister he wished to talk to, not him, he waved Crerar aside and took King into the house, leaving Crerar alone to walk in the garden.

Subsequently, Monty gave me an account of his talk with the Prime Minister. In brief, Monty was concerned as to how Crerar would perform in command of an invasion army, having under command not only a Canadian Army HQ, army troops and a Canadian corps, but also a Polish armoured division and several British formations. While he realized the political importance of a Canadian being in command, Monty pointed out that Crerar had no previous experience commanding an army in action, and in that respect, Monty had considerable reservations about Crerar's abilities.

Monty explained that he was fully aware of the rumpus over McNaughton's removal, and he certainly wished to avoid any further rows, should Crerar prove unfit for the job. Monty assured King that he would do everything possible to help Crerar on the job and would "hold his hand" at critical periods if necessary; but in the final analysis, Monty's job was to defeat the German armies, at all cost. He hoped the situation would never arise, but if it proved necessary he would have no alternative but to remove Crerar. There was too much at stake, and other units besides Canadian were involved. Monty would be held responsible.

As Monty put it, he didn't ever wish to be in a position of having to fight, at the same time, the Canadian government as well as the Germans. And so, Monty asked, what would be the position of Mr. King and his government in the unfortunate circumstances that Monty had to sack Crerar halfway through a battle.

King was taken very much aback by Monty's direct question. After thinking the matter over carefully for some minutes, King gave his answer. He fervently hoped it would never be necessary to fire Crerar, but if Monty had no other recourse, the Canadian government would support Monty completely.

That question settled, Monty concluded the visit in short order with a few pleasantries and a cup of tea, for which Crerar was asked to join, quite unmindful of the earlier matter of discussion.

When Prime Minister King had arrived in London, I was surprised to learn that he was accompanied by my former colleague, the late Grant Dexter, Ottawa editor of the *Winnipeg Free Press* and widely recognized for many years as Canada's foremost political writer. This had been at King's specific invitation, which curiously repeated a precedent established at the end of World War I, when the Canadian Prime Minister of those days had asked our famous predecessor, J. W. Dafoe, editor of the *Winnipeg Free Press*, to accompany him to the Versailles peace treaty negotiations.

Grant was a dedicated Liberal, but ever since I had known him, from our early days together in the press gallery in Ottawa, he had consistently criticized many of King's policies, including his policies on conscription. Surprisingly, however, over the years Grant was one of the very few people to whom King extended any degree of personal confidence, even in the matter of his belief in spiritualism. In the prewar years, when Grant had told me privately of King's talks to him about the spirit world and how King received guidance from his dead mother, I scoffed at the idea and thought Grant was just drawing on his imagination or spoofing me. Time, of course, confirmed Grant's account completely.

Grant and I had dinner together in London immediately after he arrived, and he was able to give me all the political gossip from Canada. For reasons of security, of course, I had to be very guarded in any discussion about army matters or the pending invasion. When we did touch on the subject, however, I was horrified as Grant blandly mentioned the first week in June as the date of invasion. I couldn't believe that Grant would attempt to trick me into giving away this important secret by confirmation or denial, but I couldn't allow him to continue talking openly about it in a public restaurant. I checked to ensure we had not been overheard, then asked Grant what made him think his information was correct.

"Oh, the PM told me," Grant blandly replied.

"Well, for God's sake, shut up about it," I told him. "I can't tell you whether you are correct or not, but if either you or Mr. King broadcasts such information, you will likely end up in the Tower."

Politically, Grant was perhaps the best informed man in Ottawa, but at the same time he was delightfully naive about many practical aspects of life or the realities and frailties of human nature.

He was much concerned that I would soon be going in on another assault-landing operation and offered me some completely crazy advice, based on his own youthful experiences in the trenches of World War I, during which time he achieved the unofficial record of being perhaps the most idealistic, untidy and impractical trooper in the Strathcona Horse.

Amongst other things he gave me a small pocket edition of Shakespeare's Sonnets, which he felt I might enjoy reading during my "moments of reflection" on the beaches. This rather insane idea came to Grant because he felt I did not fully appreciate the works of the great poet.

Later, in a burst of generosity and fellowship, enhanced by those dramatic days, Grant rounded up several of his old newspaper pals who were then in uniform as war correspondents, including such characters as Fred Griffin and the irrepressible Greg Clark. He reserved a box for us all at the Haymarket Theatre, where *King Lear* was playing. He treated us first to a bang-up dinner with plenty to drink, being deeply moved by the thought that so many of his former cronies would shortly be engaged in battle again. Grant himself was a complete teetotaller, but his guests took joyful advantage of his hospitality, though they would have found greater enjoyment in a London musical than any Shakespearian drama.

The situation got a bit out of hand at the theatre. Halfway through the first act, Greg, being small, simply stretched out on the floor of the box for a contented snooze, while Griffin, whose chair was badly placed behind a great velour curtain, kept poking his head out behind the folds. When King Lear became eloquent, Griffin offered such rude remarks as, "Christ, is that old bastard still declaiming?" Grant, of course, was outraged and desolated at such barbarism.

A few days before Prime Minister King was due to return to Canada, General Montague at CMHQ sent for me. "What do we do about King visiting the Canadian troops before he goes home?" he demanded. "He can't go back to Canada on the very eve of D-Day and tell Parliament and the people of Canada he didn't visit the troops. But we can't risk the Prime Minister being booed again just before they go into battle."

It is now perhaps timely to confess to a minor act of deception. The solution to Montague's problem, I suggested, was to secure a photograph of the Prime Minister while he was looking at Canadian troops; but the circumstances would be such that the troops would be unaware of their observer's identity.

In the event, King was taken down to a coastal area where a Canadian unit was carrying out some assault-landing exercises on a beach. From a position on a cliff overlooking the beach, King was able to see the troops scrambling ashore. From this strategic position, news pictures were taken, showing King talking to a small group of senior officers in the foreground while, in the distance below, the troops on the beaches could be seen in a mock-invasion setting. An armoured regiment was also raced past King at such a speed that the drivers could not recognize the VIP watching them. The stratagem was entirely successful. The troops had no

242

idea that it was their Prime Minister on the cliff, and the folks at home were intrigued to see Mr. King pictured in such warlike settings.

During talks with Grant Dexter, before he returned home with the PM, he told me something of the fears which were already starting to haunt King should conscription become necessary after the invasion was launched. King had been considerably heartened, however, by one possibility which had been suggested to him in England: that once a bridgehead had been firmly established in Normandy, German resistance might suddenly collapse. With this hope in his heart, King returned to report to the Canadian people.

FOURTEEN

Conflicting Stories

WORLD SCENE

Invasion plans for Normandy completed — Canadians in Italy switched to 5th Army front for final attacks on Monte Cassino. Canadians break through Hitler line in Italy. U.S. troops advance on Rome. Masses of British — U.S. — Canadian — Polish and other Allied troops concentrate in south-east coast of England for Operation Overlord.

What was the truth concerning McNaughton's removal from command? Was he in fact a victim of political intrigue, service rivalries and personal feuds, or was he simply not capable of command in battle, as claimed by the War Office?

There were many conflicting stories circulated at the time of McNaughton's removal from command of the Canadian Army, and some of these false claims have persisted to the present. The posthumous publication of McNaughton's memoirs in 1968, giving McNaughton's own version of the incident, have added further confusion to the controversy. From the grave, he seemed to be aiming a final twisted thrust at Ralston and the others who supported him for so long — and let him off so easily — despite his bitter, abusive personal attacks.

It is time that more details concerning McNaughton's removal should be made public.

Ralston, despite the fact that he had in his possession information which would have completely refuted McNaughton's vicious innuendos and reproaches, and could have publicly destroyed McNaughton, remained silent.

Until the time of his tragic death from a heart attack shortly after the war, Ralston never made any public statement either to defend himself against McNaughton's claims or to slight McNaughton in any way. This was typical of his character and great stature.

I had several private talks with Ralston on these matters shortly after the war, and he undertook to read some galley proofs of *Missing from the Record,* before publication. In that book I touched, in a general way, on McNaughton's removal, together with his appointment as Defence Minister when Mackenzie King hurled Ralston from the battlements. I did not ask Ralston at that time to endorse my accounts in any way; I knew of his desire to remain silent. As an old friend, however, he did agree to let me know if there were any serious errors in my story.

After reading the proofs he said, have no worry about publication; the account was substantially correct. There was one minor error, but it was non-essential. He wouldn't tell me what it was then, as he wished to remain in the position of not directing my statements in any way.

At that same time he did agree that he would leave copies of his personal records of the episode to his long-time friend George Currie and myself, with permission to use them if at any time his integrity was ever seriously attacked.

On my last visit with Ralston in Montreal after the war, just before his death, he recalled his promise about his wartime diaries and said he would send me a copy without delay. He died before this undertaking was met. It was my intention to enquire about the copy from Mrs. Ralston after some decent interval, but before I got around to it Mrs. Ralston also died.

Feeling it was important that these historic records should not be lost to our national archives, I eventually wrote about them to Ralston's son, Stuart. He replied that there was no trace of my copy of the diaries amongst his father's effects. So there the matter rested for several years.

One day in the south of France, at Cap d'Ail, Lord Beaverbrook, whom I was visiting, casually enquired as to the whereabouts of Ralston's diaries, which he recalled from our wartime meetings. He was anxious to secure them for the Maritime archives he was helping to establish in Fredericton, New Brunswick. I recounted my unsuccessful efforts to locate the diaries and commented that I felt they belonged in the federal archives. Beaverbrook disagreed violently and said they belonged with the papers of Angus Macdonald and Ilsley, in the Maritimes. He would beat me in locating them, he boasted.

It was shortly after this that I received a telephone call one day from George Currie, in Montreal. He had just received a large brown paper parcel containing some memos by Ralston. The parcel had been found in the Woods Building when they were clearing it out and it had George's name on it. George felt that these might prove to be the lost diaries, and he asked if I would check them over on my next trip to Montreal.

When I was able to examine these papers, I discovered that they were not the diaries but instead the complete copies of Ralston's records, covering McNaughton's removal from the command.

I had copies of the documents placed in the archives of Queen's University, with the understanding that photostats would be sent to the federal archives. Now after nearly 40 years, it is perhaps time that relevant extracts from these papers be made public.

As for the diaries, these were finally located with the assistance of Kaye Lamb, formerly head of the National Archives in Ottawa, when I suggested he make further enquiries through Stuart Ralston's widow, following Stuart's death. Most of these diary papers now rest in Ottawa.

The McNaughton biography by John Swettenham was a very detailed, painstaking and valuable documentation of the McNaughton story, but only as McNaughton himself saw things. Extensive use was made of his correspondence, his speeches, his views, his actions and his reactions to events. Others viewed his actions and interpreted correspondence and speeches quite differently.

Specifically, the many reasons given by McNaughton for his removal, in various press interviews and speeches after the war, and also advanced in his biography by John Swettenham, are as follows:

- His personal feud with Ralston and Ralston's jealousy.
- A conspiracy by other Canadian generals, ambitious for promotion and power, such as Crerar and Stuart.
- Political resentment in Ottawa, when he resisted splitting up the Canadian Army for the Sicily invasion.

- Jealousy and personal spite of senior officers in the British War Office, including the British CIGS, General Brooke and GOC South East Command, General Paget.

- The personal enmity of Monty.

- That Brooke and Paget had been pressured by Churchill, to report officially that McNaughton was unfit for command, due to his resistance in placing Canadian troops under British command at times.

- That General Sansom, commanding a Canadian corps in the major exercise Spartan (to test invasion planning) had let him down, and he had been unfairly blamed for this failure.

- Speaking in Saskatchewan in March 1945, McNaughton gave another explanation: "As I thought that orders given me were not right for Canada," he said, "I asked to be relieved. When the history of these events is written, what I did will be justified in the mind of every right thinking Canadian."

In short, McNaughton alleged every conceivable reason for his dismissal in denial of the formal statements made by the British War Office.

In his own mind, McNaughton was convinced that everyone was out to get him: the British Army, the Canadian higher command, the politicians, jealous members of the British Ordnance Board.

It was even argued, in some private quarters, that McNaughton had been back of a motion of censure against Churchill in the British Parliament.

Both during and after the war years, I endeavoured to check, as fully as possible, the validity of these multitude of charges made by McNaughton. I engaged in talks and correspondence with most of the principals involved and those in a position to know, including Churchill, Alanbrooke, Monty, Alexander, Ralston and Currie, as well as Sandy Dyde, Victor Sifton, Charles Vining, Stuart, H. D. G. Crerar, members of the Army Council, and members of the Canadian war cabinet at the time — among them, Chubby Power, Angus Macdonald and Tom Crerar. The memoranda and documentation left by Ralston have also been studied.

The weight of evidence conclusively rejects the variety of reasons advanced by McNaughton. Indeed, those most closely informed were outraged at the unfounded attack on the reputations of Ralston, Stuart and others.

McNaughton was certainly a strong and forceful personality, of very considerable ability, who, with great dedication, made a tremendous contribution to Canada's war effort. As one qualified observer put it, "To meet Andy McNaughton, even though purely professionally, was to fall immediately under his spell."

At the same time, McNaughton's own judgment was frequently flawed, due to an overwhelming vanity and, at times, vindictiveness. He was quite incapable of tolerating the views of those who saw the world differently from himself. As he interpreted matters, he was labouring with loyalty and dedication in what he conceived to be the national interest, and anyone who opposed his views was his enemy, scheming to destroy him, motivated by jealousy and a greed for power.

One cannot but speculate whether, like U.S. General Douglas MacArthur, as the war progressed he simply came to resent any civilian or government control, regardless of political implications.

In the words of his biographer, however, it was early in the war that, "the politicians started to sharpen their knives" to get McNaughton. This was indeed McNaughton's belief.

Almost without exception, most authorities questioned on the McNaughton dismissal paid generous tribute to McNaughton's wartime contribution but conceded, as charged by the British War Office, that he had not the capacity or temperament to command in action. Typical of such observations were the comments of the noted historian, Cyril Falls, Chichele Professor of the History of War at All Souls' College, Oxford. Professor Falls knew McNaughton during the war and was in a privileged position for access to British war records. Writing to the author in September 1947, he commented as follows:

"I gather you feel, as I did, that it was in the long run, best that Andy should have been removed. I greatly regretted it from one point of view because I admired him very much. Intellectually, he was ahead of any soldier I have ever met. But on the practical side, it seems doubtful if he would have filled the bill in North-West Europe."

How valid were McNaughton's charges against Ralston, Stuart, Paget and Brooke? How accurate was the claim that it was the British, supported by Ralston and the Canadian Chief of Staff, who were determined to thwart McNaughton by breaking up the Canadian Army and placing Canadian formations under British command?

The truth was quite the reverse. Many of these principals were the very men who did everything possible to cater to McNaughton's vanity in the Canadian interest and to let him down easily.

It was the Canadian cabinet which insisted that Canadian formations be uprooted from southern England and be given some battle experience in Sicily before the Normandy invasion. Indeed, the request went direct to Churchill, with the endorsement of Mackenzie King. Contrary to McNaughton's claim, the British, as well as the Americans, opposed this step at first. McNaughton, however, deluded himself with the conviction that this was part of a personal vendetta to remove him from command. More than once McNaughton threatened to resign if his army was broken up, despite the clear decisions taken in Ottawa by the government. The records clearly establish that Brooke, the British CIGS, at first opposed breaking up the Canadian Army and subsequently worked hard to have all the Canadian formations brought together again, under Canadian command, as soon as the units from Italy came north to the South of France.

Charges were also made by McNaughton that Ralston tried to interfere with his command of the army. Again the situation was quite the reverse. McNaughton repeatedly assumed powers for himself, far exceeding his actual authority and without reference to either Ralston or the government. Time after time, Ralston was obliged to check McNaughton when he made commitments in England without any approval from the Defence Department, the Treasury Board or the cabinet in Ottawa.

It should also be noted that while early in the war Ralston recognized Canada's need for a hero figure — a Kitchener — as a rallying point to help morale and recruiting, he consistently kept himself in the background and urged a publicity build-up for McNaughton. The claim that Ralston was jealous of McNaughton's popularity was sheer nonsense. The writer, in fact, on Ralston's directions, helped arrange for numerous magazine articles about McNaughton, as well as press photographs, film sequences and cover pictures, not only in Canada but also in the U.K. and the U.S.; his coverage included *Time* magazine and *the March of Time* newsreels.

Claims are also made in the McNaughton biography, that Brooke made "slurring remarks" about General McNaughton in Washington, so that the CGS, General Stuart, would overhear them; this "ambitious lieutenant general" would pass the comments along to Colonel Ralston and Mr. King.

Here again the story is quite inaccurate. In point of fact, General McNaughton's "lack of fitness" to command in the field had been well recognized in England much earlier and had been the subject of consultation among Paget, Brooke, Grigg (the British Secretary of State for War) and Prime Minister Churchill. If there were snide side remarks dropped at Washington, they never reached Ralston's ear.

As far as General Stuart being ambitious (presumably for McNaughton's job), this is quite ludicrous. General Stuart, as Canada's Chief of the General Staff, was already General McNaughton's senior.

He was also too old and not physically fit to serve overseas in the field. He had nothing to gain from McNaughton's removal. To the contrary, it presented him with a most serious problem in finding a qualified replacement for McNaughton to command the army in action.

Anyone giving the matter thought would realize that a British general on his own initiative would not formally suggest the removal of General McNaughton, the senior overseas officer of another Commonwealth country, without the very fullest prior consultation on the highest military and political levels.

At those levels, it was the considered and recorded view that McNaughton could not be accepted as a commander in the field. It was felt that: "He neglected many of his chief responsibilities as commander, was interested largely in mechanical rather than the human side of command, was excitable and very highly strung, or in other words lacked most of the attributes of high command."[*]

Prime Minister King is also on record at the time as "wholly agreeing" with the need for General McNaughton's removal and also being "deeply grateful" to Colonel Ralston for handling this most difficult situation.[**]

The first evidence I had personally of McNaughton's dislike of Ralston and his resentment of any direction from Ottawa was, as related earlier, during the brittle meeting at Taplow hospital in England. Some years after the war, Colonel H. A. (Sandy) Dyde, a wartime Secretary of the Defence Council, who knew the principals well, informed me that although not realized by Ralston, McNaughton had formed a deep hatred of him much earlier in the war. This happened even before Ralston took over the Defence portfolio, following the death of the Hon. Norman Rogers early in 1940.

Dyde, then acting as Staff Secretary, had accompanied Rogers to England in the early days of the war, to consult with the British

---

[*] General Stuart's formal notes of discussion with British Chief of General Staff, General Sir Alan Brooke, November 13, 1943. Signed by General Brooke as being an accurate statement.
[**] Cypher signals, Prime Minister to Colonel Ralston, via External Affairs, dated November 13, 1943.

authorities and visit the first Canadian contingent under McNaughton's command. By chance, Mackenzie King was briefly absent from Ottawa then, and Ralston was deputy Prime Minister.

Dyde related the story as follows:

On reaching London, Rogers and I had a meeting almost at once with General McNaughton and another officer, who I think was Crerar, who was then senior officer at CMHQ. McNaughton announced to Rogers that he had detailed two Canadian battalions for the British expedition to Norway, the Princess Patricias and the Edmonton regiment, and that these two battalions were in Scotland ready to embark. This was a complete surprise to Rogers, and it turned out that the government at Ottawa had not been informed of this action by McNaughton. At first Rogers thought McNaughton might have cabled Ottawa during the time Rogers was on the sea.

Rogers took most of an evening composing a cable to the Prime Minister at Ottawa, in which he reviewed the circumstances and indicated some sympathy for McNaughton, who had been under pressure from the British government to allocate Canadians to the expedition. Rogers recommended to the cabinet at Ottawa that McNaughton's action should be approved.

This cable reached Ottawa at a time when Mackenzie King was away in the United States for a brief period and Ralston was acting Prime Minister. A rather abrupt but perfectly proper cable came back to Rogers from Ralston approving the Norway plan on behalf of the cabinet but making a comment, which I cannot now remember, on the impropriety of the action taken by McNaughton without first referring the matter to Ottawa. McNaughton undoubtedly saw both the cable from Rogers and the reply. It was obvious to several of us in London at the time that McNaughton was resentful of the attitude taken by the cabinet with respect to himself, and Ralston was clearly the object of his resentment.

Mrs. McNaughton was in England at the time and the day following this exchange of cables the McNaughtons gave a cocktail party in the Carlton Hotel. Mrs. McNaughton made several remarks of a critical kind about Ralston. Her remarks were made in my hearing and in that of a number of others who should not have been informed in any way of the circumstances. McNaughton must have informed her of all that had taken place.

While McNaughton himself resented the tone of the cable from Ottawa, there is no doubt in my mind that at that time and from then on, Mrs. McNaughton's influence on her husband was most unfortunate, at least insofar as the relationship between her husband and Ralston was concerned.

In retrospect, I have sometimes wondered to what extent we may have unwittingly contributed to this situation through the great publicity build-up of McNaughton as Canada's Kitchener.

But what of the gossip that McNaughton had run afoul of Winston Churchill? Was there in fact any truth to the allegation that, through his active role in weapon research and development, he had incurred the displeasure of Winston Churchill, by way of Churchill's personal scientific advisor, Professor Lindemann? The story went that McNaughton had been involved with a British parliamentary group which sought to weaken Churchill's political power through a vote of lack of confidence.

Swettenham's biography of McNaughton fully documents the truly great contribution McNaughton made in many fields of weapon research, despite the opposition of the moribund British Ordnance Board and the science research people in the British Ministry of Supply. He worked closely with such people as Sir Frederick Pile and the millionaire banker Sir Albert Stern.

Churchill was coming under very heavy criticism in Parliament and the press at that time, with the serious British defeats by Rommel in North Africa and by the Japanese in the Far East largely due to inferior tanks and guns. As Hore-Belisha charged in the British House, ". . . in a hundred days Britain had lost an Empire in the Far East. What will happen in the next hundred days?" Despite this, it should be noted in passing that Churchill defeated the vote of censure by an overwhelming count of 475 to 25, and from this point forward the tide started to run in Britain's favour.

The rebel group had Sir John Wardlaw-Milne as their spokesman in the House of Commons. Privately, this group urged that Britain secure McNaughton's services to revitalize their Ordnance Board. Consequently, McNaughton's name was falsely linked with this rebel group and their efforts to censure Churchill — forcing him to give up the Defence portfolio and remove Lindemann's influence. There has been no evidence come to light, whatever, that McNaughton was ever involved in any way with this scheme.

Touching on the McNaughton-Ralston relationship, the late George Currie, one of Ralston's executive assistants at Defence HQ during the war, and later deputy minister, provided me with the following written comment in 1963:

> I knew Ralston since the First Great War and I feel that I had the honour and privilege of being his personal friend. As such, I believe that he confided in me some of his personal problems. At any rate, he did discuss with me personalities and some intimate thoughts.
>
> On many occasions we discussed McNaughton. He admired McNaughton for his good qualities, which he appreciated were many, as well as the magnificent contribution which he [McNaughton] was making to the cause. However, Ralston worried terribly because he knew that McNaughton hated him, which feeling he felt was aided and abetted by Mrs. McNaughton. He would often say to me that he wished he could find out what was wrong with their relationship. He could not understand it nor the underlying cause. I think this is important to know about because Ralston, far from being McNaughton's enemy or critic, did his level best to support McNaughton and further his career. It was McNaughton and not Ralston who was to blame for the lack of co-operation and good relationship between them. I know of no man whom I have admired more for his honesty and integrity than Ralston. On occasion his conscience carried him to bend over backwards.
>
> McNaughton just did not understand Ralston and resented what I suppose he felt was the civilian interfering with the military. Ralston never did anything with an ulterior motive such as to undermine McNaughton's military authority. Ralston was McNaughton's boss and he was most conscientious in trying to maintain the proper relationship.

McNaughton at one moment claimed it was the British who instigated his removal, starting with their snide remarks to the Canadian Chief of Staff, General Stuart, when in Washington. Later he implied that it was Ralston who first initiated steps toward his removal. Consequently, General Stuart was asked to report officially what did transpire between himself and the British CIGS, Brooke, in Washington, and subsequently. Stuart reported as follows:

1. In June 1943, in the course of a casual conversation in Washington, U.S.A., the CIGS made certain remarks to me on his own volition concerning McNaughton. These remarks indicated to me that the CIGS had some doubt as to McNaughton's fitness to command in the field. We did not have an opportunity in Washington to continue the discussion.

2. In July 1943 I was in the U.K. on my way to North Africa. I asked for an appointment with the CIGS to discuss the possibility of the despatch of additional Canadian troops to the Mediterranean area. Our discussion led to a consideration of the future of First Canadian Army in the event of 1 Corps proceeding abroad. This, in turn, led to the CIGS giving me his views regarding McNaughton's suitability to command in the field. I cannot remember whether I raised the point resulting from the remarks the CIGS made in Washington and consequent on my having studied Paget's report on 'Spartan' exercise. I am inclined to think, however, that the CIGS raised the point himself and without any prompting on my part. In any event I cannot see that it makes the slightest difference. If the CIGS had not elaborated his remarks made in Washington, I should have asked him to do so. Otherwise I should have failed in my duty to the Canadian Army and to the Canadian Government. The following represents a summary of the views of the CIGS as told to me in our conversations in July and November 1943.

3. The CIGS always spoke very frankly. He said that McNaughton's case had been worrying him for a considerable time. His doubts as to McNaughton's suitability for high command first arose when McNaughton was commanding 1 Div. These doubts became certainties during the period that McNaughton commanded 1 Cdn. Corps and First Cdn. Army. McNaughton, he said, was a good organizer and had contributed much in the way of weapon development. He was more interested in the development side than in command. His command was a full-time job, but his interests covered such a wide field that he neglected his responsibilities as a commander and spent too much time in attending to the other interests referred to. He said that McNaughton did not handle his command well on exercises; he was not a good trainer and seemed to lack both the interest and ability to conduct and supervise the training of its commanders; he was interested in the mechanical rather than in the human side of his command; he was excitable and very highly strung. In other words, the CIGS stated, he lacked most of the attributes for high command.

4. The CIGS was equally emphatic regarding McNaughton's future. He stated that he could not accept him as a commander in the field. He had discussed the case of McNaughton with Paget, with the Secretary of State for War and with Mr. Churchill. He felt that McNaughton's feelings should not be hurt and that he should be let down as easily as possible.

At the bottom of the report is the notation:

"The above is a fair and accurate statement of my conversation with General Stuart." It is signed, Alan Brooke.

Ralston later assured me that the first intimation he had that the British were unhappy with McNaughton came direct from the British CIGS. During the Quebec summit conference, Brooke spoke frankly to Ralston.

As Ralston related, the discussion took place after dinner one evening at the Chateau Frontenac. The British CIGS asked if he would care to go for a brief walk on the promenade outside.

After talking pleasantries at first, Brooke then bluntly asked, "How highly does Canada rate McNaughton as a field commander?" Taken by surprise and rather disturbed by the question, Ralston countered by asking how McNaughton was regarded in England. It was only then that Ralston learned of the serious reservations the British had regarding McNaughton's capacity to command.

Only an abridged version of the official report on the disastrous Exercise Spartan had been relayed on to Canada. It was accepted that most of the failure was due to lack of training on a divisional scale by Canada's 5th Armoured Division and a lack of experience by General Sansom, the Canadian Corps commander. Brooke confided, however, that the principal weakness lay in McNaughton's own inability to control and direct large forces in the field operations. Far too much of his time, the British felt, had been devoted to such things as weapon research, bridge building and new explosives.

Ralston was deeply concerned at hearing these frank revelations, which Brooke confirmed were the considered views not only of himself but also of Grigg, Britain's Secretary of State for War, Churchill and the chiefs at the War Office.

Until that time, Ralston had always felt that despite McNaughton's resentments and difficult personality, he was the best qualified to command the Canadian Army. Indeed, no serious consideration had ever been given to any alternative.

To suggest that Crerar was behind this or had been manoeuvring with Ralston and Stuart, to grab McNaughton's job, is quite erroneous. It was only after the decision that McNaughton must be removed had been taken, that Ralston even considered Crerar as a replacement. Even then it was rather in desperation, despite Crerar's seniority. During my various talks with Ralston in Italy and later in London and Antwerp, he confided to me that Stuart was the only one who strongly supported Crerar for army command at any time.

Shortly after his talk with Brooke at the Quebec conference and following talks with Prime Minister King about McNaughton and the despatch of further troops to Italy, Ralston left for England, to consult with the War Office and Churchill.

Before talking to either Churchill or Brooke at the War Office, Ralston, accompanied by General Stuart, met with McNaughton to hear his views. At first McNaughton seemed agreeable to the idea of sending a corps to Italy, though he insisted that the Canadian Army HQ be maintained. He agreed that some of the functions of Canadian Army HQ might be combined with those of Canadian Military HQ in London, and that there might not be a place for himself. However, he said that "the winning of the war was bigger than any man." He "would have to accept some other post."

At this meeting Ralston was upset to learn that McNaughton was still not aware of the British views on his own ability as a field commander.

Ralston did not feel he should raise the subject till he had further talks with Churchill and Brooke. The final decision regarding the corps for Italy was also delayed, pending these talks.

Ralston next met with Churchill, who agreed with Ottawa's suggestion that a Canadian corps should go to Italy but felt that Washington should be consulted before any further troops were withdrawn from the U.K., as he had commitments with them.

A meeting was next held with Brooke. As the invasion threat to the U.K. had diminished, he next agreed to a Canadian Corps going to Italy. He said he now wanted more rather than fewer troops in the Mediterranean. Privately, like Churchill, he still nursed the hope that Washington might still recognize the importance of an Allied drive through the Balkans, to secure Prague, Vienna and Berlin ahead of the Russians. Brooke, however, did not see much purpose then in maintaining a Canadian Army HQ structure in England. Ralston took an opposite view about the Army HQ, envisioning the Canadian troops in Italy ultimately returning for operations in north-west Europe.

The subject of McNaughton then came up. Brooke's views remained unchanged; McNaughton did not have the capacity to command in action. Ralston said that Brooke should see McNaughton himself and make Britain's views known to him. Brooke gave no commitment on this but pointed out, "It wasn't the same as if he [McNaughton] was a British general."

In Ralston's next talk with McNaughton, he discovered that the General had changed his mind about the corps going to Italy. He in fact now threatened to resign — "to make room for someone else" — if a policy of dispersal was adopted.

Then McNaughton, becoming heated, charged Ralston with being against a Canadian Army. Ralston said that if this feeling was in McNaughton's mind, it was wholly unjustified. He had approved McNaughton's recommendation for the army set-up and secured approval of his colleagues in cabinet, after many conferences. The meeting broke up rather abruptly.

In the following days Ralston held further meetings at the British War Office, with Brooke and Paget, over how the Canadian forces left in England would be fitted into the 21st Army Group structure for the Normandy invasion if a corps was despatched to Italy. At these meetings the question of McNaughton was raised repeatedly.

Ralston pointed out that Canada owed a debt to McNaughton for his outstanding service and asked if a senior job could not be found for him when he had to step down from Army Command. He again suggested that either Brooke or Paget should tell McNaughton very frankly their views about him as a commander. Paget said he had refrained from saying anything to McNaughton about command, wanting to keep strictly regular in not interfering with McNaughton's relations with his government.

Ralston took the position that it would not be fair to delay informing McNaughton. He should be told frankly rather than go on in the belief that everything was all right. Paget reasoned that it was up to Ralston to tell him after he had been advised of the War Office view. It was just a matter of timing, and it might be more opportune if Canada had some alternative post to suggest.

Ralston spent a troubled weekend at the Dorchester Hotel and, first thing on Monday, drove down to McNaughton's HQ at Leatherhead and presented the British view. He emphasized Britain's appreciation for everything McNaughton had done for them, and he assured him there was no personal enmity whatever on the part of Brooke or Paget. He told McNaughton he was most sorry to have to be the one to bring him the news but he felt it was due him, to know the situation.

McNaughton listened quietly; then there was silence for a few moments. Ralston mentioned that Paget had suggested that a British general might be found to command the Canadians as Byng had done in World War I, though Ralston himself had taken the position that this would not be satisfactory to Canada; a Canadian Army, he believed, should be commanded by a Canadian.

McNaughton said he would make it his business to see both Brooke and Paget at the earliest opportunity, to get from them their reasons for their conclusions. Ralston assured him this would be quite in order and that both Brooke and Paget were ready to meet with him.

Back at the Dorchester, Ralston despatched a top secret signal to Mackenzie King, advising the Prime Minister that matters had been resolved concerning McNaughton's removal and that he had accepted the situation. He then recorded in his diary: "McNaughton took it like a soldier . . . the interview was the most painful I have had since I took over the Department. I was deeply sorry for him and admired the quiet soldierly way he discussed the prospect of losing what to him must have been the height of his ambition and the fruition of over four years of ceaseless, faithful, untiring effort."

Unhappily, after brooding over the situation and not being prepared to accept the verdict, McNaughton completely reversed his attitude within the next 48 hours. Convincing himself that Ralston was acting entirely from spite and was out to get him, McNaughton went storming up to London to confront Brooke at the War Office.

He first saw Stuart, the Canadian CGS, and argued with him that as Canadian Army Commander he was not entirely subordinate to Brooke; indeed, in some aspects he represented the government of Canada. He then went on to charge that Stuart's discussions with Brooke had been behind his back. He also charged Stuart with not being frank with him.

In his own memoranda on these events, McNaughton added the observation: "I think that Stuart then perhaps for the first time realized the wrongness and unethical character of his action."

This was clearly imagination on McNaughton's part. Nowhere did Stuart ever express this thought, either in his subsequent talks with the author or in any of his memos or records at the time. To the contrary, he told McNaughton very clearly, and repeatedly, that as Chief of the General Staff, he had no alternative in his responsibilities but to advise the Canadian government of the official British view.

After seeing Stuart, McNaughton proceeded to see Brooke and Paget at the War Office. He demanded to know whether Brooke and Paget really did say he was incompetent and not fit to command, or whether Ralston had been simply lying to cover his own schemes.

Taken aback by this awkward situation and McNaughton's vehemence, Paget attempted to pacify the irate commander with a diplomatic reply, saying he had not put things in quite that manner. As Brooke confessed to the writer some years after the war, when visiting Winnipeg, this was Paget's mistake. Only later did Paget realize that he should have been as frank with McNaughton as he had been with Ralston; but at the time, he was anxious not to get involved in any Canadian dispute, if it could be avoided.

McNaughton at once seized on Paget's mollifying statement as clear evidence of treachery by Ralston. In this belief, he hotted off a violent signal via Vincent Massey's diplomatic code, direct to the Canadian Prime Minister in Ottawa and over the heads of both his minister and the Canadian Chief of Staff. His signal stated that he had "lost all confidence in Ralston... I can no longer remain in command of First Canadian Army responsible to any government of which he is a member."

McNaughton then went on to claim that he had discussed the matter with Paget, who "stated in the most emphatic terms that Ralston opened his conversation with him by expressing doubts over his [McNaughton's] fitness to command... Paget said he had felt in a very difficult position and perhaps had not been definite in his replies to Ralston and Stuart... resented the position he had been put in... gave me his most categorical assurance that everything had always been clear between us... not the least reserve that we could continue to work together... welcomed my remaining in command of Canadian Army both now and later in N.W. Europe..."

He then went on: "The situation we have to face is that a Minister of the Crown, on whom I have every right to rely on for support, comes here and by suggestions and suppositions casts doubts in the minds of senior officers of another country with whom I have to work, as to my fitness."

In conclusion, McNaughton stated: "I regard Ralston's actions as one of the meanest and most despicable of my whole experience...

"... I have given a copy of this telegram to The Hon. Mr. Ralston and with the greatest regret for any trouble it may cause you I place my resignation in your hands."*

Mackenzie King, badly confused and alarmed by the conflicting signals from Ralston and McNaughton, replied to them both immediately in the following terms.

To McNaughton: "... I hope you will not find it necessary to take any further step until I have heard from Ralston and have had a chance to communicate with you again..."

To Ralston: "... Matter referred to is of such gravity that I think it would be best if both you and McNaughton could be here at the earliest possible moment so that War Committee may all share responsibility of any decision..."

In response to the Prime Minister's signal, McNaughton agreed that "no further step of any sort in this matter will be taken by me until I know your wishes." Ralston took the position that he should not return to Canada as suggested but complete his mission in the U.K. and then, in the national interest, go on to Italy to see first hand the conditions faced by the Canadian troops in action there, regarding rations, equipment and personnel. He pointed out that no minister had so far visited our troops in action.

Immediately the next day Ralston met with Paget at the War Office and, in very concise terms, explained to him the situation created with

*Signal, McNaughton to Prime Minister, November 10, 1943.

Prime Minister King. Ralston pointed out that while Paget had told him one thing in very clear terms, he had seemingly told McNaughton quite the reverse. He demanded to know which version was correct.

Paget was shocked and outraged that McNaughton had misinterpreted his views in the manner stated to Mackenzie King. He claimed he had tried to be diplomatic but had certainly never made the statements credited to him by McNaughton. What Paget had said to Ralston was accurate, and he at once agreed to put his views to McNaughton in writing so that there could be no further twisting or misunderstanding of his views. This Paget did without delay, stating once more that he did not consider McNaughton fit for command in active operations.*

At this stage a further urgent signal was received from Mackenzie King endeavouring to prevent "an open break" and stressing that "the highest interests of the state must be the first consideration" in dealing with the painful situation. If at all possible, a public controversy should be avoided, as it "would be certain to leave disastrous effects upon the morale of the Canadians at home and abroad, and gravely affect our whole war effort."

Then to doubly ensure that Paget was not further misrepresented or misunderstood, it was arranged that McNaughton would see him person-ally and that a witness would be present to hear what was said. This meeting was duly arranged. Stuart attended as the witness, and Paget did not mince his words.

McNaughton was then asked if he had any comments to make. He had none, he replied; the facts were clear and he was prepared to accept them. It was then pointed out to McNaughton that his signal to the Prime Minister had been based on a false premise and his attack on Ralston had been without justification. McNaughton admitted this and agreed that steps should be taken to correct matters. He would contact Ralston to see what could be worked out, and he was prepared to cable the Prime Minister, admitting that his previous wire had been based on a misunder-standing of the facts.

On receipt of McNaughton's message of explanation and regrets, together with a report on McNaughton's meetings with Paget in the presence of a witness, King was greatly relieved and cabled his apprecia-tion to Ralston and Stuart, saying how much he appreciated their efforts in resolving matters under most trying and difficult circumstances and wishing Ralston well in his forthcoming visit to Italy. King also asked Ralston to "express my warmest thanks to Stuart, whose very difficult and honourable part in this matter has been of inestimable value."

King also wrote a long letter to McNaughton, following a text suggested by Ralston, saying: "It is evident to me that you have been under a terrible strain and that it is in this light we must all view this very painful episode. I realize what your anxieties and feelings are and how anxious I am to be of what assistance I can in seeking every possible honourable means of overcoming existing difficulties and thereby avoid-ing the appalling series of consequences which otherwise would be inevitable."

With these exchanges, the situation cooled down and Ralston left for Italy to visit the Canadian troops in action and to ascertain whether or

---

*General Paget's memorandum to McNaughton and Stuart, dated November 13, 1943; and General Stuart's memorandum covering this same interview, dated November 13, 1943.

not Crerar might be considered a suitable replacement for McNaughton. Meanwhile, McNaughton would continue on temporarily to command the Canadian Army. There would be no public statement made concerning McNaughton's pending retirement.

It was not long, however, before McNaughton again returned to his original charge. Despite his previous admission that he had misinterpreted Paget and been unfair to Ralston in his signal to the Prime Minister, he privately promoted the view that Stuart and Ralston had deliberately undermined him with the British, had not been frank with him, had operated behind his back. It was as though his face-to-face meeting with Paget in the presence of witnesses had never transpired; as though the official British position, which had been place before him in formal written terms, had never been expressed. None of this became public at the time.

Toward the end of November, however, complications arose. Rumours of a change in command of the Canadian Army began to circulate in Ottawa, and there was speculation in some Canadian newspapers. At the same time, McNaughton had a recurrence of a respiratory infection he had suffered the previous winter, and he was suffering from fatigue. The idea then arose that the date of his retirement should be advanced, due to reasons of ill health. This suggestion was agreeable to both McNaughton and Ralston, and King was advised accordingly. It was considered essential, however, that McNaughton undergo a proper medical examination in hospital by two senior doctors. This was carried out by Colonel L. C. Montgomery, the consulting physician for the Director of Medical Services, and Lieutenant-Colonel G. C. Ferguson, commanding the medical division of No. 12 General Hospital. They reported that McNaughton had a respiratory tract infection ... was definitely below par. They strongly recommended a three months' leave of absence, with McNaughton freed from all military responsibility.

Accordingly, a draft announcement of McNaughton's retirement was worked out in consultation with him. In this respect, General Montague saw McNaughton in hospital, as Ralston was still away in Italy.

On December 7, McNaughton formally wrote Montague, saying, "... the past few days have shown me conclusively that I have not the strength left to look after the army properly ... will you please give this message to Mr. Ralston for me when he arrives ..."

It was then decided to make a public announcement that "The Minister of National Defence announced today that as a result of an infection, due to influenza, Lieutenant-General A. L. G. McNaughton has developed a physical condition that has made him temporarily unfit to command an army in the field ..." The announcement would be withheld until just after Christmas.

In light of McNaughton's subsequent claims in Canada that there was nothing wrong with his health, it should be noted that he underwent a further medical examination on December 11. Again the doctors found that he showed definite signs of exhaustion and advised a period of three months' rest. McNaughton and his doctors considered that he would be able to return to Canada by mid-January.

The German propaganda, missing no opportunity to sow discord among the Allies, seized on the announcement of McNaughton's retirement to broadcast immediately the following report over the radio:

"As soon as the Americans had succeeded in getting the post from Commander-in-Chief of the Allied forces in England for their General Eisenhower the Commander of the Canadian army in England, General McNaughton announced that he would retire from his post. As usual he referred to his bad state of health. In the official statement announcing this retirement the unusual remark was made that the --- of the Canadian General was only accepted after the --- doctor had convinced the authorities of the necessity of McNaughton's step. It was taken for granted that this special craving was used to hide the real motive for McNaughton's retirement. During the past few years ever since there has been talk about the second front, McNaughton was put down as the favorite for the post of Commander-in-Chief of the invasion forces. Apparently McNaughton had no desire to command Canadian troops under American superiors. In view of the experiences made at Dieppe and elsewhere in this war where Canadians were slaughtered when under foreign command. The Canadian government has nominated no successor to McNaughton and the Deputy Commander-in-Chief for the time being is to be General Stuart the Chief of Staff of the Canadian forces stationed in the British Isles. It is understood that McNaughton is going back to Canada to take a long holiday."*

It is perhaps now timely also to record that the British were not alone in their opinion that McNaughton was not fit for command of an army in active operations. Nor were they alone in their determination not to have any of their own divisions serve under his command.

Not generally known was the fact that the U.S. defence chiefs, quite independently, had arrived at similar conclusions. At one stage it was being touted that McNaughton would command the Allied land forces for the Normandy invasion and anticipated that U.S. divisions would be placed under McNaughton's command for the assault. Reversing this proposal, the Americans subsequently wished to see McNaughton's abilities devoted entirely to research and the development of new weapons.

After the war, George Currie gave the following account:

> Pressure came from many quarters that McNaughton should be given a special appointment for his ability to invent and develop new modern weapons.
>
> McNaughton really did make a serious mess of his handling of large bodies of troops in the exercises in England prior to D-Day. After they had taken place, I had a very interesting call and talk with an opposite number of mine from Washington. He was a civilian attached to the American army for special duty and he came to me to inquire as to what we thought of the senior command as at that time appointed to carry out the invasion of D-Day. They had grave doubts particularly about Montgomery and also McNaughton. One reason was that it was proposed that McNaughton should have under his command a body of American troops. General Stuart was with me at this interview and it was very frank and really quite disturbing. The point I wish to make is that McNaughton was under criticism from more sources than we realize. However, the Americans did make an effort to have him transferred to Washington to head up some type of American Weapons Research Branch.

*This text is as monitored in London and Ottawa at the time, in which a few words were missed.

Nothing came of this proposal of employing McNaughton in Washington, or of the British idea for using his talents in Ordnance research. Early in the new year, passage was booked for General and Mrs. McNaughton to return to Canada via New York.

Apprehensive about McNaughton's sometimes unpredictable behaviour or what he might say or do when he returned to Canada, Mackenzie King arranged, through Ralston, for George Currie to go to New York to meet the General and Mrs. McNaughton on their arrival. What transpired next is best told in Currie's own words.

> When McNaughton came back to Canada after the change in command, both Mackenzie King and Ralston were most anxious to so arrange his arrival that the press would not interview him before he had had a talk with the Prime Minister. For this purpose Jack Mackenzie, representing the Prime Minister, and myself, representing Ralston, were sent to New York to meet McNaughton. General Murchie and one or two staff were in our party, plus a public relations officer. With the help of the U.S. Army we arranged that McNaughton be seen on the ship before disembarking and advised of the travel arrangements. He was very co-operative and assured us that he would not talk to anyone before seeing the Prime Minister. We whisked him off to a small private hotel and, with the help of the U.S. security forces, in the evening we boarded the private cars on the Montreal train, not proceeding through the main lobby of the station. Arriving at Point St. Charles, we were switched to a private train for the Seigniory Club. I had breakfast with McNaughton, which we finished as we arrived at the Seigniory Club station. I was right behind him as we went down the steps to get off the train. There in front of us on the platform was a member of the press, who greeted McNaughton and immediately interviewed him. McNaughton spoke openly and freely, assuring them that he was in perfect health and made other remarks which were quoted in the Ottawa paper that afternoon. As you know, Ralston then had in his possession the medical officer's report on McNaughton's health and also his file containing correspondence and memoranda of interviews with the British higher command and U.K. ministers. I called Ralston from the club and told him what had happened. He was very disturbed and asked me to come to Ottawa at once, which I did. Although Ralston never told me what happened in his interview with the Prime Minister, I had reason to believe that is was not friendly.

H. R. MacMillan, who saw McNaughton soon after he reached Ottawa, commented in a letter to the author, "McNaughton was beside me talking to someone else and declaring that he had never been in better health. That caused me to look at him and I came to the conclusion that at that moment he looked far from well."

Shortly after McNaughton reached Ottawa, in outright contradiction to his statements in the press that there was nothing wrong with his health, he made a written application for extensive sick leave, supported by his own doctor's recommendation. Ralston approved this request without comment or any public statement.

Had the McNaughton drama ended on this note, unquestionably his reputation and acclaim would have remained intact as the man who, with great dedication, welded together the Canadian overseas army.

In the months ahead, however, as the conscription issue developed, McNaughton was to be found negotiating with leaders of the opposition Conservative party on plans to topple the Mackenzie King government and destroy Ralston, by leading the parade for overseas conscription in Canada. He was in fact walking both sides of the political street.

Meanwhile, preparations were being completed in England for the Canadian forces to take the field, for the first time in history on an army scale, in the Normandy invasion.

A Brief Who's Who

ALANBROOKE, Field Marshal, Viscount (formerly General Sir Alan Brooke). Considered by many as the master strategist of World War II. Served in World War I with distinction, with British Army. Prior to World War II successively commanded British Mobile Division, Anti-Aircraft Command and Southern Command. On outbreak of WW II commanded 2nd Army Corps in France with British Expeditionary Force. Appointed Commander-in-Chief British Home Forces in 1940 and Chief of Imperial General Staff in 1941. As chairman, Chiefs of Staff Committee, accompanied Winston Churchill to wartime summit meetings. Greatly respected by Montgomery and other senior British generals, as well as by U.S. military chiefs. While seldom in the headlines, widely considered to be Britain's ablest professional soldier. At one time he was proposed as Commander-in-Chief for the Normandy invasion, but it was felt he could not be spared from his responsibilities as CIGS at British War Office. Retiring from the army after the war, he frequently visited Canada in his capacity as a director of the Hudson's Bay Company.

Although a deeply sensitive man, he was seen by many of his contemporaries as a man of iron, without nerves or feeling. Unquestionably one of the chief architects of the Allied victory.

ALEXANDER, Field Marshal, Viscount of Tunis (Alex). Distinguished soldier, statesman. Regular British Force officer, graduate of Sandhurst, served with distinction in World War I in France with Irish guards, then in India in 1935. Appointed to command 1st British Division 1938-40 with BEF in France. In charge of evacuation from Dunkirk. Then appointed to command Burma front in March 1942.

When British forces forced to retreat by German African Corps under General Rommel in North Africa, he was appointed Commander-in-Chief Middle East, at the time that Montgomery took command of the legendary 8th Army. In 1943 became Deputy Allied Commander-in-Chief, North Africa, and subsequently Commander-in-Chief Italy. A popular and highly respected general, noted for coolness in action and sound judgment. Following the war appointed Governor General of Canada.

BEAVERBROOK, Baron (Max Aitken). Canadian-born, British newspaper publisher. Close confidant of Sir Winston Churchill in both world wars. After building a fortune with various Canadian business enterprises, moved to England prior to WW I and became active in British politics and newspapers. A confidant of the Duke of Windsor during the abdication crisis. Served in British government as Minister of Information during World War I and Minister of Aircraft Production in World War II. A highly controversial and colourful publisher and owner of the *Daily Express* and other newspapers.

CRERAR, General H. D. G. (Harry). Canadian Permanent Force officer, Royal Military College graduate. Served in World War I as artillery officer and staff officer at HQ Canadian Corps. Following the war he served successively at Canadian Defence HQ, Ottawa, and at British War Office in London. Appointed Director Operations and Intelligence at Canadian Defence HQ, Ottawa, in 1935. Attended Imperial Conference in 1937. Became Commandant RMC in 1938. On outbreak of World War II appointed senior staff officer, Canadian Military HQ, London, England. Returned to Canada 1940 to become Chief of General Staff, accompanying Defence Minister Ralston to U.K. to co-ordinate mobilization plans late 1940. Appointed GOC 2nd Canadian Division 1941 and GOC 1st Canadian Corps 1942. After a short period of service in Italy in 1943, returned to England to replace General McNaughton in command of Canadian Army for the Normandy invasion and campaigns in north-west Europe.

CRERAR, Hon. T. A. (Tom). A senior member of Mackenzie King's wartime cabinet. (Not related to General H. D. G. Crerar, Canadian Army Commander.) Appointed to Senate in 1945. Was Canada's longest-serving Privy Councillor. A much respected elder statesman. A contemporary of Sir Clifford Sifton and a member of the legendary "Sanhedrin" in Winnipeg, a politically powerful, informal group of associates of J. W. Dafoe, editor of the *Winnipeg Free Press.* Before entering politics as Member of Parliament for Marquette, Man., in the Union government of 1917, was active in farming circles of western Canada, serving as president of United Grain Growers. Was appointed Minister of Agriculture in 1917. Resigned from the government in 1919 over disagreement on tariff policies. Became leader of the Progressive party, which captured 66 seats in 1921 election.

In subsequent Liberal governments between the years 1929 and 1945, he held such cabinet portfolios as Mines, Immigration, Indian Affairs; then became Minister of the combined Departments of Mines and Resources. A supporter of Canada's Defence Minister, J. L. Ralston, in the great conscription controversy.

CURRIE, George S., CMG, DSO, MC. Partner in accounting firm of McDonald, Currie & Company. Close associate of Canada's wartime Defence Minister, J. L. Ralston. Served in World War I with PPCLI in France and subsequently as staff captain 1st Infantry Brigade, and DAQMG of 4th Canadian Division. Offering his services again in World War II, he was appointed executive assistant to J. L. Ralston during the years 1940-42 and became Deputy Minister of Defence 1942-44.

de GUINGAND, Major-General, Sir Francis (Freddie). British Regular Force officer, Sandhurst graduate. Commissioned in Prince of Wales' own West Yorkshire Regiment in 1919. Seconded to King's West African Rifles, 1926. On instigation of then Colonel B. L. Montgomery nominated to Staff College Camberley and in 1939 became Military Assistant to British Secretary of State for War, Leslie Hore-Belisha. He was arrested and silenced for predicting Allied losses in 1940 and was posted to Middle East. Under General Wavell, as military planner, he protested against the defence of Greece and was overruled. When General

Auchinleck became C-in-C Middle East, de Guingand was appointed head of intelligence. After Auchinleck was sacked and Montgomery assumed command of 8th Army, an historic partnership was formed when de Guingand was appointed Monty's Chief of Staff. He served Monty all through the desert campaign and during the invasions of Sicily and Italy, returning as part of "Monty's team," when Monty was appointed GOC 21st Army Group, to command all Allied land forces for the Normandy invasion. de Guingand served as Monty's Chief of Staff till the end of the war and repeatedly played the role of diplomat in smoothing out serious differences between Montgomery and Eisenhower, who greatly respected de Guingand's judgment. Regarded as Britain's most successful Chief of Staff during the war years, he contributed greatly in maintaining harmony among the Allied armies.

After the war, when Montgomery became Chief of the General Staff, he failed to appoint de Guingand his vice-chief as promised, and de Guingand retired to Civvy Street.

HOWE, Rt. Hon. C. D. Canada's colourful and vigorous Minister of Munitions and Supply during World War II. A civil engineer prior to the war. Founded a large construction firm located at Port Arthur, Ont., undertaking large-scale building projects, grain elevators, pulp mills and docks. Developed new concrete construction techniques, acted as advisor to Argentine government. Entered politics as Liberal in 1935 and was appointed Minister of Railways (subsequently Minister of Transport), having under his direction Canadian Broadcasting Corporation. He reorganized administration of Canadian National Railways and founded Trans-Canada Airlines.

On outbreak of World War II, made responsible for War Supply Board. Became Minister of Munitions and Supply when this department formed in 1940.

When proceeding to the U.K. in late 1940, together with his senior assistants (E. P. Taylor, William Woodward and others) to join Defence Minister Ralston, to co-ordinate mobilization plans, his ship, the *Western Prince,* was torpedoed in the North Atlantic. Was rescued and continued his mission. In 1946 appointed Minister of Reconstruction and Supply and later Minister of Trade and Commerce.

Was also member of the British Supply Council in North America and active with international aviation organizations. Sponsor in House of Commons of Act to create Trans-Canada pipeline. Highly regarded during war years both in London and Washington. A close friend of Ralston, Beaverbrook and others. Was responsible for attracting many prominent business executives for wartime service in Ottawa as "dollar-a-year-men."

MACDONALD, Hon. Angus L. Canada's wartime Minister for Naval Affairs. Served with Canadian Army overseas in World War I. Professor of Law Dalhousie University, 1924. Elected to Nova Scotia legislature 1933 as Liberal member; sworn in as Premier and Provincial Secretary the same year. Resigned at request of Prime Minister King to enter federal government in 1940, to become Minister of National Defence for

Naval Affairs. Closely associated with Ralston, Power and Howe in the cabinet. Resigned in April 1945 to become Premier of Nova Scotia again, in August 1945.

McNAUGHTON, General the Hon. Andrew G. L. Controversial Commander Canadian Army overseas 1942-43. Identified as "Father of the Canadian Army"; also, noted scientist. Commissioned in Regular Army 1909. Served in World War I with Artillery. Twice wounded and twice mentioned in despatches. Rose to command Canadian Corps Heavy Artillery, with rank Brigadier General. Expert in counter-battery operations. Assisted in reorganization of militia after war. Appointed director Military Training and Staff Duties Defence HQ in Ottawa 1920 and subsequently. Deputy Chief General Staff, DOC Military District No. 11 Victoria and Chief of General Staff, Ottawa 1929. Inventor of cathode ray direction finder.

President of National Research Council 1935-39. Returning to the army on outbreak of war in 1939, appointed to command 1st Canadian Division, which he took to England. Promoted Lieutenant General to command 7th Corps in England 1940 and to command 1st Canadian Corps 1941; subsequently General Officer Commanding Canadian Army in 1942.

Was relieved of his command in 1943 as considered unfit to command in the field. Resisted dispersement of Canadian divisions; returned disgruntled to Canada. Disagreed with Defence Minister Ralston. Planned to join Conservative party in opposition to government but during conscription crisis prevailed on by Prime Minister King to accept Defence portfolio when Ralston was fired. Failed to get elected to House of Commons.

Following the war served as Canadian representative UN Atomic Energy Commission, president of Atomic Energy Board of Canada, permanent delegate to UN and Canadian representative on Security Council 1948-49. In 1950 was appointed Commissioner, Canadian Section, International Joint Commission.

PAGET, General Sir Bernard. British Regular Army officer, Sandhurst graduate. Served in World War I. Commanded Quetta Infantry Brigade 1937-38. On outbreak of war, commanded 18th British Division and participated in Norway Expedition. Appointed Chief of General Staff British Home Forces 1941-43, C-in-C 21st Army Group, June-December 1943 and C-in-C Middle East 1944-46. Canadian Army, while in an anti-invasion role in the U.K., came under his direction 1941-43.

POWER, Hon. C. G. (Chubby). Canada's popular wartime Minister of National Defence for Air. Served as a private soldier in World War I, was twice wounded and awarded MC. Elected to House of Commons in 1917; re-elected in eight successive federal elections. Appointed Minister National Defence for Air in 1940 and also Associate Minister of National Defence. Largely responsible for development of the great Empire Air Training Scheme during war. Resigned from the government in 1944, during the conscription crisis. Subsequently appointed to Canadian Senate.

RALSTON, Hon. J. L. Soldier, corporation lawyer and dedicated public servant. Canada's Minister of National Defence during the war years, 1940-45. A veteran of World War I, during which he commanded the Nova Scotia Highlanders. Was severely wounded, awarded DSO for gallantry, created Commander of the Order of St. Michael and St. George. Returned to his law practice after WW I and entered politics in 1926.

As Defence Minister in the period 1926-30, represented Canada at the London naval conference in 1930. A strong believer in the importance of aviation to Canada, he did much during his first tenure of the Defence portfolio to encourage flying.

When the Mackenzie King government was defeated in the Dominion elections of August 1930, Ralston was returned in Shelburne-Yarmouth and sat in opposition with Mr. King. He acted as financial critic for the opposition and also was his party's authority on defence.

Before the general elections of 1935 Ralston, deciding to return to his profession, entered the legal firm of Mitchell, Ralston, Kearney and Duquet in Montreal.

With the outbreak of war on September 3, 1939, he offered his services in any capacity, preferably on active service. Prime Minister Mackenzie King appointed him Finance Minister on September 7, 1939. When Hon. Norman Rogers, Minister of National Defence, was killed in an airplane accident on June 10, 1940, King chose Ralston as his successor.

Shortly after Ralston took the Defence portfolio, a ministry for naval services was set up and another post, that of Associate Minister for Defence, was authorized.

Ralston was given general supervision over all branches of the services, with particular responsibility for the army. Major C. G. Power, his old colleague in the House of Commons, became Minister for Air and Associate Minister for Defence, and Hon. Angus L. Macdonald, former Premier of Nova Scotia, became Navy Minister, giving Canada a defence ministry trio of First Great War veterans.

Ralston was fired from the cabinet by King in 1944 over the conscription issue and was replaced by General A. G. L. McNaughton.

SANSOM, Lieutenant-General Ernest William (Sammy), CB, DSO. Served in World War I, 1914-19; Lieutenant-Colonel in command of 2nd Battalion and 1st Battalion, Canadian Machine Gun Corps. Appointed to Canadian Permanent Forces 1920. Staff College, Camberley, 1924-25. GSO 2, Halifax, 1926-27. National Defence HQ, Ottawa, 1928-30. Assistant Adjutant and Quartermaster-General, MD No. 12, 1931-34. GSO 1 MD No. 4, Montreal, 1935-36. Director of Military Training for Canada, 1937-39. Proceeded overseas 1939 as AA and QMG, 1st Canadian Division. CO 2nd Infantry Brigade and served as DAG, Canadian Military HQ, London, July-November 1940. Promoted Major General and to command 3rd Canadian Division, November 1940; 5th Armoured Division, March 1941-January 1943. Promoted Lieutenant General and to command 2nd Canadian Corps on organization. Invalided to Canada February 1944. Inspector General Canadian Army overseas January 1945.

SIFTON, Colonel Victor, CBE, DSO, LLD. Son of Sir Clifford Sifton. Served with Canadian Army in World War I, rose to command 4th Canadian Mounted Rifles. After that war, entered publishing business and was successively publisher of Regina *Leader-Post* and *Winnipeg Free Press*. A close associate of J. W. Dafoe, the celebrated Western editor. Was also president of Canadian Press and vice-president of Great-West Life. Following outbreak of World War II was appointed an executive assistant to National Defence Minister J. L. Ralston in Ottawa, and subsequently Master General of Ordnance. Returning to the publishing business after the war, he later formed a partnership with Max Bell of Calgary and R. S. Malone, to found F.P. Publications Ltd., which expanded to include such newspapers as Victoria *Times, Colonist*, Vancouver *Sun*, Lethbridge *Herald*, Calgary *Albertan*, *Winnipeg Free Press, The Globe and Mail* (Toronto), Ottawa *Journal*, Montreal *Star*, and various broadcast and printing interests.

SIMONDS, Lieutenant-General Guy Granville, CC, CB, CBE, DSO, CD. Brittle Permanent Force officer, widely recognized as Canada's ablest field commander in WW II, rose to command the Canadian Army overseas. Rated by Field Marshal Montgomery as one of the ablest Corps Commanders to serve under him during and after the war.

A graduate of Canada's Royal Military College in 1925, with Sword of Honour and other top awards, he joined Canada's Permanent Force. Prior to World War II held appointments with RCHA and attended gunnery staff course in England and became instructor at RMC.

On outbreak of war was appointed GSO 2, 1st Canadian Division, then commanded 1st Field Regiment RCHA. Was Commandant 1st Canadian War Staff College in 1940.

Subsequently he was appointed Brigadier-General Staff (Chief of Staff), 1st Canadian Corps and promoted Brigadier, 1941; detailed to special duties as Head of Planning Staff to study operations in Norway and in this connection flew to Washington on special mission 1942. Appointed to command of 1st Canadian Infantry Brigade, 1942; Chief of Staff, 1st Canadian Army, January 1943; attached to 8th Army in North African Campaign; promoted Major General to command 2nd Canadian Division, 1943. On death of General Harry Salmon, transferred to command 1st Canadian Division detailed for Sicilian campaign. GOC 1st Canadian Division, Sicily and Italy until November 1943, when transferred to command 5th Canadian Armoured Division. Promoted Lieutenant General to command 2nd Canadian Corps, January 1944. Commanded 2nd Canadian Corps in north-west Europe and 1st Canadian Army during Battle of Scheldt. Appointed to command Canadian forces in Netherlands, and responsible for repatriation of Canadian Army after return of General Crerar to Canada. Chief Instructor, Imperial Defence College, London, 1946-49. Commandant, National Defence College and Canadian Army Staff College, 1949-51. Chief of General Staff, 1951-55.

STUART, Lieutenant-General Kenneth, C.B., D.S.O., M.C. Permanent Force Officer, served in France and Belgium in World War I. RMC graduate, commissioned in Royal Canadian Engineers 1911. Was wounded and won M.C. and D.S.O.

In 1938 appointed Director of Military Operations and Intelligence at Defence H.Q. in Ottawa; Commandant RMC 1939-40. Appointed Deputy Chief of General Staff 1940 and served as member of the Canada-U.S. Permanent Joint Board on Defence. Appointed Chief of General Staff December 1940.

Involved in bitter dispute with General McNaughton, Commander of Canadian Army overseas, when McNaughton forced to resign, pending the appointment of General H. Crerar to replace McNaughton, Stuart assumed temporary command of overseas army just prior to Normandy invasion. Remained in London afterwards as Chief of Staff at CMHQ but retired from the army during the conscription crisis, in which he supported Defence Minister Ralston against Prime Minister Mackenzie King and General McNaughton.

VOKES, Major-General Christopher, CB, CBE, DSO. Colourful and fiery commander of 2nd Infantry Brigade during Sicily invasion and 1st Division during Italian campaign. Graduate of Royal Military College in 1925; Staff College, Camberley, 1934-35. Served in World War II, 1939-45, in England, Sicily, Italy, north-west Europe; command and staff appointments include Assistant Adjutant, Quartermaster General, GSO 1, OC, PPCLI, 1st Canadian Division up to May 1942; Commander, 2nd Canadian Infantry Brigade, from June 1942; GOC 1st Canadian Division, November 1943-November 1944; GOC 4th Canadian Armoured Division, November 1944-June 1945; GOC of Canadian Occupation Force in Germany, 1945-46. GOC, Central Command, 1946-50; W. Command, 1950-59. Affectionately described by Montgomery as "a good plain cook."

Index